Challenging, insightful and thought provoking, this book draws on a wealth of experience to provide a multiplicity of perspectives on the most essential public services. It's a brilliant ensemble of critical perspectives on both theory and practice. It captures the current dynamism and the uncertainty that the sector currently faces.

—*Philip Seccombe, Police and Crime Commissioner for Warwickshire and Chair of the Emergency Services Collaboration Working Group, UK*

Asking the question as to where the ambulance should align itself, more emergency service or the urgent and emergency aspect of the NHS? Appreciation of this question and how the ambulance service needs to develop going forward, is a fundamental question as to its future and how it can ensure sustainable service provision with increased activity and a reduced funding envelope. Additionally, as Paramedicine continues to mature as a profession and the role of the paramedic diverges away from just the traditional role of simply the ambulance paramedic, this book takes stock of the progress of the progress to date, the challenges ahead and how paramedics can play a larger role in urgent and emergency care.

—*Andy Swinburn, Assistant Director of Paramedicine, Welsh Ambulance Service NHS Trust, UK*

Critical Perspectives on the Management and Organization of Emergency Services

This volume makes an important contribution to the subject of emergency services management and to public administration and organization studies more generally. It critically assesses developments in emergency services management by examining the multi-dimensional nature of the provision of emergency services and their connectedness in advanced western democracies. The effective management of emergency services has never been more important than in today's high-pressured and cost-conscious public sector. The authors of this volume forensically analyse the challenges of delivering emergency services within this context. This book provides an in-depth, scholarly and comprehensive analysis of the changing landscape of emergency service provision and clearly addresses a gap in the market for a critical volume on the emergency services.

For anyone seeking to understand why and how the management of emergency services matters, this collection is essential reading.

Paresh Wankhade is Professor of Leadership and Management at Edge Hill University, UK.

Leo McCann is a Professor of Management at University of York, UK.

Peter Murphy is a Professor of Public Policy and Management at Nottingham Trent University, UK.

Routledge Critical Studies in Public Management
Edited by Stephen Osborne

The study and practice of public management has undergone profound changes across the world. Over the last quarter century, we have seen

- increasing criticism of public administration as the over-arching framework for the provision of public services,
- the rise (and critical appraisal) of the 'New Public Management' as an emergent paradigm for the provision of public services,
- the transformation of the 'public sector' into the cross-sectoral provision of public services, and
- the growth of the governance of inter-organizational relationships as an essential element in the provision of public services

In reality these trends have not so much replaced each other as elided or co-existed together—the public policy process has not gone away as a legitimate topic of study, intra-organizational management continues to be essential to the efficient provision of public services, whist the governance of inter-organizational and inter-sectoral relationships is now essential to the effective provision of these services.

Further, whilst the study of public management has been enriched by contribution of a range of insights from the 'mainstream' management literature it has also contributed to this literature in such areas as networks and inter-organizational collaboration, innovation and stakeholder theory.

This series is dedicated to presenting and critiquing this important body of theory and empirical study. It will publish books that both explore and evaluate the emergent and developing nature of public administration, management and governance (in theory and practice) and examine the relationship with and contribution to the over-arching disciplines of management and organizational sociology.

Books in the series will be of interest to academics and researchers in this field, students undertaking advanced studies of it as part of their undergraduate or postgraduate degree and reflective policy makers and practitioners.

Crossing Boundaries in Public Policy and Management
Tackling the Critical Challenges
Edited by Luke Craven, Helen Dickinson, and Gemma Carey

The Projectification of the Public Sector
Edited by Damian Hodgson, Mats Fred, Simon Bailey, and Patrik Hall

Critical Perspectives on the Management and Organization of Emergency Services
Edited by Paresh Wankhade, Leo McCann, and Peter Murphy

For a full list of titles in this series, please visit www.routledge.com

Critical Perspectives on the Management and Organization of Emergency Services

Edited by Paresh Wankhade,
Leo McCann, and Peter Murphy

Routledge
Taylor & Francis Group

LONDON AND NEW YORK

First published 2019 by Routledge

2 Park Square, Milton Park, Abingdon, Oxon, OX14 4RN
605 Third Avenue, New York, NY 10017

Routledge is an imprint of the Taylor & Francis Group, an informa business

First issued in paperback 2020

Library of Congress Cataloging-in-Publication Data
Names: Wankhade, Paresh, editor. | McCann, Leo, 1976– editor. |
    Murphy, Peter, 1954– editor.
Title: Critical perspectives on the management and organization of
    emergency services / edited by Paresh Wankhade, Leo McCann,
    and Pete Murphy.
Description: New York, NY : Routledge, 2019. | Series: Routledge
    critical studies in public management | Includes index.
Identifiers: LCCN 2019008453 | ISBN 9781138097650 (hardback) |
    ISBN 9781315104447 (ebook)
Subjects: LCSH: Emergency management. | First responders. | Municipal
    services—Management.
Classification: LCC HV551.2 .C756 2019 | DDC 363.34068—dc23
LC record available at https://lccn.loc.gov/2019008453

ISBN: 978-1-138-09765-0 (hbk)
ISBN: 978-0-367-78630-4 (pbk)

Typeset in Sabon
by Apex CoVantage, LLC

Contents

PART 2

PART 3

PART 4

Editor Biographies

Paresh Wankhade is Professor of Leadership and Management at Edge Hill University Business School, UK. He is the Programme leader for the UK's first bespoke Professional Doctorate in Emergency Services Management. He is also the Editor-In-Chief of *International Journal of Emergency Services*. His research and publications focus on analyses of strategic leadership, organisational culture, organisational change and interoperability within the public services with a focus on blue light services. He has published in major journals including: *Work, Employment and Society*, *International Journal of Management Reviews*, *Public Management Review*, *Regional Studies*, *Public Money and Management* and *International Journal of Public Sector Management*. His recent work (co-authored with professionals) has explored leadership and management perspectives in the Ambulance, Police and Fire & Rescue Services. He is currently working on a monograph analysing the interoperability and collaboration challenges for the emergency services.

Leo McCann is Professor of Management at the University of York. His academic background is in the disciplines of sociology and history. His research and teaching interests range over the following areas: work and employment; globalization and social change; and management history. His research is usually based on qualitative, ethnographic investigation and writing, often exploring the everyday struggles and rewards of professional working life across many occupations. He is particularly interested in the organizational conflicts that often arise between professional discretion versus centralized control and measurement. His recent research has focused in particular on white-collar and uniformed professionals, and he is currently working on a new book on NHS ambulance paramedics, to be published by Oxford University Press. He has published his research work in journals such as *Journal of Management Studies*, *Organization Studies*, *Organization*, *Work, Employment & Society*, and *Public Administration*. He is the author of *A Very Short, Fairly Interesting, and Reasonably Cheap Book About Globalization* (London, Sage).

Peter Murphy is Professor of Public Policy and Management and Head of Research at Nottingham Business School, Nottingham Trent University. He is Vice Chair (Research) of the Public Administration Committee of the Joint Universities Council, and a member of the Advisory Board of the Centre for Public Scrutiny. Prior to joining the business school in 2009, he was a senior civil servant in four Whitehall departments, was a director of the Government Office for the East Midlands and is a former Chief Executive of Melton Borough Council in Leicestershire. Originally a planning officer by profession he was responsible for emergency planning and co-ordinating the response to emergencies at local, regional and national levels for over 30 years. His current research focusses on public policy, public assurance and the governance, scrutiny and value for money arrangements of locally delivered public services.

Acknowledgements

There are a number of people to thank who have contributed towards the publication of this ambitious volume in a timely manner. To our authors, who shared their expertise, knowledge and insight, we extend our sincere gratitude. To our professional experts, who shared their experiences and knowledge for this academic endeavour, we thank them wholeheartedly. To the team at Taylor and Francis and, in particular, the Routledge Critical Studies in Public Management Series editor, Prof Stephen Osborne and the publication team of David Varley, Brianna Ascher and Mary Del Plato, we are grateful for trusting us to make a contribution to a thinly explored field. To our respective institutions, we acknowledge the support for this project. Finally, to our families, we thank them for their patience and understanding.

Paresh Wankhade, Lancashire, UK
Leo McCann, York, UK
Peter Murphy, Nottingham, UK

1 Introduction to Critical Perspectives on the Management and Organisation of Emergency Services

Paresh Wankhade,* Leo McCann and Peter Murphy

Background

Emergency services (in this book we focus primarily on police, fire and ambulance services) represent complex and diverse occupational fields. While each service has its own distinct history and way of operating, they are all widely known to be challenging environments for management, organisation and work. Workloads and responsibilities can be extremely demanding for employees and professionals given the common objective of reducing and managing risks of harm to the public. Public services have been undergoing substantial change in many societies since at least the 1980s and the onset of various, often controversial, reforms. Uniformed emergency services in many countries have a strong historical connection to notions of public service and duty: the very idea of an emergency service has connotations of being indispensable or 'essential'; blue light services can be the only public service available to rapidly respond to those in the direst need. Its absence or shortage can have potentially catastrophic effects on public order, as in the policing metaphor of 'the thin blue line'. In a time of reforms, cutbacks and ten years of austerity measures, an exploration of this particularly fundamental form of public service can be highly instructive; if major changes are being made to 'essential' emergency services then what does that say about government's views about what is 'essential' for it to provide?

Despite emergency services being a worldwide phenomenon with an increasing number of scholars and practitioners actively researching and investigating these services, a critical understanding of these services is only recently beginning to emerge. Systematic understanding is also hampered by a 'theory-practice' divide and the dominance of occupational literature at the cost of balanced inquiry (Wankhade and Murphy, 2012). The need for an engaged and *critical* analysis of management in this sector is apparent. Much of the current literature on management in emergency services tends towards *practical*, mainstream and even common-sense treatments of notions such as 'leadership', 'risk management' and 'professionalism';

* Correspondence E-mail ID: Paresh.Wankhade@edgehill.ac.uk

concepts that in a critical perspective are considered loaded terms with a multiplicity of interpretations. Vast critical literatures about these concepts exist (Alvesson et al., 2009; Grey and Mitev, 1995) in parallel to the more practical publications emanating from emergency services education and training. There is a pressing need to complement and better integrate the more practical educational approach of the emergency services world with the more reflexive, critical, academic disciplines of business and management, organisation studies, criminology, public administration or sociology.

This need is even more important when one considers the prevalence of failure, controversy and struggle in the daily management of police, fire and ambulance services. Low morale, perceptions of remote and/or bullying management, industrial relations conflict, a lack of a research culture, failures to 'learn lessons' from untoward incidents, limited diversity in the workforce and blame cultures are all arguably severe problems in emergency services workplaces (Andrews and Wankhade, 2016; Charman, 2013; Granter et al., 2015; Murphy et al., 2017; McCann et al., 2013, 2015; Spencer et al., 2018; Wankhade et al., 2018). There is an urgent need to openly acknowledge and address some deep controversies around management failures in uniformed services. For this to have any chance of happening, there needs to be an acceptance of a need for reflexivity and critical understandings of workplace structures, behaviours, power relations and identities (Buchanan et al., 2013; Gascoigne et al., 2015; Granter et al., 2019; McCann et al., 2008).

Contested Policy and Organisational Terrain

Emergency services provision is increasingly global in nature but there are huge variations in the way they are commissioned and organised. A combination of delivery models including public, private and mixed is in vogue, making it difficult to make any meaningful international comparisons and identify best practices. In England alone, there are ten ambulance trusts working within the National Health Service (NHS); more than 40 fire and rescue services and authorities and over 40 police forces. They operate under different departments and ministers with different governance, management and organisational structures. The lack of a nodal agency further creates a fragmented policy and service delivery framework, which is discussed by Carl Daniels and Peter Murphy et al. in their chapters in this book.

Recent statutory changes to the services in England resulting from the Policing and Crime Act 2017 have placed increasing scrutiny on the emergency services and call for a critical analysis of their role, responsibilities and contribution to the wider public and society. Current evidence points to several fundamental shifts in the nature of the work undertaken by the three services, with all three facing significant operational problems. Ambulance demand is now rising at an annual rate of about 10% every year, creating massive organisational challenges (National Audit Office, 2017). Police services are working in a climate of overall reductions in recorded crime, but are grappling with very different types of crime, or crimes and social problems that have recently become much more significant priorities, such as modern slavery, cybercrime, childhood sexual exploitation, domestic violence, and mental health and vulnerability (College of Policing, 2015). The fire and rescue services have been very successful in preventing fires in recent years (although numbers of fire incidents are once again rising), but as a result have faced the challenges of new duties and funding cutbacks. Current models of service delivery and management are being challenged by the changes in the nature of demand and new workforce dynamics emerging in these services.

The overall picture of the performance of emergency services and their legitimacy with the public is mixed. Emergency services and the professionals who staff them have an increasingly prominent profile in news media and public discourse given the scale of such incidents as the Grenfell Tower fire in London as well as the recent terror attacks in London and Manchester. The services' response to multi-casualty incidents has attracted praise but has also highlighted serious concerns about resources, funding levels, operational doctrine, effectiveness of leadership and the sustainability of these organisations. The Keslake Report (2018), an independent review commissioned to look at the response of the emergency services to the Manchester Arena suicide bomb incident in 2017, praised the overall response of the services but also expressed concerns about coordination and communication between various agencies involved.

Another very prominent issue has been the potential impact of the organisational, financial and cultural challenges of emergency work on the health and well-being of its staff. Cases of stress, poor mental health and post-traumatic stress disorder (PTSD) are on the increase in the emergency services (Bentley & Levine, 2016; Granter et al., 2019; MIND, 2016; Sterud et al., 2011). Cases of harassment and bullying are also well known and feature significantly in many inspection reports (Care Quality Commission CQC, 2016; NHS Improvement, 2018). Recruitment of black and minority ethnic staff remains a challenge, and staff retention is also proving difficult (NAO, 2017). The risks of sickness absence, burnout, conflict and low morale are among the biggest challenges facing the emergency services worldwide (Bigham et al., 2014; Brady, 2015; Maguire et al., 2018; Wankhade, 2016).

In approaching this volume, we took a broad approach to providing a critical understanding of emergency services given the significant organisational and cultural differences between them. The field is further complicated if we include more specialised services such as the coastguard, air-sea and mountain rescue. The editors chose to focus on the three main 'blue light' services, namely the ambulance, police, and fire and rescue services, acknowledging that further research into other uniformed services is an area for future development. The chapters in the book take a descriptive, normative and reflexive approach in order to generate critical understandings of the emergency services landscape. We also include case studies to help the reader understand key issues across different policy and organisational settings.

This book is a part of Routledge's 'Critical Studies in Public Management' book series. It is probably useful at this stage to explain what we mean by 'critical' in this context. Critical Management Studies (CMS) is a broad field of writing and teaching contributed to by scholars who, for various reasons, are dissatisfied with the kinds of 'mainstream' business and management knowledge and practice that tends to dominate large organisations, is taught in business schools and is circulated by corporate consultants. All too often the 'solutions', 'toolkits' or 'gold standards' provided by those who claim to best understand and practice management and leadership are simplistic and inadequate (Alvesson et al., 2009). CMS literature often highlights the importance of the context and structures in which 'management' takes place, drawing attention to the conflicts and contradictions between groups and perspectives in organisations that are often very pronounced. Our approach is to try to be as honest as possible about organisational problems and conflicts rather than to deny or erase them from the discussion. Emergency services organisations have largely been somewhat isolated from university teaching and research—until rather recently—and there are dangers associated with applying expert knowledge (which can include business consulting as well as research emanating from universities) to new and unfamiliar fields. Texts in this Routledge series aim to present, critique, explore and evaluate the emergent, existing and developing nature of public administration, management and governance in a wide range of settings. The principle aim of this volume is to establish a comprehensive understanding of the organisation and management of the emergency services while critically explaining the distinct organisational issues they face. Areas of debate that repeatedly resurface include the changing meanings of 'professionalism' in the workforce, the difficulties of leadership style and means of decision-making, problems around establishing safety and quality cultures, the changing identity of emergency services workers, and the critical importance of professional mental health and well-being.

This book is a timely and critical inquiry into the functioning of emergency services in a dynamic policy environment dictated by very considerable cuts in public service budgets. The continuing climate of austerity has forced emergency services organisations to explore new forms of management and service delivery in order to do 'more for less' while protecting the public from increased risk.

The chapters are written by academics, experts and practitioners of acknowledged scholarship in a language accessible and suitable to a range of audiences. The themes covered in the book will resonate with various stakeholders engaged in emergency services planning, organisation, service delivery, education and professional development. We hope that the book will be of interest to a wide audience including professionals, practitioners, policymakers and university students. We are confident that this book provides an in-depth, scholarly and comprehensive analysis of the changing landscape of emergency service provision and clearly addresses a gap in the market for a critical volume on the organisation and management of emergency services.

Outline of the Chapters

The book is divided into four parts. Part 1 provides an overview of the issues along with contextual background to the blue light field in general.

Chapter 2, "Emergency Services Architecture: JESIP and Interoperability" by Carl Daniels, clarifies the emergency services architecture in the UK, including the Joint Emergency Services Interoperability Programme (JESIP), which provides a framework for collaboration or interoperability between the emergency services. Drawing from his personal experience of working in the Cabinet Office and having the responsibility for the delivery of the JESIP programme, the author provides an historical context for the legislative and organisational set-up of the three services. Citing recent evidence on the experience and evaluation of the JESIP framework, the author cautions against the persistent failure to learn from past incidents for want of a clear mechanism with which to audit or monitor any progress taken against these incidents.

Chapter 3, "History of the UK Paramedic Profession" by Bob Fellows and Graham Harris, provides a fascinating account of the development of the paramedic profession in the UK. Ambulance services predate the creation of the NHS 70 years ago, but the real growth in the development of the paramedic profession took place in the 1970s once the ambulance services became part of the NHS family. As the leading lights in the development of the paramedic curriculum and establishment of the professional body for the service, the College of Paramedics, our authors review the key historical aspects from the 60s to the present day while charting key milestones. Implications for future direction of travel and the trajectory for further reforms are discussed and analysed.

Chapters 4–6 provide reflections from three senior practitioners, each representing one of the three blue light services and looking at a particular issue.

Chapter 4, "Personal Reflections on Fire and Rescue Service Incident Command" by Roy Wilsher, explores the role of incident command as a mainstay of an operational fire officer's role. Reflecting on personal experiences, the author narrates his own perspective in dealing with a building fire, a terrorist attack, a depot fire and a rail crash in his fascinating career. He highlights the importance of some key issues, namely understanding operational principles, who is in charge, the incident command structure and how one fits into the operational plan. Drawing support from the JESIP principles, he demonstrates how incident command is vital to a multi-agency approach to tackling major and complex incidents.

Chapter 5, "Quo Vadis: Eight Possible Scenarios for Changes in the Ambulance Services" by Andy Newton, provides a critique of the current structure and condition of the ambulance services. It highlights unreformed organisational and managerial practices accompanied by fundamental shortcomings and variation in the performance of the NHS ambulance service in England. Questioning the 'fitness for purpose' of the organisational and management structures within the ambulance service in its current form, eight possible scenarios are outlined, each with possible issues and implications for the ambulance services and the broader blue light landscape.

In Chapter 6, "Galvanising Partnership and Communities to Tackle Domestic Violence and Abuse: Why Wicked Problems Have No Easy Solutions", Linda Reid tackles the 'wicked' problem of domestic abuse—the characteristics of which are complexity, ambiguity and uncertainty—that requires a collective response. Detailing the scale of the problem and the effects it has for victims and families, the author, a former Detective Chief Inspector, argues a case for a more strategic response to this problem. She makes a strong plea for a future reform agenda based on a greater understanding of family violence and how it differs from other forms of violence and which addresses the needs of survivors from diverse communities.

Part 2 of this book covers theoretical perspectives and examines two key issues for emergency services. The controversial issues of police discretion and professionalisation are tackled in Chapter 7: "Beyond the Scope of Managerialism: Explaining the Organisational Invisibility of Police Work". Written by Cliff Bacon, formerly a British police officer at the rank of Inspector, the chapter explores the ways in which policing has undergone significant change in the last ten years. While much of the practitioner and academic literature on police professionalisation suggests that British policing has gone through a successful and much-needed change programme, the chapter suggests that organisational, cultural and behavioural change in policing has actually been profoundly difficult. Based on interviews and observations within a UK police force, Bacon describes a demoralised and confused organisation, in which the rhetorical, operational and professional shifts from 'fighting crime' to 'handling vulnerability' have not matched the optimistic appraisals of much of the practitioner literature, suggesting that well-meaning reforms have paid insufficient attention to the practical levels of daily operation.

Chapter 8, "Reaching Out Across the Theory-Practice Divide?" by Yiwen Lin, Mihaela Kelemen and Lindsay Hamilton, deals with the all-important issue of meaningful impact in the field of emergency services and disaster management. The authors take an international perspective and explore their argument by presenting a case of collaborative research undertaken with a Japanese community devastated by the 2011 tsunami. This chapter asks how to build relationships between academic work and hands-on emergency response and suggests that participatory and collaborative research techniques provide an ideal vehicle for doing so. Their analysis focuses on the efforts of the community to 'build back better' not only in terms of physical infrastructure but, more importantly, with regard to individual and collective well-being. The chapter provides new insights into understanding the aftermath of a natural disaster by analysing evidence about an empirical approach, something often missing from theoretical academic discussions of impact.

Part 3 of the book provides a critique of what we describe as current orthodoxy in the efforts to modernise and reform the sector. Five key issues pertaining to the three main emergency services are examined with a critical lens.

Chapter 9, "The Professionalisation of the Police in England and Wales: A Critical Appraisal" by Simon Holdaway, examines the notion of the police as a 'profession' within the wider policy context. The sociological literature about professions is then analysed to clarify, criticise and refine police common-sense ideas of their occupational status, including the idea of a profession as a form of regulation. The chapter argues that police professionalisation is central to a new framework of police governance in England and

Wales, raising significant policy and related theoretical questions including the regulation and related accountability of constabularies.

The issue of changing professional culture(s) is examined next by Sarah Charman in Chapter 10, entitled "Changing Landscapes, Challenging Identities—Policing in England and Wales". The academic literature on the prevailing cultures within the police remains overwhelmingly negative as police culture(s) are routinely described as being sites of 'hegemonic masculinity, racism, prejudice, discrimination and exclusion'. The author challenges this notion and makes reference to the recent British Crime Survey figures and the police response to the recent terrorist attacks in the UK, which suggest increasing confidence in policing. This chapter considers the changing policing landscape over recent years which have faced the challenges of a reduced workforce, an increased workload and increasing efforts to pursue an agenda of 'professionalisation'. The changing external policing environment is then considered alongside the changing internal policing cultures which together form a 'new policing identity'.

In Chapter 11, "From Extreme to Mundane? The Changing Face of Paramedicine in the UK Ambulance Service", Jo Brewis and Richard Godfrey turn their attention to ambulance services and provide a fascinating account of the shifting perception of paramedicine from an 'extreme' to a more 'mundane' profession, an under-researched topic in the management and organisational studies (MOS) literature. The scope of the profession is expanding generally to encompass community-based assessment, management and treatment of patients. The authors argue that research on paramedics is overwhelmingly focused on issues such as burnout and stress, with emergency response characterised as a site of 'extreme work'. Paramedicine is a field that is rapidly changing, in ways that might give us reason to reconsider some of the traditional characterisations of blue light work as dramatic, life-saving and 'heroic'.

Chapter 12, "Decision-Making at the Front Line: Exploring Safety Culture, Safety and Moral Conflicts" by Andrew Weyman and Rachel O'Hara, further analyses the important but under-researched issue of the roles and responsibilities of front-line ambulance professionals in making clinical decisions. Broadening ambulance personnel skill sets has led to significant and fundamental changes in roles and responsibilities. Rather than simply conveying patients to hospital, a key policy drive has been to increase the volume of patients treated at scene in a context of organisational pressure to minimise rates of conveyance. Structural and workplace climate moderators and mediators of priorities and clinical decision-making (e.g. service performance criteria; resources; blame and accountability) impact on paramedic stress and well-being, and implications for patient safety are then analysed and implications discussed.

In Chapter 13, "A Comparative Appraisal of Recent and Proposed Changes to the Fire and Rescue Services in England and Scotland", Peter Murphy, Katarzyna Lakoma, Kirsten Greenhalgh and Lynda Taylor discuss the controversial issue of governance arrangements in fire and rescue services. Adopting a comparative methodology, the authors present a critical account of the antecedents, policy and assurance frameworks and more recent and proposed changes to the fire and rescue services in England and Scotland. The recent experience of a single service model in Scotland throws some new and interesting perspectives, and the account is both timely and opportune with the introduction of the new framework and inspection regime in England.

Part 4 of this book sets to provide alternative narratives for a few of the burning problems and 'wicked issues' confronted by emergency services personnel. We address both the policy and organisational aspects of reform and focus on four key themes ranging from innovation in governance arrangements to organisational themes of leadership, public trust, roles of curriculum in professional development and workforce health and well-being issues.

Our first theme is explored in Chapter 14 by Mark Learmonth who, in his piece "Rethinking the New 'Leadership' Mainstream: An Historical Perspective From the National Health Service", makes a compelling argument against the hegemony of the language of 'leadership' in use today. Drawing from a particular reading of the history of administration, management and leadership in healthcare settings, he speculates on the implications of its historical interpretation for current practices of 'leadership' and what he calls 'leaderism'. This analysis has important lessons for the emergency services, which have faced significant management and operational problems and scandals and which exhibit entrenched cultures of conflict, such as bullying and blame cultures, and hyper-masculinized traditions of authoritarianism and hierarchy.

In Chapter 15, Basit Javid and Kevin Morrell in "Public Confidence in the Police: A Critical Review and Interrogation of Construct Clarity" tackle the contentious question of public trust and confidence. Trust and confidence are widely seen as an essential part of modern-day policing reflecting a view that improved public confidence leads to better policing outcomes. Critically reviewing the literature on public confidence, the authors identify a number of potential problems with defining and measuring confidence—what they refer to as a problem of 'construct clarity'. While identifying and teasing apart various sources of ambiguity in relation to confidence, the authors also identify common, overlapping themes such as 'trust' and 'legitimacy' and the willingness of the public to help the police. A strong plea for the improvement of public confidence in policing is one of the highlights of the chapter.

Chapter 16, "Balancing Formal and Informal Support for Psychological Health in Emergency Services: Creating Multiple Pathways for Ambulance Staff" by Ashlea Kellner, Keith Townsend, Rebecca Loudoun, Tiet-Hanh Dao-Tran and Adrian Wilkinson, examines the formal and informal support systems of two Australian state emergency services cases with a specific focus on formal employee assistance and peer support officer programs, as well as informal colleague, family and front-line manager support. It is well accepted in the literature that ambulance work is characterised by employee burnout, high stress, work intensification and exhaustion, an issue highlighted and argued in Chapters 11 and 12 of the current volume. The authors propose a balance of complementary formal and informal support mechanisms that can temper the climate and provide a holistic approach to supporting employees that is responsive to individual preferences.

Chapter 17, "Commissioners, Mayors and Blue Lights: Reviewing the Prospects for Integrated Emergency Service Governance" by Rachel Ashworth, draws our attention to the important but complex issue of governance and accountability of the emergency services. The elected commissioner and mayoral models of governance are not without problems, and the proposals for joint governance of the emergency services by the police and crime commissioners have also faced controversy. The chapter draws on recent research on police and crime commissioners and presents a critical assessment of new accountability mechanisms for blue light services. It reviews the prospects and potential of future integrated emergency service governance systems.

Chapter 18, "Conclusion: Understanding Emergency Services in Austerity Conditions" by Leo McCann, Paresh Wankhade and Peter Murphy, is the final chapter which draws out the implications and assumptions that follow from the chapters in this book. This volume aspires to contribute to a critical understanding of the organisation and management of the emergency services with a call for more systematic research by management and organisation studies scholars in these settings. This final chapter draws on the key arguments advanced in the book—those of the limitations of an academic–practitioner divide—and identifies avenues for a fruitful research agenda.

Together, these chapters offer a rich account of recent research and critical thinking on the organisation and management of emergency services. Chosen topics do not aim to cover the whole gamut of issues, and some questions and gaps (methodological as well as empirical) remain. However, they reflect the core issues faced by the individual services and hopefully will stimulate discussion and debate as well as further research and scrutiny. This book is a contribution towards a better understanding of these important but underresearched public services. We hope that this volume will trigger a greater academic, practitioner and organisational interest in the understanding of emergency services professions and will motivate management scholars (both new and experienced) to join us in developing this new, emerging and exciting field.

References

Alvesson, M., Bridgman, T., and Willmott, H. (2009) 'Introduction', in Alvesson, M., Bridgman, T., and Willmott, H. (eds), *The Oxford Handbook of Critical Management Studies*, Oxford: Oxford University Press, pp. 1–26.

Andrews, R. and Wankhade, P. (2016). Regional variations in emergency service performance: does social capital matter? *Regional Studies*, 49 (12): 2037–2052.

Bentley, M.A. and Levine, R. (2016). A national assessment of the health and safety of emergency medical services professionals. *Prehospital and Disaster Medicine*, 31 (s1): s96–s103.

Bigham, B.L., Jensen, J.L., Tavares, W., Drennan, I.R., Saleem, H., Dainty, K.N., and Munro, G. (2014). Paramedic self-reported exposure to violence in the emergency medical services (EMS) workplace: A mixed-methods cross-sectional survey. *Prehospital Emergency Care*, 18 (4): 489–484.

Brady, M. (2015). Death anxiety among emergency care workers. *Emergency Nurse*, 23 (4): 32–36.

Buchanan, D.A., Parry, E., Gascoigne, C., and Moore, C. (2013). Are healthcare middle management jobs extreme jobs? *Journal of Health Organization and Management*, 27 (5): 646–664.

Care Quality Commission. (2016). *South East coast ambulance service NHS foundation trust quality report*. London: CQC.

Charman, S. (2013). Sharing a laugh: The role of humour in relationships between police officers and ambulance staff. *International Journal of Sociology and Social Policy*, 33 (3/4): 152–166.

College of Policing. (2015). *College of policing analysis: Estimating demand on the police service*. Ryton, England: College of Policing.

Gascoigne, C., Parry, E., and Buchanan, D. (2015). Extreme work, gendered work? How extreme jobs and the discourse of 'personal choice' perpetuate gender inequality. *Organization*, 22 (4): 457–475.

Granter, E.J., McCann, L., and Boyle, M. (2015). Extreme work/normal work: Intensification, storytelling and hypermediation in the (re)construction of 'the new normal'. *Organization*, 22 (4): 443–456.

Granter, E.J., Wankhade, P., McCann, L., Hassard, J., and Hyde, P. (2019). Keyed up: Intensity in ambulance work. *Work Employment and Society*, 33 (2): 280–297.

Grey, C. and Mitev, N. (1995) 'Management education: A polemic'. *Management Learning*, 26 (1): 73–90.

The Keslake Report. (2018). *An independent review into the preparedness for, and emergency response to, the Manchester Arena attack on 22nd May 2017*. Available at: www.kerslakearenareview.co.uk/media/1022/kerslake_arena_review_printed_final.pdf (accessed 15 April 2018).

Maguire, B.J., O'Meara, P., O'Neill, B.J., and Brightwell, R. (2018). Violence against emergency medical services personnel: A systematic review of the literature. *American Journal of Industrial Medicine*, 61 (2): 167–180.

McCann, L., Granter, E., Hassard, J., and Hyde, P. (2015) ' "You can't do both—something will give": Limitations of the targets culture in managing UK health care workforces'. *Human Resource Management*, 54 (4): 773–791.

McCann, L., Granter, E., Hyde, P., and Hassard, J. (2013). Still blue-collar after all these years? An ethnography of the professionalization of emergency ambulance work. *Journal of Management Studies*, 50 (5): 750–776.

McCann, L., Hassard, J., and Morris, J.L. (2008). Normalized intensity: The new labour process of middle management. *Journal of Management Studies*, 45 (2): 343–371.

MIND. (2016). *One in four emergency services workers has thought about ending their lives*. MIND, 20th April 2016. Available at: www.mind.org.uk/news-campaigns/news/one-in-four-emergency-services-workers-has-thought-about-ending-their-lives/#.W5-OhehKjIU (accessed 17 July 2018).

Murphy, P., Eckersley, P., and Ferry, L. (2017). Accountability and transparency: Police forces in England and Wales. *Public Policy and Administration*, 32 (3): 197–213.

National Audit Office NAO. (2015). *Financial sustainability of fire and rescue services*. HC 491, Session 2015–16. London: Stationery Office.

National Audit Office NAO. (2017). *NHS ambulance services*. London: Stationery Office.

NHS Improvement. (2018). *Operational productivity and performance in English NHS ambulance trusts: Unwarranted variations*. London: NHS Improvement.

Spencer, T., Hayden, J., Murphy, P., and Glennon, R. (2018). Stating the obvious: evaluating the state of public assurance in fire and rescue authorities in England. *International Journal of Emergency Services*.

Sterud, T., Hem, E., Lau, B., and Ekeberg, O. (2011). A comparison of general and ambulance specific stressors: Predictors of job satisfaction and health problems in a nationwide one-year follow-up study of Norwegian ambulance personnel. *Journal of Occupational Medicine and Toxicology*, 6: 10.

Wankhade, P. (2016). Staff perceptions and changing role of pre-hospital profession in the UK ambulance services: An exploratory study. *International Journal of Emergency Services*, 5 (2): 126–144.

Wankhade, P., Heath, G., and Radcliffe, J. (2018). Culture change and perpetuation in organisations: Evidence from an English ambulance service. *Public Management Review*, 20 (6): 934–948.

Wankhade, P. and Murphy, P. (2012). Bridging the theory and practice gap in emergency services research: case for a new journal. *International Journal of Emergency Services*, 1 (1): 4–9.

Part 1

2 Emergency Services Architecture
JESIP and Interoperability

Carl Daniels

Introduction and Background

Interoperability is frequently described as the ability of differing technological solutions to talk to each other and share data seamlessly, or it is referred to as the ability of the military to operate different units, often from different countries in a collaborative way (Dictionaries, 2018). In this chapter, interoperability is discussed as the ability of the emergency services of the United Kingdom and their employees to work together in response to either pre-planned or spontaneous emergency situations.

The UK's emergency services are admired and respected around the world for the professional service they provide. The work they do keeps our country safe and secure as well as protecting the public.

As with services in other countries, they have faced many challenges over the years and have had to adapt to face these. Whether it be from increased demand, natural disasters, terrorist incidents or reductions in financial and physical resources, the constant requirement is to provide a professional service that meets or exceeds the expectations of the end user.

Unlike many other countries, the three main services of police, fire and rescue (FRS) and ambulance[1] are mainly funded directly from central government, with governance and oversight provided by the relevant government department. Until 2017, this oversight was provided by three separate government departments, the Department of Health (DH) (ambulance service), Department for Communities and Local Government (DCLG)[2] (FRS) and the Home Office (police service).

In January 2016, the responsibility for fire service policy, and therefore governance, moved from DCLG to the Home Office, this was "in order to support a radical transformation of how the police and fire and rescue services work together" (Government, UK, 2016). This has simplified the oversight structure with two government departments now involved.

The Policing and Crime Act 2017 provided a significantly new landscape within which the emergency services in England could collaborate; indeed, it placed a duty on them to do so by stating,

> A relevant emergency service in England ("the relevant service")
> must keep under consideration whether entering into a collaboration

agreement with one or more other relevant emergency services in England could be in the interests of the efficiency or effectiveness of that service and those other services.

(UK Parliament, 2017)

The act also went on to allow for fundamental changes to the way the fire and rescue services are governed locally, allowing for the police and crime commissioner (PCC), who is an elected official, to act as the fire authority for the co-terminus fire and rescue service. This means they could either form part of and chair the existing fire and rescue authority (FRA) or replace the whole panel of elected officials with the PCC as the sole FRA body.

Challenges in Response

The emergency services responding together is not new; they have done so pretty much since each of their inceptions. As with any dynamic, evolving incident, however, things have not always gone as well as they could. Many public and independent inquiries and coroners' inquests into past major incidents and disasters have highlighted issues where interoperability wasn't as effective as it should have been. A key challenge is understanding the difference between joint working and interoperability. Joint working involves agencies and responders working together in pursuit of achieving a common goal; however, this will often not involve working to a common doctrine or way of working, which in turn can lead to competing priorities, duplication of effort or even an incoherent response. Interoperability is defined by JESIP as "the extent to which organisations can work together coherently as a matter of routine" (JESIP, 2016a); to achieve this, there needs to be agreed common doctrine, models and ways of working. This reduces the risk of duplication and competing priorities and promotes a coherent response.

A Vision for Improvement

In 2012, the home secretary pledged that the emergency services would learn lessons from these incidents and put into place systems to effect real change. Working with the national lead officers for the emergency services, the Joint Emergency Services Interoperability Programme (JESIP) was launched. The remit for JESIP was to understand what key issues were hindering interoperability to be able to improve multi-agency working between the police, fire and ambulance services.

Established as a programme for the emergency services run by the emergency services, the vision for JESIP, "working together, saving lives", is supported by the aim, "To ensure that the blue light services are trained and exercised to work together as effectively as possible at all levels of command in response to major or complex incidents so that as many lives as possible can be saved" (JESIP, 2013).

A full-time central programme team consisting of a mixture of experienced police, fire and ambulance commanders, with non-operational staff in support, came together in September 2012. Understandably, this team came with individual, single-sector views and assumptions of what the issues affecting interoperability and joint working were. Assumptions, however, can be very dangerous, and there was a requirement for some robust academic research to support or dispel these assumptions. JESIP structured its programme around four thematic workstreams: doctrine, training, testing and exercising, and joint organisational learning (JOL). It was through these that improvement would be delivered. The outputs of these workstreams are described in detail later in the chapter.

JESIP, thorough the Cabinet Office, Civil Contingencies Secretariat (CCS), approached the Emergency Planning College[3] (EPC), who were requested to research joint working between the emergency services at major incidents in the UK. The report was to identify recurring themes, any perceived failures to learn from previous lessons identified and what the key challenges to interoperability might be. The EPC subsequently commissioned Dr Kevin Pollock to conduct this research. Alongside this report, JESIP also commissioned Skills for Justice (SfJ) to conduct a series of workforce surveys. These were designed to gain some ground truth from commanders in the emergency services around the issues affecting interoperability.

Pollock Findings

The Pollock report[4] looked at 32 incident reports that contained issues affecting interoperability from 1986 to 2010. The 32 events were selected for research because they were subject to a public inquiry or because the event impacted significantly the public consciousness (Pollock, Dr Kevin, 2013). The findings laid bare a significant number of recurring themes across the wide range of incidents that affect interoperability.

The key issue was the persistent failure to learn from past incidents. Pollock went on to say, "The consistency with which the same or similar issues have been raised by each of the inquiries is a cause for concern" (Pollock, Dr Kevin, 2013). This failure to act on lessons and recommendations from the past was augmented by the fact that, whilst there is a significant number of reports produced following incidents and events, there was no system or mechanism with which to audit or monitor any progress taken against these. This leads to a lack of audit and the ability to demonstrate if progress or action has occurred. Moreover, there was an issue where the same or similar lessons were reoccurring, a point highlighted critically by Lord Justice Taylor in his report on the Hillsborough stadium disaster where 96 football fans lost their lives in a crush. Justice Taylor highlighted,

> It is a depressing and chastening fact that mine is the ninth official report covering crowd safety and control at football grounds. After eight previous reports and three editions of the Green Guide[5] it seems astounding that 95[6] people could die from overcrowding before the very eyes of those controlling the event'.
>
> (TAYLOR, 1989)

The failure to learn from past incidents was not just down to the lack of a system for tracking lessons and progress. Pollock also identified that leaders in affected organisations had not led by example, specifically through the development of a no blame culture that embraces learning from past mistakes. Furthermore, they had not provided those in their charge with adequate direction and support to be able to report near-miss events and mistakes. During the 1990s, there was a rise in organisations adopting the phrase 'no blame culture'. Whilst the concept is often well meant, it's also quite misleading, since no one can truly, from a point of ethics or morality, offer a culture which is blame- free, where any kind of behaviour can be reported without reprisal. The issue is that when people have wantonly exited from what is acceptable in terms of personal behaviour and professional practice, there exists culpability, so here we see that there cannot be 'no blame'. Unpicking deliberate or culpable acts from genuine mistakes is often difficult, especially if the people involved do not feel that there is an open and fair culture at play. In recent years, 'no blame' has been replaced by the 'just culture'. This is one in which people are encouraged, sometimes rewarded, to provide information which pertains to issues of safety, whilst supported by an environment of trust, but one which also has clearly defined lines between what is acceptable and not (Reason, 2000). The 'just culture' contains a process to decide whether an act is culpable or non-culpable; this is often referred to as the 'culpability or decision tree' (Figure 2.1). This process asks a number of questions, each with a simple yes or no answer. As the investigator works through the questions, the degree of culpability will become clear. The scale or level of diminishing culpability ranges from sabotage or malevolent damage through to blameless error; whilst the actual language will change based on organisational interpretation, the principles remain the same.

The airline industry has for many years been at the forefront of a culture that seeks to learn from incidents and not to automatically apportion blame, and in recent years the National Health Service (NHS) in the UK has been adopting this approach. A report by a panel of experts into the establishment of the Healthcare Safety Investigation Branch (HSIB) recommended that a 'just culture' be adopted by the branch for conducting investigations. The NHS improvement agency has also issued guidance on the implementation of a 'just culture' for NHS employers. It says,

> the fair treatment of staff supports a culture of fairness, openness and learning in the NHS by making staff feel confident to speak up when things go wrong, rather than fearing blame. Supporting staff to be open about mistakes allows valuable lessons to be learnt so the same errors can be prevented from being repeated. In any organisations or teams where a blame culture is still prevalent, this guide will be a powerful tool in promoting cultural change.
>
> (NHS Improvement, 2018)

Having an airline industry or 'just culture' approach across the emergency services would certainly assist in addressing the issues identified by Pollock.

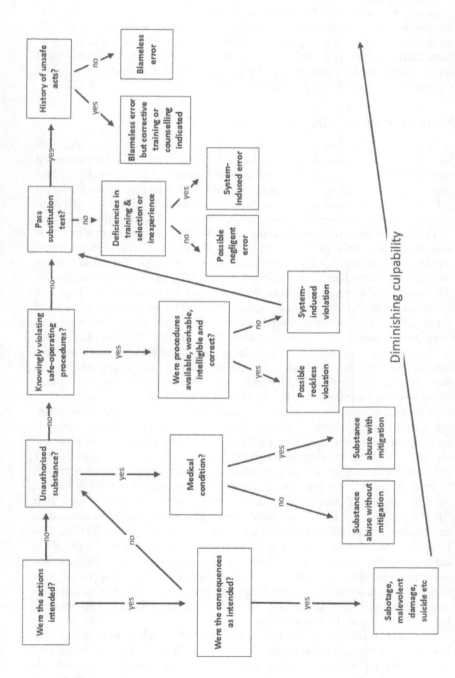

Figure 2.1 The culpabilit decision tree

Returning to the Pollock report, it went on to highlight that organisational planning was poor, and this led to staff not being trained in previous recommendations or neglecting to provide the necessary skills for individuals to become competent in providing a coherent and effective response. Some organisations displayed a reluctance to provide the appropriate resources in terms of time and finances to build this capability and capacity to respond efficiently; no doubt this contributed to further failings.

Workforce Survey Findings

A further building block to understanding the issues with interoperability were the two workforce surveys conducted by Skills for Justice. They surveyed nearly 2000 emergency service responders to further build a picture of the barriers to interoperability and to support JESIP in the development of suitable solutions. The intention was to conduct an initial survey as a pre-JESIP position, with a further survey to follow once the solutions had been put into place.

The lack of joint training was identified by 95% of respondents as a barrier to effective interoperable working, with a further 71% of operational commanders stating that they had either never been on a joint training course or that when they had, it was over two years ago (Skills for Justice, 2013). The concept of having those from the emergency services, who are expected to respond together, in a room being taught together, was considered to be of great benefit. This would allow participants to discuss some of their perceptions and assumptions of what should happen during a response, gaining an understanding of each other's core roles and responsibilities, as well as capabilities and limitations. There is further benefit if joint training has an element of practical application to further test these and allow the participants to understand how their role fits into the joint response space.

Whilst joint training is rightly seen and positioned as critical to developing a joint, interoperable response, it offers no guarantees that the models and principles presented will be used in high reassure, time critical response scenarios, if these are already competing against ones that are significantly engrained in the response arrangements of organisations. Responders will simply fall back to a position of comfort and familiarity; that is human nature. The JESIP assurance programme conducted in 2017 found that "JESIP models can still be superseded by single service models in areas such as situational awareness, briefing and decision making" (JESIP, 2017a). The issue of culture in the emergency services has been considered as the main reason for this; however, the SfJ survey suggested that the willingness for joint working was consistently ranked as one of the lowest levels of concern for respondents. What wasn't measured was the willingness to abandon single-sector models that perform the same function as that of JESIP models; this is where a key challenge exists.

The joint training of responders in interoperable working practices is only one step to building an interoperable capability. Without the opportunity to practice this training in an appropriate exercise with specific objectives and outcome measures, it is unlikely the training will be enacted or applied effectively or consistently (if at all) at an incident. Joint exercises were considered by survey respondents as the most valuable aspect over all other practical activities. These allow responders to practice the knowledge that they have gained in the training environment and work through any issues and conflicts that may be highlighted in the joint response. It is much safer to highlight these issues in this safe, controlled environment than to find out about them at the incident.

The Pollock report and Skills for Justice surveys provided robust evidence that there were some significant challenges with interoperable working between the emergency services. Whilst there was a positive approach to working together (Skills for Justice, 2013), there was a lack of systems and tools to foster this.

Interoperability

Whilst the concept of interoperability is reasonably simple to describe, achieving it is much more difficult. It requires the harmonisation of the individuals who are tasked with working with others, organisations which must foster a collaborative approach to joint working and, finally, technology. Turning to technology, which organisations will often do for an immediate solution to issues with joint working, is often the wrong approach. Whilst technology can be a huge asset, there is no single technical solution to operational interoperability in terms of multi-agency response to an emergency. Many systems assist in enabling interoperability, whether it be a radio system that allows responders from different agencies to talk to each other or a common information sharing platform that allows for the safe and quick dissemination of information to multiple users at once. Nevertheless, none of these is the panacea to interoperability; instead, each is an important piece of the puzzle.

Arguably, the most important aspect of interoperability are the individual responders who are expected to deliver life-saving actions through a joint, coherent response. But to enable the responders to do this, there needs to be an environment which embraces this approach, through the provision of common systems and processes.

JESIP consciously stayed away from technical solutions, since UK responders have had an interoperable communications system and a secure platform for sharing information for many years. The programme concentrated instead on the development of systems, processes and products to support the development of responders and their ability to work together. As mentioned previously, the approach to the issues was set out across four key areas: doctrine, training, testing and exercising, and joint organisational learning (JOL), all of which required very specific solutions to be developed.

The joint doctrine, of which the interoperability framework was the first of these areas, provided a structure for services to work to through a set of simple principles, a common reporting framework for situational awareness and a joint decision model. There are five principles for joint working: co-location, communication, coordination, joint understanding of risk and shared situational awareness (Figure 2.2). Whilst they are presented in

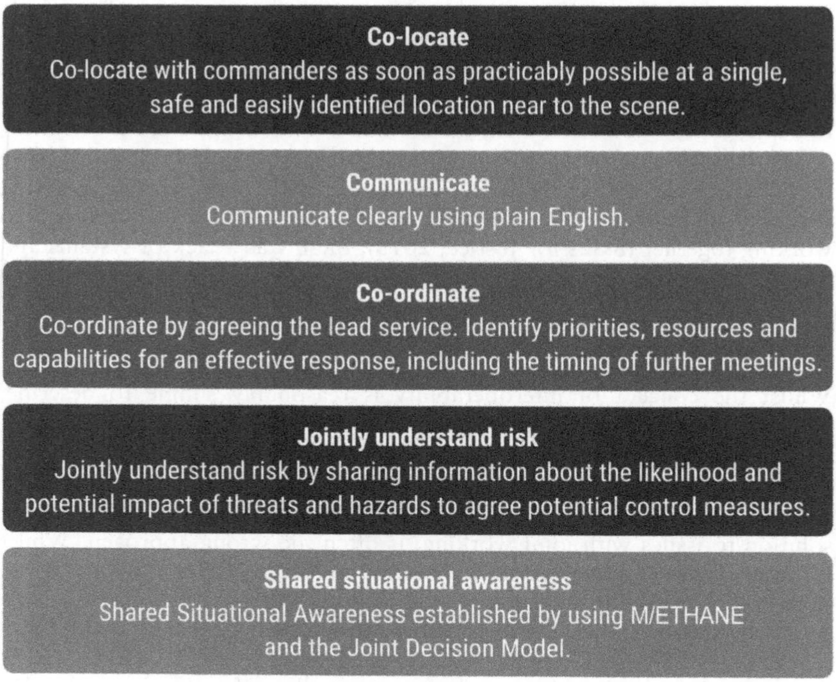

Co-locate
Co-locate with commanders as soon as practicably possible at a single, safe and easily identified location near to the scene.

Communicate
Communicate clearly using plain English.

Co-ordinate
Co-ordinate by agreeing the lead service. Identify priorities, resources and capabilities for an effective response, including the timing of further meetings.

Jointly understand risk
Jointly understand risk by sharing information about the likelihood and potential impact of threats and hazards to agree potential control measures.

Shared situational awareness
Shared Situational Awareness established by using M/ETHANE and the Joint Decision Model.

Figure 2.2 The principles for joint working

this order, it is important to note that they are not a hierarchy and may be achieved in any order. For example, a responder who has mobilised to an incident can, through the use of interoperable communications, begin communicating with responders from other agencies to begin building their situational awareness, which would inform a joint understanding of risk, therefore allowing them to coordinate activities before they actually arrive at the incident and co-locate.

The joint doctrine also introduced the joint decision model (JDM), which can be seen in Figure 2.3. This tool assists responders in bringing together information and reconciling differing priorities.

Feeding into the JDM and helping to build shared situational awareness is M/ETHANE (Figure 2.4). This common situational reporting tool is used by responders to provide critical reports from the scene of an incident. The first M/ETHANE report should be sent by the first resource on scene from any of the emergency services.

A key aspect of M/ETHANE are that it asks the sender to consider the declaration of a major incident. An early declaration is important, as it will allow for the early establishment of an appropriately resourced response. If it isn't a major incident, then an ETHANE message should be passed. Following the model provides a structured path, starting with the exact location

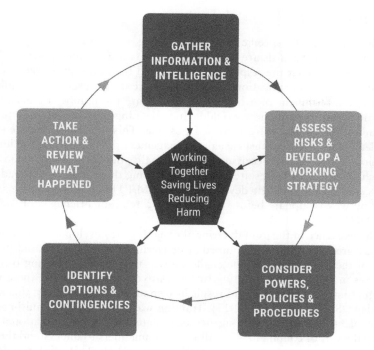

Figure 2.3 The joint decision model (JDM)

M	MAJOR INCIDENT	Has a major incident or standby been declared? (Yes / No - if no, then complete ETHANE message)	*Include the date and time of any declaration.*
E	EXACT LOCATION	What is the exact location or geographical area of the incident?	*Be as precise as possible, using a system that will be understood by all responders.*
T	TYPE OF INCIDENT	What kind of incident is it?	*For example, flooding, fire, utility failure or disease outbreak.*
H	HAZARDS	What hazards or potential hazards can be identified?	*Consider the likelihood of a hazard and the potential severity of any impact.*
A	ACCESS	What are the best routes for access and egress?	*Include information on inaccessible routes and rendezvous points (RVPs). Remember that services need to be able to leave the scene as well as access it.*
N	NUMBER OF CASUALTIES	How many casualties are there, and what condition are they in?	*Use an agreed classification system such as 'P1', 'P2', 'P3' and 'dead'.*
E	EMERGENCY SERVICES	Which, and how many, emergency responder assets and personnel are required or are already on-scene?	*Consider whether the assets of wider emergency responders, such as local authorities or the voluntary sector, may be required.*

Figure 2.4 M/ETHANE Mnemonic

of the incident; the specific type, which helps to identify the appropriate resources; what hazards are present, which may also include potential hazards based on what the responder can see; and the most appropriate access point, although identification of an egress route is also useful as this allows for the establishment of a blue route.[7] Next are the number of casualties; additional information here would include the range and severity of injuries, including the number of deceased if possible. This will allow for the early implementation of a robust casualty management plan, including the identification of appropriate receiving centres. Finally, the sender should consider which emergency services are required, including those who may already be on scene. As the incident develops, further M/ETHANE messages may be sent by way of update before switching to a relevant briefing tool such as IIMARCH.[8]

The existence of the joint doctrine allowed for the development of training and awareness products, all aimed at delivering the key models and principles of the joint doctrine. The challenge was that whilst delivering training courses in a single-sector setting was a relatively simple process, there were no guarantees that this would result in responders then applying this at an incident (Skills for Justice, 2013). Training was delivered by a multi-agency team of facilitators to multi-agency candidates across the operational and tactical levels of command. This allowed commanders to understand the priorities, actions and capabilities of other responders. This joint training is fundamental in building an interoperable capability (Skills for Justice, 2013). The confidence among individuals was also highlighted in the second Skills for Justice survey, with commanders stating that they feel their 'organisation's ability to work interoperably has improved over the past year' (Skills for Justice, 2014).

Learning From the Past

"There is no point in holding inquiries or publishing guidance unless the recommendations are followed diligently. That must be the first lesson" (Taylor, 1989). Being open and honest about shortcomings or failings in operational response is one of the hardest things for any organisation. Whilst actions which are malicious or negligent need to be dealt with appropriately, the emergency services need to be able to operate in an environment which allows them to be transparent about genuine mistakes or errors without fear of punishment, so that lessons identified can be processed and learnt.

The steps which take lessons from identified to learnt can be considered in five phases. Firstly, change national policy or doctrine to reflect the recommendations. These may have come from a public enquiry, coroner's report or other appropriate source. Services then need to change their policies and procedures at the local level to reflect the national direction. Once new policies and procedures exist, responders need to be trained in them before they move to the next phase and practice the new ways of working in relevant exercises, underpinned with appropriate objectives. The final phase is monitoring the implementation of the changes and addressing any arising issues, looping these back into the relevant phase of the process, such as tweaks to policy, training or the exercise. If we have learnt and followed the process, we shouldn't see a reoccurrence of the same issues.

The lack of a common system or platform for both the sharing of lessons and the tracking and auditing of progress around implementation was highlighted in the Pollock report. JESIP introduced a national system called Joint Organisational Learning Online (JOL Online). This secure system sits on the UK government's web platform, ResilienceDirect (RD), and is available to anyone with an RD account. The JOL process is a very simple three-step one which is highlighted in Figure 2.5. The inputs could be a lesson identified from an incident, exercise or training scenario that requires improvements to be made, or it could be a piece of notable practice. This is something that has been identified to significantly improve interoperability between responders (JESIP, 2017b).

Whilst the single, secure system is a significant step forward, the governance arrangements that sit around it are as, if not more, important. There is a full-time JOL Secretariat (the JOL coordinator), organisational points of contact for the emergency services, an interoperability board and ministerial oversight through government departments (Figure 2.6).

The Secretariat is responsible for analysing all the inputs which go into the system; these inputs are moderated and subject to a thorough risk assessment. The risk assessment process is looking for risks across the whole spectrum of impact versus likelihood, with those coming out as a medium or above requiring a more detailed analysis and investigation. However, those which are recorded as 'low impact, high frequency' events may be treated in much the same way, since this can be evidence of a developing trend (JESIP, 2017c) which may lead what appear to be small, insignificant issues becoming larger and more significantly impactive events in the future.

Regardless of the nature of the risk, all those which require remedial action will be reported to the interoperability board. A national-level strategic board which comprises chief-level officers from across emergency services and other Category 1 and 2[9] responder agencies, as well as senior civil servants. Here, decisions can be made on recommendations and directions on further actions provided.

JOL Online employs a double loop learning approach (Figure 2.7). While most learning processes look at 'what we do' and how it can be improved, double loop learning requires you to take a full, reflective look at 'why you do what you do', assessing effectiveness, in order to do better things, not just to do things better (JESIP, Oct 2017d).

Figure 2.5 JOL Process steps 1–3 (JESIP, 2017b)

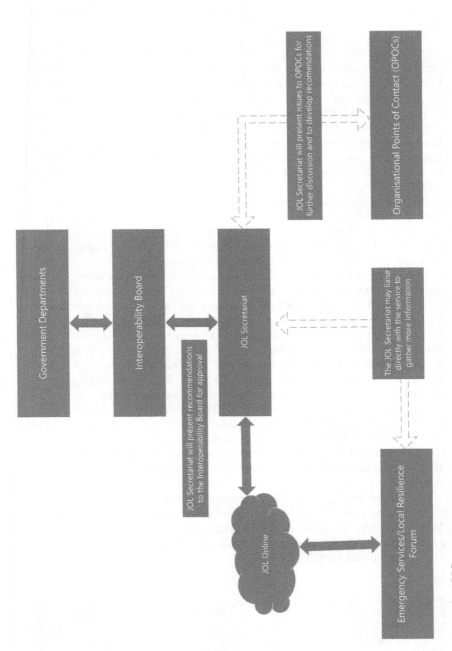

Figure 2.6 JOL governance process

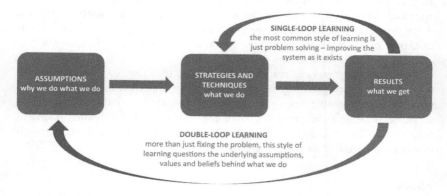

Figure 2.7 Double loop learning

A key aspect of the JOL arrangements are the ability to distribute action notes to services, setting out very specific activities that are required to be undertaken in relation to a lesson. The greatest improvement with the system over previous arrangements is the requirement of services to report back to the interoperability board on progress against the action note, which will itself contain the timescales for updates to be provided. This has now closed the loop on not being able to audit the progress of lessons as highlighted in the Pollock report.

Future Challenges

Joint working has nearly always been evident between the UK emergency services; however, true interoperability, based on a joint doctrine and using common language and models had been difficult to achieve prior to the inception of JESIP in 2012. Since then, there have been significant improvements in interoperability and the way the services work together. Moving forward, the challenge is for the JESIP ways of working to become part of the emergency services business as usual arrangements, so that regardless of the incident, its location or the services responding, JESIP principles and ways of working are at the heart of the response.

This will only be achieved when JESIP is part of organisational DNA, achieved by the JESIP ways of working being engrained into responders' career development, from new entrant all the way through to chief officer, across all agencies.

Services invest a significant amount of time, effort and money in debriefing in order to identify the pertinent learning points; however, without the sharing and management of these lessons through JOL, it is difficult to see how they will lead to sustained organisational change and improve any future response. Whilst it is strikingly obvious that services need to learn from past failures, there needs to be a philosophical shift in the way the emergency services are perceived to allow for an airline industry–style culture of mistakes and errors being treated differently to malice or neglect. The benefits of this approach have been obvious in the airline industry, and no doubt hundreds, if not thousands, of lives have been saved through the open and honest identification of mistakes by front-line operators themselves, which have led to changes in procedures, design and operations.

The emergency services train and prepare so that they can keep our communities safe by responding to emergencies. The biggest challenge is to maintain the interoperable response capability and ensure that the emergency services continue to respond together, creating a 'Team of Teams' (General Stanley McChrystal, 2015), all with different roles at an incident, but with one common goal, "working together, saving lives".

Notes

1 Currently the ambulance service is considered an essential service, not an emergency service, but that's for another time.
2 DCLG changed its name to the Ministry for Housing and Local Government (MHCLG) in January 2018 following a ministerial reshuffle (www.gov.uk/government/news/government-renews-focus-on-housing-with-ministry-of-housing-communities-and-local-government)
3 The Emergency Planning College, now known as the EPC, is a Cabinet Office-owned training facility.
4 The Dr Kevin Pollock report—Review of Persistent Lessons Identified Relating to Interoperability From Emergencies and Major Incidents since 1986.
5 Guide to Safety at Sports Grounds, often referred to as the Green Guide due to the colour of its cover.
6 A further person died after the publication of the Taylor report.
7 Blue Route—A dedicated route for emergency vehicles to access and egress from the scene of an emergency or major incident.
8 IIMARCH briefing—information, intention, method, administration, risk assessment, communications, humanitarian issues.
9 Category 1 responders are subject to all duties under the CCA 2004, whilst Category 2 responders, who are classed as 'cooperating bodies', have a lesser set of duties, which are co-operating and sharing relevant information with other Category 1 and 2 responders.

References

Dictionaries, O. L. (2018, September 21). *Oxforddictionaries.com/definition/interoperability*. Retrieved from oxforddictionaries.com/: https://en.oxforddiction aries.com/definition/interoperability
Fire and rescue policy to move to the Home Office. (2016, January 05). Retrieved from gov.uk: www.gov.uk/government/news/fire-and-rescue-policy-to-move-to-the-home-office
General Stanley McChrystal, D. S. (2015). *Team of teams: New rules of engagement for a complex world.* New York: Portfolio Penguin.
Government, UK. (2016, January 05). *www.gov.uk/government/news/fire-and-rescue-policy-to-move-to-the-home-office*. Retrieved from www.gov.uk/government/news/: www.gov.uk/government/news/fire-and-rescue-policy-to-move-to-the-home-office
JESIP. (2013). *Engagement & communications strategy.* London: JESIP.

JESIP. (2016a). Briefing. In JESIP, *Joint doctrine—the interoperability framework* (p. 22). London: JESIP.

JESIP. (2016b, September 21). *jesip.org.uk/glossary*. Retrieved from www.jesip.org. uk/: www.jesip.org.uk/glossary

JESIP. (2017a). *JESIP assurance programme report on findings*. London: JESIP.

JESIP. (2017b). JOL online. In JESIP, *Joint organisational learning guidance* (p. 9). London: JESIP.

JESIP. (2017c). Scope. In JESIP, *Joint organisational learning online* (p. 7). London: JESIP.

JESIP. (2017d, October). Assessment stage 2 — Further analysis. In JESIP, *Joint Organisational Learning Guidance* (p. 14). London: JESIP.

NHS Improvement. (2018, March). *A just culture guide*. Retrieved from NHS Improvement: https://improvement.nhs.uk/resources/just-culture-guide/

Pollock, Dr Kevin. (2013). *Review of persistent lessons identified relating to interoperability from emergencies and major incidents since 1986*. York: The Emergency Planning College.

Reason, J. (2000). Safety paradoxes and safety culture. *Injury Control & Safety Promotion*, 10–12.

Skills for Justice. (2013). *Emergency services interoperability survey report and recommendations executive summary*. Sheffield: Joint Sector Skills Councils.

Skills for Justice. (2014). *Emergency services interoperablilty research wave 2*. Sheffield: Joint Sector Skills Council.

Taylor, R. H. (1989). *The hillsborough stadium disaster*. London: The Home Office.

UK Parliament. (2017). *Policing and crime act 2017*. London: United Kingdom Government.

3 History of the UK Paramedic Profession

Bob Fellows* and Graham Harris

Introduction and Background

Expressions like 'the good old days' or 'the dispute changed everything' are common in the older generation paramedic. The 1989/1990 ambulance dispute (Government, 1990) brought an abrupt halt to the traditional ways of the ambulance service, and so many new brooms appeared that the 'sweep clean' process (McGraw-Hill, 2002) was unpleasant and indeed brutal, albeit some aspects were long overdue and necessary. New money appeared to modernise the ambulance drivers through extended training into what Americans now called 'paramedics'. Whilst the dispute between staff and employers started from a standpoint of the need to gain a significant improvement in basic wages and the attempt to index link them to something tangible, it soon became a much bigger issue of working men and women standing firm against an intransigent Conservative government who were watching on as the ambulance service received clear public support. The government were losing 'face' and were looking for something to trade with, and much-needed items such as kit (defibrillators) and training became a centre to the many pages of Hansard as it was thrashed out week by week. Expressions such as 'glorified taxi drivers' really didn't help the government and just inflamed the situation, and yet the comments seemingly helped fire the braziers and ambitions of the war-torn staff after many months of standing on picket lines.

So, let's swing back to the mid-60s briefly to examine what these good old days meant and how we evolved from Civil Defence Training of the 1950s to proud, well-trained and experienced ambulance staff who were rough diamonds but amazing in a real crisis, unflappable and dependable.

The well-known and often quoted (Millar, 1966, 1967) reports chaired by Prof E. J. Millar on behalf of the Home Office produced a two-section report. Section 1 was to standardise kit and equipment and section 2 to improve and standardise the training of ambulance drivers and attendants. Interesting how this returned in 1990 to the central part of the ambulance dispute resolution table. Millar stated in two of the 67 recommendations the encouragement of extended training for the attendant and not for the driver, so that

* Correspondence E-mail ID: bob.fellows@collegeofparamedics.co.uk

the focus of future development into direct patient care and not the generic interchangeable roles. That recommendation was ignored, even when it used expressions such a paramedical to describe the possibility of developments or selected experienced staff changes in training. Was it too forward? Yes, probably. But it was clear the role needed drastic changes and developments into basic and extended training. What Millar did was ensure that the training in 'Manchester' was almost identical to that provided in 'Bristol' or 'Brighton'. The training entailed two weeks of induction, a six-week course of ambulance aid and, if required, a two-week driving course, which was a provision that was not mandated, but following a driving assessment was offered if truly required. Perhaps we could all still learn from that approach today.

Medicine was also developing exponentially, and a new pattern of hospital-based coronary care units arrived in 1963 in places such as Kansas City, Toronto and Belfast, and far-sighted cardiologists were recognising that taking care into the community was the way forward and maybe, just maybe, ambulance staff might be a key component of the future.

An Ulster cardiologist, Frank Pantridge, worked out that there was an eight-hour delay to admission for cardiac patients in Belfast after first presenting with cardiac symptoms; not surprisingly, most deaths occurred outside of hospital. It is interesting that Pantridge (Geddes, Adgey, & Pantridge, 1967) commented in the *Lancet* in 1967 that this delay was similar to the plight of Baron Dominique Larrey and the battle wounded who were left on battle fields for up to 24 hours and inevitably bled to death. French army regulations insisted that all medics be one league (2.8 miles) behind battle lines, a delay resulting in the lack of effective life-saving treatment.

So, getting a portable defib and reducing transport and hospital delays was the next challenge. In that era, the defibrillator batteries were charged from mains electricity and a brilliant cardiac technician from Queens University called Alfred Mulwhinney who converted a mains to a crude portable with two car batteries and a static invertor.

It was December 1965 when the scheme was set up using a discarded ambulance, and a grant from the British Heart Foundation (BHF) paid for the Senior House Officer Geddes and an ambulance driver supported by a cardiac trained nurse. It went live on 1 January 1966, and a paper was published on 5 August 1967 with preliminary results printed in the *Lancet*. The scheme changed the cardiology world regarding pre-hospital care; it was copied worldwide and in effect the jump made us all rethink how ambulances responded and started the concept of taking healthcare to the patient and reducing the unnecessary delay to treatment.

The Irish heart foundation set up a cardiac ambulance in September 1967 and trained the Dublin Fire Brigade ambulance staff to deliver cardiac monitors and vehicle-based (Bedford SP2) defibrillators to patients in Dublin who were in ventricular fibrillation (VF). Commencing in December, they attended 1973 calls in the next 35 months and conveyed into five different hospitals in an area 460 square miles and a population of 800,000. VF was treated in 20 of the patients, 17 successfully, and is recognised as the earliest known use of ambulance staff in defibrillation in the UK or Ireland. Of the calls received,

78% were from GPs whilst 18% came from the 999-ambulance service and 4% from police and industry. It is still worthy of note that most patients didn't call 999 or use this private ambulance service but preferred the delay of going to their GP.

Kit was carried in the Dublin ambulance, much of it for the specific benefit of a GP who might be at scene on arrival and not for the ambulance crew (see Table 3.1), other than the defibrillator and monitor, which could easily be typical of the equipment seen 30–40 years later.

The conclusion of the report from the cardiology team Gearty et al., (1971) concluded, "The use of paramedical staff in cardiac resuscitation can be extended to ambulance personnel" and went on to suggest, "We envisage a further improvement in the efficiencies of the service when radio telemetry is incorporated to provide immediate and continuous transmission of ECG information about the patient prior to admission". In conclusion, "In light of this experience, the routine deployment of Doctors may be unnecessary and involve an uneconomical use of specialist skills".

Dr (now Professor) Douglas Chamberlain (Consultant Cardiologist) and Dr Peter Baskett (Consultant Anaesthetist) were starting to consider how ambulance staff could do so much more than just defibrillate, such as the Dublin model, if given the chance. Chamberlain, a Brighton cardiologist, got his programme off the ground with a first cohort in December 1971 trained to use a defibrillator and undertake ECGs and in addition provide a venous cannulation as a drug and fluid route. The scheme was off and running and known as the Brighton Scheme (White, 1973; Briggs et al., 1976). Peter Baskett from Frenchy Hospital in Bristol started training staff in advanced stepwise airway management, including intubation, and added cannulation and defibrillation, launching that scheme in early 1972. It is worth noting that 50 ambulance staff in South Gloucestershire were trained to administer Entonox in 1969, believed to be the first in the UK (Baskett & Withnell, 1970).

Further cohorts were added year on year to the schemes, and further developments occurred in London with Dr Margaret Hague (late 1972), in Dorset with Dr Bernard Lucas, in Nottingham with Dr Hampton and in Leeds with Mr Lea, a regional chief officer, as well as others in 1973. The focus and content of these schemes, and the many others that followed, often differed according to local medical opinion, but the original projects shared the essential features of strong medical direction and absolute commitment from the volunteer ambulance staff who were subsequently recruited to the schemes. Enthusiasm and a pioneering spirit characterised these early projects and proved to be important ingredients to the considerable local success that followed.

Table 3.1 Equipment carried on the Dublin Ambulance

ECG writer	Fixed & portable monitor	DC defibrillator
Entonox	Cardiac and emergency drugs	Endotracheal tubes
Oxygen	Fixed sphygmomanometer	Suction unit

In 1973, the NHS Reorganisation Act, more fully implemented on 1 April 1974, transferred all ambulance services, including those services with experimental 'paramedic' schemes, from local authority control to the NHS. In addition, it also separated social care and health care; 45 years later we are still attempting to re-join these vital components.

Following this transition, there was considerable discussion regarding the merit of 'paramedics' or, as they were referred to at the time, 'extended trained ambulance staff'. In 1979, Dr Bernard Lucas of the Medical Commission on Accident Prevention (MCAP) considered the potential of ambulance staff to undertake an expanded 'paramedic'-type role. Dr Lucas' committee expressed the opinion that 'as ambulance staff were frequently the first to arrive at an accident scene, it would be logical to train them in advanced resuscitation techniques'. This recognition that the plagues of the late 20th century—heart disease and traumatic injury—could benefit from treatment before the service user reached hospital played a part in creating conditions for change.

The Department of Health and Social Security remained cautious and recommended that 'ambulance authorities defer the introduction of further schemes'. In the health circular LHAL34/73 (73 indicating the year), and again in HN(76)204, the official position was made clear. The 1976 communication states,

> There is as yet no firm evidence that such schemes have made a significant contribution to saving life. The Department therefore recommends that these schemes should continue to be regarded as experimental and pending further evaluation should not be extended at present.
>
> (p. 3)

The Department of Health commissioned an analysis into the potential benefits of such training. The research by the committee which included Dr Chamberlain, Mr Lea and Roland Furber of Surrey Ambulance Service and conducted by the University of York's Institute for Research in the Social Sciences was published in 1984 and proved extremely positive, providing a compelling and economically sound vision for extended paramedic training.

> The saving of between four and five lives each year for every ambulance staffed 24 hours per day for 365 days per year, would, the report suggested, be a reasonable and conservative estimate.

The *Health Service Journal* ran a brief article entitled 'More Than Mercy Men'. This commented on the York report and noted the more enlightened international approach in developing paramedics. It went on to state,

> We would challenge the negative label applied to most ambulance crews of them being little more than glorified taxi drivers and instead go for positive developments.
>
> (Wright, 1984, p. 121)

We certainly all wondered where Kenneth Clarke obtained his famous quote from.

Despite some resistance, acceptance of the need for more highly trained ambulance crews grew rapidly and led to the Department of Health establishing a UK-wide pilot scheme in 1985 under the national leadership of Roland Furber at Banstead in Surrey, which was ultimately adopted by all UK ambulance services. This initiative brought the many disparate schemes in operation together into a standardised package of training taught within regional ambulance training schools and involving their local hospitals.

Descriptions used included 'Additional Training', 'Extended Training', 'Further Training' and 'Advance Training'. The word 'paramedic' was resisted by many, including unions, managers and many staff, only coming into general usage in the early 1990s. An American-born technician on an ambulance station in the 80s had a rear car window sticker that said, "Paramedics save lives!" He was mocked mercilessly by all concerned; our time had not yet come.

The dispute that followed during the winter of 1989–1990 proved to be the bitterest ever fought between ambulance staff, employers and government and has been recognised as unique in British industrial relations, principally for the level of public support it generated. Media attention was ubiquitous; ambulances blockading central London made for good news footage. Nightly news updates featured three leading protagonists, one being the Right Honourable Kenneth Clark QC, the then Secretary of State for Health, whose famous comment that ambulance staff were merely professional 'taxi drivers' proved highly inflammatory. Duncan Nichol, the NHS's chief executive, and Roger Pool, the leading negotiator for the trade unions, also proved to be rather effective, being described as 'leaden footed' in Conaghan's analysis of the disputed Coach and Horses (2010).

The police and voluntary aid societies were recruited to operate a makeshift ambulance service. However, it soon became apparent that additional resources would be needed, particularly in the larger metropolitan areas. In consequence, troops were brought in to fill the shortfall, primarily drawn from the army, but also with representation from the navy and the RAF medical establishments. The standards of training between both the military and non-military groups soon attracted comment from senior members of the medical community, who had more insight than most regarding the effects of the dispute upon patient care.

The following letter, written by two of the most senior medical figures involved in Emergency Medicine, Dr Williams, President of the Casualty Surgeons Association, and Dr Glucksman, Chairman of the London A&E Consultants Group, appeared in the press describing the seriousness of the situation.

> Sir, it is now four weeks since the ambulance pay dispute began to affect the emergency services in London and there are many signs that the pre-hospital emergency health service is becoming increasingly precarious throughout the country. No less than 50 percent of 999 patients are

being transported to hospital by police cars or vans, whilst the Army (30 percent) and the LAS (20 percent) share responsibility for the rest. These contingency arrangements may appear to be working, but it is only ambulance crews who have the requisite training skills, equipment and vehicles to provide an acceptably safe civilian service. The current system of pre-hospital care is therefore causing distress to many and danger to some, and there are also doubtless those whom it has completely failed. That people are not lying in the streets is no consolation.

(Ridley, 2013, p. 42)

The letter went on to urge both sides to move to a rapid resolution. The public provided massive psychological and monetary support for ambulance staff, which enabled many ambulance men and women to continue their industrial action without incurring disastrous financial consequences. One of the reasons for this fidelity was a feeling that injustice was being done to ambulance staff. It was also recognised that many ambulance crews, although suspended, were endeavouring to operate a minimum level of service using their own vehicles in response to direct calls from the public, and sometimes from the police.

In an article entitled 'Third Among Equals: An Analysis of the 1989 Ambulance Dispute' which appeared in the *British Journal of Industrial Relations* one year after the conclusion of the dispute, Kerr and Sachdev (1992) described it as the most important industrial conflict since the miners' strike which occurred only four years earlier. Indeed, NHS officials described it as 'the miners' strike for the NHS'. Kerr and Sachdev noted that, while its aim was redolent of many similar disputes, the tactics were revolutionary in that staff declared themselves suspended, not on strike; hence, the action was always referred to as a 'dispute'. Response to such media-worthy incidents, such as the Deal bombing and large-scale motorway incidents that occurred at the time, reinforced a positive image. The dispute also proved to staff that their work was valued, a direct contrast with the earlier findings of the 1979 Clegg Commission (p. 115) that reported that [ambulance staff] "believe that society does not recognise the importance of the ambulance service".

To some extent, the respective attitudes and public personas of the key protagonists helped the public make up their minds and, in many cases, actively supported ambulance crews; Mr Clarke was described as a bully in media reports of the time and Roger Pool, the chief union negotiator, who appeared conciliatory, appeared like a 'company manager'. Duncan Nichol, the NHS's chief executive during the period, acted as chief negotiator for the NHS. Subsequently reflecting upon the events (Hansard, 1990), he described the dispute 'unnecessary', but did accept that "the dispute concentrated minds and gave the impetus that was needed. It is now clearly recognised that early action by properly trained and equipped staff at the scene of accidents and emergencies can save many lives". The penny had finally dropped.

When a settlement was eventually concluded in 1990, the ambulance service was at the threshold of yet another metamorphosis.

We (paramedics) all knew in the spring of 1990 that change would come; talk in the negotiations of only a handful of paramedics and the haphazard voluntary approach to extended training was the 'get out of jail' card required. Did we really get the pay deal we hoped for? You may remember Roger Poole stating, "A Coach and Horses through the Conservative Pay Policy" (Workers.org, 1990).

Well, it resulted in a 16.9% over two years, an extra 2% for productivity, increases in the London allowance and the funding for training of paramedics. In return for this, the staff side agreed to not pursue the annual pay formula linked to pay systems of firefighters and police officers. By 13 March 1990, over 81% of ambulance workers nationwide had accepted the offer.

'Paramedic Skills' payment arrived in wages in June 1990 and was worth 17p an hour.

On 31 July 1990, Secretary of State for Health Kenneth Clarke announced £3.8 million was made available to buy defibrillators to equip 2350 front-line ambulances. Prior to that, ambulance crews had been fund raising for the previous four years to buy defibrillators to put on the ambulance. The British Heart Foundation would match a new defibrillator for each one purchased by ambulance services.

In the next ten years, consistent management reshuffles would disrupt the transition into this bold brave new world. The staff felt aggrieved that 33 years of underfunding had allowed the ambulance world to fall into the doldrums and block natural and obvious clinical development from 1966 to 1989 (23 years), and then constant management changes left much distrust in the new brooms named 'performance' and 'modernisation' that had arrived. The dust cloud was impressive.

The ambulance fleet was now very old and so new vehicles were required. The dispute had been a big financial drain on the ambulance service, and the out-of-date Vauxhall CF Bedfords were not a real option moving forward, so around the UK each service had its own cab chassis favourites and its own saloon builder. The London Ambulance Service (LAS) for example had Leyland Daf diesels with manual gear boxes and no door between cab and saloon. After a brief attempt to 'try them', the LAS switched back to a cab/saloon door and automatics and included petrol engines.

Uniforms arrived from Scotland as boiler suits, a bright green one piece that gave no regard to the user other than they were cheap. The uniforms were a mixed blessing for the staff, and within a year or two they were switched back to trousers and shirts, albeit by now ambulance services had lost ties and hats for road staff, whilst officers clung on to that military 'disciplined' past heritage.

A national Programme for paramedic training was being rolled out across the country, initially for existing intubation and infusion, or ambulance service trained extended trained staff to take on a two-week upgrade course to paramedic and then later a grand plan for having a paramedic on every ambulance by 1995 (DH, 1993). It was neither practical at that stage or even desirable to place a paramedic on every ambulance, as we needed to know what we were going to, and great efforts were employed to improve the emergency control system from paper and pen to full computer-aided dispatch (CAD) with algorithms to anticipate which street corner the next 999 call would appear from.

The role of paramedic had been established and was starting to flourish under a unified NHS Training Directorate (NHSTD) scheme. Extended training was now in the mainstream, and the weight of the extra skills required was causing several educationalists to question the quality of the underpinning knowledge base, to continue the building programme into the next century.

So, during the mid-1990s, two higher education institutions (HEIs) (Hertfordshire and Coventry) formed partnerships with ambulance services (London and Warwickshire) to develop degree schemes in paramedic science, setting the future pattern of development that would see a much wider role for HEIs in the preparation of paramedics. Hertfordshire went live with a top up programme for paramedics in 1996 and a full pre-registration degree for 18 new students in 1999, who would graduate in 2001. Coventry delayed for a few more years until the next millennium and were soon joined by many other HEIs.

The modern-day UK paramedic has seen key changes to their clinical practice, and career development has evolved from the early days of a simple first aid qualification and the status of manual workers through the progression of paramedic education, which has seen far-reaching improvements in the standards and quality of patient care.

There is now a much greater emphasis on critical clinical decision-making, treatment and management, and a greater responsibility for appropriately assessing service users to enable effective evidence-based decisions on where service users are best managed or referred to within the healthcare system. To do so requires paramedics to have routine access to community health and social care services to enable them to safely manage more patients at scene. A graduate profession was the way forward; however, there would be another 20 years of resistance from employers and regulators who preferred a simpler quick-fix training framework.

In the final years of the decade, 1999, paramedics voted to become registered as healthcare professionals (Saunders, 1998).

The year 2000 saw the arrival of not only the millennium, but also UK paramedics becoming registered as healthcare professionals with the Council of Professions Supplementary to Medicine (CPSM), using the protected title 'State Registered Paramedic'. This was in accordance with the Professions Supplementary to Medicine Act 1960 (the act), which provided for

> the establishment of a Council, boards and disciplinary committees for certain professions supplementary to medicine; to provide for the registration of members of those professions, for regulating their professional education and professional conduct and for cancelling registration in cases of misconduct; and for purposes connected with the matters aforesaid.
>
> (Professions Supplementary to Medicine Act 1960)

Another development regarding the education of the paramedic profession in 2000 was the proposed 'practitioner in emergency care' (PEC) concept (JRCALC-ASA, 2000), which started the debate on practitioner (*paramedic*) development in pre-hospital care. During the next three years, the wording of the PEC was reviewed and eventually set as 'emergency care practitioner' (ECP). In the same year, the University of Hertfordshire appointed the first paramedic academic Paul Burke in a UK university delivering paramedic education, whilst Andy Newton, also another past University of Hertfordshire senior tutor, later went on to become the first consultant paramedic and accept an appointment as chair of the professional body.

The CPSM provided a register for those 'registrants' who were members of their professional bodies; unfortunately, however, at that period this did not exist. Consequently, there was a requirement for a professional body for paramedics to be developed, and this was subsequently established and founded in 2001 by Richard Lane and Stephen Dolphin on 14 December 2001 as the British Paramedic Association (BPA) (Companies House, 2001). The paramedic profession now had its own professional body, run by paramedics, for paramedics. The very slow start to membership for the first five years was attributed to a paramedic workforce who had just got used to paying for registration in addition to union fees and were cautious to take on this new concept; however, membership accelerated after the headquarters were moved to Bridgwater.

The motto *Meditatio per Eruditio* loosely translated means 'We gain skill through study'—an extremely suitable motto for the paramedic profession.

Figure 3.1 British Paramedic Association—original logo: 2001–2005

COLLEGE OF PARAMEDICS
British Paramedic Association
Meditatio per Eruditio

Figure 3.2 British Paramedic Association—College of Paramedics logo: 2006–2011

Table 3.2 *Number of registrant paramedics 2001–2018*

Year	2001	2002	2003	2004	2005	2006	2007	2008	2009
Paramedics	8892	8778	9334	10,224	11,316	12,343	13,183	13,703	15,019
Year	2010	2011	2012	2013	2014	2015	2016	2017	2018
Paramedics	16,562	17,652	17,913	19,995	21,185	22,380	23,992	24,722	25,637

In the same year, the Health Professions Order 2001 (Legislation.gov.uk) was made under Section 60 of the Health Act 1999. This legislation established the Health Professions Council (HPC) as the regulatory body for UK paramedics and the other allied health professionals. In that first year, we started paramedicine with a small number of paramedics 8892 transferred from the CPSM register to the HPC register (Health and Care Professions Council, 2018a). The HPC came into force in February 2002, and the protected title was changed to 'paramedic'. However, in 2002, the number of paramedic registrants are recorded as only 8778; this lower figure was due to the adjustment of the late removals from the register. This year also saw the introduction of the first foundation degree in paramedic science at the University of Hertfordshire (a new funding pathway into higher education) and paramedics commencing employment in NHS walk-in centres and GP practices.

Education—Professional, Regulatory and Statutory Body Publications

By 2003, the HPC published several standards that specifically pertained to paramedic registrants and pre-registered student paramedics. These included the first editions of the *Standards of Proficiency, Paramedics* and *Standards of Conduct, Performance and Ethics* (Health Professions Council, 2003a, 2003b). These documents identified the generic standard for all registrants. The first (Health Professions Council, 2003a) identified in bold the standard for all registrants, whilst the normal text explained the sub-elements of the standard, and the blue text was specific for paramedics. The second document contains the standards that all registrants with the regulatory body must adhere to as part of maintaining registration and re-registration. In the same year, paramedics and the other allied health professionals (AHPs) were recognised as part of the multi-professional health workforce (Department of Health, 2003). This document identified the roles that AHPs played in delivering a wide range of services for patients, including first contact services, self-care, integrated care, ambulatory care, referral to other professionals, promoting expert patients, prescribing and care of chronic conditions. From the professional body perspective, 2003 saw the British Paramedic Association introduce a formal regional council structure and publish the first newsletter to members (College of Paramedics, 2018a).

On 3 March 2004, the title 'College of Paramedics' was registered with Companies House to protect our interest in a future change of title, away from BPA which was unpopular in Northern Ireland, Wales and Scotland. Later that same year, on the 1 December 2004, Richard Lane resigned as chair of the College of Paramedics. Bob Fellows was voted in as chair at the December board meeting. The College of Paramedics were consulted on by the regulatory body as part of the HPC *Continuing Professional Development— Consultation paper* (Health Professions Council, 2004). In 2004, B. Fellows, A. Newton and D. Whitmore, with others, produced and published the first Quality Assurance Agency for Higher Education (QAA) *Paramedic Science— Benchmark statement* (Quality Assurance Agency, 2004).

This subject benchmark statement, set at certificate, diploma and degree levels, would remain in force for education providers and higher education institutions until the second edition was published in 2016. There were other milestones in the development of the paramedic profession in 2004; one of these was the publication and introduction of the *Clinical Practice Guidelines* (Ambulance Service Association, 2004), for use in the UK ambulance services. These guidelines covered the full range of paramedic treatments then available across the UK. Another milestone was the publication of *The ECP Report: Right Skill, Right Time, Right Place* (Modernisation Agency, 2004). The latter document caused controversy from the professional and regulatory bodies' perspective, as the title 'ECP' did not identify the profession of the individual treating the patient. Whilst the report acknowledged the need for emergency care practitioners to be registered with an appropriate professional body to undertake autonomous clinical work, with three possible professional bodies recommended, this objective was not achieved. The titles nurse and paramedic returned, and the battle was won. The title has been superseded by the introduction of the *Paramedic Career Framework* authored by John Martin (College of Paramedics, 2018b), which demonstrates progression from paramedic to specialist, advanced and consultant paramedic.

In 2005, the regulatory body finalised and published the *Standards of Education and Training*. These standards set the threshold entry to the register for paramedics at the 'Equivalent to Certificate of Higher Education' (Level 4 on the Framework for Higher Education Qualifications (FHEQ); Level 7 on the Scottish Credit and Qualifications Framework (SCQF)) (Health Professions Council, 2005a). The HPC also published its key decisions on the continuing professional development which explained that the first CPD audit would occur between 31 July 2008 and 30 December 2008, with a focus on the activities undertaken in the two years preceding this (Health Professions Council, 2005b). The same year saw the publication of *Taking Healthcare to the Patient* (Department of Health, 2005), which saw the introduction of various recommendations, including a move to higher education–delivered models of education and training, with employers working in partnership with higher education institutions to introduce direct-entry higher education programmes as an entry route into the paramedic profession, rather than through the previous vocational route in an ambulance service. The report mentioned the College of Paramedics six times, which was a key benchmark for the professional body. The other benchmark was the college's first national conference held at the Royal Centre for Defence Medicine, Keogh Barracks, Aldershot (College of Paramedics, 2018a).

In 2006, the first edition of the professional body's curriculum, *A Curriculum Framework for Ambulance Education* (British Paramedic Association—College of Paramedics, 2006), was published. The same year also saw the publication of the *UK Ambulance Service Clinical Practice Guidelines* (Ambulance Service Association, 2006). The key changes within these guidelines from the 2004 edition included consent, patient confidentiality, pain management in adults and children, drugs, medical emergencies, specific treatment options, obstetrics and gynaecology, treatment and management of assault and abuse, emergencies in children, and cardiac arrest and arrhythmias; the latter were based on the *Resuscitation Guidelines 2005* (UK Resuscitation Council, 2005) which were derived by international consensus. During the same year, the HPC published *Continuing Professional Development and Your Registration* (Health Professions Council, 2006). This document was part of the communication process to inform registrants of the requirement for paramedics and other healthcare professionals to undertake continuing professional development (CPD) as part of the re-registration audit process, although the first audit of paramedics did not occur until the re-registration period of 2009 (Harris & Fellows, 2012).

The following year, a major publication was made by the regulatory body (HPC) which affected paramedics; this was the second edition of the *Standards of Proficiency, Paramedics* (Health Professions Council, 2007). The key changes from the 2003 edition related to Standard 3a.2, which no longer required paramedics to be able to use specific airway management, resuscitation, fluid resuscitation and replacement techniques. The reasoning provided by the HPC for the change was that these standards were covered in other publications relating to the paramedic profession. In the same year, the College of Paramedics, in partnership with several professional bodies and organisations, produced *A Joint Statement on Continuing Professional Development for Health and Social Care Practitioners* (Royal College of Nursing, 2007).

The purpose of the joint collaborative statement was to influence health and social care employers and influence UK-wide health and social care policymakers to support workplace representatives and the union learning agenda whilst facilitating the healthcare quality and the workforce modernisation agendas.

Another document published in 2007 affecting the development of the paramedic profession was *The Competence and Curriculum Framework for the Emergency Care Practitioner* (Skills for Health, 2007). This document impeded the development of the paramedic profession, as this assumed that paramedics were developing through the emergency care practitioner route, should local organisations wish to introduce ECPs into their service provision. However, not all employers of paramedics either utilised or developed this role. From the professional body perspective, the College of Paramedics was developing a career framework that was based upon the Skills for Health career framework, which included specialist, advanced, consultant and director levels post registration.

In 2008, the professional body published the *Paramedic Curriculum Guidance & Competence Framework*, second edition (College of Paramedics, 2008). This document had a career framework for paramedics which outlined a clear progression from paramedic to consultant paramedic and clinical director of services and contributed to defining a career pathway for paramedics. It also saw Bob Fellows resigning as chair after written criticism by his employer relating to his involvement in the professional body. In the same year, the college appointed the late Professor Malcolm Woollard as chair.

The regulatory body published the second edition of the *Standards of Conduct, Performance and Ethics* (Health Professions Council, 2008). The changes within this version focused less on the role of the standards in fitness to practise procedures and more on how registrants could use and meet the standards. In the same year, *Modernising Allied Health Professions (AHP) Careers: A Competence-Based Career Framework* (Department of Health, 2008) was published. This document also impeded the development of the paramedic profession in line with other non-medical and allied health professionals (AHPs), because paramedics were not included in the project. The reasoning behind this decision was because of their inclusion in the competence and curriculum framework for the emergency care practitioner document published in the previous year. Although paramedics were AHPs, as a profession they still did not have similar commissioning and education routes as other professions.

In 2009, the HPC published the second edition of the *Standards of Education and Training* (Health Professions Council, 2009). These are the standards which education providers must meet to ensure that all those completing an approved programme meet the respective standards of proficiency. The professional body appointed John Martin as vice chair of the College of Paramedics, and along with other directors reviewed the executive committee, and it was 2009 that saw the college send its first tweet. Sadly, in June 2009, the college was informed of the death of Carol Furber, wife of Roland Furber (chief executive). Carol was a remarkable lady who gave so much to so many, not least to the paramedic profession. From 2004 when Roland became chief executive of the college, Carol undertook a major unpaid role in supporting and promoting the professional body for paramedics. Her work included membership administration, minute taking and secretarial, assisting with conferences and amongst many other things, catering for meetings and conferences to help keep costs to a minimum. She was also a major advocate for the college through the many hours she would spend talking to people from a wide range of professional levels about the work of the profession and the development of the college. The college struggled for a year or two after Carol's death, and we missed her administrative and organisational skills.

On 27 March 2010, Roland Frederick Furber resigned as chief executive of the College of Paramedics due to ill health. The following month on

19 April, Professor Malcolm Frederick Woollard resigned as the chair. May saw the registered office change from Derby to Bridgwater. The stewardship of the college was held by the vice chair and members of the executive until the appointments of Professor Andrew Newton as chair and Dave Hodge as the chief executive. The College of Paramedics joined Facebook in the same year. The year 2010 saw the publication of the UK Resuscitation Council guidelines (UK Resuscitation Council, 2010), which included changes to basic, advanced and new-born life support, all of which affected paramedics, both registrants and students.

In December 2011, the College of Paramedics as the professional body for UK paramedics celebrated its tenth birthday. At the council meeting in January, it was agreed to update the professional body's logo (Figure 3.3).

(For use on white backgrounds, see Figure 3.4.)

During the same year, the college introduced regional groups and CPD events across the UK. Some events were hosted independently and others in partnership with higher education institutions. Most of the events were with the support of the college's then corporate sponsor, Bound Tree Medical. The college's professional standards directorate implemented an 'Endorsement' process, which allowed education providers to apply for their pre-registration paramedic science programme to be endorsed against the college's Paramedic Curriculum Guidance.

In 2012, the University of Greenwich, BSc (Hons) Paramedic Science programme was 'Endorsed' against the paramedic curriculum guidance—the first to do so. The college appointed Ewan Armitage as the Head of Endorsements. During the same year, the college applied to the Department of Health for paramedics to be included in the NHS Bursary system. This was successful for Stages 1–4; however, this was overtaken by the spending review of

Figure 3.3 College of Paramedics logo: 2011—present day

Figure 3.4 College of Paramedics logo: 2011—present day (for use on white backgrounds)

2015, which ended the NHS Bursary system in England. At the June council meeting, Professor Mary Lovegrove and June Davis provided a presentation regarding the evidence-based case for the strategic aims of the College of Paramedics. The council formally approved the work across all four nations to commence, and that report was published in 2013. The HPC changed their name to the Health and Care Professions Council (HCPC) (Health Professions Council, 2012) and was brought about by the Health and Social Care Act 2012, which also required the regulation of social workers in England to be undertaken by the HCPC.

In 2013, the College of Paramedics launched its medical malpractice and public liability insurance as a benefit for full members. In 2013 the Francis Report (Her Majesty's Government, 2013) was published, which included recommendations for healthcare professionals, including paramedics. The year 2013 also saw the publication of the *Paramedic Evidence-Based Education Project (PEEP) Report* (Lovegrove & Davis, 2013). The study was commissioned by the Department of Health (England) National Allied Health Professional Advisory Board and funded by the College of Paramedics. The report made several recommendations regarding the education and development of paramedics and the professional body that would be implemented and achieved during the next five years. The college as the professional body for paramedics were consulted by the regulatory body during 2013 on the review of the *Standards of Proficiency—Paramedics*.

In 2014, the College of Paramedics appointed its first executive officer (Martin Berry); the position was to support the chief executive and provide continuity with the then council executive. In the same year, the college published the *Paramedic Curriculum Guidance,* third edition, and the career framework diagram (College of Paramedics, 2014a). The college also published its five-year Strategic Plan 2014–2019 and advised members of the national conference being held at the University of Warwick on 6 and 7 October 2014 (College of Paramedics, 2014b). In 2014, the HCPC published *Professional Indemnity and Your Registration* (Health and Care Professions Council, 2014a) in readiness for future professional indemnity requirements, and the third edition of the *Standards of Proficiency—Paramedics* (Health and Care Professions Council, 2014b).

In 2015, Dave Hodge retired as chief executive and Gerry Egan was appointed as the new chief executive. The college published its first podcast and published the *Post Registration—Paramedic Career Framework,* third edition (College of Paramedics, 2015a), and the revised third edition of *Paramedic Curriculum Guidance* (College of Paramedics, 2015b). The latter was due to an independent review of the third edition undertaken by the UCL Institute of Education on behalf of Health Education England. In the same year, the college published *Paramedic—Scope of Practice Policy* (College of Paramedics, 2015c). The college became a registered charity [Number 1164445] as part of its objective in obtaining Royal College status, and the structure changed accordingly. The College of Paramedics—Council now became known as the Board of Trustees, which included trustee officials and representatives, and the executive team comprising of paid employees. The college, following consultation with its members, renamed its newsletter to *Paramedic INSIGHT* (College of Paramedics, 2015d). In 2015, the Migration Advisory Committee Report (Centre for Workforce Intelligence, 2015) was published, which recommended that paramedics were added to the shortage occupation list (SOL). Whilst the number of UK paramedics had increased by over 13,000, from 8892 to 22,380, since becoming a registered profession in 2001, there was now a shortage of paramedics within UK ambulance services, the previous mainstay employer. In 2015, the HCPC introduced a professional indemnity requirement which advised that, by law, registrants (other than social workers in England) must have a professional indemnity arrangement in place as a condition of registration. For those already HCPC registered, the HCPC incorporated a similar professional declaration as part of the renewal process (Health and Care Professions Council, 2015). The college in response to these changes amended its medical malpractice and public liability insurance to include indemnity cover for full members.

The College of Paramedics in 2016 had another productive and busy year, commencing with the recruitment and appointment of Graham Harris as the first National Education Lead; this appointment was a recommendation of the PEEP report. The college worked with various agencies and published the *Digital Paramedic Career Framework* (College of Paramedics, 2016a), which provided case studies of paramedics across the four career pathways. This was followed by the recruitment and appointment of Bob Fellows as head of Professional Development (College of Paramedics, 2016b). The college advertised and appointed Kerry Crawley as Clinical Lead e-Learning for Health (eLfH). The posts oversaw the development of an e-learning programme package for registered and pre-registered paramedics according to the modern scope of practice, which included the following subjects: Mental Health, Clinical Decision Making, End of Life Care, Paramedics Ethics and the Law, and Pain Management. The project was launched at the 2017 national conference.

In 2016, the College of Paramedics launched the *British Paramedic Journal (BPJ)*, a quarterly electronic journal committed to publishing high-quality research and increasing the evidence base for the paramedic profession. The *BPJ* is freely accessible to members of the college at www.collegeofparamedics.co.uk or on the *BPJ* website at: http://britishparamedicjournal.co.uk.

Representatives from the Education Advisory Committee chaired and worked collaboratively with the QAA and other agencies in producing the second edition of the *Subject Benchmark Statement—Paramedics* (Quality Assurance Agency, 2016). In 2016, the college also provided medical malpractice and public liability insurance for student members whilst undertaking elective placements. The college also sent its first Instagram and achieved 10,000 full paramedic members. The HCPC published the revised *Standards of Conduct, Performance and Ethics* and the *Guidance on Conduct and Ethics for Students* (Health and Care Professions Council, 2016a, 2016b). The first affected all registrant paramedics and the second all student paramedics on pre-registration programmes.

In 2017, the college published the *Paramedic Post-Graduate—Curriculum Guidance* (College of Paramedics, 2017a), and launched phase 1 of the e-learning programme for paramedics at the national conference (College of Paramedics, 2017b). At the national conference, the college provided all delegates with a conference edition of the *Practice Educator Guidance Handbook*, which was then reviewed and published in August 2017 (College of Paramedics, 2017c). The year 2017 also saw the change of chair from Professor Andy Newton to John Martin, and the college recruited and appointed Gary Strong as the National CPD Lead responsible for all CPD delivered by the College of Paramedics (College of Paramedics, 2017d). The college published the fourth edition of the *Paramedic Curriculum Guidance* (College of Paramedics, 2017e), and the 2017 *Digital Paramedic Career Framework* (College of Paramedics, 2017f). During the period of September to December 2017, the HCPC undertook a public consultation on the threshold level of qualification for entry to the register for paramedics (Health and Care Professions Council, 2017). However, 2017 will be remembered in the history of the paramedic profession as the year that the Commission on Human Medicines (CHM) supported the case for independent prescribing by paramedics (College of Paramedics, 2017g); this was the culmination of several years' work by the professional body and other agencies.

To date, 2018 has seen the HCPC Education and Training Committee publish its executive summary and recommendations on the threshold level of qualification for entry to the register for paramedics (Health and Care Professions Council, 2018b). In summary, the executive proposed the following.

The threshold level for paramedics to change to degree level (level 6/9/10 on the qualification frameworks).

The change to be implemented in two stages:

1   With immediate effect, we will not accept any new applications for approval of paramedic programmes that are delivered at below degree level (level 6/9/10).
2   From 1 September 2021, we will withdraw approval from existing programmes delivered below the new threshold level. They will not be able to take on any new cohorts.

The attainment of the threshold level for paramedics to degree level has been the culmination of several years' work by the professional body and another recommendation of the PEEP report. On 1 April 2018, the Human Medicines (Amendment) Regulations 2018 came into force that enabled paramedics to become independent prescribers (Legislation.gov.uk). The college released phase 2 of the e-learning programme for paramedics at the national conference (College of Paramedics, 2018c). The module titles for phase 2 are 'Maternity Care for Paramedics', 'Urgent Care for Paramedics—Illness', Urgent Care for Paramedics—Injuries', 'Long-term Conditions for Paramedics' and Paediatrics for Paramedics.

The College of Paramedics is currently chairing work in partnership with several professional bodies and organisations in reviewing the 2007 joint statement on continuing professional development for health and social care practitioners, which will be published later in 2018.

Conclusion

At the point of writing in 2018, a total of 25,637 paramedics were registered with the HCPC (Health and Care Professions Council, 2018a), a threefold increase since the council became registered in 2001. The paramedic profession and professional body is less than two decades old, yet it has transformed from being a vocational role, able to provide first aid at scene and transportation, into a profession that delivers healthcare to the UK population in primary, urgent, unscheduled, emergency and critical care settings. The College of Paramedics, through the diligence and dedication of its members and elected representatives, has achieved numerous milestones and continues to lead the development of the paramedic profession. At the time of writing, 41.4% of all UK paramedics are full members of the College of Paramedics—the growth is phenomenal, at over 18% increase year on year for the past decade.

Bibliography

Ambulance Service Association (2004) *Clinical Practice Guidelines—For Use in U.K. Ambulance Services.* [online] Available at: www.nelh-ec.warwick.ac.uk/JRCALC_Guidelines_v3_2004.pdf. Accessed. 17.08.18.

Ambulance Service Association, Fisher, J.D., Brown, S.D., and Cooke, M.W. (Editors) (2006) *UK Ambulance Service Clinical Practice Guidelines* (2006). [online] Available at: https://warwick.ac.uk/fac/sci/med/research/hsri/emergencycare/prehos pitalcare/jrcalcstakeholderwebsite/guidelines/clinical_guidelines_2006.pdf. Accessed. 23.07.18.

Baskett, P.J.F., and Withnell, A. (1970) Use of Entonox in the Ambulance Service. *British Medical Journal*, 2, 41–44.

Briggs, R.S., Brown, P.M., Crabb, M.E., Cox, T.J., Ead, H.W., Hawkes, R.A., Jequier, P.W., Southall, D.P., Grainger D.P., Williams, J.H., Chamberlain, D.A. (1976) *British Medical Journal*, 2, 1161.

British Paramedic Association—College of Paramedics (2006) *A Curriculum Framework for Ambulance Education.* Derby: British Paramedic Association.

Centre for Workforce Intelligence (2015) *Migration Advisory Committee (MAC)—Healthcare Occupation Submission. Main Report for the 2014 Shortage Occupation List (SOL).* London: Centre for Workforce Intelligence.

Clegg, H.A (1979) Local Authority and University Manual Workers NHS Ancillary Staff, and Ambulancemen. Standing Commission on Pay Comparability, Report number 1. Cmd 7641: HMSO.

College of Paramedics (2008) *Paramedic Curriculum Guidance & Competence Framework.* 2nd edition. Derby: College of Paramedics.

College of Paramedics (2014a) *Paramedic Curriculum Guidance.* 3rd edition. Bridgwater: College of Paramedics.

College of Paramedics (2014b) July 2014 Newsletter. [online]. Available at: www.col legeofparamedics.co.uk/news/jul. Accessed. 03.09.18.

College of Paramedics (2015a) *Post Registration—Paramedic Career Framework.* 3rd edition. Bridgwater: College of Paramedics.

College of Paramedics (2015b) *Paramedic Curriculum Guidance.* 3rd edition (Revised). Bridgwater: College of Paramedics.

College of Paramedics (2015c) *Paramedic—Scope of Practice Policy.* Bridgwater: College of Paramedics.

College of Paramedics (2015d) *Paramedic INSIGHT*. August 2015, Vol.1, No.1. [online]. Available at: www.collegeofparamedics.co.uk/member-services/newsletters. Accessed. 03.09.18.

College of Paramedics (2016a) *Email News Digest*. 9 July 2016. College of Paramedics launches interactive Career Framework [online]. Available at: www.collegeof paramedics.co.uk/member-services/email-news-digest Accessed. 06.09.18.

College of Paramedics (2016b) *Paramedic INSIGHT*. June 2016, Vol.2, No.2. [online]. Available at: www.collegeofparamedics.co.uk/member-services/newsletters. Accessed. 03.09.18.

College of Paramedics (2017a) *Paramedic Post-Graduate—Curriculum Guidance*. [online] Available at: www.collegeofparamedics.co.uk/publications/post-graduate-curriculum-guidance. Accessed. 04.09.18.

College of Paramedics (2017b) *e-Learning CPD*. [online]. Available at: www.col legeofparamedics.co.uk/member-services/cpd-hub/access-the-free-e-learning-cpd. Accessed. 04.09.18.

College of Paramedics (2017c) *Practice Educator Guidance Handbook*. Bridgwater: College of Paramedics.

College of Paramedics (2017d) *Paramedic INSIGHT*. September 2017, Vol.3, No.3. [online]. Available at: www.collegeofparamedics.co.uk/member-services/newsletters. Accessed. 04.09.18.

College of Paramedics (2017e) *Paramedic Curriculum Guidance*. 4th edition. [online]. Available at: www.collegeofparamedics.co.uk/publications/professional-standards. Accessed. 06.09.18.

College of Paramedics (2017f) Digital Paramedic Career Framework. [online] Available at: www.collegeofparamedics.co.uk/publications/digital-career-framework. Accessed. 06.09.18.

College of Paramedics (2017g) *Independent Prescribing by Paramedics to be Recommended for Implementation*. [online]. Available at: www.collegeofparamed ics.co.uk/news/independent-prescribing-by-paramedics-to-be-recommended-for-implementation. Accessed. 06.09.18.

College of Paramedics (2018a) *The Journey of the College of Paramedics*. [online]. Available at: www.collegeofparamedics.co.uk/about_us/the-journey-of-the-college. Accessed. 23.07.18.

College of Paramedics (2018b) *Post Registration—Paramedic Career Framework*. 4th edition. [online]. Available at: www.collegeofparamedics.co.uk/publications/post-reg-career-framework. Accessed. 20.08.18.

College of Paramedics (2018c) *Free eLearning CPD for Paramedics—Phase 2 Now Live! Paramedic INSIGHT*. June 2018, Vol.4, No.2. [online]. Available at: www.collegeofparamedics.co.uk/member-services/newsletters. Accessed. 06.09.18.

Companies House (2001) *The British Paramedic Association—Company Number 4340181. Incorporation*. [online]. Available at: https://beta.companieshouse.gov.uk/company/04340181/filing-history?page=2. Accessed. 28.08.18.

Companies House (2004) College of Paramedics—Company Number 05062387. Incorporation. [online]. Available at: https://beta.companieshouse.gov.uk/company/05062387/filing-history?page=5. Accessed. 17.08.18.

Conahan, J. (2010) *A Coach and Horses*. London: Blackwell Publishing.

Department of Health (1993) *The Health of the Nation: Key Area Handbook: Accidents*. London: Department of Health.

Department of Health (2003) *The Chief Health Professions Officer's Ten Key Roles for Allied Health Professionals*. [online]. Available at: www.acprc.org.uk/Data/Resource_Downloads/10_key_roles.pdf. Accessed. 24.07.18.

Department of Health (2005) *Taking Healthcare to the Patient: Transforming NHS Ambulance Services*. London. Department of Health. Available at: www.dh.gov. uk/publications. Accessed. 23.08.18.

Department of Health (2008) *Modernising Allied Health Professions Careers: A Competence Based Career Framework*. London. Department of Health.

Gearty, G.F., Hickey, N., Bourke, G.J., and Mulcahy, R. (1971) Pre-hospital coronary care service. *British Medical Journal*, July 3, 3 (5765), 33–35.

Geddes, J.S., Adgey, A.A.J., and Pantridge, J.F. (1967). Cardiac Ambulance Model. *Lancet*, 2, 273.

Government Hansard (1990) Kenneth Clark. Available at: https://api.parliament.uk/historic-hansard/commons/1990/jan/11/ambulance-dispute. Accessed.14.09.18.

Harris, G., and Fellows, B. (2012) Continuing professional development: Pre and post registration. In Blaber, A. (ed) *Foundations for paramedic practice: A theoretical perspective*. 2nd edition. New York: McGraw Hill, Open University Press.

Health and Care Professions Council (2014a) *Professional Indemnity and Your Registration*. London: HCPC.

Health and Care Professions Council (2014b) *Standards of Proficiency—Paramedics*. London: HCPC.

Health and Care Professions Council (2015) *Professional Indemnity*. [online]. Available at: http://hpc-uk.org/registrants/indemnity/. Accessed. 03.09.18.

Health and Care Professions Council (2016a) *Standards of Conduct, Performance and Ethics*. London: HCPC.

Health and Care Professions Council (2016b) *Guidance on Conduct and Ethics for Students*. London: HCPC.

Health and Care Professions Council (2017) *Consultation on the Threshold Level of Qualification for Entry to the Register for Paramedics*. [online]. Available at: www.hcpc-uk.org/aboutus/consultations/index.asp?id=225. Accessed. 06.09.18.

Health and Care Professions Council (2018a) *Historic Registrant Statistics*. [online]. Available at: www.hpc-uk.org/aboutregistration/theregister/oldstats/. Accessed. 23.07.18.

Health and Care Professions Council (2018b) *Threshold Level of Qualification for Entry to the Register for Paramedics—Executive Summary and Recommendations*. [online]. Available at: www.hcpc-uk.org/assets/documents/100056F2Enc02-Thresholdlevelofqualificationforparamedics.pdf. Accessed. 06.09.18.

Health Professions Council (2003a) *Standards of Proficiency, Paramedics*. London: HPC.

Health Professions Council (2003b) *Standards of Conduct, Performance and Ethics*. London: HPC.

Health Professions Council (2004) *Continuing Professional Development—Consultation Paper*. [online]. Available at: www.hcpc-uk.org/assets/documents/10000575cpd_consultation_document.pdf. Accessed. 21.08.18.

Health Professions Council (2005a) *Standards of Education and Training*. London: HPC.

Health Professions Council (2005b) *Continuing Professional Development—Key Decisions*. www.hcpc-uk.org/assets/documents/100008F3CPD_key_decisions.pdf. Accessed. 21.08.18.

Health Professions Council (2006b) *Continuing Professional Development and Your Registration*. London: HPC.

Health Professions Council (2007) *Standards of Proficiency, Paramedics*. London: HPC.

Health Professions Council (2008) *Standards of Conduct, Performance and Ethics*. London: HPC.

Health Professions Council (2009) *Standards of Education and Training*. London: HPC.

Health Professions Council (2012) *We Have Changed Our Name*. [online]. Available at: www.hpc-uk.org/aboutus/namechange/. Accessed. 28.08.18.

Her Majesty's Government (1960) *Professions Supplementary to Medicine Act 1960*. [online]. Available at: www.legislation.gov.uk/ukpga/Eliz2/8-9/66. Accessed. 23.07.18.

Her Majesty's Government (2001) *The Health Professions Order 2001*. [online]. Available at: www.legislation.gov.uk/uksi/2002/254/contents/made. Accessed. 23.07.18.

Her Majesty's Government (2013) *Report of the Mid Staffordshire NHS Foundation Trust Public Inquiry – Executive Summary*. [online]. Available at: https://assets. publishing.service.gov.uk/government/uploads/system/uploads/attachment_data/ file/279124/0947.pdf. Accessed. 28.07.18.

Her Majesty's Government (2018) *The Human Medicines (Amendment) Regulations 2018*. [online]. Available at: www.legislation.gov.uk/uksi/2018/199/made. Accessed. 06.09.18.

Joint Royal Colleges and Ambulance Liaison Committee and the Ambulance Services Association (2000) *The Future Role and Education of Paramedic Ambulance Service Personnel, Emerging Concepts*. London: A Subcommittee of the Joint Royal Colleges and Ambulance Liaison Committee and the Ambulance Services Association.

Kerr, A., and Sachdev, S. (1992) Third Among Equals: An Analysis of the 1989 Ambulance Dispute. *British Journal of Industrial Relations*, 30 (1).

Lovegrove, M., and Davis, J. (2013) *Paramedic Evidence-Based Education Project (PEEP) Report*. Buckinghamshire: Allied Health Solutions.

Ministry of Health, Scottish Home and Health Department (1966) *Report by the Working Party on Ambulance Training and Equipment: Part 1 – Training*. HMSO: London.

Ministry of Health, Scottish Home and Health Department (1967) *Report by the Working Party on Ambulance Training and Equipment: Part 2 – Equipment*. HMSO: London.

Modernisation Agency (2004) *The ECP Report: Right Skill, Right Time, Right Place*. Available at: http://minney.org/Publications/The_ECP_Report_Right_Skill_Right_ Time_Right_Place.pdf. Accessed. 20.08.18.

New Brooms Sweep Clean (2002) *McGraw-Hill Dictionary of American Idioms and Phrasal Verbs* (n.d.). https://idioms.thefreedictionary.com/ New+brooms+sweep+clean. Accessed. 22.08.18 and 14.09.18.

Quality Assurance Agency for Higher Education (QAA) (2004) *Paramedic Science— Benchmark Statement: Health Care Programmes Phase 2*. Gloucester: QAA.

Quality Assurance Agency for Higher Education (QAA) (2016) *Subject Benchmark Statement—Paramedics*. [online]. Available at: www.qaa.ac.uk/docs/qaa/subject-benchmark-statements/sbs-paramedics-16.pdf?sfvrsn=9594f781_12. Accessed. 04.09.16.

Resuscitation Council (UK) (2005) *Resuscitation Guidelines 2005*. [online]. Available at: www.resus.org.uk/archive/guidelines-2005/. Accessed. 21.08.18.

Resuscitation Council (UK) (2010) *Resuscitation Guidelines 2010*. [online]. Available at: www.resus.org.uk/archive/guidelines-2010/. Accessed. 04.09.18.

Royal College of Nursing (2007) *A Joint Statement on Continuing Professional Development for Health and Social Care Practitioners*. London: Royal College of Nursing.

Saunders, R. (1998) "Yes" To State Registration—How Paramedics are Moving Towards Registered Professionals. *Ambulance UK*, 13 (4), 206–209.

Skills for Health (2007) *The Competence and Curriculum Framework for the Emergency Care Practitioner*. Bristol: Skills for Health.

White, N.M., Parker, W.S., Binning, R.E., Kimber, E.R., Ead, H.W., and Chamberlain, D.A. (1973) Mobile Coronary Care Provided by Ambulance Personnel. *British Medical Journal*, 3, 618–622.

Workers.org (1990) [online]. Available at: http://www.workers.org.uk/features/feat_1010/ambulance.html. Accessed. 14.03.19.

Wright, K. (1984) *Extended Training of Ambulance Staff*. Institute for Research in the Social Sciences Centre for Health Economics, University of York.

4 Personal Reflections on Fire and Rescue Service Incident Command

Roy Wilsher

Introduction and Background

Incident command is a mainstay of an operational fire officer's role. It is something we pride ourselves in, something that is learnt and considered from the first time one becomes a member of a firefighting crew and stays with you until the day you leave. Being part of a crew means you need to understand the operational principles, who is in charge, the incident ground structure and how you fit into the operational plan. Incident command and operational practice are critical; if they go wrong, people, including tragically sometimes firefighters, can be lost.

But it is not only about life risk; good operational command can help mitigate property, economic, environmental and societal damage. Something that makes fire and rescue services adept at incident command is the fact that the same model is used whether it is a single car alight or one of the biggest fires seen in the United Kingdom, including Buncefield (HSE 2011) and Grenfell (The Grenfell Tower Inquiry 2018). Fire service incident commanders know the system.

They use the system and adapt it as necessary, but within the recognised framework. Although, with the fall in the number of fires, on-the-job training and experience has reduced, so training and assessment needs to increase. Criticising a fire officer's ability to command an incident is taken very seriously, and no one wants to be seen as not competent in this vital role. The incident commander can very quickly become directly responsible for the lives of others, including their own colleagues.

My intention is to explore some of my own incident command experiences, from the very first incident to my biggest. I will recount some of my own thoughts and experiences, consider the new thinking on incident command psychology and theories, how incident command is vital to a multi-agency approach to tackling major and complex incidents, and then explore some of the new innovations, including virtual reality.

I joined London Fire Brigade in November 1981 and was posted to my first station, Hornsey in north London, in April 1982. About three years later, I was in charge of a fire engine for the first time. In fire and rescue services today, the aim is to train people to take charge of a fire engine before they actually do so, often colloquially known as 'a ticket to ride'. But in 1984, it was just as likely that a willing crew member would take temporary promotion for the night to enable a colleague to take leave.

That is exactly the position I was in as a temporary leading firefighter barely turned 22 as we came across a road traffic accident (road traffic collision, RTC). Questions rushed through my head, What message should I send control? What should I tell the experienced crew to do, should I stop the traffic? Do we need the police? How do I ensure my crew remain safe whilst they assist the trapped driver? What bit do I do first? I knew most of the questions; fortunately, my experienced crew knew the answers. The driver radioed control; "running call, road traffic accident, one person trapped, ambulance and police required". The crew in the back were straight into high-visibility jackets and off the fire engine with what passed as RTC equipment in the early 1980s, directing traffic and starting to stabilise the car and the casualty.

I am not so sure I actually commanded that incident—it was more making sure I helped and did not get in the way. I thanked the crew afterwards and mumbled a short explanation of why I was not more dynamic. They were supportive as ever, said I would learn and it was my turn to make the tea. I remember the incident vividly; I even remember three main members of the crew, driver Brian Partridge with Ian Scott, apologies Scott and Dennis Huckle in the back. The lessons from that incident stayed with me. I knew I had to learn my incident command craft and always recognised the importance of well-trained and motivated fire crews.

It wasn't much further into my career when I found myself with more temporary promotion as a leading firefighter at Tottenham Fire station Red watch. Like my first station, Hornsey, Tottenham in the early 1980s was a busy area for fires, especially in derelict buildings. I was in charge of a fire engine one night, Tottenham had two full-time crewed fire engines and the first machine was out on a call when we received a call to a factory fire. This turned out to be my first 'make up'. A make up in fire service parlance is when you make a priority call for assistance as the incident appears to require more resources. We had two fire engines attending, so I sent a priority message to control to make pumps four. This required another set of skills, a larger attack plan to deal with a larger fire, liaising directly with the officers in charge of the extra fire engines so worked together to resolve the incident, putting into practice the need for a plan of attack, spans of control and clear, concise, regular communication.

When developing a plan and providing control and communication, something that has embedded itself in my own command skills and is now widely recognised across the emergency blue light services and beyond, is situational awareness. I know that different reports going into a single point, whether it is an on-scene command unit or a strategic co-ordination group (SCG), can cause confusion and lead to different, or worse, conflicting decisions being made. Hence the importance of a common recognised picture of what the incident is and what is affected. I will cover this in more detail later, but one of my first realisations of the importance of situational awareness was when I was in charge of a fire in a theatre in the Haymarket in central London.

For various reasons, I spent most of the time on the back of the control unit working with the command team to deal with the incident. It was only later when the fire was reported to be almost out that I stepped down from the control unit to look round the incident ground. I realised that the fire I had been fighting from the back of the unit was not quite the same size and shape of incident the firefighters had been fighting on the ground—another lesson learned.

Situational awareness and good communication with other emergency services was always important but was driven home to me when I was a station officer at Soho fire station, my last role on a watch before joining the ranks of the flexible duty officers as an assistant divisional officer, now known as station managers or commanders. Being born and growing up in London, I had lived with the threat of IRA terrorism and whilst at Soho fire station had dealt with IRA fire bomb attacks. But the call we received in early February 1991 was a new dimension; there had been a mortar bomb attack on Downing Street and we were the first fire service resource in attendance (see Dillon 1996). A really good example of you never know what you will be called to, it was an incident that certainly got the mind racing, a new dimension in the way terrorists were bringing their fight to the UK mainland. Over 25 years ago we had procedures for terrorist incidents, but they were not as well developed as they are now with the onset of counterterrorism hubs and the Joint Emergency Services Interoperability Programme (JESIP 2018). Liaison with police colleagues was vital; was there a possibility of a secondary explosion? Downing Street and Whitehall were in lock down, and it wasn't long before the world's media were alerted. To be honest, we didn't do much firefighting; the danger of the van from which the mortars were launched exploding was too great, we made sure there was no undue spread of fire and held back whilst army bomb disposal experts checked the area. It is a vivid memory, with one of the overriding images being the hundreds of media people held at the top of Whitehall as we drove back to Shaftsbury Avenue through Trafalgar Square; the role of media and press was a developing theme throughout the rest of my career.

Life as a Flexible Duty Officer

The next phase of my career, as a flexible duty officer, added new skills, experience and knowledge in incident command. Becoming a flexible duty officer brings different demands. Not only do you manage more people, but you also attend and take charge of larger incidents, becoming part of a team when you need to, but travelling to and from incidents by yourself, picking up what information and situational awareness you can via a briefing from control or over the main scheme radio. It was vital to learn the skills of gathering information from control during the initial call. What is the incident, are any people involved, who is in attendance, who is in charge, are there any risks associated with the building or location, have there been any messages? You ask these questions and others that might help build a picture, or gain situational awareness. Then whilst travelling to the incident going through this information in your mind, assessing what might be taking place—you might even know the current commander and their strengths and weaknesses—you start to formulate a plan.

On arrival, I learnt early on to park a little way from the incident and use the time whilst you get your fire gear on to assess the situation, using sight and sound to try to improve situational awareness. It is easy when first starting on this route to rush and not put yourself in the best possible position. It sounds a bit trite, but a piece of vital advice I received in my early days on 'flexi' was, 'an officer never runs'. This was a way for an experienced assistant chief fire officer to tell me to take time to gather the information and to remain calm. What the people on the control unit and wider incident ground do not want to see is an officer who does not appear to be in control or know what they are doing.

As a flexi duty officer attending an incident, I would likely find that there would already be a control point, quite possibly a control unit with a command support team in place. Certainly there would be an incident commander in place, and at the right time a full and coherent briefing from this commander would be vital; What is the situation, how are the resources, what is the plan, any priority actions or risks? This would become a handover if the incident was large enough or you decide to take command. Often the previous commander would become part of the command support team that grows and shifts depending on the needs of the incident, sector command, both operational and functional; functional being where a particular task or resource needs some control, for example, water supply for firefighting or breathing apparatus. A good command support team is important to any commander with a larger incident to command. If you do not take command, as the oncoming officer then you will monitor and support the incident commander, being another set of eyes that can offer support, but also monitoring performance in order to feedback at later debriefs. Many fire and rescue services, if not all, have arrangements for this formal monitoring. When I was in London Fire Brigade, this became very formal and was known as Operations and Training Performance Inspection, or OTPI.

OTPI was a dedicated performance team that would attend incidents to monitor performance and would be in addition to any officer attending as a flexible duty officer. Some members of OTPI became infamous, I remember one particular Christmas eve when I was on duty, I had already taken charge of two four-pump (fire engine) incidents, one where unfortunately a member of the public died, and was then called to take charge of a six-pump fire at a church on Kingsway London. I found myself at lunch time on Christmas day on the church roof, having been up most of the night, being questioned by a member of OTPI. It made me think.

Monitoring and debriefing are vital components of the need to maintain performance and constantly improve. Much as it may seem that firefighting is pretty much the same year after year, modern methods of construction, different fire loads and different levels of skill and experience make it vital to learn from every incident. We now have a national tool, National Operational Learning (NOL), that captures information from across the UK to feed into our national operational guidance and also links in to the multi-agency JESIP tool, Joint Organisational Learning (JOL), so JESIP doctrine (JESIP 2018) can stay up to date. The formal debriefing is vital and is conducted using tools such as a performance review of command. This type of learning and the analysis of the issues led to the first development of the linear decision-making model that appeared so clearly in the second edition of the fire and rescue service incident command manual (DCLG 2008).

Also important are the 'hot debriefs' that will often see firefighters and officers gathered on the incident ground after an incident to identify immediate learning or issues to follow up on. As important is the informal debrief that often happens back at the fire station over a strong hot cup of tea, a time for the team to talk and wind down from often stressful situations. It is this last type of debrief I missed most as a new flexi-duty officer. One incident in particular springs to mind. It was a four- or six-pump fire at a house in Mayfair, a significant fire; there were bars on the windows and more than one staircase inside that led to different bedrooms. Unfortunately, we lost children to the fire that night. I drove back to my base alone in the early hours of the morning and had to get petrol. I can remember looking through the security glass at the cashier and thinking, you don't know what I have just seen and done. I can also recall returning to base alone, not wanting to disturb anyone else and sitting alone, without that debrief over a cup of tea and wishing I had gone back to the fire station instead. As Grenfell has shown, looking after the mental well-being of all involved, including the emergency responders, should not be overlooked.

Kentish Town High Street

One consideration of the monitoring role is making the decision whether to take over as incident commander. Often it was straightforward, as service orders would dictate when you took over, depending on the number of fire engines in attendance. It was possible to leave a lower rank in charge if the incident was suitable and could also be used as a learning opportunity; a fire in a derelict house with no people involved would be a clear example. It was only once that I had to take over at a level below which my rank dictated I should. It was an eight-pump fire in Kentish Town High Street in a medium-size builders merchants. I met with the incident commander, whom I knew well. I was confident in his abilities, but issues on the incident ground were not going well, and after my second tour of the incident I confirmed that I would take over as incident commander and wanted the current incident commander to take charge of the forward firefighting.

Taking over like this was a rare event and I was questioned by OTPI. It was my decision, and as an officer, leader and incident commander, you must make decisions and stand by them; the worse decision is no decision. This incident was notable for another aspect of leadership and incident command—'confirming understanding'. Cylinders at a fire create a particular hazard; they can fail dramatically and cause extensive damage to life and limb.

That is why when a person from the builders merchants came on to the control unit to tell us that the back of the building was absolutely full with shoulder-high cylinders that where a dark colour, it sounded very much like acetylene cylinders, probably our biggest cylinder hazard and demanding a 400-metre exclusion zone. Gathering information from on-site individuals who know the building layout, whether people are inside and the hazards involved, is a standard process for any incident commander and helps formulate the tactical plan. But just as important is confirming the information being given and understanding what is being said. It turned out, after many minutes questioning that the individual was describing new empty cooper hot water tanks, which were actually of little or no hazard to the firefighters. Getting that information correct prevented even more chaos to that area of north London.

The IRA Bombing of Canary Wharf in 1996

Having said it was laid down in service orders at what stage a different rank of officer would take over as incident commander, this did not happen on one particular occasion for me. It was the night of another IRA attack, the bombing of Canary Wharf in 1996 (Oppenheimer 2009). I was a divisional officer (group manager) on duty that night and was called to a fire in a warehouse in Edgware. By the time I got there, it was a 15-pump fire which would normally have a principal officer, assistant or deputy chief in charge, at least two ranks above my own. But then Canary Wharf happened and all eyes were turned to the docklands and the major incident there. I was left in charge of the 15-pump fire. To be fair, both the on-duty assistant chief and deputy chief stopped at my control unit to check that everything was alright before travelling on to Docklands on blue lights, but they were fairly fleeting visits. At this incident, I learnt to trust the systems and procedures that made up the Fire and Rescue Service Incident Command System (ICS), a system that could flex and grow to meet the requirements of the incident in front of you.

The Risks of Firefighting

One important aspect of having such a system is the training, exercising and assessment that goes alongside. Acquiring the skills through on-station and other training, applying them whilst taking charge of drills and exercises, then learning from the use of ICS on the incident ground help make incident command a central and risk-critical skill for every FRS incident commander. Risk critical because it is during incidents and particularly at fires which can develop rapidly, weaken structures and flashover or backdraught dramatically, that lives are at risk. Unfortunately, I have known colleagues to die at incidents—Jeff Wornham and Michael Miller at Harrow Court on 2 February 2005 (Hertfordshire Fire and Rescue Service 2007). They had already rescued one resident from a 14th-floor flat when they and a second occupant were overcome by a rapid and fatal development of the fire. Then two years later, the watch commander from the same watch as Jeff and Michael was killed by an out-of-control car on the A1(M) during what was really a routine car fire on the hard shoulder.

There is no feeling worse as a fire officer than to be told one of your colleagues has been killed. This can still happen even when you feel that all the ICS processes are in place. I recall being in charge of a large fire at the old Football Association building in Lancaster Gate London in 1998. I was silver commander at the front of the building. We had breathing apparatus crews inside who were having some difficulty locating the fire. We later discovered there were voids between ceilings and floors of 3–4 feet through which the fire was travelling. As I stood monitoring the incident, a messenger came across from the breathing apparatus (BA) control entry point to say that a breathing apparatus crew were missing. They were overdue on their time of whistle, a whistle that sounds on the BA set when the available air is becoming low. It is at times like these when your next decision becomes vital—Do I send in an emergency crew, do I signal a full evacuation, do I do both or can I give the crew a bit more time to appear, have firefighters lost their lives at a fire where I am in charge? These sort of questions and decisions take a matter of seconds, but a barrister can look at them years later, with the benefit of 20–20 hindsight and hours of questioning to dissect and imply you didn't know what you were doing. Fortunately, the missing crew appeared at a top floor window and waved to attract our attention; we were able to recover them with little more drama, but it was a heart-stopping moment.

Although the welfare of firefighters and firefighting crews is always considered, the incidents in the last paragraph emphasis this fact and made real for me the fact we do have to take some risks to deal with incidents. At every incident we consider the benefit of any action, as the current National Operational Guidance foundation document for incident command states, "At every incident, the greater the potential benefit of fire and rescue actions, the greater the risk that is accepted by commanders and firefighters" (National Operational Guidance 2015).

Paddington Rail Crash (Ladbroke Grove)

We expect safe, assertive and effective commanders to lead crews to bring incidents to a safe conclusion. The need to have effective systems, to be assertive, to be calm under pressure, to bring order to chaos, to work with other emergency responders and to consider the welfare of firefighters and the people we are trying to save was never more real than at an incident in which I was the silver commander for seven hours in October 1999. It should have been a day off for me; I was a senior divisional officer (area manager) responsible for fire safety for Western Command, consisting of 11 boroughs in north and west London. I went into my office at Wembley to catch up on some work when fire control rang me to ask if I was available to attend an incident.

I replied that I was and was asked to attend a rail crash at Ladbroke Grove London, more commonly known as the Paddington rail crash (Cullen 2001). I went through the usual procedure of gathering what information I could, two trains in collision, unknown number of people involved, fire and severe crash damage, incident was currently at make pumps eight, major incident declared, assistant divisional officer (station commander) in charge. I left immediately to travel the few miles to the incident.

I listened to my main scheme radio on the way to the incident but messages were unclear and breaking up on the way. When I arrived, it was clear that something very serious was happening. I parked and took in as much information as I could whilst rigging in fire gear, asked a firefighter where the control unit was and walked there to book in attendance. On the way I met a divisional officer (group commander), Kevin Heymer, whom I knew well as a solid operational officer. Kevin informed me the incident was now 12 pumps and, as the most senior officer at the incident, I would be in charge.

Remembering the importance of a command team, I told Kevin to stick with me as part of my team as we got our first briefings. Having booked in with the control unit, I put on my incident command jerkin and learnt all the information I could. I formally took over, asking for a message to that effect to be sent to fire control and the incident ground. I was informed there were no sectors at that time and the command support staff were not entirely sure where the current incident commander was located. I no longer controlled incidents from the back of a unit without seeing them first. I had checked the electricity to the site was off and then asked Kevin to accompany me to the scene of the crash.

It was a scene I will never forget, like something from a disaster movie or major training exercise—walking wounded, teams of paramedics, firefighters and police officers working with casualties, debris as far as the eye could see. I recall two things I said to Kevin, "[expletive], followed by this one is for real" and "we need to get some order into this chaos".

I found the incident commander, and he became a sector commander for one of two operational sectors I put in place either side of the crash. The fire was virtually out, but each carriage needed searching for casualties as soon as possible, but we also needed to ensure each carriage was searched systematically and not searched again, wasting time and resources. I asked for the carriages to be marked with paint, B1, B2, A1, A2 etc. so we could record the search and location of casualties and deceased. I also set up functional sectors, one for equipment, one for casualty clearing, another for firefighter welfare. We ensured that police and ambulance control vehicles were located near the fire control unit to facilitate joint meetings. This was a common theme in the London Emergency Services Liaison Plan (LESLP) and is now enshrined in the Joint Emergency Services Interoperability Principles (JESIP 2018) doctrine as co-location.

I recall many images. It was the early days of mobile phones, but everyone seemed to have one, and it was the first time I experienced the network go down. I also vividly recall the time it took for the last live casualty to be cut free from the wreckage. It was hours into the incident, the fire rescue unit crew that had been working with her for hours and should, by all procedures, now be relieved because tiredness was a factor. I kept asking the sector commander "how much longer?" as the crew should be relieved;

"a few more minutes" I kept being told. The crew had developed a bond with the trapped woman. What was the right decision—leave them there as they got more and more tired, liable to make mistakes or order them to be relieved and break that bond with the severely injured casualty with unknown consequences? I left them in the end, and the woman was freed, a great outcome, but what would a barrister have said with a different outcome? I also recall the way I felt when relieved of my command after seven hours. I stepped off the unit and do not think I have ever felt so tired, I felt shattered as soon as the responsibility was lifted and the adrenaline had stopped flowing.

Guvnor Buncefield's Alight

Multi-agency working has always been important and has proved its worth to me time and time again and never more than when I was fire gold, the highest level of command, for the Buncefield fuel depot fire in 2005 (HSE 2011). I have often been asked how I approached this fire. My usual response is that I knew how to put out a fuel fire and knew about incident command, I just had to scale both to deal with the situation. This was a time before the complete rollout of the New Dimensions project and before the National Co-ordination and Advisory Framework (NCAF), National Resilience Adviser Team or tactical advisers, although a number of past and present members of the New Dimensions project took up these roles at the incident.

There was an interim National Co-ordination Centre in West Yorkshire and the Fire Emergency Information Centre (FEIC, an innovation for the 2002/3 national strikes and forerunner of the emergency room), but neither was as developed as they are today. Her Majesty's Fire Service Inspectorate was being wound down, the position of chief fire and rescue adviser did not exist, JESIP was years away; fire service was in the Office of the Deputy Prime Minister, John Prescott; the fire minister was Jim Fitzpatrick MP, the local MP was Mike Penning and my county councillor responsible for fire was David Lloyd, now the Police and Crime Commissioner for Hertfordshire. Wheels within wheels.

The explosion that occurred at just after 0600 on Sunday 11 December 2005 engulfed 20 tanks across seven bunds, later spreading to just two more tanks as fire service action was taken to reduce spread. The fires created a massive smoke plume that rose several thousand feet. The control rooms in Hertfordshire and adjoining services received two hundred and twenty-one 999 calls as the explosion was heard across many counties and measured 2.4 on the Richter scale. The response of all the agencies and private industry partners involved was magnificent. The 31 fire and rescue services, the oil industry firefighters and specialists, local and county councils, voluntary sector, and companies such as Angus and Tesco all played their part.

Gold command remained in place for five days, and Hertfordshire Fire and Rescue continued to work on site until 5 January 2006. In successfully extinguishing one of the largest fires of its kind in Europe and co-ordinating the multi-service response, Hertfordshire clocked up some significant statistics; the incident required 786,000 litres of foam concentrate to extinguish the fire and maintain foam blankets. Both 'clean' and recycled water was used to extinguish the fire and maintain cooling water jets, 53 million litres of clean water and 15 million litres of recycled water were used. In addition, 10 million litres of contaminated water were held on site and only removed in February 2006 under direction of the Environment Agency (EA). There were 642 fire appliance movements to Buncefield.

The response to the Buncefield incident was a multi-agency and national response that worked extremely well. I was soon on the way to gold, or Strategic Co-ordinating Group[1] at police headquarters in Welwyn Garden City while my deputy at the time, Mark Yates, went to the scene as silver commander. I worked in tandem with the police chair, Assistant Chief Constable Simon Parr, at the formal gold meetings and outside. Gold is not just about sitting around the SCG table making strategic decisions, it is also about the work within your own agency and with other agencies about planning and reporting to ensure the strategic decisions are taken forward and implemented.

A good example were the meetings between myself, police and Environment Agency that worked through the detail and requested changes to the fire response plan formulated by Mark and a team at the silver level. Police established their silver at Watford Police station, with multi-agency partners and a fire liaison, probably called a tactical co-ordinating group today. This way of working with fire tactical (silver) command at the scene and police tactical being remote is still with us and is why JESIP developed the term 'on-scene commander' and introduced police command tabards. So promoting co-location and shared situational awareness with use of the joint decision model and METHANE (JESIP 2018).

Some other previous lessons came back to me immediately. The first phone call at just after 6AM to tell me "Guvnor, Buncefield's alight", I gathered all the information I could and didn't rush to the SCG. It was a Sunday morning; I knew the incident would take days to resolve and it gave me time to think, "an officer never runs". There were many lessons from the incident itself which helped shape many of the systems we have in place now. I knew how many resources had to be gathered and marshalled so the old M10 (now the A414) was used as a rendezvous point with the marshalling officer, a forerunner of a strategic holding area and Enhanced Logistics Support (ELS) officer. It was these actions—the review, lessons identified and recommendations made to the Lord Newton enquiry (HSE 2011) along with learning following the 2007 floods—that developed into NCAF and the way we now coordinate national resilience.

But one lesson particularly sticks in the mind, to confirm understanding. When the scientific analysts told us that within 24 hours the smoke from the fire would be over Paris, we needed to confirm they meant smoke particles in the upper stratosphere and not the thick black smoke that had bought midnight to central London at midday that Sunday.

Joint Emergency Services Interoperability
Programme (JESIP)

The origins of JESIP were probably many years or even decades in the past as emergency responders identified the need to work closer together. But for the actual JESIP initiative, the start was a letter from Home Secretary Theresa May dated 27 October 2011. This was addressed to a number of lead offices, including Her Majesty's Chief Inspector of Constabulary (HMIC), the Chief Fire and Rescue Adviser (CFRA) and the leads of the professional associations. The letter invited representatives to a meeting on 7 November 2011 to discuss improving blue light interoperability at complex or large-scale incidents, citing 7/7, the Norway and Derrick Bird shootings as events demonstrating the need for improvement. There was also a particular focus on the Olympic Games, which already had extensive planning and preparation in place but were less than a year away. Even at this early stage, the areas of focus were command, control and coordination, communications, training and exercise. That meeting set off a chain of events, meetings and team development that now sees JESIP almost fully embedded in the emergency services.

The first stages were delivered on time; these were the pre-Olympic awareness package and the Olympic assurance conducted by HMIC, the Chief Fire and Rescue Adviser and Association of Ambulance Chief Executives, a model established for future JESIP assurance. The awareness package was developed and along with an aide-memoir was delivered to all fire, police and ambulance services in the UK for them to present to their commanders prior to the Olympics. It was at this stage that it became common to talk about delivering this interoperability to 105 organisations, each with their own leadership and local culture, just one of the challenges to be faced over the coming years. The Olympic package was a real precursor to the JESIP products and covered common hazard analysis, on-scene command, situational awareness and joint decision-making.

With the go-ahead from the Ministerial Board, the Blue Light Interoperability Team was established. It is fair to say that in these early days, with the formation of a new team, other external pressures and some scepticism from some of the blue light organisations, it was not always an easy time. One of the early decisions that has proved worthwhile was to develop a positive brand for the programme. Blue Light Interoperability Programme or BLIP did not have the right ring to it, so Joint Emergency Services Interoperability Programme or JESIP was developed. Particular mention at this point goes to Deputy Chief Constable Charlie Hall as senior responsible officer and Assistant Chief Ambulance Officer Steve Wheaton as deputy SRO, followed by Carl Daniels, who along with a focused JESIP team helped make JESIP the success it became. I have now chaired the JESIP Interoperability Board for over six years.

Having the joint doctrine in place now allows all subsequent operational guidance developed by any of the emergency services and others to be based on the same foundations. The whole process has undergone assessment and evaluation through two skills for justice surveys, before and after the joint training, exercising and the HMIC/CFRA/ACCE reviews. All three methodologies have shown the JESIP process to be a success, and key to this success was the willingness of all the ambulance, police and fire organisations to embrace the JESIP principles, namely:

- JESIP Champions established across all services as single points of contact
- All products developed centrally by multi-agency working groups which included recognised professional organisations (e.g. the College of Policing)
- For training: learning outcomes, course content and design completed in conjunction with all three services and subject matter experts
- Train the Trainer Programme to establish a network of JESIP trainers across all services
- Joint local delivery to multi-agency delegates

Much of the JESIP work needed a breakdown of cultural barriers and compromise, seen in the adoption of the joint decision model, based very much on the national police model, and the adoption of METHANE for messages and situational awareness across all three services.

M	MAJOR INCIDENT	Has a major incident or standby been declared? (Yes / No - if no, then complete ETHANE message)	Include the date and time of any declaration.
E	EXACT LOCATION	What is the exact location or geographical area of the incident?	Be as precise as possible, using a system that will be understood by all responders.
T	TYPE OF INCIDENT	What kind of incident is it?	For example, flooding, fire, utility failure or disease outbreak.
H	HAZARDS	What hazards or potential hazards can be identified?	Consider the likelihood of a hazard and the potential severity of any impact.
A	ACCESS	What are the best routes for access and egress?	Include information on inaccessible routes and rendezvous points (RVPs). Remember that services need to be able to leave the scene as well as access it.
N	NUMBER OF CASUALTIES	How many casualties are there, and what condition are they in?	Use an agreed classification system such as 'P1', 'P2', 'P3' and 'dead'.
E	EMERGENCY SERVICES	Which, and how many, emergency responder assets and personnel are required or are already on-scene?	Consider whether the assets of wider emergency responders, such as local authorities or the voluntary sector, may be required.

Figure 4.1 METHANE model for incident communication (JESIP)

But there is more to be done. The original blue light work, which became JESIP, was deliberately aimed at the emergency services, with some familiarisation for the wider Local Resilience Forum; this certainly needs to be developed further. Another key outcome still to be finalised is the Joint Organisational Learning system, which will bring together learning from the three services to inform future policy, guidance and training, a key deliverable for the legacy team. Embedding JESIP as a consistent approach across the emergency services and then with Local Resilience Forum partners is vital and we need to maintain the doctrine, ensuring appropriate training and exercising at all levels for a 40-year career firefighter, police officer or paramedic.

The National Coordination and Advisory Framework (NCAF) is part of the mechanism to provide the coordination of fire and rescue assets. Home Office (HO) National Resilience & Fire Directorate (NRFD) and the Office of Security and Counter Terrorism (OSCT) work with other government departments, partner organisations and the devolved administrations during 'no notice' and 'rising tide' major incidents to provide policy reach back and advice, ministerial briefings, coordination across government and management of communications. NCAF enables decision makers, both locally and nationally, to receive clear and unambiguous advice on how best to coordinate the fire and rescue service response to relevant emergencies.

Japan

My experience and learning of incident command was put to good use in a totally different environment when I joined the 54-person-strong UK International Search and Rescue team as strategic lead following the 2011 tsunami (Rafferty and Pletcher 2018). Although a different environment, many of the issues I learned over many years were relevant: information gathering, situational awareness, multi-agency working, coordination, communication, joint location, joint risk assessments and logistics all came into play. We flew into an American airbase in the north of Japan and joined teams from Fairfax Virginia, and Los Angeles County before convoying to our base of operations in Ofunato and then Kaimaishi on the coast. We were self-sufficient for ten days and liaised with the local emergency services before entering the zones devastated by the earthquake and subsequent tsunami. Utilising our incident command and search and rescue procedures, we searched an area for survivors and bodies to be recovered. We were in Japan for a week, showing the Japanese they had not been forgotten, providing reassurance and recovering the bodies of those overcome by the devastating waters. The need for good communication, logistic support, joint working and excellent command procedures were never more evident and put my years of incident command experience to the test.

Reflection

I have covered the major incidents and experiences that formed my ability in incident command and shaped the way I think about the subject which is so important to the fire and rescue services and our partners. When I first became an incident commander in the early 1980s, incident command procedures were similar but local, and it wasn't for a decade or more that national recognised procedures were put into place. Like the original decision-making model as set out in Figure 4.2, it was a linear process originally developed in London with an almost classic Plan-Implement-Evaluate-Review cycle, but effective all the same.

Whatever the model, a few learning points stuck with me beyond the formal structures of an incident command system. The need for timely and accurate information that is shared by others and commonly understood and the need for situational awareness. The importance of understanding risk and weighing any risk against the benefit that could be gained can be different among individuals as well as organisations, so trying to get a common understanding of risk is important. When you are in charge of an incident, it is imperative to be confident in your own ability, remain calm under sometimes extreme situations and have confidence in the people and crews under your command.

Working in a multi-agency environment is commonplace, but JESIP has sought to improve this by introducing command decision models and common information flows through METHANE and promoting the need to collocate, communicate and coordinate. We also have more incident command research that has put some of the human elements into the fire and rescue command system, recognising that we don't always receive information or make decisions in a linear way. Introducing decision controls ensures that the incident commander understands what effect they are trying to achieve and what the consequences of a decision might be as reflected in the latest fire and rescue decision model that links into the JESIP joint decision model.

Although the number of fires has fortunately decreased over the last decade or so, there are signs that this trend is at a plateau and may start to rise again, especially as more people live alone and for longer. Modern materials and methods of construction also need to be considered. There has been a lack of real fire research in the UK but anecdotally fire loading seems to be increasing, and the insurers tell us that fire losses in terms of financial loss are definitely getting larger. As the nature of incidents is changing, with an ever-changing terrorist threat, more weather-related events and more pressure on transport systems, the fire and rescue service is needed as much as it ever was. What a reduction in fires definitely means is that we need to train and assess our incident commanders more than before to make sure they are confident and safe when called upon to take charge. We have better training methods, including the increasing use of virtual reality, that show real possibilities in all aspects of fire training, including incident command. We also have better equipment than ever before and I am sure innovations will keep coming.

But even when all this is taken into account, the individual still needs the skills, knowledge and experience—not experience in number of incidents, but experience in what they learn from each incident—to be an incident commander. No matter what training and experience is behind you, when you are in charge with colleagues inside a burning building looking for possible casualties, you must be confident in yourself, the crews, the procedures and the equipment; it is what the public expects.

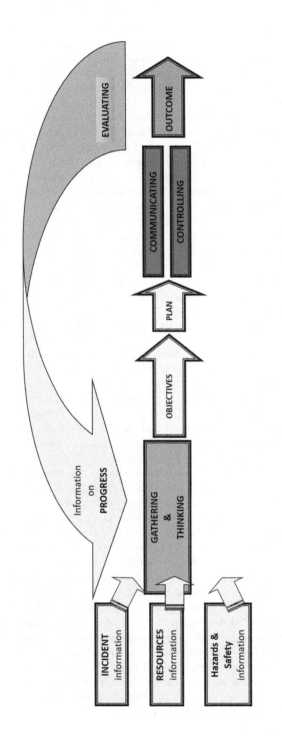

Figure 4.2 Original decision-making model (JESIP)

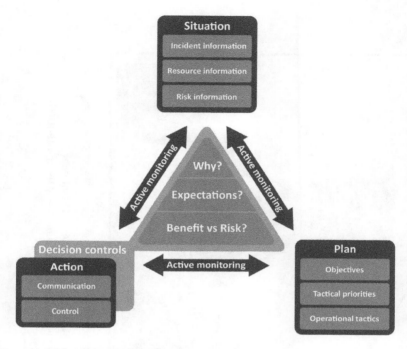

Figure 4.3 The decision control process (JESIP)

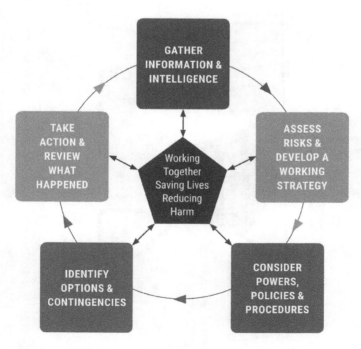

Figure 4.4 The joint decision-making model (JESIP)

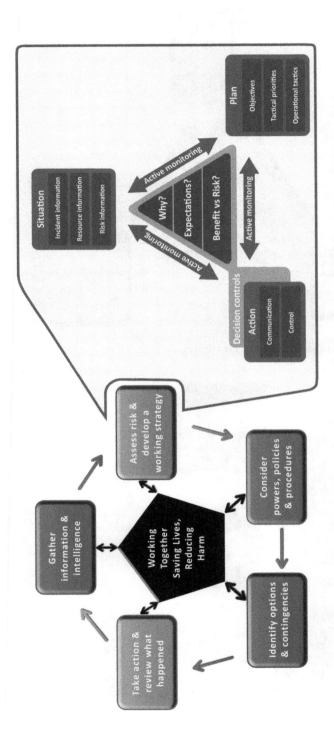

This helps to feed information into the JDM process, and as a process to plan and implement activities to achieve the fire and rescue objectives that have been agreed collectively using the JDM.

Figure 4.5 How the two models fit together (JESIP)

Note

1 Strategic Co-ordination Group, usually chaired by the police, is where the Category 1 responders, emergency services, local authority etc. and Category 2 responders, utilities and voluntary organisations meet to coordinate the response to a major incident.

References

Cullen (Rt Hon Lord Cullen PC) 2001. *The Ladbroke Grove Rail Inquiry.* Health and Safety Executive. HMSO, Norwich.

DCLG 2008. *Incident Command - 3rd Edition - Fire and Rescue Manual - Volume 2: Fire Service Operations.* Available at: www.gov.uk/government/publications/fire-and-rescue-manual-volume-1-incident-command [Accessed 09/09/2018].

Dillon, M. (1996). *25 Years of Terror: The IRA's war against the British.* Bantam Books, London.

The Grenfell Tower Inquiry 2018 (ongoing). *The independent public inquiry, set up to examine the circumstances leading up to and surrounding the fire at Grenfell Tower on 14 June 2017.* Available at: *www.grenfelltowerinquiry.org.uk/* [Accessed 09/09/2018].

Health and Safety Executive 2011. *Buncefield: Why did it happen?* (Newton Report) [Online]. Available at www.hse.gov.uk/comah/buncefield/buncefield-report.pdf [Accessed 09/09/2018].

Hertfordshire Fire and Rescue Service 2007. *Harrow Court Investigation.* Available at: www.highrisefire.co.uk/case/harrowct/HRSR%20Inquiry%20into%20the%20fire%20at%20harrow%20court.pdf

JESIP 2018. *Joint Emergency Services Interoperability Principles [Online].* Available at: www.jesip.org.uk/home, www.britannica.com/event/Japan-earthquake-and-tsunami-of-2011

National Operational Guidance 2015. www.ukfrs.com/foundation-knowledge/foundation-incident-command

Oppenheimer, A. R. 2009. *IRA: The bombs and the bullets. A history of deadly ingenuity.* Irish Academic Press.

Rafferty, J. P., and Pletcher, K. 2018. *Japan earthquake and tsunami of 2011.* Encyclopaedia Britannica [Online]. Available at: www.britannica.com/event/Japan-earthquake-and-tsunami-of-2011 [Accessed 09/09/2018].

5   Quo Vadis

Eight Possible Scenarios for Changes in the Ambulance Services

Andy Newton

Introduction and Background

Foretelling the future can be something of a 'mugs' game, and as Niels Bohr, the renowned Danish physicist, famously said, "prediction is very difficult, especially if it is about the future". Many of those who have stepped into this arena have failed badly, with arguably two of the best examples being, "The horse is here to stay but the automobile is only a novelty", which was attributed to Henry Ford's bank manager, as well as the more recent 1977 prophesy by Mr Ken Olsen, of the US Digital Equipment Company, that "there is no reason why anyone would want a computer in their home".

Nevertheless, throughout the centuries, oracles, visionaries, soothsayers, fortune-tellers and, more recently, professional futurologists have been in demand. The techniques available to these and other practitioners have moved on a little from the Roman predilection of butchering a goat and examining its entrails, tarot cards, palm reading or the 18th-century use of reconnaissance balloons to satisfy the military desire to see, as General Lord Wellington desired, 'over the hill'.

Today there are many new approaches grounded to one degree or another in academia and science, all promising to provide insight to a customer with the irresistible promise of strategic, commercial, military or other advantage. Drawn from the general designation of 'foresight studies', these methods include scenario planning, health technology assessment and horizon scanning, to name but a few, and it isn't even necessary to be Jules Verne or H. G. Wells to tap into them.

However, sometimes common sense and a review of ideas in circulation, which are not necessarily visible, is enough of a basis to frame important questions and possible scenarios as to what the future could possibly hold. Few techniques from futurology or, for that matter, systematic speculation have been applied to ambulance services in the UK. This is somewhat surprising, given the extent to which health has become an ever-present preoccupation today. One aspect which is difficult to be unaware of is the close media attention that has been expended in relation to ambulance services, which increasingly suggests that the organisations' future should be of concern to all who might one day need to call upon it. While decidedly not a blatant exercise in prediction, eight scenarios, set out in the form of options, are presented. Perhaps one or a combination of several represents a probable, or even preferable, version of the future that might offer some prospect of imaginative opportunities for the change that is so acutely needed in the ambulance service across England today.

Current State of the Ambulance Services

Before delving into the future, it is worth briefly considering the direction of thought and policy in this area, which is more capacious than might be imagined. During the last two decades, there has been an ever-increasing number of policy and other key documents. The Bradley Report, 'Taking Health Care to the Patient' (2005a), and the follow-up Association of Chief Ambulance Officers subsequent 'progress' report on the 2005 recommendations (2011) are probably the best known. These documents largely echoed the less visible 'Future of Ambulance Services in the United Kingdom (1999)', authored by Nicholl et al., and the Audit Commission's 'Life in the Fast Lane' a year earlier (1998).

There have also been frequent changes in national ambulance performance response time targets, the last revision being the 'Ambulance Response Programme' (Turner et al., 2017), and most of these have seemingly been, at least partially, motivated by a desire to make them easier to achieve. Together with a veritable deluge of publications, numbering over a dozen major contributions, most notably the Department of Health's 'Reforming Emergency Care' (2000) and the Office of the Strategic Health Authority's Emergency Services Review (2009) (a comparative review of international ambulance service best practice). Another is the Audit Commission's report, 'Transforming NHS Ambulance Services' (2011), as well as NHS England's 'Transforming Urgent & Emergency Care in England' (2015) and the National Institute for Health Research 'Care at Scene' (2016). Yet another offering is from the Audit Commission, the imaginatively named 'NHS Ambulance Services' (2017), followed by a House of Commons Committee of Public Account report into NHS Ambulance Services (2016), not to mention countless academic and other papers and books on similar themes. Most recently the Lord Carter review, 'Operational Performance and Productivity in the Ambulance Service; unacceptable variation' (2018), has taken centre stage.

Lord Carter found that the ambulance service currently employed 40,000 staff in England alone, making it considerably larger than either the Royal Navy or the Royal Air Force, who have 32,880 and 32,830 regular personnel respectively (MoD quarterly statistical bulletin, 2018). With annual costs, again in England only, of £2.3 billion, the ambulance services absorb more than ten million 999 calls, using 22 control centres with differing computer-aided dispatch systems annually (a ten-fold increase over the last 50 years since the publication of the seminal Millar report, 1966), with approximately seven million receiving a physical response which were achieved by means of 32 different types of ambulance, with a variety of equipment. A remarkably similar observation to that was made 50 years earlier by the then Ministry of Health, 'Report by the Working Party' ('Equipment and Vehicles, part 2'

1967), and an unspecified variety of response cars, sending both classes of vehicles to the scene in some cases, thereby contributing to the wide disparity in productivity which has been observed.

Lord Carter also noted, again in line with the conclusion reached in previous reports, that the service, which was originally designed to respond to those with life-threatening conditions, now only encountered such cases in 10% of 'emergency' 999 calls, while the bulk of activity is made up of a complex mix of generally less urgent cases, many of which would have been managed within primary care in previous decades. Tactfully, he omitted to mention that the burgeoning air ambulance services have, to a considerable extent, gradually taken on the role of championing the needs of more seriously injured patients and some seriously ill ones too, thereby challenging the ambulance service's historic raison d'etre of being primarily a life-saving intervention and transport service. Today's reality is one where the major role of the service is to function as primarily an urgent care and transport provider and as a 24/7 safety net for a general under-provision of primary and social care services; while, less frequently, being called upon as the sole professional service available to save life. In this sense, much of its work is caused by wider avoidable failures in other parts of the system, a phenomenon termed 'failure demand' by Seddon (2009).

Collectively, the many reports into the ambulance service have ensured an increasingly firm grip on what has been patently obvious since at least the late 1990s and probably a good deal earlier. First, that patient demand has grown and morphed fundamentally for a myriad of reasons outlined in countless other publications, exemplified by Snooks et al. (2002), and Edwards (2014) who considered demography, specifically changing population age profiles and other well-established factors, to be of significance, in a study funded by the Association of Ambulance Executives. A heightened emphasis on patients with long-term conditions, deprivation, population growth, lifestyle factors and changes to out-of-hours service provision were added to an ever-growing list of suspected reasons for escalating call volumes. Secondly, while the paramedic profession has risen to the challenge, professionalising and diversifying, ambulance services have been less successful in adapting to the level of change and modernisation required. Even the most charitable observer would feel obliged, therefore, to question its current fitness for purpose.

At various times over the last few years, it has been fashionable to simply blame 'underfunding' (although here, again, Lord Carter found plenty of scope for savings) or patients, for the increasing demand, and, by implication, the cause of the poor performance of ambulance services. While there is often a mismatch in supply and demand for ambulance services, it is relevant to develop the theme of raising efficiency referencing past attempts to do so, including early work trialled with success in Staffordshire during the mid- to late 1990s. These draw upon a range of quality improvement methods, referred to as 'high performance methods', adapted by Stout and the American Ambulance Association (1994), and were based on 'lean' techniques, which gained the acceptance of American Medical Directors (Kuehl,

1994). Staffordshire Ambulance Service's success was independently audited, and the results were found to be valid and suitable for wider dissemination (Turner & Nicholl, 2002). The Staffordshire Ambulance Service was merged with the West Midlands Service in 2006, and this lucky inheritance may be one of the reasons for their better performance in some areas when compared to most other ambulance trusts.

Challenging the appropriateness of many 999 calls (Palazzo et al., 1998; Victor et al., 1999; Wrigley et al., 1999; Peacock et al., 2005) is nonetheless of significance to any discussion in this area, with such concerns of 'misuse' or 'overuse' of ambulance services, no doubt, playing a role. The threshold at which individuals are prepared to call 999 has unquestionably reduced over time, but this is driven by complex socio-economic factors, and definitions are rarely considered the patient's perspective (Ahl, 2006). Neither is the phenomenon new or one that is confined to the UK, with plenty of other countries experiencing similar trends, as diverse as Japan (Kawakami et al., 2007; Hagihara et al., 2013), Australia (Lowthian et al., 2011) and Camasso et al. (1997) in the United States. Passing responsibility on to the customer for any shortfall in service provision is a shabby way to tackle chronic underperformance of the service and should therefore be assessed in the context of broader organisational and psychosocial factors.

Today, there seems to be a greater acceptance of the advice offered by Snooks et al. (2002) which suggests that services should worry less about 'appropriateness' and devote more effort to providing appropriate care and alternative pathways. Given that the 999 system has always acted as a safety net and, notwithstanding the value of well-conceived triage services such as the Advanced Medical Priority Dispatch System (AMPDS), or the other commonly employed sorting product, 'NHS Pathways', there are few 'road blocks', eligibility requirements or restrictions to making a 999 call. Much demand, like water or electricity, will inevitably flow to the line of least resistance, thereby helping to paper over cracks and deficiencies in other parts of health and social service provision.

What, therefore, seems to be happening is that, whilst the paramedic profession has developed rapidly during the last four decades and has considerably enhanced the range of their skills, largely as a function of a rising professional consciousness, better education, curriculum frameworks (College of Paramedics, 2017) and, what might be considered to be broadly an adaptation due to evolutionary clinical pressures, the ambulance service has not progressed at the same rate. This is sometimes a source of friction between paramedics and the ambulance service, but it is a testimony to paramedics and other ambulance staff that they can retain public confidence and keep a creaking system functioning. Nevertheless, these tensions may well be exacerbating the organisational problems that are making accessing health care and the experience of working in health care less positive than might have been the case previously, due to its increasingly atavistic organisational factors, a lack of a clear leadership or role identity and a failure to construct a suitable doctrine upon which to base the future concept of operation of the service (Newton & Harris, 2015).

Paramedics, although only making up 38% of the service in Lord Carter's review, are the clinical 'backbone' of the service and could legitimately be termed an example of 'disruptive innovation', a term coined by Clayton Christenson, a Harvard academic, *Harvard Business Review* (Bower & Christensen, 1995) and outlined in his book the *Innovator's Prescription* (Christensen et al., 2009). This has enabled paramedics to gain increasing competency, while doing so at comparatively low cost, providing the agility necessary to work not only in the ambulance service, but also increasingly across the spectrum of health care. This process has been facilitated by a more comprehensive undergraduate and postgraduate curriculum framework, developed by the College olf Paramedics (2013, 2017), which recognises that paramedics now work in a wider range of settings than the ambulance service and require comprehensive and appropriate preparation.

By contrast, ambulance services have failed to adapt at the same speed, demonstrating a schism with some of its clinical staff and a yawning 'implementation gap' that often fails to heed policy advice, and which exhibits wide variations in many performance metrics. Those areas, found most recently by Carter to be of the greatest concern, included differing rates of telephone triage ('hear and treat') and on-scene assessment ('see and treat'), the absence of which often result in transporting patients to hospital, simply to determine whether the patient needs to be there. This result is often a poor outcome for individual patients, potentially exposing them to greater risk, while adding to the burden of emergency departments (EDs), their personnel and taxpayers alike.

Ambulance services can also be quite ugly and even, at times, oppressive places to work, obsessed with a performance-driven culture (Wankhade, 2011, 2012), unsupportive and often hindering the professional growth of paramedics (McCann et al., 2013), with sometimes toxic organisational cultures (Wakefield, 2014b). The obsession with time-based process standards, rather than focusing upon measures that are clinically relevant, is a source of additional stress for ambulance crews. All clinicians recognise that some time-related targets are important, but a too general application of such measures, at the expense of more sensible approaches, such as an approach based on clinical outcomes, exemplified by the Pre-hospital Outcomes for Evidence Based Evaluation Phoebe, proposals (Coster et al., 2017) is not helpful. Bullying (Twist, 2014) and bullying coupled with sexual harassment (Lewis, 2017) compound and contribute to high rates of sickness and equally high staff turnover, which have been increasingly recognised as a 'crisis' (Wakefield, 2014a), as well as predictably low staff satisfaction; among the worst in the NHS. These factors create an organisational culture that is often the very opposite of what is needed and also displays the 'tyranny of command and control approaches to management' that the architect of quality management, Edward Deming, sought to eliminate (Hunter, 2013). They are also the polar opposite of what is required for a 'learning organisation' popularised by (Senge, 1990) and widely recognised as an essential prerequisite for effective service delivery. Even more concerning is the fact that poor rates of physical and mental health among paramedics and ambulance crews generally are trends observed in literature since at least the 1990s (Young & Cooper, 1997), and these are not improving.

If past and existing behaviour and performance were to be used as a guide, a question might reasonably be asked as to why decades of underperformance and the poor experience of staff should be rewarded with yet greater public funding to ensure the continuation of the ambulance service in its current form? This, it might be argued, could simply be a receipt for keeping alive yesterday's way of doing things badly, while nourishing and perpetuating the sort of harmful culture frequently described by staff. Perhaps it is time to consider breaking the mould, but not necessarily by amalgamating ten mostly poorly performing organisations into one monopolistic nationally underperforming one (an option, nonetheless, but a notion sensibly rejected by Lord Carter). Could the time be right for something more radical and more attuned to the needs of patients in the 21st-century health care and for those who deliver the service?

Possible Scenarios for the Future

Eight possible scenarios are outlined, each with possible issues and implications for the ambulance, along with wider blue light services.

Option 1: No Change

The last major change in configuration was heralded by the Department of Health in 2005. The proposals were set out in a consultation document and were implicit within 'Taking Health Care to the Patient' or, as some described it, somewhat harshly but with an element of truth at the time, 'taking away local services and any responsibility for them'. It was implemented the following year and has changed little since, except for the merger of the Great Western and South West Ambulance Services, resulting in a greater 'South Western' service.

Adopting this stance would likely ensure a continuation of at least the majority of the ten English ambulance services (and the Isle of Wight service, which is attached to the local hospital trust). This option might be expected to seek to adopt some of the recommendations of the Lord Carter report to reduce waste and improve productivity, thereby echoing entreaties repeated almost annually over the last two decades and possibly with similar prospects of success. Nonetheless, a no-change option, given the level of inertia in large bureaucracies like the NHS, is a realistic prospect and certainly, for now, the outcome of Lord Carter's review.

Option 2: Single Nation (English) Ambulance Service

During the last half century, the number of ambulance services has fallen dramatically from 142, prior to the services' incorporation into the NHS in 1974, to 44 thereafter, with subsequent further reductions to 32 and, more recently, 11 in the 2006 restructure. The number of services in England today is 10, following the merger of Great Western into the South West Ambulance Service NHS Foundation Trust (SWASFT), as noted in the previous option.

There are potential services and economic advantages in a single national service, as England, Scotland, Wales and Northern Ireland are all single systems, although none gives great encouragement to England adopting this approach. An England-wide NHS model has been achieved for the National Blood Service, and the coastguard operates at a UK level. In Canada, Japan and Australia very large 'regional', but not national, ambulance services operated successfully. Denmark is close to operating as a national service, as is the Republic of Ireland, although Dublin is served by a Fire Service model. Portugal, too, has the benefit of fire service support. Israel and Qatar, while organisationally different, are effective national services. New Zealand offers a model that has many similarities with the UK, and operates a near National Ambulance Service with high clinical standards and good response time reliability; it represents a good reference point for what could possibly be achieved. A similar model for ambulance services, termed a 'National Ambulance Authority', has been suggested by the Larrey Society (Davis, 2015). A single service would yield cost reductions in the number of Trust Boards while also streamlining procurement, a goal that has largely eluded all efforts at resolution thus far.

An amalgamation of ten regional ambulance services into a single national very large, almost inevitably underperforming, organisation would seem to be an exercise in 'hope over experience'. Guided by the history of earlier amalgamations of ambulance services, it is hard to make a convincing case that such a move would be beneficial, and it is unlikely that the calibre of leadership or competence of systems that would be required would lead to an improved situation for patients, taxpayers or staff working within the

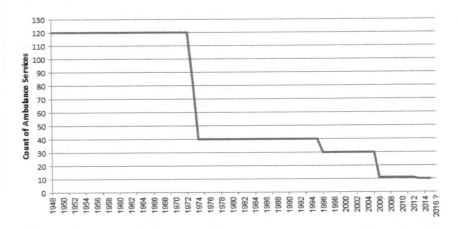

Figure 5.1 Ambulance services 1948 to 2018 showing a stepwise reduction in the number of services over the last 40 years, with a trend in only one direction

new arrangement. Such a model, or even one moving from the current ten to perhaps four 'super' regional units, as something of a 'half-way' house to a national model, would be difficult to reconcile with the need for greater integration with local NHS or local authority services. Integration and closer working between different NHS and social care organisations are likely to be prerequisite to improving patient care and efficiency. Further centralisation might be expected to lead to even less accountability to the public and politicians than exists today.

Option 3: Ambulance Services Become Integrated into a Single National (English) 'Urgent and Emergency Care' Service

One of the important issues in any consideration as to the shape and structure of future ambulance service models is the relationship of the service with the wider NHS. This fact has been repeatedly recognised, and access to services, such as general practice and community services, was cited in the Carter Report, as with its predecessors.

Some ambulance services incorporate at least some relevant elements, the most common being NHS 111. There are also examples of participation in out-of-hours and other services, but this is far from universal. 111 represents a sizable duplication of NHS telecommunications provision with 999, to which out-of-hours services and, potentially, a clutch of other related services all provide some degree of avoidable overlap, which could be streamlined.

A larger scale amalgamation of ambulance 999, NHS 111 and out-of-hours GP services into a single clinical hub, possibly arranged on a regional basis, is feasible, and there are limited examples of such arrangements having been piloted, which are operated on a multi-professional basis. If these emerging examples were scaled up, it would conceivably be a pathway to the creation of a larger 'ambulance and urgent care service', which could be established in a variety of ways and at varying degrees of size, up to and including a national service and, although the challenge at that level would be considerable, one likely result would be some level of economy resulting from merging the currently largely duplicated 999 and 111 telecommunications system.

The diagrammatic illustration below offers a visual indication of the services that might be incorporated in such a model.

The most important point when considering this option is the potential appeal of integration with other services at the local level, achieved by means of smaller and more diverse organisational units, whether called ambulance services or something else is less important, under the aegis of a larger, notionally national organisation. Taking actual demand into account, and the fact that much of this would hitherto have been dealt with by primary care and community services, there is an obvious attraction to being able to provide care in a lower cost setting, including a policy priority, sometimes described as 'shift left' (Rasmus, 2009; Newton & Hodge, 2012; Newton & Harris, 2015).

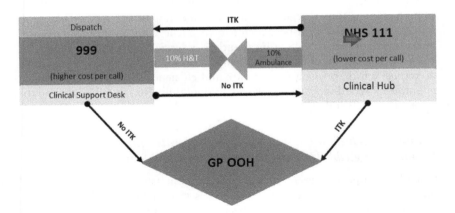

Figure 5.2 A possible National NHS urgent and emergency care and out of hours call handling service, incorporating the ambulance service

Option 4: Privatisation of Ambulance Service Provision

Many ambulance service trusts in England are now sub-contracting significant proportions of front-line emergency ambulance services, and this is becoming increasingly common and more necessary, to fill the shortfall in NHS capacity. Nevertheless, the approach has attracted some media criticism (Campbell, 2017), giving general concern over the long-term sustainability of outsourcing and its role in the NHS (BMJ, McCartney, 2018), which has privatised service accounts for 7.7% of total spend (Kings Fund, Mckenna, 2017). Although sometimes controversial, the use of private sector ambulance resources to augment public ambulance provision emulates a well-established pattern in other countries, such as the United States, Denmark, Sweden, India, Germany, South Africa, Switzerland and many other parts of the globe.

Probably the best international example is unquestionably the Danish Falck organisation, an organisation that has been extensively researched by Murdock (2017), resulting in his book *Private Action for Public Purpose*. Falck is an interesting model, which has been operating within Denmark since 1906 and now has a 'footprint' in 44 countries including the UK, where it holds both NHS Accident and Emergency cover support contracts, while also operating patient transport services.

Murdock describes an organisation that embraces ambulance, fire, rescue and automobile assistance services and which appears to be almost a hybrid between a public and private organisation. It holds a near monopoly in Denmark and yet also seems to retain public confidence. It is a fascinating model which shows that the paramedic personnel are not yet independently registered clinicians and have not so far developed to the level of, for example, the UK or Australia, in achieving high levels of patient and staff satisfaction. According to Murdock, this embodies the elements that LeGrand (2010) has associated with the best features of the public sector; high levels of trust, [patient voice] and choice, attributes which he characterises as 'knightly', rather than the less selfless or 'knavish' characteristics sometimes ascribed to the private sector.

Private ambulance operators providing emergency response were virtually unknown even a decade ago in England. They are still largely absent from Scotland, Wales and Northern Ireland, at least in terms of regular emergency services provision. However, the market in England is slowly maturing, with a larger number of operators each year becoming active, although some attrition has occurred, with tight profit margins and other factors, sometimes cited as the cause of going into administration (Marsh, 2017). Scaling up to provide the totality of services in England would seem premature, but it is entirely plausible, subject to the direction of government thinking in the future, that they might seize larger market shares in the years ahead.

Option 5: Develop a Closer Working Relationship With the Fire Service

Prior to Brexit dominating the political agenda, this option has received a higher level of scrutiny due to the recent H.M. Government Consultation (H.M. Government, 2016), government encouragement for collaboration through the Joint Emergency Services Interoperability Principles (JESIP) programme (2012), creating JESIP principles and the finding of Sir Ken Knight's 'Fire Futures Report' (2013). Any suggestion of ambulance services working more closely with fire and rescue services (FRS) raises severe antibody reaction among some; hence, this area requires a little more explanation than some of the other, better known, options.

High priority medical and trauma related 999 calls related to everyday instances of road and industrial accidents which, by definition, were very time sensitive. This was also the case with an even smaller proportion of cases which were generated from major incidents from whatever cause, including major transportation or industrial accidents, serious fires, terrorism and the like. In both planning and responding to these cases, there is a natural affinity with the fire service and the police service, given the shared first-order priority to save life. The FRS is unusual in the public sector in having what is euphemistically called 'latent' (spare) capacity, and there is a logic to utilising existing resources more intensively.

Media attention, such as Matt Ridley's 'London Isn't Burning' (Ridley, 2013) and the even more critical commentary by the American economist Fred McChesney (McChesney, 2002, 2015), have highlighted the dramatic reduction in fires and the consequent low levels of fire service productivity complicated by, allegedly, sometimes intransigent fire unions who have been accused of refusing to take on additional tasks (Beckford, 2018). McChesney notes that where fire services also operate as emergency medical first or 'co-responders', such work accounts for up to 96% of all responses. His preferred solution is to reduce full-time paid firefighters in favour of volunteer staff, a resolution that is strongly challenged by Statter (2015), but a direction of travel generally agreed with by Stromberg (2015).

From an evidence-based perspective, 'fire medical responding' can sometimes play a potentially useful role in saving life and achieving health gain. Academic research has confirmed this to be the case (Lerner et al., 2003; Claesson et al., 2012). As shown in Williams et al. (2016), who found similar potential for life saving through utilisation of UK fire services, as well as in 'New Economy' (2017), the research, when repeated in a UK context, suggests that improvements in cardiac arrest survival were feasible and economic benefits were likely through the provision of more fire service 'emergency medical responding' activities.

McKinstry, writing in *The Spectator* (2015), has made similar arguments suggesting that firefighters should receive more medical training and adopting the view that fire services are 'heavily staffed fire services and are anachronistic', operating with more than double the number of staff in the ambulance service, but with only a small fraction of the call volume, while also being better paid. These assertions are stridently rejected by the Fire Brigade Union (*The Spectator*, 2015):

> There are benefits, such as drawing upon the Fire Service's success with prevention and other aspects of collaboration, some of which have been aired in the recent 'Fire Work's publication (Mansfield, 2015). All of this indicates that there is a potential for FRS to play a useful role in, at the very least, augmenting the existing ambulance service response, or possibly going further. There is a synergy between the FRS culture of rapid response to the albeit small number of serious fire incidents, whereby

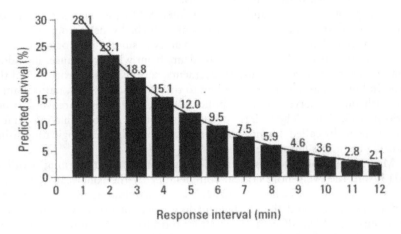

Figure 5.3 Fire services can sometimes reach victims of sudden collapse more rapidly than can ambulance services. Cardiac arrest survival rates showing an increased probability of patient survival directly related to the speed that defibrillation takes place (De Maio et al., 2003).

serious cases of injury and illness, such as cardiac arrest, need just as much help, but cannot always be reliably obtained from ambulance services. Cross training firefighters to provide some emergency medical care taps into an existing pool of emergency service workers adding resources to combat the current and likely future shortages of ambulance service clinicians/technicians and paramedics. It is an approach cleverly employed in Portugal, which operates a national Ambulance Service with the ability to call upon local 'basic life support' firefighter staffed ambulances at a time when operational pressures exist is an admirable example of placing patient need before concerns over demarcation.

Option 6: Large-Scale Restructuring of the Emergency Service, With Central Political Control and the Development of an 'Emergency Response Service'

The creation of an 'Emergency Response Service' as part of a major reappraisal and reorganisation of all the emergency services is distinct from the earlier notion of fire and rescue services taking a greater role in emergency medical response and involves much broader considerations relating to the whole emergency service sector.

The proposal would lead to a high level of integration and the appointment of a 'chief of Emergency Services', to whom police, fire and ambulance services would report and the creation of new 'Department of Homeland Security'. Other aspects include a national emergency coordination centre, the establishment of a 'College of Emergency Service Excellence' and the formation of a Parliament Scrutiny Committee to oversee the work of the emergency services.

The idea evolved from the work of Ellwood & Phillips (2013) as part of an All-Party Group and was developed by this cross-party committee comprising members of the House of Lords and MPs, including Tobias Ellwood (currently a defence minister), who championed the work. It is a very interesting concept, is far more ambitious in scope than any previous proposal in respect of the emergency services and is one which would lead to a wholesale reconstruction of all services and, arguably, a much clearer and more direct line of accountability that reports directly to central government.

The development of an 'Emergency Response Service', created by the merger of fire and ambulance services, which creates a new single identity for both organisations, is a step beyond what has been created anywhere in the world, certainly at the scale suggested. The size of the resulting restructure is, perhaps, such a project's biggest barrier, and it is difficult to see it attracting the level of political support or legislative time required, while also overcoming likely concerns over the potential loss of local accountability, which could result in substantial objections.

If, however, international tensions became sufficiently concerning to enhance the country's civil and other preparedness arrangements, this option would be the logical choice. There are precedents, including the creation of a National Fire Service during World War II and the development of an

'Emergency Medical System', embracing most healthcare capabilities, which also occurred during the 1930–1945 period. This was an innovation that was influential in the subsequent development of the National Health Service (Rivett, 2018).

A proposal to merge a proportion of ambulance services with FRS, thereby offering the opportunity for the greater portion of non-urgent 999 calls to be addressed in some other way, might be more achievable. Nevertheless, given that considerable thought has already been extended to this concept, which clearly has some level of political interest, it stands as an option for possible exploitation in the future and embodies an all-encompassing approach to reform in the emergency services.

Option 7: A Federated Model

A 'federated model', in which an ambulance service becomes part of a network of provider organisations typically arranged around a centre of excellence similar to, for example, a large teaching hospital with major trauma centre status and/or other acute cardiac and other services, acts as the centre piece of a network. The Dalton Review (2014) identifies 'federation' as a step beyond a 'network', adding more direct responsibility and control. It is becoming a more frequently used and useful arrangement for NHS organisations that are in difficulty, and there are plenty of examples of underperforming hospitals being taken under the wing of better performing ones.

Federated models, involving a lead organisation, together with several similar or smaller sized partner providers, are therefore becoming a more common arrangement in the NHS and in that sense are a known quantity. They have not yet been formally employed with ambulance services but could be exploited and might also help to overcome the legal and other organisational difficulties caused by the relative independence of ambulance services that are foundation trusts. As such, they are more difficult to 'unpick', and rebuild.

It is conceivable that such a model might help the drive to greater integration within the wider NHS, although this might be partly at the expense of diluting the core service and possibly hampering functions such as emergency planning and coordination. There is one example, briefly cited above, in the UK whereby the ambulance service has achieved full integration in a 'federation like' manner, although in this case the reality is more closely one of full merger. The Isle of Wight Acute Trust (St Mary's) has adopted this approach, with the island's ambulance service being effectively a separate, but integrated, department. If this example was taken to the extreme, it is possible to conceive of a large network of similar 'bonsai' ambulance services, each centred on their local hospital emergency departments, and such models do exist in the United States and elsewhere. In some ways, it would reflect what is occurring with air ambulance services, which are progressively moving toward co-location with many regional trauma centres.

Creating over a hundred small ambulance services would turn the clock back a hundred years and, while superficially attractive, would be difficult to coordinate, creating many interfaces, complicating mutual aid and the response to major incidents. Any attempt at central control or planning would be immensely complex and it would create many fiefdoms which, unless it could be effectively coordinated, would evolve in different directions according to the preferences of local personalities; these might not necessarily be fully aligned with local population needs. Nevertheless, one quite successful model already exists, and aspects of the benefits derived from close alignment might be usefully built into any future optimal system design.

Option 8: A Charitable Model

Historically, the primary stimulus for the development of ambulance services stems from conflict and the practical necessity to remove those with infectious disease from population centres. The French military surgeon Baron Dominique Jean Larrey, Napoleon's Chief Medical Officer to the Imperial Guard, is credited with the 'modern' concept of the ambulance, although in his case the meaning was also related to what would be considered a more mobile field hospital unit. The term 'ambulance' became more specific to a single wheeled horse-drawn vehicle in the mid-19th century, with civilian 'ambulance service' organisations servicing large cities in North America coming into being immediately after the American Civil War. However, paralleling these developments were the efforts of philanthropically minded individuals, such as Henri Dunant, ultimately leading to the development of the Red Cross and in the UK charitable institutions, including the order of St John and the formation of the St John Ambulance Brigade. Both the Red Cross and St John delivered front ambulance services to the community in the UK well into the 20th century, but do so now generally on more commercial terms. In that sense, they are an implicit part of Option 4.

While this is the case in the UK, Third Sector organisations, including both the Red Cross and St John, continue to provide ambulance services in some countries around the world, in the case of examples such as New Zealand on a near country-wide basis, with government grant support, membership subscriptions and voluntary donations. In the United States, smaller communities are still often heavily dependent upon volunteers operating within locally constituted ambulance organisations or as part of volunteer fire departments. For these reasons, charitably based ambulance services cannot be ruled out as an option even though, in the UK, the move to professionalisation and integration with the public services has been a well-established trend for a century. There may yet be some merit in determining if there might be a role for some level of contribution, extending what has been achieved in the use of 'community responders'. However, in a modern society with the scale of regulation and the many demands upon the time of individuals, it is hard to see how this could be a complete solution, unlike some of the others listed above.

Conclusion

If the quality of ambulance services in England were judged by the quality or quantity of investigations available detailing its shortcomings, the service would be the finest in the world. National Health Service Improvement (NHSI), the latest version of many overseeing NHS bureaucracies (Carter Report), while a creditable contribution in itself, seems to lack an organisational memory. It maintains and adds to the established tradition of scholarly enquiry that characterises the ambulance services' continuing and often identified deficiencies, many of which have been repeatedly characterised over half a century and others more recently. Even for those with the most charitable and enduring of dispositions, the advent of a further report, once again chronicling the misfortunes of the service, is a wonderful example of irony-laden British bureaucracy parodying Charles Dickens' Little Doritt and the dystopian officialdom of the 'Office of Circumlocution'.

Sadly, no amount of analysis, however lavishly employed, almost to the point of inviting near paralysis, can miraculously transform low performance into high performance. Resolution is not, primarily, a matter of simply 'investing', as some would wish to call it, more money; this is not the principle issue, but it is the treatment of first resort when NHS organisations find themselves in the sort of difficulty that the ambulance service is in. Any lack of funding normally has one of two effects; acting as incentive for innovation or driving a compromise in service delivery, bureaucracies dislike innovative ideas or change and therefore favour the latter. In most cases the result is a transitory injection of cash, which acts as a palliative, keeping alive yesterday's way of doing things badly for a little bit, or probably quite a lot longer, certainly long enough until the next investigative report arrives, which itself will likely act as an incentive to the loosing of purse strings, starting this far-from-virtuous cycle once again.

For many of those entering either the paramedic profession or the ambulance service, the work they undertake in their communities is far more than simply a job or even a career. There are frequent rewarding moments, and patients, their families and the public at large often recognise the efforts that are made on their behalf. Patients and staff are also often aware that there are many inadequacies in the service they receive as either users or providers of care; concerns often related in the media, as well as being catalogued in reports that testify to the need for urgent change and improvement. When the ambulance service fails to provide a prompt response, patient harm can result. Equally, when staff experience a toxic, performance-driven culture that can be unwelcoming towards a professionally minded workforce, they are at risk of suffering physical and mental consequences to their health.

The gap between policy and other encouragement to implement reforms and re-engineer the service for the needs of patients with the full spectrum of conditions encountered continues to grow to the detriment of patients and staff alike; repeating the long-established tradition of organisations sustaining themselves to the disadvantage of their service function. There is a need to tackle the root causes of growing demand, much of which is 'failure demand', i.e. failure of the wider system resulting in calls flowing to the ambulance service, when other options might provide superior outcomes at lower cost. There is also a real need to integrate care provided by paramedics in the ambulance service more seamlessly with health and social care.

This will need a clearer and more widely shared view of what the services' primary role should be. Equally, a priority must be placed on meeting the aspirations of staff and make ambulance services less hostile places in which to work, and this must ultimately become an overriding priority in order to prevent staff, who are now better trained and educated and more marketable, from leaving the profession in large numbers. Improving staff retention means making ambulance services at least marginally more palatable places in which to work than in other parts of the NHS.

While organisational form is only one factor that will dictate future success or failure, it is a relevant one. During the last 50 years, mergers and amalgamations have resulted in ever-expanding ambulance services, and the result has not been a resounding success. Nor has it led to the expected benefits that are arguably the easiest to achieve, such as streamlining of purchasing and resulting economies or a reduction in management costs. It is disconcerting that relatively simple tasks, such as reducing duplication in the type of ambulances in use today or providing more standardisation, remain points to be highlighted in contemporary reports just as they were 50 years ago, despite the ambulance service having been part of the NHS since 1974. As the 1967 national report into ambulance equipment discovered (and Lord Carter, 50 years later, rediscovered), there is scope for more standardisation and less duplication in supply chains, but this must occur without compromising opportunities for innovation. It is, given the scale of challenges and the longevity of these ongoing concerns, legitimate to question whether the service should continue, for the most part, as a regional public sector monopoly that is poorly integrated with other health and care services and which lacks a clear view as to how to focus and discharge its responsibilities, or the right concept of operation for its role in the 21st century.

Alternative options are available, and none represents a panacea, although at least some offer potential value, which could improve the lot of patients and staff. Of the scenarios presented here, at least some seem to be worthy of closer consideration. Developing a service constituted as one that is focused on the realities of urgent care demand which predominates, and is integrated within, the wider NHS and social care also has its attractions and is logical. To some extent, this is happening in some places at ground level due to local initiatives of general practitioners and paramedics, thereby speeding the movement of paramedics into primary care to accelerate this trend.

A segmentation of the service, with FRS playing a greater role by adding further capacity, at little or no cost, and bringing the proven capability of a reliable and fast response will unquestionably aid life saving, for those patients who are time critical this is likely to improve their outcome. It is a well-established model elsewhere in the world, and ideological hostility should not preclude its consideration as part of a wider solution. Equally, a more federated model also suggests benefits and has a track record elsewhere in the NHS and beyond. Ultimately, the questions of service model, the resulting concept of operation and the future focus of the ambulance services must be coupled with the reality of patient demand and close attention to the variables that impact on patient outcome and staff welfare.

Addressing these problems and opportunities in an open-minded, imaginative manner and reshaping the service needs new thinking directed at creating a highly reliable organisation. It is the challenge that should preoccupy those charged with delivering ambulance services and those with political responsibility for the strategic delivery of health services. Seismic changes are required; the alternative is another 20 years of annual reports and investigations that will add little further illumination on how to improve matters, but much by way of hand-wringing exhortations, no doubt to equally insignificant effect.

References

Ahl, C., Nystrom, M., Jansson, L. (2006). Making up one's mind:- Patients' experiences of calling an ambulance. *Accident & Emergency Nursing* 14(1), (January) 11–19.

Association of Ambulance Chief Executives (2011). Taking Healthcare to the Patient 2. A review of 6 years' progress and recommendations for the future.

Audit Commission for Local Authorities and the National Health Service in England and Wales (1998). Life in the fast lane; Value for money in Emergency Ambulance Services (National Report) ISBN 10: 1862400644, ISBN 13: 9781862400641.

Beckford (2018). Mail on-line. Militant union blocks plan to put firemen on terror front line after criticism in Manchester atrocity enquiry. www.dailymail.co.uk/news/article-5565993/Militant-union-blocks-plan-firemen-terror-line.html

Bower, J. L., & Christensen C. M. (1995). Disruptive technologies: Catching the wave. *Harvard Business Review*, 73(1) (January–February 1995), 43–53.

British Medical Journal, McCartney, M. (2018). As outsourcing has become normal the debate on what "privatisation" of the NHS amounts to, or what it would look like, is magnified. www.bmj.com/bmj/section-pdf/971433?path=/bmj/360/8142/Comment.full.pdf

Camasso-Richardson, K., Wilde, J.A. & Petrack, E.M. (1997). Medically unnecessary pediatric ambulance transports: A medical taxi service? *Academy of Emergency Medicine*, 4(12), 1137–1141.

Campbell (2017). The Guardian. NHS Spends £80 million, on ambulances a year, data shows. www.theguardian.com/society/2017/sep/19/nhs-spends-80m-on-private-ambulances-a-year-data-shows.

Christensen, C., Grossman, J. & Hwang, J. (2009). *The Innovator's Prescription*. New York: McGraw Hill.

Claesson, A., Lindqvist, J., Ortenwall, P., & Herlitz, J. (2012). Characteristics of lifesaving from drowning as reported by the Swedish Fire and Rescue Services 1996–2010. *Resuscitation*, 83(9) (September), 1072–1077. doi:10.1016/j.resuscitation.2012.05.025. Epub: 2012 June 2015.

College of Paramedics Career Framework (2017). file:///D:/OneDrive%20-%20Andy%20Newton/Downloads/DigitalCareerFramework2017v2%20(1).pdf

College of Paramedics Curriculum Framework. 3rd edition (2013).

College of Paramedics, Post-graduate Curriculum Guidance (2017).

Coster, J., Irving, A., Turner, J., Phung, V.-H., & Siriwardena, N. (2017). Prioritizing novel and existing ambulance performance measures through expert and lay consensus: A three-stage multimethod consensus study. *Health Expectations*, 21(1) (August 25), 249–260. doi:10.1111/hex.1261. Epub 2017 Aug 25.

Dalton Review (2014). Examining new options and opportunities for providers of NHS care.

Davis, D. (2015). The Larrey Society. https://twitter.com/larreysociety?lang=en

De Maio, V.J., Stiell, I.G., Wells, G.A. & Spaite, D.W. (2003). Optimal defibrillation response intervals for maximum out-of-hospital cardiac arrest survival rates. *Annals of Emergency Medicine*, 42(2), 242–250. doi:10.1067/mem.2003.266

Department of Health (2000). Reforming Emergency Care.

Department of Health (2005a). Taking Healthcare to the Patient. Transforming NHS Ambulance Services. *The Bradley Report*, 18, 29–35.

Department of Health (2005b). Configuration of NHS Ambulance Trust in England, Consultation Document.

Edwards (2014). Association of Ambulance Chief Executives (2014). Academic Review of Demand 2013/14.

Ellwood, T., & Phillips, M. (2013). Improving Efficiency, Interoperability and Resilience of our Blue Light Service. *The All Party Parliamentary Group on Homeland Security*.

Hagihara, A., Hasegawa, M., Hinohara, Y., Abe, T., Motoi, M. (2013). The aging population and future demand for emergency ambulances in Japan. *International and Emergency Medicine*, 8(5), 431–447.

HM Government (2016). Enabling closer working between the emergency services. https://assets.publishing.service.gov.uk/government/uploads/system/uploads/attachment_data/file/495371/6.1722_HO_Enabling_Closer_Working_Between_the_Emergency_Services_Consult. . . .pdf

HMSO (1966). Report by the working party on ambulance training and equipment.: Part 1—training. Ministry of Health, Scottish Home and Health Department. London: Chaired by Millar, E.L.M.

HMSO (1967). Report by the Working Party on Ambulance Training and Equipment Part 2; Equipment and Vehicles. Chaired by Millar, E.L.M. August 2013.

House of Commons Committee of Public Accounts NHS ambulance services Sixty-second Report of Session (2016–17). Report, together with formal minutes relating to the report ordered by the house of commons to be printed 24 April 2017.

Hunter, J. (2013) Tyranny of the prevailing style of management, the essential Deming, includes material from Dr Deming's letters, speeches and articles. Several are from his lectures at Fordham University, including: Tyranny of the Prevailing Style of Management (pp.184–185). The W. Edwards Deming Institute Blog, Cedar City Utah.

JESIP Principles (2012). www.jesip.org.uk/home.

Kawakami, C., Ohshije, K., Kubotu, K., & Tochikubo, O. (2007). Influence of socioeconomic factors on medically unnecessary ambulance calls. *Journal of Health, Population & Nutrition*, 7, 120.

Kings Fund (2017). Mckenna, H. Is the NHS being privatised? www.kingsfund.org.uk/publications/articles/big-election-questions-nhs-privatised?gclid=Cj0KCQjw9NbdBRCwARIsAPLsnFb3kJcQjgtvrPVhwJgZkHy2QsrZRp-NkByv_K7hvkVcSsB2o1S-PcUaAlS4EALw_wcB

Knight, K. (2013). Facing the Future, report for the Department for Communities and Local Government Eland House Bressenden Place London SW1E 5DU. www.gov.uk/dclg

Kuehl, S. (Editor). (1994) Prehospital systems & medical oversight. Second Edition. National Association of EMS Physicians. Published by Mosby Lifeline.

LeGrand, J. (2010). Knights and knaves return. Public service motivation and the delivery of public services. *International Public Management Journal*, 13(1), 56–71.

Lerner, E.B., et al. (2003). The time first-response fire fighters have to initiate care in a midsize city. *The Journal of Emergency Medicine*, 25(2), 171–174.

Lewis (2017). Plymouth University and Longbow Associates. Bullying and Harassment at South East Coast Ambulance Service NHS Foundation Trust.

Lord Carter (2018). Operational Performance and Productivity in the Ambulance Service; unacceptable variation.

Lowthian, J.A., Cameron, A., Johannes, U., Stoelwinder, A., Curtis, A., Currell, B., Cooke, M., McNeil, J. (2011). Increasing utilisation of emergency ambulances. *Australian Health Review*, 35(1), 63–69. https://doi.org/10.1071/AH09866

Mansfield, C. (2015). Fire works. A collaborative way forward for the fire and rescue service. New Local Government Network.

Marsh, S. (2017). Private Ambulance Firm Contracted to the NHS Goes into Administration. *The Guardian*.

McCann, L., Granter, E., Gyde, P., & Hassard, J. (2013). Still blue-collar after all these years? An ethnography of the professionalization of emergency ambulance work. *Journal of Management Studies*, 50(5), 750–776.

McCartney, M. (2018). Should the NHS rely on outsourcing? As outsourcing has become normal the debate on what "privatisation" of the NHS amounts to or what it would look like, is magnified. *British Medical Journal*.

McChesney, F.S. (2002). Smoke and errors. Library of Economics and Liberty. https://www.econlib.org/library/Columns/Mcchesneyfire.html

McChesney, F.S. (2015). Fewer fires, so why are there far more firefighters? *Washington Post*. https://www.washingtonpost.com/opinions/2015/09/04/05316abe-517c-11e5-933e-7d06c647a395_story.html?noredirect=on&utm_term=.4c19389841ff

McKinstry, L. (2015). Why can't fire fighters double as paramedics? *The Spectator*. London, UK. https://www.spectator.co.uk/2015/09/why-cant-firefighters-double-as-paramedics/

Ministry of Defence (MoD) (2018). UK Armed Forces Quarterly Service Personnel Statistics. (July 1). https://assets.publishing.service.gov.uk/government/uploads/system/uploads/attachment_data/file/735105/20180701-_SPS.pdf

Murdock, A. (2017). Private Action for Public Purpose. Examining the Growth of Falck, The World Largest Rescue Company. Published by Palgrave Macmillan. UK

National Audit Office (2011). Transforming NHS Ambulance Services Public Accounts Committee, House of Commons. https://publications.parliament.uk/pa/cm201012/cmselect/cmpubacc/1353/1353.pdf

National Audit Office (2017). NHS Ambulance Services. HC 972, Session 2016–17.

National Health Service England (2015a). Transforming urgent and emergency care services in England. Urgent and emergency care review. *End of Phase 1 Report*. Sir Bruce Keogh.

National Institute for Health Research (NIHR) Dissemination Centre (2016). Care at scene. Themed report, research in the ambulance service.

New Economy (2017). Emergency Medical Response by the Fire and Rescue Services. www.local.gov.uk/sites/default/files/documents/workforce%20-%20fire%20and%20rescue%20services%20-%20EMR%20CBA%20Executive%20Summary.pdf

Newton, A., & Harris G. (2015). Leadership and System Thinking in the Modern Ambulance Service. In Ambulance Services Leadership and Management Perspectives, Edited by Wankhade, P. & Mackaway-Jones, K. pp. 81–93. Springer, Cham, Heidelberg, New York, Dordrecht & London. https://link.springer.com/chapter/10.1007/978-3-319-18642-9_7

Newton, A., & Hodge, D. (2012). The ambulance service: The past, present and future (Part 1). *Journal of Paramedic Practice*, 4(5).

NHS England (2015). Transforming urgent and emergency care services in England. [Benger Report].

Office of the Strategic Health Authorities (2009). Emergency services review—A comparative review of international ambulance service best practice.

Palazzo, F.F., Warner, O.J., Harron, M., & Sadana, A. (1998). Misuse of the London ambulance service: How much and why? *Journal of Accident and Emergency Medicine (now published as Emergency Medical Journal)* 15, 368–370.

Peacock, P.J., Peacock, J.L., Victor, C.R., & Chazot, C. (2005). Changes in the emergency workload of the London ambulance service between 1989 and 1999. *Emergency Medicine Journal* 22, 56–59. doi:10.1136/emj.2004.016741

Rasmus, W. (2009). Listening to the future, why it is everybody's business. Microsoft Executive Leadership Series. Wiley, New Jersey.

Ridley, M. (2013). London isn't burning, don't fetch the engines. *The Times*.

Rivett, G. (Retrieved 7/10/18) NHS History. Emergency Medical Service (1939–45) www.nhshistory.net/ems_1939-1945.htm.

Seddon, J. (2009). Failure demand. Rethinking lean service; 'from the horse's mouth. *Customer Strategy*, 2(1) Winter, 33–34.

Senge, P. (1990). *The fifth discipline: The art and practice of the learning organization.* Doubleday, New York.

Snooks, H., Williams, S., Crouch, R., Foster, T., Hartley-Sharpe, C., Dale, J. (2002). NHS emergency response to 999 calls: Alternatives for cases that are neither life threatening nor serious. *The British Medical Journal.*, 325(7359) August 10, 330–333.

Snooks, H., Wrigley, H., George, S., Thomas, E., Smith, H., & Glasper, A. (1998). Appropriateness of use of emergency ambulances. *Journal of Accident and Emergency Medicine,*15(6), 368–370.

Statter, D. (2015). Truly one of the dumbest articles ever written about firefighting & The Washington Post should be ashamed for publishing it. (Response to McChesney article above). Statter 911.

Stromberg, J. (2015). Firefighters do a lot less firefighting than they used to; here's what they do instead. Vox, USA. https://www.vox.com/2014/10/30/7079547/fire-firefighter-decline-medical

Stout & The American Ambulance Association (1994). *Contracting for emergency ambulance service; a guide to effective system design.* Washington, DC.

Turner, J., Jacques, R., Crum, A., Coster, J., Stone, T., & Nicholl, J. (2017) Ambulance response programme: Evaluation of phase 1 and phase 2. Final Report to NHS England. Centre for Urgent and Emergency Care Research, University of Sheffield. July.

Turner, J., & Nicholl, J. (2002). A review of the Costs and Benefits of Helicopter Emergency Ambulance Services in England and Wales - Final Report to the Department of Health. *An independent study carried out by the Medical Care Research Unit of the University of Sheffield on behalf of the Department of Health.* www.sheffield.ac.uk/polopoly_fs/1.44077!/file/MCRU-staffs-2002.pdf

Twist, A. (2014). London Ambulance Service Bullying and Harassment Review. The University of Sheffield. Ambulance Outcomes Programme. Pre-hospital Outcomes for Evidence Based Evaluation PhOEBE. www.sheffield.ac.uk/scharr/sections/hsr/mcru/phoebe

Victor, C.R., Peacock, J.L., Chazot, C., Walsh, S., & Holmes, D. (1999). Who calls 999 and why? A survey of the emergency workload of the London Ambulance Service. *Journal of Accident & Emergency Medicine.* 16, 174–178.

Wakefield, M. (2014a). The Ambulance Service is in a state of emergency. Frontline paramedic staff are leaving their jobs in droves. *The Spectator*.

Wakefield, M. (2014b). Revealed: Why paramedics are fleeing the NHS. *The Spectator*.

Wankhade, P. (2011). Performance measurement and the UK emergency ambulance service: Unintended Consequences of the ambulance response time targets. *International Journal of Public Sector Management*, 24(5), 382–402.

Wankhade, P. (2012). Different cultures of managements and their relationship with organisation performance: evidence from the UK ambulance service. *Journal of Public Money and Management*, 32, 381–388.

Williams, J., Newton, A., Talbot, J., Skedgel, C., Herbrand, A., Skinner, A., Mikrut, T., Willmore, J., & Jones, K. (2016). Broadening responsibilities, consideration of the potential to broaden the role of uniformed fire service employees. *University of Hertfordshire Research Archive*. https://uhra.herts.ac.uk/bitstream/handle/2299/20482/Broadening_Responsibilities_of_FRS_Main_Report_Final_with_Summary_Formatted.pdf?sequence=2&isAllowed=y

Wrigley, H., Snooks, H., Thomas, E., Smith, H., Glasper, A., & George, S. (1999) Epidemiology and demography of 999 ambulance calls: A review. *Pre-hospital Immediate Care*, 3, 94.

Young, M., & Cooper, C. (1997). Occupational stress in the ambulance service: A diagnostic study. *Health Manpower Management*, 23(4), 140–147(8). Emerald Publishing Group.

6 Galvanising Partnership and Communities to Tackle Domestic Violence and Abuse

Why Wicked Problems Have No Easy Solutions

Linda Reid

Introduction

Domestic violence and abuse (DV&A) is a significant problem in the UK and in many societies across the world. A study by the Early Intervention Foundation (EIF) (2014) found that eight million people in the UK (24.4% of people between the ages of 16 and 59) have been victims of DV&A and 25% of young people have witnessed at least one episode by the age of 18. The EIF identified a key barrier to effective prevention of DV&A as a lack of uniformity and clear integrated pathways in the approaches used across services and recommended a collaborative approach between providers, funders, researchers, central and local government and the voluntary sector.

The costs of DV&A have been calculated in 2001/2 (Walby, 2009) in the UK at £22.9 billion. Of these costs, £3.1 billion (13.5% of all DV&A costs) were to services largely funded by the government, including the criminal justice system, health care, social services, housing and civil legal services. Economic output losses were calculated at £2.7 billion (11.8% of all DV&A costs) and human and emotional costs at £17.1 billion (76.7% of all DV&A costs). In 2009, Walby estimated that the total cost of DV&A had declined to £15.7 billion, but there was an increase in service use of 24%.

The definition of domestic violence and abuse determined by the UK Home Office (2013a, p. 1) is

> Any incident or pattern of incidents of controlling, coercive or threatening behaviour, violence or abuse between those aged 16 or over who are or have been intimate partners or family members regardless of gender or sexuality. This can encompass but is not limited to the following types of abuse: psychological, physical, sexual, financial and emotional.

Accurate knowledge about the extent of DV&A is hampered by the reluctance of victims to report their experiences. The Crime Survey for England and Wales (CSEW) is considered a more accurate picture of the true extent of the problem than is police data. The CSEW collects data from face-to-face interviews and from confidential self-completion modules. The most recent set of data brings together different data sets across England and Wales, and the Office of National Statistics (2018) estimates that 26% of women aged between 16 and 59, an estimated 4.3 million females, have experienced some form of domestic abuse since the age of 16 years. Fifteen per cent of men, an estimated 2.4 million males, have experienced some form of domestic abuse since the age of 16 years to the year ending March 2017. In that year, 1.9 million adults aged 16–59 years experienced domestic abuse in the last year: 1.2 million women and 713,000 men (Office of National Statistics, 2017). The police recorded 1.1 million domestic violence and abuse related incidents in the year ending March 2017. Of these, 46% were recorded as domestic violence and abuse related crimes, and it accounted for 32% of all violent crimes recorded (Office of National Statistics, 2017).

Domestic violence is a 'wicked' problem, the characteristics of which are complexity, ambiguity and uncertainty that require a collective response (Rittel and Webber, 1973). This wicked societal problem requires qualitatively different ways of thinking and working for multi-agency partnerships. The strategic response needs to be appropriate to the complex nature of the issue and must address the needs of survivors from diverse communities. Grint (2010) suggests that individual leaders cannot address wicked problems and must engage the collective. Leadership of wicked problems is not a science, but an art, 'the art of engaging a community in facing up to complex collective problems' (2010, p. 171).

This chapter will examine whether the policy and systems that have been created and developed to tackle domestic violence and abuse are sufficient to address the complexity of the problem and the diverse needs of communities. It will look particularly at some of the issues in multi-agency working, mobilising the community and policing, as recourse to law enforcement remains the predominant response to reported incidents. It will highlight a difficult contradiction between the impetus for multi-agency working, collaboration and local devolution (Reid, 2014) versus the drive to centralise decision-making, remove front-line discretion and variation, calculate risk and measure progress against centralised standards. Policy frameworks designed to tackle DV&A have oscillated confusingly between these two impetuses, and the overall progress in addressing the wicked problem of domestic violence has been patchy at best.

The Response From the Government: Structures, Systems, Policies and Legislation

The first major policy impetus for multi-agency working in the UK was the Crime and Disorder Act of 1998, which placed a duty on local authorities and the police to establish Community Safety Partnerships and to develop crime and disorder strategies. Crawford (2001, p. 57) argues that New Labour's politics offered more plural understandings of and social responses to crime, drawing together a variety of stakeholders, which allowed a "systemisation and co-ordination of effort, expertise and information and a democratisation of control through greater community empowerment".

But by 2003, Loveday and Reid suggested that this system of accountability should be scrapped because research had shown that the Crime and Disorder Reduction Partnerships (CDRPs) were ineffective, and the tripartite arrangement of the Home Office, Chief Constable and Police Authority was unsatisfactory (2003). They recommended it should be replaced with a system of direct accountability to the mayor and council leaders, because that form of accountability would be more focused and effective than the plurality of the CDRPs. Police and crime commissioners (PCC) were introduced by the Police Reform and Social Responsibility Act (2011) and replaced Police Authorities, which were established under Section 3 of the Police Act (1996) and were not democratically elected by the public. Since the introduction of police and crime commissioners in 2012, there have been significant developments in terms of their role and responsibilities, amid a significantly changing governance environment which also includes the introduction of elected mayors and the Conservative government's devolution policy.

In September 2014, the government announced additional devolution for Scotland, Wales and Northern Ireland, and in May 2015 legislation to provide devolution of powers to cities with elected mayors was announced in the Queen's Speech, in the form of the Cities and Local Government Devolution Bill. Prime Minister Teresa May (2016) said that there would be significant changes in future reforms, and there would also be a merger of the roles of the PCCs and elected mayors, which would enable them to join up with local services. Paun, Rutter, and Nicholl (2016) claim that devolution reflects the desire for policy decisions to be taken closer to home and to provide greater alignment with local preferences, needs and values. However, the parliamentary report (2016) identifies a number of issues with the process. There was a significant lack of public consultation about the devolution process, and there are objections to elected mayors in some areas, reflected in the low turnout for the PCC elections in 2012. The report expressed concern that the public could be confused by too much bureaucracy and too many politicians, and recommended much more public engagement and consultation, involving residents in designing more open and transparent processes.

Government strategies are intended to create the infrastructure to enable local partnerships to effectively tackle DV&A. In July 2018, the Secretary of State for Communities announced a Domestic Abuse Fund 2018–2020, in which councils working in partnership with organisations such as charities are able to bid for funding to support survivors. The council response must be collaborative and meet the need of diverse communities. The criteria for funding are clear that partnerships are to be led locally, with services joining up and pooling resources for maximum flexibility.

Coordinated Community Responses

Coordinated community responses to domestic violence have a longer, but not untroubled, history. One of the first such approaches was introduced in what is known as the 'Duluth Model', in Minnesota, USA, in 1980. It shifted the approach from offender theories and frameworks to a pluralist, multi-agency approach (Shepard and Pence, 1999). The Duluth model changed the way the system is structured to respond and requires each practitioner to work as part of an organisational network that produces consistency, rather than using differing tools and discretion to screen a case in or out of their system.

The UK government's new model of Open Public Services (2011) creates a complex set of relationships and partnerships and is driven by a competitive commissioning framework. The Localism Act (2011) devolves greater powers to councils and neighbourhoods and gives local communities more control over housing and planning decisions. The new approach is an end to the top-down model of public services, and is intended to give people more control and choice over the public services they receive and open up the delivery of those services to new providers. The commissioning framework and payment by results are central to the policy and are intended to open provision to all potential providers, with the aim of getting good value for money for taxpayers.

There is also a Home Office (2010a) programme of police reform underway. After extensive consultation nationally, the aim is to subject the police service to greater local democratic accountability whereby citizens are involved in the local governance of public services. The primary mechanism for this is the police and crime commissioners and elected mayors (see Ashworth, this volume).

Amid this changing environment, the government policy that sets the strategy and direction for tackling domestic abuse and violence in the UK is the Violence Against Women and Girls (VAWG) strategy and subsequent action plans (Home Office, 2010b). The strategy is intended to ensure that central and local oversight, local focus and local drive come together to create a stronger response for women and girls. The localism agenda is evident in the strategy, with a government leadership role at national level to provide strategic direction, and local areas able to work together to develop an approach that addresses their local needs and to optimise their existing services and the capacity of the local community to respond effectively. They argue that greater decentralisation will give local people a stronger voice in setting local priorities, and that the voluntary and community sector, the statutory sector and communities will work together.

The Multi-Agency Risk Assessment Conference (MARAC)

The MARAC was introduced as a mechanism for agencies to share information and manage the risk of harm from domestic violence and abuse. Agencies, including the police, have adopted a risk management approach, often using a risk management tool, the most common being the Domestic Abuse, Stalking and Harassment, and Honour-Based Violence risk assessment tool (DASH) (Richards, 2009). The MARAC is widespread good practice, and the focus is on managing the risk to victims using a multi-agency approach. It is a forum for sharing information and taking action to reduce future harm to high-risk victims and their families. Robinson (2006) and Robinson and

Tregidga (2007) evaluated the MARAC and concluded that the MARAC "produced a positive, measurable impact in victims' lives" (2006, p. 784). There is evidence (Robinson et. al., 2016), however, that the MARAC may not be working effectively, and there are inconsistent practices such as the criteria for referral to MARAC. There are also difficulties in successfully integrating the established MARACs into the newer processes of public protection, such as the Multi-Agency Safeguarding Hubs (MASH). The safeguarding hubs have a wider remit and different models of service delivery.

The DASH (Richards, 2009) is the single risk assessment tool which has been implemented by the Association of Chief Police Officers (ACPO) and multi-agency partners in England and Wales. It was developed on understandings of risk for the most likely victim, that is, heterosexual females. The aim is to identify and manage high risk at the outset of an incident, so that early referrals can be made to give appropriate support and a partnership approach to managing the risk can be put in place, usually in the form of a MARAC. Risk is determined at standard (low), medium or high. There has been an increase in the number of incidents considered medium and high risk after risk assessment was introduced, creating significant increase in demand on resources. McLaughlin and Robbins (2014) found a 24% increase in cases referred to MARAC from 2010 to 2013:

2010/11: 935   2011/12: 1014   2012/13: 1162

In the year ending March 2017, there were 260 MARAC partnerships across England and Wales and 83,136 cases were discussed, which equates to 36 cases per 10,000 adult females (Office of National Statistics, 2017). Sixty-five per cent of the cases were referred by the police, with the next highest at 12% referred by specialist independent domestic violence advocates (IDVAs). (Office of National Statistics, 2017). Healthcare and the voluntary sector referrals were less than 10% of the total.

There is a significant adaptive challenge (Heifetz, 1994) of working differently to add value for the community in tackling domestic abuse in a partnership context. The challenge is to align values across public sector services and agencies and within the communities themselves. The PCC or elected mayor is the infrastructure by which public value can be created, and their role should be to orchestrate the competing stakeholder interests. For the moment, the multi-agency management of domestic violence and abuse is strongly reliant on police attendance and action at domestic incidents and law enforcement strategies. The following section will explore this issue in more depth, as it is often at the point of police response at 'street level' where the complexities around and multi-agency working and discretion versus standardisation and risk management are most prominent and problematic.

Policing Domestic Violence and Abuse

When a member of the public makes an emergency 999 call to request police assistance at an ongoing domestic incident, the call taker decides whether the nature of the call fits the criteria for domestic violence and abuse. Police policy requires officers to be dispatched immediately to the scene when an incident is in progress.

On arrival at the scene, the front-line police officer will conduct a primary investigation, which includes speaking to everyone involved, safeguarding the victim and any children or vulnerable family members, arranging medical assistance and gathering evidence about what has happened. If they establish a domestic incident or crime has taken place, they will complete the risk assessment process with the victim and decide which level of risk is posed at this time: standard, medium or high. If offences have been committed and the perpetrator is present, they will be arrested. The officer will create an electronic record of the incident, including the details from the risk assessment and the level of risk they have determined from their professional judgement. The details are then reviewed by specialist domestic abuse officers, who will decide whether they agree with the risk level set by the front-line officer, raise or lower the level if they feel appropriate and take action based on their review of the incident.

Measuring the extent of domestic abuse criminally has been difficult because there was no specific criminal offence of domestic violence or domestic abuse until 2015, when a new offence of controlling or coercive behaviour was introduced. Other offences associated with domestic abuse are recorded as other types of criminal offences, for example assaults, damage to property or theft. Other legislation that is commonly used includes the Protection from Harassment Act 1997, threats to kill contrary to Section 16 Offences Against the Person Act 1861, false imprisonment contrary to Common Law, and sexual assaults contrary to the Sexual Offences Act 2003.

Domestic abuse is complex and can encompass several forms of action involving harm and risk, such as stalking, harassment, honour-based violence and forced marriage. Some of these issues can be straightforwardly classified as offences and some cannot. Like many other problems confronting emergency services, domestic abuse is often deeply connected to other social and health problems such as people missing from home, mental ill health, self-harming, substance abuse and suicide. There are a range of civil powers that can be used to tackle domestic abuse: the Family Law Act 1996 provides for non-molestation orders and occupation orders; the Crime and Security Act 2010 gave the power to issue a Domestic Violence Protection Notice (DVPN) which excludes the perpetrator from the home of the victim and from contact with the victim for up to 28 days. The Children Act 1989 provides for care orders, contact orders, exclusion orders, residence orders and emergency protection orders, all of which help safeguard victims and families from an abusive perpetrator.

Front-line officers face very complex situations when attending incidents. There is often a history of calls to the address and differing accounts to unravel. For the purposes of illustration, the following is a real example from a police incident dataset gathered during research undertaken for a doctoral study from 2011 to 2017 (Reid, 2017).

Case study

On 28 July 2011, the police in this city force were called to this domestic abuse incident:

A neighbour has called police after hearing loud shouting and a child crying from a nearby address. On arrival the police knock at the address and find an extremely intoxicated male and female, both covered in blood. The female appears to have a broken nose and a broken hand, which is swollen and bruised. The male does not have any obvious injuries.

Both parties state that there has been an incident with the female's ex-partner, who allegedly turned up at the address and attempted to gain entry via the kitchen window. Inside the address there was a large amount of blood all over the floor and it was obvious that a physical altercation had taken place. Both parties were adamant that the incident and injuries had been caused by the female's ex-partner.

In the bedroom was a three year old child, and she too had blood on her arm, which she stated was her Mum's. She said that the male present had hit her Mum. The male, aged 32, was arrested on suspicion of assault. The female refused to give any details and insisted that her injuries had been caused by her ex-partner, but refused to make a complaint against him.

The child was taken into Police Protection in order for Social Services to conduct an assessment. The mother, aged 29 years, was left at the address.

The DASH risk level for this incident was classified as Medium.

This female victim had been reported as a victim of domestic abuse to police on 47 previous occasions. The victim was involved in a custody battle with her ex-partner and the father of her three year old child, as he wanted custody. Forensic evidence eliminated the ex-partner from the assault investigation.

The outcome from this incident was that she refused to support a prosecution against the perpetrator, her current partner, and wanted him back home with her. The perpetrator was released without charge, and it was found that there was a Crown Court Curfew requiring him to live at the victim's home. There was a subsequent incident at the address on 7th August 2011 and the same man was arrested, charged and remanded in custody. He had a history of committing domestic violence against previous partners.

A foster placement was found for the three year old.

This is emblematic of a very difficult DV&A case where front-line officers are faced with ambiguity and complexity. The officers exercised front-line leadership in dealing with this wicked problem by safeguarding the child and arresting the correct perpetrator. There are, however, failures by the multi-agency partnership to manage this abusive relationship. The court determined he must live with the victim, perpetuating the violence and risk. The officers set the risk level at medium rather than high, despite her having been victimised on 47 previous occasions and the perpetrator having a history of violence towards other partners. This case would not have been referred to MARAC for partnership intervention, so this family were also failed by the system.

Walklate and Mythen (2011) believe there are a number of dynamics in relation to risk assessments, and criminal justice professionals use their experience, professional culture and their 'feelings' about the case to inform their decisions. Robinson, Pinchevsky and Guthrie (2016) found that factors explicitly related to physical violence are in the forefront of officers' minds. Research suggests that the perceptions of victims are more important and potentially more accurate in predicting future domestic violence than risk assessment instruments (Heckert and Gondolf, 2004). In this doctoral study (Reid, 2017), the information required to complete the DASH was refused by 22.1% of victims. Without the cooperation of the victim in answering the questions, the front-line officer has to base their decisions on their professional judgement with limited information. Many of the officers who took part in the study were critical of the DASH tool, claiming that a box-checking, standardised system is in reality often unworkable.

Moreover, only reports considered high risk are subject to further action and multi-agency arrangements. In this study of police incident data in a major UK city (Reid, 2017), the majority of incidents were reported to be standard risk: 71% standard; 21% medium and 2% high risk. Only high-risk cases and a few medium-risk cases are referred to a MARAC, where multi-agency information sharing and a coordinated response take place. The remaining medium risk and standard risk are referred to domestic violence and abuse support agencies, usually voluntary agencies or charities, to seek advice. In reality, a very small percentage of reported DV&A is being effectively tackled by society.

The Nature of the Police Organisation

Lipsky (2010) says that each encounter of a citizen with a teacher, police officer or social worker is an example of policy delivery, and the policy delivered is immediate and personal because public service street-level workers have "substantial discretion in the execution of their work" (2010, p. 8). In recent years the effects of austerity have resulted in a considerable reduction in police resources. In processing large amounts of work with inadequate resources, front-line workers develop shortcuts and simplifications, and there may be a degree of non-compliance with policies. The supervisors and managers of street-level workers find it difficult to monitor or scrutinise decisions made by the front line because of the high degree of discretion.

Vinzant and Crothers (1998) applied the theory of tame and wicked problems to police leadership at street level. A police constable, by virtue of his or her authority, exercises discretion, power and legitimacy over members of the public and is in a unique position to adopt a leadership role. For example, when a constable decides to arrest a perpetrator at the scene of a domestic abuse incident, they are making a discretionary decision based on professional judgement. In contemporary parlance, they are exercising 'leadership' by committing public resources and seeking to influence others, in an environment of competing norms and values. The constable has made a discretionary choice at a complex (wicked) level of problem. Grant and Rowe found a discrepancy between risk assessment policy created by senior management and front-line implementation and suggests that "street level police use their discretion to negotiate and resist reforms imposed by management" (2011, p. 61).

Rowe examined the impact of a positive arrest policy for domestic abuse on police officer discretion, professionalism and decision-making. Officers make arrests because of a risk aversion: if they did not arrest they would have to justify their actions; and if the perpetrator committed further violence after the officers left the scene there would be serious repercussions for them. Rowe argues that officers resent the impact on their discretion, however they continue to implement the policy, thus experiencing considerable 'cognitive dissonance' on some occasions (2007, p. 288).

Strategic leaders assume that the introduction of a law or policy will be followed by a programme of implementation as set out in the strategy. However, front-line use of discretion creates a pattern of agency behaviour which cannot be eliminated by their first- and second-line managers (Lipsky, 2010). Managers can try to narrow the gap between performance at the front line and the desired policy outcomes, and some of the ways of doing this include narrowing the job role to constrain discretion, the use of technology such as body-worn cameras and remote monitoring, and the introduction of sanctions and compliance processes. But, as we shall see below, none of these measures will ever fully close the circle when it comes to removing variation in street-level practice or restricting professional judgement. Police work (like many kinds of public service work) involves interaction with the public in complex 'grey areas' that will always involve front-line judgement calls and what Lipsky calls 'dilemmas of the individual' (Lipsky, 2010; Maynard-Moody and Musheno, 2003).

Data Collection and Recording Issues in Police Reports

When it comes to something seemingly as straightforward as measuring the prevalence and outcomes of DV incidents via police reports, we once again see political reforms around localism and devolution coming into conflict with pressures to remove variation, reduce risk and raise standards of practice in public services. Robinson et al. (2016) found inconsistent and incomplete recording of domestic abuse incidents in police data. Measures such as local force performance indicators, Her Majesty's Inspectorate of Constabulary (HMIC), the Audit Commission, the Independent Office for Police

Conduct (formerly the Independent Police Complaints Commission) and community surveys have been introduced in order to increase the scrutiny of and reduce the scope for discretion of individual officers. Applegate (2006) suggests that policing domestic violence is a policy area where central and external influences are greater than those exerted from a local level, and that top-down control tends to be more effective in overcoming the difficulties of direct supervision. Conversely, Myhill and Johnson (2016) found that even with National Crime Recording Standards (NCRS), the National Standard for Incident Recording (NSIR) and a standardised risk assessment process (DASH), it is still possible for police officers to minimise the seriousness of domestic incidents or not report them at all. However, the HMIC inspection of police domestic abuse arrangements (2014) found that officers require greater discretion to ensure that the police response is "targeted to address the particular risk that they find" (2014, p. 37).

Reid (2017) found that in a survey of front-line police constables in a major UK city, when asked about their use of professional judgement at domestic incidents, 61% agreed they needed more freedom in deciding how to handle situations at domestic abuse calls, with only 18% disagreeing. There are conflicting views about the amount of discretion that police officers should have the authority to use in policing domestic abuse, and a tension about whether they can be trusted to enact policies to meet the expectations of their senior leaders and interested stakeholders. The HMIC (2014) report into police arrangements of domestic abuse exposed failures and weaknesses and denounced the police service for treating domestic abuse as a 'poor relation' to other police activity.

Conclusion

Walklate (2008) argues that there is a continued focus on criminal justice solutions to domestic abuse, despite the evidence that suggests that they do not work. HMIC (2015) found that chief officers are taking personal responsibility and making domestic abuse a priority and recommended that chief constables should review how action to tackle domestic abuse is prioritised and valued, and how staff are given the appropriate level of professional support and encouragement. Another recommendation is that there should be further multi-agency inspections of partnership organisations, to consider how local services contribute to keeping victims safe and the quality of partnership working.

There is a gap between the representation of family violence in police data and the real amount of violence taking place. Stanko (2001) introduced an innovative methodology to capture an audit of calls about domestic violence over a period of 24 hours to the police, other public sector agencies and charities such as women's refuges, telephone helplines and victim support, and concluded that "domestic violence is highly visible in the day-to-day workload of public services" (2001, p. 222). Smeenk and Malsch (2005) argue that instruments that measure abuse, and the legislation that defines abuse, differ around the world and so it is difficult to make comparisons about prevalence internationally, and that measurement independent of legal definitions would be more accurate and enable better allocation of resources. Research in an international context would also assist with hard-to-reach communities and the factors that prohibit victims from seeking help.

Smeenk and Malsch (2005) suggest that when police are properly trained in a multi-agency context, they may use their discretionary powers to "provide flexibility in their response, and a combination of legal and assistive interventions that meet the needs of victims" (2005, p. 254). Kelly et al. (2005) also argues that future reform needs to be based on a greater understanding of family violence and the way it is different from other forms of violence. In 2014, Australia declared family violence as a national emergency and made a $100 million funding package available.

Devolution is facing a considerable challenge in engaging with communities, and the domestic abuse context is no exception. In 2014, two national consultations about domestic abuse received little engagement from the public.

The introduction of policies and processes, and changes in political and partnership structures to tackle domestic violence and abuse, is a tame response to an intractable, wicked societal problem. The adaptive leadership challenge is to work differently, involving the community in designing services that will work for them, rather than a 'one size fits all' approach. The new devolution arrangements offer opportunities to really align services and resources; however, there needs to be fundamental changes. For example, scrutiny and accountability is largely dependent on performance regimes led by what is measurable, rather than measures which seek evidence about the quality of service delivered and the impact the interventions have had on the domestic abuse. Scrutiny needs to be more focused on the whole partnership response rather than the police in isolation. The extent of the problem is overwhelming and much more investment is needed, particularly to secure the engagement and support of the community and victims.

References

Applegate, R. J. (2006). Changing Local Policy and Practice Towards the Policing of Domestic Violence in England and Wales. *Policing: An International Journal of Police Strategies & Management*, 29 (2), 368–383 [online]. Available at: http://dx. doi.org/10.1108/13639510610667718 (accessed 15 May 2015).

Crawford, A. (2001). Joined-up but fragmented. In R. Matthews and J. Pitts (Eds.), *Crime, Disorder and Community Safety. A New Agenda?* London: Routledge, pp. 54–80.

Early Intervention Foundation (2014). *Domestic violence and abuse review*, Early Intervention Foundation [online]. Available at: www.eif.org.uk (accessed 22 April 2014).

Grant, S., and Rowe, M. (2011) Running the Risk: Police Officer Discretion and Family Violence in New Zealand. *Policing and Society: An International Journal of Research and Policy*, 21 (1), 49–66 [online]. Available at: doi:10.1080/ 10439463.2010.540662 (accessed 15 May 2015).

Grint, K. (2010c). Wicked problems and clumsy solution: The role of leadership. In S. Brookes and K. Grint (Eds.), *The New Public Leadership Challenge*. Basingstoke: Palgrave Macmillan, pp. 169–186.

Heckert, D. A., and Gondolf, E. W. (2004). Battered Women's Perceptions of Risk Versus Risk Factors and Instruments in Predicting Repeat Reassault. *Journal of Interpersonal Violence*, 19 (7), July, 778–800 [online]. Available at: doi:10.1177/0886260504265619 (accessed 23 January 2015).

Heifetz, R. A. (1994). *Leadership Without Easy Answers*. Massachusetts: Harvard University Press.

HMIC (2014). *Everyone's business: Improving the police response to domestic abuse*, HMIC [online]. Available at: www.hmic.gov.uk (accessed 6 June 2014).

HMIC (2015). *Increasingly everyone's business* [online]. Available at: www.justiceinspectorates.gov.uk/hmic/wp-content/uploads/increasingly-everyone's-business-domestic-abuse-proges-report.pdf (accessed 17 February 2016).

Home Office (2010a). *Policing in the 21st century: Reconnecting police and the people* [online]. Available at: www.gov.uk/government/uploads/system/uploads/attachment_data/file/118233/response-policing-21st.pdf (accessed 2 March 2014).

Home Office (2010b). *Call to end violence against women and girls* [online]. Available at: www.homeoffice.gov.uk/publications/crime/call-end-violence-women-girls/vawg-paper?view=Binary (accessed 14 February 2011).

Home Office (2011). *Open public services* [online]. Available at: http://files.openpublic *services.cabinetoffice.gov.uk* (accessed 2 March 2014).

Home Office (2013a). *Home office circular 003/2013* [online]. Available at: www.gov.uk/government/publications (accessed 18 February 2014).

Home Office (2013b). *Guidance domestic violence and abuse* [online]. Available at: www.gov.uk/guidance/domestic-violence-and-abuse (accessed 14 July 2013).

House of Commons (2016). *The parliamentary report, devolution: The next five years and beyond* [online]. Available at: https://publications.parliament.uk (accessed 10 February 2017).

Kelly, L. in Smeenk, W., and Malsch, M. (Eds.) (2005). *Family Violence and Police Response*, 83–103, Hampshire: Ashgate Publishing Limited.

Lipsky, M. (2010). *Street-Level Bureaucracy*. New York: Russell Sage Foundation.

Loveday, B., and Reid, A. (2003). *Going local. Who should run Britain's police?* Policy Exchange, London [online]. Available at: www.policyexchange.org.uk (accessed 14 February 2004).

Maynard-Moody, S., and Musheno, M. (2003). *Cops, Teachers, Counselors: Stories from the Front Lines of Public Service*. Ann Arbor: University of Michigan Press.

McLaughlin, H., and Robbins, R. (2014). Presentation 3rd March, *MARAC and Adult Social Care* [online]. Available at: http://sscr.nihr.ac.uk/PDF/AdultSafeguarding 030314/HughMcLaughlin.pdf (accessed 18 January 2015).

Myhill, A. and Johnson, K. (2016). Police Use of Discretion in Response to Domestic Violence. *Criminology & Criminal Justice*, Vol. 16(1) 3–20 [online]. Available at: DOI: 10.1177/1748895815590202 (accessed 26 January 2016).

Office of National Statistics (2017). *Domestic abuse in England and Wales: Year ending March 2017*, The Crime Survey of England and Wales [online]. Available at: www.ons.gov.uk/peoplepopulationandcommunities/crimeandjustice (accessed 14 August 2018).

Office of National Statistics (2018). *Domestic abuse: Findings from the Crime Survey for England and Wales: Year ending March 2017* [online]. Available at: www.ons.gov.uk/peoplepopulationandcommunities/crimeandjustice (accessed 4 September 2018).

Paun, A., Rutter, J., and Nicholl, A. (2016). *Devolution as a policy laboratory*, Nesta [online]. Available at: www.nesta.org.uk/sites/default/files/devolution_as_a_policy_laboratory_alliance_report.pdf (accessed 2 February 2016).

Reid, L. (2014). Adding Value Through New Public Leadership. *The International Journal of Leadership in Public Services*, 10 (4), 233–242.

Reid, L. (2017). *Why is Leadership Important in Policing Domestic Abuse?* A case study of the leadership issues in tackling domestic abuse in a major city in the U.K. PhD. Thesis, University of Manchester.

Richards, L. (2009). *Domestic Abuse, Stalking and Harassment and Honour Based Violence (DASH, 2009) Risk Identification and Assessment and Management Model* [online]. Available at: www.dashriskchecklist.co.uk (accessed 10 July 2010).

Rittel, H., and Webber, M. (1973). Dilemmas in a General Theory of Planning. *Policy Sciences*, 4, 155–169 [online]. Available at: doi:10.1007/BF01405730 (accessed 20 November 2010).

Robinson, A. L. (2006). Reducing Repeat Victimization Among High-Risk Victims of Domestic Violence. The Benefits of a Coordinated Community Response in Cardiff, Wales. *Violence Against Women*, 12 (8), 761–788 [online]. Available at: doi:10.1177/1077801206291477 (accessed 20 October 2010).

Robinson, A. L., Myhill, A., Wire, J., Roberts, J., and Tilley, N. (2016). *Risk-led policing of domestic abuse and the DASH risk model* [online]. London: College of Policing. Available at: www.college.police.uk/News/College-news/Documents/Risk_led_policing_of_domestic_abuse_and_the_DASH_risk_model.pdf (accessed 21 November 2011).

Robinson, A. L., Pinchevsky, G. M., and Guthrie, J. (2016). Under the Radar: Policing Non-violent Domestic Abuse in the US and UK. *International Journal of Comparative and Applied Criminal Justice*, 40 (3), 195–208 [online]. Available at: doi:10.10 80/01924036.2015.1114001 (accessed 21 November 2016).

Robinson, A. L., and Tregidga, J. (2007). The Perceptions of High-Risk Victims of Domestic Violence to a Coordinated Community Response in Cardiff, Wales. *Violence Against Women*, 13 (11), 1130–1148 [online]. Available at: doi:10.1177/1077801207307797 (accessed 20 October 2010).

Rowe, M. (2007). Rendering Visible the Invisible: Police Discretion, Professionalism and Decision-making. *Policing and Society*, 17 (3), 279–294 [online]. Available at: http://dx.doi.org/10.1080/10439460701497352 (accessed 26 July 2011).

Shepard, M. F., and Pence, E. L. (1999). *Coordinating Community Responses to Domestic Violence. Lessons from Duluth and Beyond*. Sage Series on Violence Against Women. California, Sage.

Smeenk, W., and Malsch, M. (Eds.) (2005). *Family violence and police response*, Hampshire: Ashgate Publishing Limited.

Stanko, E. A. (2001) The Day to Count: Reflections on a Methodology to Raise Awareness About the Impact of Domestic Violence in the UK. *Criminal Justice*, 1 (2), 215–226.

Vinzant, J. C., and Crothers, L. (1998). *Street Level Leadership*. Washington, DC: Georgetown University Press.

Walby, S. (2009). *The Cost of Domestic Violence: Up-Date 2009*. Lancaster: Lancaster University [online]. Available at: www.lancaster.ac.uk/fass/doc_library/sociology/Cost_of_domestic_violence_update.doc (accessed 18 January 2012).

Walklate, S. (2008). What Is to be Done About Violence Against Women? Gender, Violence, Cosmopolitanism and the Law. *British Journal of Criminology*, 48 (1), 39–54 [online]. Available at: doi:10.1093/bjc/azm050 (accessed 16 July 2016).

Walklate, S., and Mythen, G. (2011). Beyond Risk Theory: Experiential Knowledge and Knowing Otherwise. *Criminology and Criminal Justice*, 11 (2), 99–113 [online]. Available at: doi:10.1177/1748895811398456 (accessed 14 December 2014).

Part 2

7 Beyond the Scope of Managerialism

Explaining the Organisational Invisibility of Police Work

Cliff Bacon

Introduction

Organisational control mechanisms focusing on performance and outputs are often essential factors in determining the scope and direction of working practice. A significant literature on professional work focuses on the limitations and boundaries of control, from both a conceptual and structural perspective (Bannick et al., 2016; Evetts, 2003; Frey et al., 2013; Gundhus, 2012; Power, 2007), and the practical realities of how street-level workers adapt to the various iterations of instruments of control (Lipsky, 2010; McCann et al., 2013; Maynard-Moody and Musheno, 2003). While much of the historical roots of organisational control mechanisms lie in the private sector (Power, 2007), the integration of New Public Management (NPM) metrics and control systems into the public sector (from the 1980s) has spawned discussion on the extent to which public sector professional interests and expertise have been co-opted, curtailed or have resisted integration into a managerialist framework (O'Reilly and Reed, 2011). In particular, the control of professional autonomy and discretion in everyday working practice is seen as a crucial factor in attempts to change occupational cultures linked to historical failure and outdated modes of work (Charman, 2017; Holdaway, 2017; Fournier, 1999). The ways in which these new mechanisms are operationalised and how employees adapt to its requirements will have significant impacts on the nature and quality of service delivery (Power, 2007).

This chapter examines the factors that impact on an organisation's ability to successfully operationalise control measures to standardise working practice to a level that allows task regulation, audit and scrutiny—the ability of management and regulators to monitor employee compliance and to view change in action, from a distance. The empirical data used are derived from an ethnographic study of a police force in England and Wales. Policing in England and Wales is currently in the midst of adapting to significant, austerity-driven structural change. Its operational challenge is the prioritisation and distribution of work, in an era of increased demand, changing demand and reduced staffing levels (Boulton et al., 2017). Parallel to this challenge is a politically driven agenda to 're-professionalise' policing, to unravel the old 'occupational closure' model of policing and to replace it with a managerialised, harm reduction, vulnerability reduction model required to adapt to current requirements and to rectify service delivery mistakes of the past (Holdaway, 2017). Both a pragmatic approach to austerity cuts and the skillset adjustment to professional status require tight institutional control of finances, resources and the transfer of new knowledge into practice. This chapter's focus on control of policing practice explores the extent to which the physical working environment and the task characteristics of police work place restrictions on the extent and type of managerial control that the organisation will attempt to exercise over officers. The invisibility (to the organisation) of the policing environment (Rowe, 2007) and the ambiguity and complexity of tasks (Bannick et al., 2016) place boundaries on the visibility of outcomes and the degree of prescriptive regulation applicable. This, in turn, raises the thorny question of the extent to which experiential knowledge and discretion are effectively ineradicable (Evans, 2016; Lipsky, 2010), suggesting that managerial attempts to control every aspect of policing cannot work as intended. Many aspects of police work cannot be rendered visible, standardised and controllable.

Drawing on empirical evidence relating to interactions between operational police officers and individuals with mental health issues, the chapter will highlight the complexity of practice issues in two distinct operational settings—in the community and in police custody—and the variable consequences for all of those involved: police officers, support staff and the wider public. The chapter continues in five further sections. The first section focuses on the concept of managerialism as a means of organisational control and a way to restrict and shape the practice environment and task characteristics. In the second section, the research design is outlined. The findings are presented in the third and fourth sections, analysing policing practice in the community and in police custody, highlighting the unintended and undisclosed consequences of policing complex issues. Finally, the conclusion discusses the flaws in a managerialist approach to practice change and argues that to maintain public safety and minimise injustice, application of professional attributes of autonomy, discretion and experiential knowledge will always be required in the complex practice environment of street-level, public sector work.

Managerialism as Control Mechanism in the Public Sector

A key element of this chapter is the ways in which, since the 1980s, the public sector in general and policing in particular has been controlled by the discourses, systems and logics of managerialism (Gilling, 2014). Evolving in its current iteration, through NPM reforms, conflicting logics of enterprise and auditability are realised through demands for accountability and transparency, demanding, as Power (2007, p. 197) states, "cultural ideals of precision, proof and calculability". Applying principles widely used in the private sector, NPM strategies have determined and controlled public sector resource provision, incorporating measurement and scrutiny largely via metrics-driven audit and risk management systems (O'Reilly and Reed, 2011; Power, 2007). Emphasis is placed on the use of standards and performance measures with the requirement for managers and employees to work on quantifiable and measurable tasks (Hood, 1991). The potentially negative consequences of focusing on quantifiable output controls based on efficiency, rather than the social and equitable value of operational practice, is particularly significant in the public sector given the importance of public legitimacy (Skinns, 2009; Power, 2007) and the 'policy alienation' experienced by employees who fail to comprehend the relationship between newly imposed NPM practices and the greater public good (Tummers et al., 2009, p. 690).

Managerial control, in its public sector guise, provides mechanisms of authority that go alongside (and in the policing case form a central part of) professionalisation programmes, in particular where tight control is required to impose new employee standards, behaviours and practice and to remove variation and discretion. Principles of accountability via external regulation, legal legitimacy, standardised practice and performance-related measures are trademark traits of the kinds of control mechanisms used to influence and regulate professions and occupations (Evans, 2016; Gundhus, 2012; Power, 2007). Control 'from above' is often a means of enforcing change, a disciplinary logic to transform and reformat practice and expertise (Fournier, 1999). Policing is currently undergoing a 'top-down' transition from occupational to organisational professionalism, enforced, in part, by historic institutional failures (e.g. systemic national occurrences of child sexual exploitation, the Saville enquiry, the Stephen Lawrence case, Hillsborough; see Holdaway, this volume). Since 2013, a politically driven transformation programme has changed the institutional landscape of policing in England and Wales with the reconfiguration of regulatory bodies and their senior management. Independent oversight has replaced police control of managerial posts regulating training, standards, scrutiny and discipline, creating a network of institutional control (Holdaway, 2017). A discourse of cultural change through the prioritisation of a vulnerability agenda (focusing on those most vulnerable in society as opposed to dealing with universal crime and disorder) has required a move from the historical concept of police professionalism as a craft-based occupation, requiring autonomous and discretional practice (Bartkowiak-Theron and Asquith, 2014; Reiner, 2000a; Rowe, 2016), to a more scientific and evidence-based version of practice (Gundhus, 2012; Myhill and Johnson, 2016; Willis and Mastrofski, 2014). In this iteration of professionalism, the fear of 'loose cannon' street-level workers controlling, evolving and ultimately changing practice is replaced by managerial control of what needs to be done, how it should be done and how it is inspected, measured and enforced.

In the context of new control measures, managers are potentially more able to restrict the freedom of workers, including expert professionals (Evans, 2016; Evetts, 2011). Sociology of work literatures contain numerous examples of implicit and explicit worker resistance to managerial control in an effort to sustain professional autonomy (McCann et al., 2013; Maynard-Moody and Musheno, 2003; Moskos, 2008). The literature implies a manager-worker power struggle with, at its core, a breakdown in principles, communication and general resistance to change for economic, social, professional and political reasons. Yet, in many working environments, the ability of managers to control working practice and the extent to which it can be controlled is equally as reliant on environment and task characteristics as it is on the will and desires of workers (Lipsky, 2010). Control, audit and scrutiny of practice are only possible as far as the tasks and associated actions and results are visible to the organisation (Bannick et al., 2016). Yet much of the working environment of public sector workers (paramedics, social workers, police officers, firefighters) takes place outside the organisation, on the streets, in neighbourhoods, where staff are scattered and dispersed, with little supervision and where external accountability is difficult. This environment gives street-level workers, whether subversive or not, scope to make their account of the reality of their actions the authoritative one, with very little corroboration possible (Reiner, 2000b; Lipsky, 2010).

Within this environment, control metrics to increase practice visibility and to reveal, uncover and standardise actions and results rely, primarily, on the type and nature of the practice task. Literature focuses on the complexity and ambiguity level of tasks as a precursor to the implementation of organisational control mechanisms (Bannick et al., 2016; Frey et al., 2013). High levels of complexity (e.g. where there are multiple options and actors or uncertainty of factual estimations of social problems), combined with high levels of ambiguity (uncertainty, for example, around legal or social problems and solutions) are often deemed unsuitable for managerialist or process-based control metrics. In this schematic, output control is only feasible where knowledge relating to the task is clear, stable, not subject to change and is, ideally, observable. Different combinations of ambiguity and complexity are seen to require different control solutions.

In reality, practice tasks carried out daily by street-level workers in the public sector are usually dynamic and multi-layered and cannot always be compartmentalised and categorised (Lipsky, 2010; Maynard-Moody and Musheno, 2003; Bannick et al., 2016). Questions such as 'what happened' and 'who did what' and 'why' are complex enough when there is only one agency involved and become yet more problematic with inter-agency working. Management control theory on the organisational response to changing environments (such as bureaucratic, professional, managerialist, with corresponding metrics of process, output and input control (Bannick et al., 2016; Frey et al., 2013)) suggests the ability for organisational flexibility and adaptation. Yet, in practice, this is often not the case. In UK policing, the professionalisation programme appears fixed on a process-controlled, standardised, managerialist approach to ensure professional requirements around the practice of priority issues (e.g. vulnerability) are adhered to. If anything, the solution to non-compliance is a stricter dose of process metrics, rather than a change in approach.

The focus of this chapter, on policing practice around mental health-related incidents, highlights the depth of the problems involved in trying to control and manage such complex, indeterminate, discretionary activity. Mental health is a clear policing priority in England and Wales within the broader vulnerability agenda (Cummins and Edmonson, 2015). Police contact with individuals deemed to have mental health issues has risen significantly during the last five years, partly due to increased police awareness and prioritisation and partly because of the impact of austerity on community services (Cummins, 2012; Leese and Russell, 2017; McLean and Marshall, 2010; Senior et al., 2014). Complexity and ambiguity in dealing with mental health calls is multi-layered. The nature of symptoms of mental health and their severity may not be apparent to officers or initially disclosed until, for example, a detainee is in custody. Legalities are often described as vague by practitioners, and there is often confusion/elision with symptoms of other health problems, notably drug and alcohol abuse (McLean and Marshall, 2010). Importantly, outcomes can be processed by officers through either a health or a crime pathway (or a combination of both). The pathway chosen, therefore, depends on complex decisions and perceptions by street-level workers, often unsupervised and working in both the invisible environment (on the street) and the highly visible environment of the custody suite (with extensive CCTV coverage and accountability through prescriptive electronic systems).

Focusing on one prioritised clientele group (individuals suffering from poor mental health), managed within one control mechanism (managerialism), should, in theory, produce standardised outcomes, whether intended or unintended. The potential for outcomes to be based only around auditable process, making auditability of practice the focus of organisational scrutiny and good practice, is well documented (Power, 2007; Hood, 1991). In this scenario, non-auditable tasks are often disregarded, with organisational performance and operational practice siloed. The creation of two strata of practice—one visible (risk averse, process driven) and the other invisible (left to the discretion of practitioners) allows the possibility of inequality of service.

Research Methods

Data were collected from an ethnographic study of policing in a metropolitan police force in England and Wales (renamed 'Eastside', for anonymity), between 2015 and 2017. The author, a retired police inspector with 30 years policing experience, interviewed 34 operational officers and spent 100 hours observing a team of 34 response officers on mobile patrol. Interviews were conducted in two Eastside divisions (one inner city, one on the outskirts) with observations and ad hoc interviews in the same inner city division. Analysis of detailed interviews directed the scope of the observations which were documented, transcribed and written in a series of vignettes to portray the full context of incidents and outcomes as well as officers' (and the researchers') comments and opinions on these incidents.

The study portrays a wide range of policing practice and roles, from serious, potentially life-threatening scenarios to routine administrative tasks. This particular chapter discusses these activities in two different policing environments, the community and police station custody and back office. It focuses exclusively on data relating to policing mental health incidents (where the condition is either known or discovered at a later point). The specific task characteristics of these incidents highlight the problems and indeterminacies of managerial control mechanisms and metrics. Firstly, data is discussed from the invisible (community) policing environment and secondly from the visible (custody) environment, describing the unintended and undisclosed consequences of managerialist control.

Controlling the Invisible Policing Environment

The invisible policing environment commences when officers leave the relative visibility of a police station on foot or vehicle and choose their direction and purpose of travel. The extent of organisational control of patrol (assignment and task requirements) can be total or minimal. They can include, for example, assignment to an incident or task by a control room operative or supervisor, a self-generated requirement to complete a task as part of an ongoing enquiry (such as collecting CCTV footage), or self-directed patrol of a high crime area as a preventative measure. Officers, working away from the station, are only visible to the small section of the public they have contact with (and who have little say on what they are doing and why). Incident allocation at Eastside was prioritised on a graded matrix, based on the potential vulnerability of people involved, e.g. victims and witnesses. Officers were directed to either specific, definable incidents (a closed task with prescribed procedural requirements), e.g. domestic violence, juveniles missing from care homes, or non-specific incidents (open, dynamic, ambiguous tasks, with limited procedural guidance), e.g. suicidal person, street disturbance. Incidents involving contact with people with mental health issues generally fell into the latter category and took up a significant proportion of officers' shift time. Calls ranged from violent disturbances in the street, to suicidal individuals carrying knives, to the daily occurrence of multiple police officers guarding individuals awaiting mental health assessment at hospital. On one evening shift, nine officers (two thirds of the available officers on duty) were at a hospital for four to five hours each.

Practice control was often initiated by other agencies, such as ambulance, mental health and social services, indirectly taking resource control from the policing domain, to the consternation of officers who often questioned the validity of non-police directives. One officer noted the following:

> We are seeing more mental health incidents. The mental health team know that if they ring us we will deal with it. The ambulance service asks for assistance with, say, a suicidal male, but it's only assistance because they can't allocate the job. So we are blue lighting to assist the ambulance service for a job they are not even at because our criteria is that someone is in immediate risk, as we have a different grading policy to them and they know we will do that.

In Eastside, supervisory oversight (a potential means of increasing organisational visibility), of operational practice on the streets, was minimal. On average, two shift sergeants, responsible for the immediate supervision of the patrol officers, remained in the station back office, checking the computerised incident log and the allocation of resources and completing myriad bureau-cratic tasks, such as reviewing crime reports. There were only three occasions (out of hundreds of allocated incidents) during the observation period when a sergeant left the station to attend an incident (a suspicious death, a gas leak in a town centre premises, and to speak to officers guarding a detainee at hospital). Sergeants universally viewed their role (with some resentment) as desk-based; part command and control, part administrative. Senior man-agement were blamed by many for over-burdening the role with paperwork. In essence, the intense scrutiny requirements of patrol control metrics (pro-cesses, reports, incident logs) left sergeants unavailable to supervise their officers on the streets. This left a vacuum where officers (many with less than two years' service) were left to fend for themselves at daily incidents where there was serious risk of harm to the public (and officers). These incidents were often complex, ambiguous and dynamic, with changing scenarios and multiple task options and outcomes. Information passed back to the control room and documented on official reports and databases was often minimal. Officers updated the results and simply moved to the next job. There were no debriefs at the station or scrutiny of actions. As such, serious incidents were routinised and virtually invisible to the organisation. Yet many of these incidents involved people displaying mental health symptoms, a categorisa-tion of police contact deemed a local and national priority within the vulner-ability agenda.

The consequences of actions in an invisible environment, beyond prescrip-tive control, without scrutiny and oversight and with multiple outcomes, were undisclosed to the organisation. In Eastside, those most vulnerable were the most likely to get poor outcomes. Officers, left to make autono-mous, discretional decisions under pressure, often displayed attributes of poor leadership, questionable decision-making and limited knowledge. One incident (of many) involving a call to a male brandishing a knife illustrates the problem. The male, suffering from severe mental health issues, had called at his ex-partner's house waving a knife, believing he was being 'ambushed'. Eight officers attended (no supervisor) and were informed by the occupant, who had left the house in fear, of the man's deteriorating mental condition. Four officers entered the house, spoke to the man, and for approximately 25 minutes were in and out of the house discussing, with officers outside, what they should do. Eventually, the man walked out of the house (without being searched), and was followed about 20 yards behind by two officers on foot and two officers in a van. They explained they were allowing him to walk to a nearby A&E department (15 minutes' walk) to get a voluntary mental health assessment and were following to ensure he arrived. Five min-utes later, on a busy main road, there was a standoff between the man and the officers, resulting in a struggle to arrest him. Two officers were assaulted. Back at the station, several officers and a sergeant gathered around a com-puter to look at body cam footage of the arrest (and police assault). The body cam had only been turned on prior to the arrest. I noted in my field notes,

> The crux of the whole incident appeared to be condensed into one vio-lent struggle and arrest. There was no discussion over the actions at

the house; the delay in making a decision and the (potentially danger-ous) rationale for letting him walk to the hospital. It was obvious to me, that after forty hours and several incidents into my observations, I was witnessing a group of officers, mostly young in service, who lacked supervision, leadership and decision-making skills at ongoing incidents where there was a risk of immediate, serious harm to people in the vicinity. These incidents were routinised, nothing special, an everyday occurrence. They were one of several incidents on a computerised list, allocated and finished, unnoticed. No paper trail or scrutiny of actions or decisions. They were beyond the scope of bureaucratic process. Yet these were every day incidents where the most serious threat of risk and harm to the public lay.

Officers dealing with individuals with mental health issues made different decisions based on the dichotomy of choosing a health or criminal course of action (detaining and taking to hospital or arresting on suspicion of commit-ting a crime). Either course of action gave officers the opportunity to turn an open into a closed task, in other words to reduce the complexity and ambi-guity (and responsibility) of action at the scene. At one incident witnessed, where a male in a house was threatening to kill himself with a knife, six officers (who were first at the scene) stood chatting in the front garden, leav-ing two paramedics (who attended five minutes later) and a neighbour inside for over 20 minutes, oblivious to what was or could occur. This incident was finalised to the police control operative as an 'ambulance job' with no details taken by the officers. Explaining the motivation for this redistribution of responsibility, which in numerous cases led to vulnerable individuals spend-ing over 24 hours in police cells, a custody sergeant said,

> There are a lot more people coming in with mental health issues, and because of austerity and driving things down, the cops do not have the time or skill sets to deal with risk on the street. So very often, they will bring risk into here (custody) and hope that one of us will manage that risk and sort out the problem for them. In many, many cases, we are the first point of supervision for lots of officers.

Standardised practice, encouraged through the policing professionalisation programme, was not achievable in most tasks allocated to officers in the invisible policing environment of Eastside. Closed, prescriptive processes, limited to less ambiguous tasks, were scrutinised post-incident, at least up to a point. Yet in the majority of practice, officers deskilled in many fac-ets of policing (notably crime scene management and crime investigation) did not display experiential skills and the characteristics of autonomy and discretion associated with occupational professions (Abbott, 1988; Lipsky, 2010). Empathetic communication skills, meticulous statement taking, use of multi-agency referrals and process compliance were all in evidence when the incident and outcomes of vulnerability incidents were specific and unam-biguous. Yet, even in these cases, the consequences of a lack of proactivity and deskilling led to poor investigations and delayed opportunities to arrest perpetrators, both affecting outcomes for victims. Where the scrutiny process increased the visibility of practice, completing processes to a high standard appeared more important than achieving justice for victims. One instructive example of this took place when a junior officer was commended for dealing with a domestic violence incident by a mentor after taking a detailed statement and updating the relevant databases. I questioned why the force wasn't attempting to immediately find and arrest the perpetrator who had recently been released from prison for the same offence. "We've done all we can, someone else will pick it up later" was the answer I was given. The officer had complied with all the elements of post-incident scrutiny including a simple, closed answer to the question—'Arrest Yes/No?' Scrutiny of any proactive attempts to subsequently find, detain and question the perpetrator was non-existent. In the invisible environment of policing in Eastside, compliance with control metrics provided some opportunities to employ good practice, standardisation and accountability. But, in general, it left officers in a practice 'black hole', trying to do their best but without a sense of direction or purpose. As an officer said, 'We're doing the wrong things for the right reasons'.

Controlling the Visible Environment

Police custody is a heavily controlled environment, governed by custody law, convention and technology—a liminal space between the community, prison and hospital (Moran, 2013). Discourse of control in carceral environments usually describes bureaucratic staff power over powerless inmates (Goffman, 1961; Skinns, 2009) who languish, abandoned in punitive spaces (Moran, 2016). The carceral environment—the cells, CCTV, the raised 'booking-in' desks and subterranean lighting—are all parts of a tight control mechanism creating a potentially highly coercive environment (Skinns et al., 2017). Sociological, organisational or criminological research rarely, if at all, focuses on the flip side of carceral control, that is, organisational surveillance of staff to enable directed outcomes and the powerlessness of staff trying to carry out their functions in a way which they believe best serves both the welfare of detainees and the effective progression of the criminal justice process.

CCTV cameras in Eastside's custody suites covered virtually every area of the staff working environment, including the van dock (where vans transporting detainees enter and leave the custody suite), entry and exit doors, cells, corridors, booking-in desks, forensic sample rooms and a portion of back office space (depending on design). Specific locations also had 24-hour audio recording. The only areas not covered were a handful of private offices. Documentation of all staff and detainee actions and movement took place on an electronic custody database that timed every input. Specific data fields with drop-down entries (whether relevant to the scenario or not) could not be avoided, which minimised the use of free text comments. Actions and movements were frequently cross-referenced from both sources (CCTV and custody record) to verify performance, complaints, adverse incidents (e.g. injury, assault, suicidal attempts or death in custody) and evidential facts. Visibility of staff practice (to the organisation) was therefore extremely high, creating a risk-averse approach by staff to daily routines, as described by a custody sergeant:

> Detainees can quite often dwell in cells between eight and sixteen hours for fairly simple offences. The cause is bureaucracy, risk assessments. The whole organisation is so risk averse it's phenomenal. Everything is gone through with a fine-toothed comb, about risks when they come in and risks when they leave the station. Nobody comes to work expecting somebody to die in custody. If someone does it's mayhem on yourself and staff for eighteen months. We are scrutinised by the Coroner, IPCC (Independent Police Complaints Commission), Professional Standards, the Home Office and everything gets scrutinised to the Nth degree. As a result, we are trying to box off all those risks before they happen. It's gone too far I think.

Many officers described a 'blame culture' in policing fuelled by the availability and subsequent misinterpretation and misuse of data by superiors and oversight authorities. Another sergeant said,

> The point is, if you scrutinise any police activity, and we have it in custody, you will find fault. [The officer goes on to describe an incident where he believed his actions had saved the life of a suicidal detainee.] Did we ever get a thanks for saving his life? No. The criticism was, you missed a visit [staff have a legal requirement to regularly check detainees]. We don't actually look at what's going wrong to stop it happening again, we just look to find someone to hang out to dry. 'We' is the whole corporate organisation.

The policing prioritisation of a vulnerability agenda has refocused custody practice requirements and changed staff perception of their role, as described by a custody sergeant:

> Our priority used to be assisting officers with the investigations, ensuring PACE (Police and Criminal Evidence Act 1984) was complied with in pursuance of a positive outcome at court, a successful prosecution. Now, our priority is not prosecution, but diverting them to other services and ensuring medical and mental health issues are addressed while they are here. The investigation bit gets a back seat.

National criticism of poor police practice in custody regarding the identification and management of detainee health issues (see HMIC, 2015; and individual police force custody inspections by HMIC (Her Majesty's Inspectorate of Constabulary) between 2011 and 2014) has led to the implementation of standardised, prescriptive processes, as an officer describes:

> You become used to it. You know the process, which route to go down. It's a standardised process. If someone presents with what you think are

serious mental health problems, the process is they initially see a nurse, who will refer it on to a duty [police-employed] doctor, then the on-duty [NHS] doctor. If they think they need a full mental health assessment they call on more specialists who decide if that person needs to be taken into care. . . . Personally, I think the seven out of ten ratio of detainees having mental health problems has changed. It's worse now than three years ago. I think it's us being more aware of what risk people pose. Having more intrusive risk assessments changes how we work. We don't do police work in here anymore. We basically look after people.

Unintended consequences of new process requirements and system changes to improve the management of vulnerability in custody impacted on staff and detainees. Staff constantly talked about the pressure of getting things right, not missing parts of the process, in particular for detainees with obvious or self-declared mental health conditions. The process includes over 50 health check questions on arrival, referrals to in-house medical staff, collection of medication, timed cell visits, referral to external agencies, exit risk assessments. One officer commented,

In the past an officer would say, "he's only here for an hour, Sarge, for a quick interview". Now, if he (the detainee) says, "I'm suicidal" or has suicidal thoughts, then that person is staying in until they have had an exit risk assessment. They will not be released. You can't reduce custody times now. The only way is not to bring them in in the first place.

In many cases in Eastside, vulnerable detainees with mental health issues were kept in custody beyond legal time limits set by the Police and Crime Evidence Act, 1984, just to be seen by an in-house doctor for an exit risk assessment, primarily because the staff and the organisation put safety and risk aversion before the legal process. Incorporating the whole medical management process in custody, those detainees most likely to suffer from prolonged spells of incarceration (those at risk of self-harm, for example), spent the longest time in custody, sometimes well beyond 24 hours. In many cases officers on the streets who had chosen the criminal route of action which placed the risk onto the custody staff, or had performed a 'mercy arrest' to get a health intervention, were potentially putting vulnerable people at risk of greater harm. Officers questioned the impact interventions in custody actually had on the lives of detainees after their release. Staff generally felt it was a 'back-covering' exercise that couldn't be deviated from, which started, in many cases, with poor actions and choices by officers on the streets (in the invisible environment where actions weren't scrutinised). As one custody sergeant put it,

We have a tier of management normally who are disinterested. They have no consequential management. They think it's a good idea. There's indifference about leadership . . . We talk around things. Achieving the task is not important, it's the method of how we do it.

Conclusion

Power (2007, p. 160), analysing the features of institutional environments in risk regulation, poses a critical question: "What are the collective institutional mechanisms by which some uncertainties and hazards become managerially and politically visible, and others do not?" This chapter, focusing on policing in England and Wales, has incorporated the crucial significance that environmental and task characteristics play in an organisation's actual capability to control practice. The imposition of a top-down, managerialist-driven change programme on policing in England and Wales, to improve standards and re-prioritise practice with increased auditability and accountability, has improved visibility of practice and outcomes in limited, carefully chosen areas. HMIC annual reports document exhaustive inspection results on prioritised themes, vindicating the progress of the change programme. My Exploration in this chapter of the everyday reality of practice at street level questions both the validity of disclosed outcomes of auditable tasks and the oversight of ignoring (intentionally or not) invisible practice. The disciplinary logic of control applied to policing, through managerialist mechanisms, fails the criteria of legitimacy and professional competence (Fournier, 1999).

Authentic and legitimate internal and external accountability of street-level worker practice in low-visibility environments is rarely viable or achievable (Reiner, 2000b). Police work requires individuals to exercise judgement and skill in the management of ambiguous and complex tasks (Bayley and Bittner, 1984). In the invisible environment, a lack of any scrutiny of the management of incidents where there was risk of serious harm to those involved, coupled with deskilling in core areas of police work, produced a toxic situation of inertia and organisational paralysis. Many of these incidents (it could be argued all) involved vulnerable people. Improving standards and practice, even within the prioritised agenda of vulnerability, was not achieved. This was backed up by observation of numerous other non-mental-health incidents. Improved visibility of street practice was partly achievable by prescribed closed tasks or where officers chose to close an open task by passing responsibility to an internal or external source. Both these scenarios tended to lead to poor outcomes for victims. Risk aversion, lack of experiential knowledge and process reliance and compliance all contributed towards weak management of incident scenes, poor investigation of crime and the injustice of lengthy incarceration of those most vulnerable. In the highly visible world of police custody, surveillance of practice and fear of scrutiny, alongside the imposition of structurally closed tasks and processes, changed the mentality and practice of staff. Personal survival of detainees was discussed in the context of staff survival from rebuke and disciplinary action. Complying with health management overruled legal and human rights compliance. In both the invisible and visible environments, concerns about the effectiveness of control metrics led to further bureaucracy to control the application of controls (Power, 2007). Overwhelmed and hemmed in by mushrooming administrative processes, supervisory and managing staff in both environments felt hindered in their capacities to fulfil their professional roles, notably when it came to mentoring and developing junior officers.

Policing is undergoing institutional and cultural change to address historical failures and new challenges. The operationalisation of change, however, has been practically limited in its ability to control practice in different environments and very problematic when it comes to the tension between autonomy and control. The challenge is how to enable knowledge management from above and utilise skills and experiential knowledge from below (Gundhus, 2012). Literature on the role of street-level bureaucrats as autonomous enablers of public policy implementation is particularly significant (Hupe and Hill, 2007; Lipsky, 2010; Maynard-Moody and Musheno, 2003) in light of organisational challenges to bridge practice gaps in the physical environments of work. Core skills of occupational professionals cannot be dismantled without consequences. Experiential knowledge and discretional decision-making, gained through mentorship, supervisory support and trust in self-regulation, could be embedded in training and practice direction on new priorities, aims and outcomes (Myhill and Johnson, 2016). Awareness of environmental and task characteristics by policymakers and collaboration between practitioners and managers on 'what really works' to improve and maintain quality of public service may provide a localised, community-based service that incorporates accountability at both local and institutional level. If the problematic scope and reach of managerialism in the public sector continues to operate in its current vacuum, with management semi-aware of what is happening in limited areas of practice but oblivious to the rest, the concerns of practitioners and academic observers around serious risk of harm and injustice will continue to reverberate across the public domain.

References

Abbott, A. (1988). *The System of Professions: An Essay in the Division of Expert Labor*. Chicago: University of Chicago Press.

Bannick, D., Six, F., and van Wijk, E. (2016). 'Bureaucratic, market or professional control? A theory on the relation between street-level task characteristics and the feasibility of control mechanisms', in Hupe, P., Hill, M., and Buffat, A. (eds), *Understanding Street-Level Bureaucracy*, Bristol: Policy Press.

Bartkowiak-Theron, I. and Asquith, N. (2014). 'Policing diversity and vulnerability in the post-MacPherson era: Unintended consequences and missed opportunities', *Policing*, 9(1): 89–100.

Bayley, D. H. and Bittner, E. (1984). 'Learning the skills of policing', *Law and Contemporary Problems*, 47(4): 35–59.

Boulton, L., McManus, M., Metcalfe, L., and Brian, D. (2017). 'Calls for police service: Understanding the demand profile and the UK police response', *Police Journal*, 90(1): 70–85.

Charman, S. (2017). *Police Socialisation, Identity and Culture: Becoming Blue*, London: Palgrave.

Cummins, I. (2012). 'Policing and mental illness in England and Wales post Bradley', *Policing*, 6(4): 365–376.

Cummins, I. and Edmonson, D. (2015). 'Policing and street triage', *The Journal of Adult Protection*, 18(1): 40–52.

Evans, T. (2016). 'Professionals and discretion in street-level bureaucracy', in Hupe, P., Hill, M., and Buffat, A. (eds), *Understanding Street-Level Bureaucracy*, Bristol: Policy Press.

Evetts, J. (2003). 'The sociological analysis of professionalism', *International Sociology*, 18(2): 395–415.

Evetts, J. (2011). 'A new professionalism? Challenges and opportunities', *Current Sociology*, 59(4): 406–422.

Fournier, V. (1999). 'The appeal to 'professionalism' as a disciplinary mechanism', *The Sociological Review*, 47(2): 280–307.

Frey, B., Homberg, F., and Osterloh, M. (2013). 'Organizational control systems and pay-for-performance in the public service', *Organization Studies*, 34(7): 949–972.

Gilling, D. (2014). 'Reforming police governance in England and Wales: Managerialisation and the politics of organizational regime change', *Policing and Society*, 24(1): 81–101.

Goffman, E. (1961). *Asylums: Essays on the Social Situation of Mental Patients and Other Inmates*, Garden City, NY: Anchor Books.

Gundhus, H. I. (2012). 'Experience or knowledge? Perspectives on new knowledge regimes and control of police professionalism', *Policing*, 7(2): 178–194.

HMIC (2015). *The Welfare of Vulnerable People in Police Custody*, London: HMIC.

Holdaway, S. (2017). 'The re-professionalization of the police in England and Wales', *Criminology & Criminal Justice*, 17(5): 588–604.

Hood, C. (1991). 'A public management for all seasons', *Public Administration*, 69(1): 3–19.

Hupe, P. and Hill, M. (2007). 'Street-level bureaucracy and public accountability', *Public Administration*, 85(2): 279–299.

Leese, M. and Russell, S. (2017). 'Mental health, vulnerability and risk in police custody', *The Journal of Adult Protection*, 19(5): 274–283.

Lipsky, M. (2010). *Street-Level Bureaucracy: Dilemmas of the Individual in Public Services*, Expanded edition, New York: Russell Sage.

Maynard-Moody, S. and Musheno, M. (2003). *Cops, Teachers, Counselors: Stories from the Front Lines of Public Service*, Ann Arbor: University of Michigan Press.

McCann, L., Granter, E., Hyde, P., and Hassard, J., (2013). 'Still blue-collar after all these years? An ethnography of the professionalization of emergency ambulance work', *Journal of Management Studies*, 50(5): 750–776.

McLean, N. and Marshall, L. A. (2010). 'A front line police perspective of mental health issues and services', *Criminal Behaviour and Mental Health*, 20: 62–71.

Moran, D. (2013). 'Between outside and inside? Prison visiting rooms as liminal carceral spaces', *GeoJournal*, 78(2): 339–351.

Moran, D. (2016). *Carceral Geography: Spaces and Practices of Incarceration*, Abingdon: Routledge.

Moskos, P. (2008). *Cop in the Hood: My Year Policing Baltimore's Eastern District*, Princeton: Princeton University Press.

Myhill, A. and Johnson, K. (2016). 'Police use of discretion in response to domestic violence', *Criminology and Criminal Justice*, 16(1): 3–20.

O'Reilly, D. and Reed, M. (2011). 'The grit in the oyster: Professionalism, managerialism and leaderism as discourses of UK public service modernization', *Organization Studies*, 32(8): 1079–1101.

Power, M. (2007). *Organized Uncertainty*, Oxford: Oxford University Press.

Reiner, R. (2000a). *The Politics of the Police*, 3rd ed. Oxford: Oxford University Press.

Reiner, R. (2000b) 'Police research', in King, D. R. and Wincup, E. (eds), *Doing Research on Crime and Justice*, Oxford: Oxford University Press.

Rowe, M. (2007). 'Rendering visible the invisible: Police discretion, professionalism and decision-making', *Policing and Society*, 17(3): 279–294.

Rowe, M. (2016). 'Learning and practicing police craft', *Journal of Organizational Ethnography*, 5(3): 276–286.

Senior, J., Noga, H., and Shaw, J. (2014). 'When two worlds collide: A twenty-first century approach to mental health and policing', *Criminal Behaviour and Mental Health*, 24: 81–85.

Skinns, L. (2009). 'I'm a detainee; get me out of here', *British Journal of Criminology*, 49: 399–417.

Skinns, L., Rice, L., Sprawson, A., and Wooff, A. (2017). 'Police legitimacy in context: An exploration of "soft" power in police custody in England', *Policing*, 40(3): 601–613.

Tummers, L., Bekkers, V., and Steijn, B. (2009). 'Policy alienation of public professionals: Application in a New Public Management context', *Public Management Review*, 11(5): 685–706.

Willis, J. J. and Mastrofski, S. D. (2014). 'Pulling together: Integrating craft and science', *Policing*, 8(4): 321–329.

8 Reaching Out Across the Theory-Practice Divide? Impact, Participation and Change in Post-Disaster Reconstruction

Yiwen Lin,* Mihaela Kelemen and Lindsay Hamilton

Introduction

Conducting research that has a meaningful impact is paramount in the field of emergency services and disaster management, because practical change and assistance is often more acutely required than new theoretical frameworks or analytical tools. This chapter asks how to build relationships between academic work and hands-on emergency response and suggests that participatory and collaborative research techniques provide an ideal vehicle for doing so. We contend that such methods generate impact through the involvement of multiple stakeholders, something which is relevant and important for emergency studies as well as communities and individuals in different forms of crisis. We explore our argument by presenting a case of collaborative research undertaken with a Japanese community devastated by the 2011 tsunami. The analysis focuses on the efforts of the community to 'build back better' not only in terms of physical infrastructure but, more importantly, with regard to individual and collective well-being. In raising the profile of this example, we contribute new insights to understanding the aftermath of a natural disaster, an empirical approach which is often missing from theoretical academic discussions of impact.

In everyday usage, the word 'impact' means the action of one body or object coming into contact with another, often forcefully. Academic work is often viewed in similarly Newtonian fashion with impact regarded as something that comes after research; an 'add-on' that materialises in pathways to practical change or in the translation into practice of research findings (Cunliffe and Scaratti, 2017). The subjects of impact and impact evaluation remain colonised by an academic discourse which equates it with knowledge transfer from academia to the 'real world'. Critics argue, however, that the evaluation of impact through the institutionalised mechanisms of academia such as the Research Excellence Framework is unhelpful and leads to the widening of the divide between theory and practice (Aguinis et al., 2014). In a recent *British Journal of Management* special issue on this theme (2017),

* Correspondence E-mail ID: y.lin@keele.ac.uk

Well and Nieuwenhuis (2017) argued that "impact can take multiple but often indistinct (and difficult to measure) forms and unfolds erratically over time" (p. 47). As such, "impact could be both a cause, consequence and context of research and it may be an outcome, output and process at the same time" (Antonacopoulou, 2010, p. 222). We support and extend this position in our empirical case, but our starting point is to set out our own definition of impact in a context of emergency and disaster management.

We see impact in three overlapping ways. First, we regard it as *output*—tangible, physical and visible changes in the recovery of individuals and infrastructure from upheaval or catastrophe (the process of reconstruction, for example). Second, we see impact as *outcome*—differences in the way individuals think, feel and know the world about them after an emergency event or involvement with a given research project on emergency (the process of reflection following an event, for example). Third, and perhaps more complex, we regard impact as *process*—the ability of a given research project to bring multiple stakeholders together and diverse voices to a conversation or project to address the inequalities of knowledge production. In this reading, an observer would perceive there to be an impact when researchers and community members appear to be equal partners, and their skills, experiences and knowledge are treated with the same respect. The process need not be tangible or immediate and may take many years to unfold. While existing literature in emergency services tends to conceive of impact in terms of the first two definitions—outputs and outcomes—in what follows we highlight and explore the process perspective.

The chapter is organised as follows. We first focus upon our empirical case, introducing the area and the community of Minami-sanriku and its efforts to 'build back better' after the tsunami of 2011. We then discuss our methodology, which consists of a mix of collaborative art-based workshops, participatory ethnographic interviews and observation. We elaborate on this by showing how the process of collaborative research makes room for diverse voices to democratise the ways in which researchers and community members relate to each other and collaborate in a process of knowledge co-creation. We end the chapter by reflecting on the need to define impact from the point of view of both academic and non-academic stakeholders and suggest an agenda for future research.

'Building Back Better' in Minami-sanriku

On March 11, 2011, the largest ever earthquake (a magnitude of 9.0) hit the north-eastern areas of Japan, causing a tsunami and nuclear crisis. The severity of the damage incurred by this triple disaster in Japan was enormous. A report by the National Police Agency (NPA) of Japan (March 2018) confirmed 15,895 deaths, 6156 injured and 2539 missing people. Damage to property was also severe with 121,776 buildings collapsed, 280,923 half collapsed and 726,574 partially damaged (NPA, 2018). In addition, roads, railways, seawalls and land were significantly damaged, and many businesses ground to a halt. The tsunami also destroyed other important living facilities:

schools, shopping facilities and hospitals. The large scale of this disaster rendered the recovery process extremely challenging, requiring the involvement of multiple stakeholders and a need for the community to self-organise and rebuild from within.

Given the scale of the reconstruction, some areas of activity had to be given priority at the expense of others due to limited resources—in terms of both time and money. In November 2013 and against this backdrop, the researchers visited Minami-sanriku, an area that had been slow in receiving help from the government. This research visit was part of an Arts and Humanities Research Council project exploring communities in crisis, which aimed to learn new ways to bridge the gap between academic knowledge and community practice. We followed this with a three-month participatory fieldwork trip carried out in June–August 2016 and funded by a Great Britain Sasakawa Foundation grant.

Prior to the disaster, the population of Minami-sanriku town was 17,666 (as of February 2011), making it a relatively small town on the Pacific coast of the Miyagi prefecture. The town is surrounded by mountains, and its living areas face the Pacific Ocean. Its main industries are fishing and marine product processing. The tsunami reached Minami-sanriku about 30 minutes after the earthquake, killing 831 people (620 accounted deaths and 211 people still noted as missing). More than 60% of households were damaged, and 9753 people were evacuated and spread across 95 different facilities such as schools and community halls (March 2011). In May 2011, many of them started to move to temporary housing over different locations (Minami-sanriku Town website, 2012). The public transportation was paralysed for some months due to the damage of main roads, railways and bridges. A great deal of farmland was inundated by the seawater; most fishing ports could not function and 94% of fishing boats were damaged, which greatly affected marine enterprises.

In this context of massive negative impact on human lives and economic infrastructure, Ferris and Solis (2013, p. 2) highlighted the merits of Japanese civil society and citizens' reaction to the disaster: "the dignity, creativity and orderly response of the Japanese population to this mega-disaster is indeed the best measure of Japan's potential". Veszteg et al.'s (2015) research on the impact of the disaster also found that mutual trust increased in the aftermath of the disaster. Aldrich (2016) suggested that the government's poor response resulted in the loss of public trust but at the same time ignited social bonding and spurred the community to self-organise in order to 'build back better' and in a bottom-up, democratically organised fashion.

The concept of 'building back better' has been at the heart of many disaster recovery projects as the guiding principle for recovery efforts. It is a term widely used in humanitarian policy work and has been applied to disaster relief projects in Aceh, Myanmar and Haiti, among others (see, for example, Humanitarian Policy Group, 2013). The concept advocates that one should not only restore what existed previously but states that everything should be built better, stronger and fairer than before. Disasters can, therefore, be seen not only as a catastrophe but as an opportunity to improve community

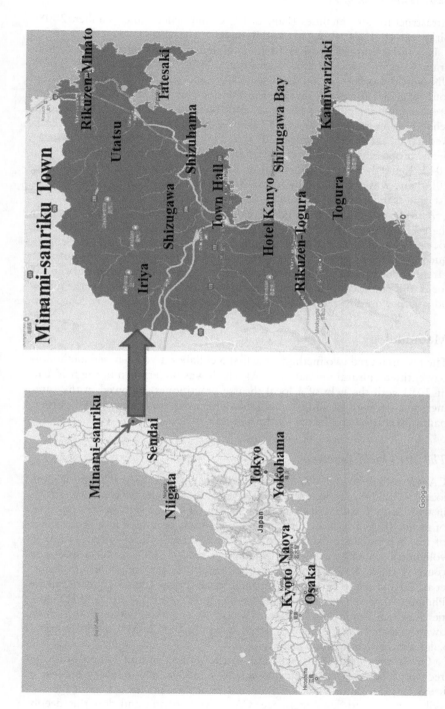

Figure 8.1 Maps of case study area, Minami-sanriku town

infrastructure and facilities (Fan, 2013; Gunewardena and Schuller, 2008; Birkmann et al., 2010; Archer and Boonyabancha, 2011).

Its critical importance has been reiterated more recently in the Sendai Framework for Disaster Risk Reduction 2015–2030 adopted at the Third UN World Conference on Disaster Risk Reduction in 2015. One of the four priorities for action outlined in the document is "to enhance disaster preparedness for effective response, and 'building back better' in recovery, rehabilitation and reconstruction" (United Nations Office for Disaster Risk Reduction, Sendai Framework, 2015, p. 21). As a concept, it has many academic proponents (see, for example, Fan, 2013; Mannakkara and Wilkinson, 2012; Kennedy et al., 2008; Clinton, 2006; Lloyd-Jones, 2007; Alexander, 2006) and was first coined by former US President Bill Clinton after the devastating tsunami across the Indian Ocean region in 2004.

As to how 'building back better' can be implemented in practice through the collaboration of international organisations, governments, NGOs and local communities, however, remains somewhat mysterious. The consequences of 'building back better' are usually expressed in terms of outputs, rarely as outcomes and almost never in terms of process, which is our central focus and empirical contribution. In the next section, we describe the methods that we used to explore the concept of post-disaster impact as a process.

Methodology

The research used two methods: the first a collaborative art-based methodology entitled cultural animation (CA) which was undertaken in the field trip of 2013 with the help of a local theatre practitioner, followed in the summer of 2016 by a period of qualitative interviews and longitudinal participant observation conducted by the first-named author.

The 2013 Field Research

CA is a methodology of community engagement and knowledge co-production, located within the broader field of creative methods. It aims to create safe spaces in which new relationships and dialogue can take place between diverse types of people (Kelemen and Hamilton, 2018). CA has been used in a broad range of research projects, including community leadership (Kelemen et al., 2017), volunteering, disaster recovery (Goulding et al., 2018), marketplace exclusion (Burgess et al., 2017), food poverty and health in the community (Kelemen et al., 2018) both in the UK context and abroad (Japan, Canada, Greece and the Philippines). Given its success in addressing these topics, the Arts and Humanities Research Council commissioned a podcast on cultural animation from an award-winning BBC filmmaker (https://youtu.be/VkFtTi6M4t8) which encapsulates its key features and processes.

Given the highly sensitive and often 'messy' nature of post-disaster recovery, the researchers felt that this was an ideal methodology because it seeks to place equal value on academic expertise, practical knowledge and skills, and day-to-day experience. CA views knowing and doing as deeply interconnected. Drama, music, poetry, art making and other creative activities are the practical vehicles by which participants become involved. Within the process, a central role is played by the 'cultural animator' who is best described as a facilitator who helps participants to advance personal and collective views about past and present circumstances as well as to imagine futures in which they could play a more central role (Kelemen and Hamilton, 2018). Participants discuss, dispute or share meanings for themselves rather than bow to the academic's privilege of abstracting accounts on their behalf (Kelemen and Hamilton, 2018). Hence, advocates of CA often describe it as a democratic approach to research which responds practically to concerns over the power inherent in authorship (Kelemen et al., 2018).

The research team ran two cultural animation workshops at the 'Isatomae Fukko Shoutengai Shopping Street' and the 'Heisei-no-mori Temporary Houses'. More than 100 community members and business leaders attended the workshops along with ten academics from the UK, Seinan Gakuin University and Osaka City University, Japan (some of the latter acted as translators). During the workshops, a central leadership role was played by the 'cultural animator', Sue Moffat, who is an award-winning theatre director based at the New Vic Theatre in the UK.

The cultural animation exercises were designed to capture and celebrate stories of people who had experienced this natural disaster within the Minami-sanriku community. They drew on ordinary and more artistic objects to broker conversations, 'break the ice' and help develop group work. During the workshop, a central focus was placed on a plain wooden tree which was self-supporting in structure and which formed the basis for the arts, crafts and conversations of the events. The tree was chosen as the central part of the CA workshops because of its symbolic value, for it represents a long-standing cultural emblem in Japan and signifies endurance and longevity. The CA facilitator encouraged participants to work together to create and produce items to decorate the tree, keeping her directions as broad as possible with the intent to enable the participants to structure the tasks in their own ways. The need for language translation was minimal because the activities were intended to be embodied and exploratory rather than technical. The facilitator from the theatre told the workshop's participants a story about the wooden tree, stating that it was sad and bare because it had lost its leaves, which had been swept away by the river (this was an indirect reference to the tsunami). In order to help it 'thrive', community members were then invited to create/recreate items, stories, poems and songs to give as a gift to the tree so that it could be filled with life again.

During the first workshop, the empty tree was placed in the middle of an outdoor temporary shopping street. Near the tree, tables and benches with a selection of everyday objects (e.g. empty picture frames, clocks, tea cups and candle sticks) as well as a collection of art and craft materials (e.g. tissue paper, ribbons and string) were set up. A simple invitation had been sent out in advance. As a result, some people had arrived with an idea of joining in with a research workshop organised by a UK university. The presence of the tree and items disrupted what participants originally anticipated but nonetheless they began making gifts for the tree and started sharing stories with other people, which was considered uncommon for Japanese people who are generally private and reserved. Through the actions of making and creating together, an environment of communal endeavour was created, something which was augmented by later workshops in which CA was used to add further gifts to the tree.

The 2016 Participant Observation

In the summer of 2016, the first author returned for a three-month field trip to Minami-sanriku. Her role as a researcher and volunteer sharpened as well as challenged her taken-for-granted understanding of Japanese culture, which had been built on her previous two-year work experience in Japan. While conducting her research, she worked as a volunteer on local farms cutting weeds, planting seeds and picking vegetables. She took part in the local market selling dumplings, promoting seafood products or working with fishermen's families, cleaning fish ropes and nets, processing seafood for morning markets or participating in tour-guide activities along with tidying and removing the weeds and rubble around the temporary housing. As researcher and volunteer in the field, she was able to understand and document everyday experience as well as establish relationships based on trust and mutual respect. The immersive approach particularly helped gain in-depth understanding of the community endeavour to rebuild from within.

Several initiatives were observed at close quarters. The Minami-sanriku Fukko-ichi (Reconstruction Market) was first initiated one month after the tsunami disaster by locals to create an atmosphere of 'normality', bringing a vision of hope for community recovery. Later, the temporary Sun Sun Shopping Village was established by a group of around 30 pre-disaster shop owners with the support of Minami-sanriku Chamber of Commerce to attempt to bring back the vitality of the town. They abandoned market-driven norms of doing business and returned to a traditional model of Kyo-jo (Japanese, meaning collaboration) and restarted their businesses collaboratively. The local Hotel Kanyo at Minami-sanriku, which acted as an emergency evacuation shelter for months after the tsunami, started to share disaster experiences by operating a 'storytelling bus' from 2012, taking hotel passengers to the areas hit by the tsunami, with hotel employees taking the role of storytellers to share their disaster experiences. They were determined to make Minami-sanriku a place where people could learn about disaster risk reduction.

The post-disaster reconstruction is clearly a complex project requiring the joint efforts of government, NGOs, the local community and general public home and abroad. The complexity of the reconstruction and sensitive nature of the traumatic experience required building close relationships between the researcher and the researched. Compared to traditional ethnographic research, the three-month fieldwork undertaken for the project was relatively short, but shorter timescales are not necessarily viewed as a limitation. As Pink and Morgan (2013, p. 351) point out, this could be an "intense route[s] of knowing", and "a route to producing alternative ways of knowing about and with people and the environment" (Pink and Morgan, 2013, p. 359). The dual role as both volunteer and researcher enabled meaningful dialogues and relationships to grow, which resonates with Pink and Morgan's argument (2013) that the intensity of the research encounter, the focus on the detail and the ethnographic-theoretical dialogue are important qualities for a short-term ethnography.

The first place the researcher visited and stayed at was the Minami-sanriku Learning Centre. She was welcomed by one of the founders of the Learning Centre, who later introduced her to many of his networks. Thus, she was granted access to the disaster learning tours held at the Learning Centre, local story-telling tours and local residents' workshops. This ensured she could meet many people including academics, research students, local university students, local residents and also key figures of the town, such as the mayor, local story tellers, disaster tour coordinators, etc. The founder of the Learning Centre himself had a lot of stories to share. She was introduced to the Beans Club, fish market factory, agricultural farms, fishery farms, Blue Tourism Initiative, local non-profit organisations and other organisations which had connections with the Learning Centre. She was busy joining in all kinds of activities and doing all kinds of volunteer activities. Her approach to the study was proactive as she tried to grasp every opportunity to be involved in local activities in order to capture all the nuances of the local practices of disaster implementation. Despite a relatively short period in the field, the researcher made constant and sustained efforts to negotiate her dual roles as researcher and volunteer in the field in order to better understand and document everyday experience.

Like most Japanese volunteers there, she armed herself with a volunteer uniform which comprised waterproof boots, working gloves, jackets, caps, masks and so on and hired a motorbike. This gave her the chance to talk with more people and visit local families. Volunteering created a natural atmosphere for dialogue as the conversation flowed naturally while doing the work together. At times, people seemed to forget that she was a researcher. As volunteer and researcher in these spaces and elsewhere, the first-named author gained insights into how the community worked together to co-design its future and set new objectives. Using her motorbike, she was able to travel from mountainous areas to coastal areas, participate in many activities and meet different people. Different voices were heard and individual accounts were captured along with collective decisions and strategies for reacting to the disaster. In the next section, we consider the findings of these two methodological approaches, considering how insights from the field enable us to see impact as a process rather than simply as outputs and outcomes.

Findings

Reflecting on our experiences in the field, we worked to refine our understanding of research impact, considering it as a process emerging in meaningful dialogue and knowledge co-production with diverse voices and across multiple perspectives but, in particular, across academic–practitioner 'boundaries'. From our observations, it was evident that this boundary crossing runs two ways, with new thinking emerging from the point of view of both the researcher and the researched. It is a continuation of connection and was not pursued as an end in itself or for instrumental purposes (i.e. to publish a paper) during the field-work. It was observed that cultural animation brokered the exchange of ideas in a subtle way, because focusing upon 'fun' craft activities ensures that those involved are not required to enter formal academic settings (the interview, the focus group, for example) to make their views known. This was important because in Japanese culture, social etiquette in the use of Honne (true/real feeling) and Tatemae (shown behaviour in public) are important elements of social harmony and are visible in the polite manner of speaking, privileging indirect communication and distinct social hierarchy. Reflecting upon these norms, our project ensured that emergent ideas and conversations at informal events were followed through using rather more traditional methods of participation, observation and conversation.

We see our approach to disaster research as effective because it sheds light upon the practicalities of the 'build back better' approach as well as the cultural, social and close-grained interactions that work together to create resilience in the face of disaster, which may not have been captured through reliance upon mainstream methods alone. Participatory collaborative research not only captured the input of those who lived at the scene of the disaster, they helped us to learn how they worked towards rebuilding their community in collaboration; observing people as they worked towards recovery was vital for demonstrating the lengthy time horizons involved.

Research Impact as Process

According to HEFCE, impact is "an effect on, change or benefit to the economy, society, culture, public policy or services, health, the environment or quality of life, beyond academia" (Higher Education Funding Council website, 2016). With this definition in mind, when the researchers started the fieldwork, they anticipated the challenges of disaster research but did not expect to make significant impact upon the recovery process itself. We were not convinced that cross-cultural researchers, outsiders, ('gaijin' or 'foreigners' in Japanese) could have enough control over the disaster reconstruction policy and practice at the site. The reason for this is not simply cultural but more importantly that top-down local governance mechanisms still dominate in Japan (Sorensen and Funck, 2009), a country which, "does not right now have a culture or set of institutional arrangements to be able to realise a bottom-up reconstruction process" (Matanle, 2011, p. 841). To transform the structure and principle of national and local governance into a bottom-up model, implementing community involvement, requires cultural shifts as well as confrontation (Matanle, 2011). In what follows we reflect on how our research approach built trust to the communities affected by the tsunami and facilitated a process by which the locals were willing to share their experiences and reflections on the disaster and post-disaster reconstruction.

Reflections on the Tree Exercise

The items that participants created in our cultural animation workshop held at the temporary accommodation centre prompted stories to emerge and appeared to generate a levelling of perceived hierarchies which might have existed beforehand. As the CA workshop progressed, the bare wooden tree became filled with poems, dolls and stories. Items such as empty picture frames were filled with colour and drawings. The participants appeared to be able to leave 'usual' ways of thinking/behaving behind, and the researcher noted that there was sharing, interacting and collaborating around this simple task. For example, the space was not dominated by a single voice or group and everyone was able to join in, equally involved through observing and enjoying the activities taking place around them. They could contribute as much or as little as they felt able. The end result of the process was an opportunity to share the labours of their creativity together. It was observed that there was a sense of camaraderie and achievement among participants who took part in the workshops. People appeared to feel genuinely proud as they could see what had been achieved and were able to make sense of it either individually and privately or by conversing with others. The atmosphere in the workshop had changed from quiet reservation to celebration by the end with people clapping and cheering each other as they presented their creative work.

To us, this demonstrated that conditions of trust and positive connectedness among participants (for more detail see Lam et al., 2018) were powerful ways to draw out experiences of the tsunami disaster and understand aims and hopes for recovery. A main reason why this worked so well was because the workshops brought together multiple stakeholders which would not normally be in dialogue with each other, and the processes involved in making and crafting meant that researchers and community members were 'equal partners' in the conversation about emergency, recovery and change. Stories about the tsunami and how people coped in the immediate aftermath flowed organically without the researchers prompting the participants to share such intimate emotions and memories.

One group of women made dolls, for example, to highlight biographical detail; they never had the luxury to own dolls when they were children. Growing up in the 1920s, they had to accompany their parents in the fields either to work or to look after younger siblings. They told stories about how they survived the Second World War when food was very scarce and how they had shared the very little there was with extended families. Finally, in turning to the more recent events of the tsunami, one of them said she felt lucky to escape via the broken roof of her house, where she waited for two days to be rescued, in freezing conditions and with no food or water. While the stories were harrowing, there was plenty of laughter and humour in the making of the dolls, naming them after favourite soap opera celebrities and teaching us their favourite Japanese songs. What might seem an unusual artistic experience enabled accounts of trauma and resilience—both historic and contemporary—to come to light. The fieldwork conducted in

2016 extended these insights with in-depth work shadowing, observation and interview.

Reflections on the Ethnographic Fieldwork

The process of research was not simply a journey of reflexivity and self-discovery as it usually is in fieldwork research, more importantly it was a collective journey in which the respondents joined in, leading to what Isaac (2008, p. 9) terms 'shared inquiry'. From this observation, we suggest that the impact of the research lies in the process of meaningful dialogue and engagement when the participants and researchers are fully involved and willing to share Honne (true/real feeling), not Tatemae (shown behaviour in public) by confronting social etiquette and institutional rules to co-produce shared knowledge. To illustrate, when participants discussed the national authority's decision to rebuild the seawall, they appeared honest about their feelings, as the following quotations reveal.

> A: I do not want the seawall to be built that height but I find it disgraceful to say no when government invests huge money on it. (Informal conversation)
> B: If we say no, government is not going to invest any money on our area. I also feel bad to say no as the opinion might differ from those who lost their family members and they might feel the need to build. (Informal conversation)
> C: I think it is more important to spend money on the relocation and evacuation training. As the areas nearby the sea are designated as only for commercial building and park, and residential area would be relocated in the higher land. (Informal conversation)

As reflected in such extracts, participants invited the researcher into their homes, opened up about their private lives and talked about their emotions with regards to the tsunami and reconstruction. The researcher records,

> I had moments when asking for 'consent was forgotten'. . . . I forgot I was a researcher, I forgot all about research ethics . . . they forgot too . . . it was just dialogue between two humans, I felt it was unethical to interrupt the stories . . . for I felt their pain.
>
> (Reflective diary, 2016)

Indeed, the researcher was acutely aware of the depth of those precious moments of human contact and valued them enormously. She felt trusted and wanted to do something special for all in the community, but all she could do was to work harder as a volunteer. Especially when she worked with elderly local people, she felt they were so willing to share their disaster experience. The story of the disaster unfolded naturally from how they survived to how they restarted their lives, the challenges faced in various conflicts such as debates about rebuilding the seawall and their concern for the future of fishery, as it can be seen from her reflexive diary:

> I was absolutely exhausted after a full day's working on the Farm and felt like I could just crawl into bed and fall asleep in seconds. I finally arrived home but I had trouble falling asleep. My mind was still in the dialogue with the farmer. I just realized that women actually played an important role in post disaster recovery and the elderly have so much wisdom to share. I was wondering whether there were any policy makers who made efforts to consult women's perspectives or record the elders' wisdoms to include their voices in the disaster reconstruction plan.
>
> (Field diary, 2016)

She reflected on the situation. Often, it was the spirit of local people that made her feel even more acutely the importance of understanding and disseminating their individual experiences and struggles and their collective efforts to revitalise their town. Impact here is reflected in the process of dialogue and engagement and it has effects on both researcher and researched.

For the researched, our approach of engagement on equal footing created a safe space to bring in diverse voices to conversations. At the same time, the researcher felt inspired by the spirit of the local community, becoming even more committed to the view that academic theory generated from the community in crisis should be useful for that community. It was paramount that the collective wisdom of diverse voices should be documented and shared in dealing with this crisis, including women and elders and their everyday existence. Two brief ethnographic examples of rebuilding and regeneration from the field help show this practically.

Example One: 'Beans Club'

The impact of an ageing society is often perceived in negative terms. However, it was clear from the fieldwork that the elders' knowledge and experience could also be a valuable asset to the community, leading the way to resilience building in crisis situations when the normal system does not function any longer. For example, a small group of local women who engaged in agriculture in the Iriya district set up a club named the 'Beans Club' by making use of fallow rice fields to produce soybeans, and their activities have been extended to making Natto (fermented soybeans), tofu (bean curd), kinako (roasted soybean flour) and a tofu-making experience project for visitors and the young generation. They enjoyed working as a group and having yearly group trips using part of their shared income from Beans Club. By volunteering in the bean field with them, the researcher experienced firsthand how this system worked. Their collaborative approach enhanced the bond between different generations of local women and brought the physical energies of the young generation and the traditional wisdom of the old generation into full play. In doing so, the long years of experience, knowledge of traditional ways of living (e.g. making traditional soybean foods, dried fruit storage for disaster use) were passed onto the young generation as Ms Sato, the 82-year-old lady said, "these skills have been passed on from generation to generation, so they will not be forgotten".

Example Two: Blue Tourism

During her volunteering in the fishing farms, the researcher was able to experience and observe the fishermen's passion for the sea and their pride in their profession, the joy of harvest and optimistic spirit for the future. Meanwhile, she also felt their pain of going to sea at 3 am, the risks of unpredictability in the weather, the harsh conditions of preparation for selling products at early morning markets and the hardship of everyday work. Interestingly, though, these concerns were not always articulated explicitly in words by the fishermen:

> There was no volunteer in the Farm today. I was the only one. I cleaned the whole pile of ropes, then, I used the machine manually to insert the specialised pins into all ropes which were prepared for attaching the baby scallop, known as ear-hanging sea scallop cultivation. There was no automatic scallop pinning machine in the farm. Even now I feel my hands still have the smell of the sea creatures from the rope. My host seemed to worry I might get bored and constantly checked whether I was ok. . . . she said, 'I was lucky to have my daughter-in-law . . . local young girls left town for more exciting city life and do not want to come back . . . not many girls want to marry fishermen as it is hard life. Some fishermen left too after tsunami.' . . . 'It was great that my son loves the sea, a small group of his fishermen friends love it too . . . They tried to revive the fishery industry'.
>
> (Field diary, 2016)

Clearly, there is marked discrepancy between the perception of a country with deep fishing roots, world-renowned for its sushi and the day-to-day realities of its production. By working alongside and having meaningful conversations with both young and elderly fishermen, the researcher was able to capture nuances and subtleties with regards to lived experience, identify the gap between different generations and understand the action taken by the young generation of fishermen to lead the changes for the future. The younger generation of workers launched a community-led initiative named Blue Tourism to counteract the environmental, social and economic hardships the locals faced after the 2011 Tohoku earthquake and following tsunami. The project yielded a gradual transformation of 'dark emotions' associated with loss of human life and property to positive engagement at communal level to rebuild from within. The Blue Tourism enterprise was a means to turn the despair to a more positive form of activity with economic benefits.

Discussion

Observing such enterprises and participating with community members through the research process enabled us to develop our concept of impact as a process based on cumulative and reciprocal interaction, a situation that leads to change in thinking or action when both the researcher and the respondents feel a sense of connection. "It is not something you do *to* another person, it is something you do *with* people. Indeed, a larger part of leaning this has to do with learning to shift your attitudes about relationships with other" (Isaac, 2008, p. 9, emphasis as in original) and understand each other. For example, participants offered the fieldwork researcher a printed book of the Shizugawa history and customs; as a trusted volunteer she was informed about the local festivals and other events and historical disaster lessons from their ancestors assuming it would be 'good for the research'.

As society has drifted away from the traditional way of dialogue to technology-based communication, it is perhaps harder and harder to engage in conversations where both participants and researchers articulate their most private feelings and treat each other as equals. In the 'publish or perish' culture that dominates academia, for example, it is daunting to approach impact as process, as the expectation is to document outputs and outcomes. The emphasis is upon immediacy rather than longevity. In the chaotic situation that followed the tsunami, however, there were logistical challenges of re-homing displaced residents as well as managerial challenges of co-ordinating NGOs and volunteers. The examples of Beans Club and Blue Tourism demonstrated a slow, gradual and collaborative means of reconstruction and, thus, recording immediate impact was not a possibility. The recovery efforts were convoluted and involved multiple stakeholders; a longer-term view of impact was necessary.

In considering the long view of impact, we reflected on our own transition from researchers to learners, being part of the environment, removing the barriers between academic and community and embracing knowledge transfer as two-way process. The research process demonstrated how we learned from community members and vice versa, in this way we felt part of the 'build back better' mission. One of us recorded, "I visited with two purposes: to learn and to contribute . . . but I was amazed by their [local people] achievements and spirit. They almost rebuilt their lives out of the debris, and they reinvented themselves and created more sustainable ways of living" (first author's reflective diary). As to the material effects and benefits of recovery, Minami-sanriku won two awards: the FSC Certification (Forest Stewardship Certification) award and the ASC Certification (Aquaculture Stewardship Certification), in recognition of the town's achievement in managing their forest and fishing farm in a sustainable way. Interestingly, our participant relationships did not end with the research, something which we consider was made possible by the method itself. The first-named author remains in close social media contact with participants and has returned to Minami-sanriku in 2017 and 2018 for social visits and further informal interviews.

Conclusions

Our study seeks to generate broader questions about the way we think about the place of participatory research methods in emergency studies as well as about the role of academics in knowledge production more generally.

Although the literature on the latter is steadily growing (Antonacopoulou, 2010; Avenier and Cajaiba, 2012; Beech et al, 2010; Bartunek and Rynes, 2014; Lorino et al, 2011), we suggest that the range of methods and techniques we have outlined in the foregoing analysis offers many new ideas for further research that builds empathy and interaction between academics and practitioners, as a way of contextualising research impact as process.

We regard research impact as a process rather than an outcome/output and, in this chapter, have demonstrated how this is embodied in meaningful dialogue and knowledge sharing between academics and community members. By extending this, we have contributed new insights to ways of thinking about disaster recovery, specifically how creative and participatory methods provide an effective and sociable approach to co-produce disaster knowledge in the support of 'build back better' initiatives. There are further areas of research that could benefit from our approach. Disaster recovery is often characterised by long-term changes and slow processes of resilience creation, which means that researchers often find it difficult to follow up changes due to time and funding constraints. By using our techniques to build and safeguard genuine relationships with community members, we think other researchers could help develop long-term projects that revolve around knowledge co-production and, as we have demonstrated, networks created during the research process can become long-term relationships, enhanced by social media platforms and electronic communications. Furthermore, studies on the impact of such dialogues and collaborations on individual and community well-being could shed more light on impact as process, which would benefit research funding bodies and policymakers as they consider the value of legacy and long-term change and how to evidence such experiences and effects. Further research is now needed to explore how unconventional art-based methodologies such as those highlighted here can be used not only as a method of data collection but also as a way of disaster intervention, which relies on a strong relationship between communities and researchers.

References

Aguinis, H., Shapiro, D.L., Antonacopoulou, E.P., and Cummings, T.G. 2014. Scholarly impact: A pluralist conceptualization. *Academy of Management Learning & Education*, 13(4), 623–639.

Aldrich, D.P. 2016. It's who you know: Factors driving recovery from Japan's 11 March 2011 disaster. *Public Administration*, 94(2), 399–413.

Alexander, R. 2006. *Tsunami build back better: Mantra aside, an aid gone wrong story? A livelihood sector review*. India: Development Constancy Group.

Antonacopoulou, E.P. 2010. Beyond co-production: Practice-relevant scholarship as a foundation for delivering impact through powerful ideas. *Public Money & Management*, 30(4), 219–226.

Archer, D. and Boonyabancha, S. 2011. Seeing a disaster as an opportunity—harnessing the energy of disaster survivors for change. *Environment and Urbanization*, 23(2), 351–364.

Avenier, M.J. and Cajaiba, A.P. 2012. The dialogical model: Developing academic knowledge for and from practice. *European Management Review*, 9(4), 199–212.

Bartunek, J.M. and Rynes, S.L. 2014. Academics and practitioners are alike and unlike: The paradoxes of academic—practitioner relationships. *Journal of Management*, 40(5), 1181–1201.

Beech, N., MacIntosh, R., and MacLean, D. 2010. Dialogues between academics and practitioners: The role of generative dialogic encounters. *Organization Studies*, 31(9–10), 1341–1367.

Birkmann, J., Buckle, P., Jaeger, J., Pelling, M., Setiadi, N., Garschagen, M., Fernando, N., and Kropp, J. 2010. Extreme events and disasters: A window of opportunity for change? Analysis of organizational, institutional and political changes, formal and informal responses after mega-disasters. *Natural Hazards*, 55(3), 637–655.

Burgess, G., Kelemen, M., Moffat, S., and Parsons, E. 2017. Using performative knowledge production to explore marketplace exclusion. *Qualitative Market Research: An International Journal*, 20(4), 486–511.

Clinton, W.J. 2006. *Lessons learned from tsunami recovery: Key propositions for building back better.* New York: Office of the UN Secretary-General's Special Envoy for Tsunami Recovery.

Cunliffe, A.L. and Scaratti, G. 2017. Embedding impact in engaged research: Developing socially useful knowledge through dialogical sense making. *British Journal of Management*, 28(1), 29–44.

Fan, L. 2013. Disaster as opportunity? Building back better in Aceh, Myanmar and Haiti. Overseas Development Institute: Humanitarian Policy Group. On-line available at: www.odi.org/sites/odi.org.uk/files/odi-assets/publications-opinion-files/8693.pdf (Accessed 05 March, 2017).

Ferris, E. and Solís, M. 2013. *Earthquake, Tsunami, Meltdown—The triple disaster's impact on Japan, impact on the world.* Washington, DC: The Brookings Institution.

Goulding, C., Kelemen, M. and Kiyomiya, T., 2018. Community based response to the Japanese tsunami: A bottom-up approach. *European Journal of Operational Research*, 268 (3), 887–903.

Gunewardena, N. and Schuller, M. eds. 2008. *Capitalizing on catastrophe: Neoliberal strategies in disaster reconstruction.* California: AltaMira Press.

Higher Education Funding Council website. 2016. Research Excellence Framework (REF impact), on-line available at: www.hefce.ac.uk/rsrch/REFimpact/ (Accessed 10 May 2018).

Humanitarian Policy Group. 2013. *Disaster as Opportunity? Building Back Better in Aceh, Myanmar and Haiti.* Available at: www.odi.org/sites/odi.org.uk/files/odi-assets/publications-opinion-files/8693.pdf (Accessed 7 July, 2018).

Isaacs, W. 2008. *Dialogue: The art of thinking together.* New York: Crown Publishing Group.

Kelemen, M. and Hamilton, L. 2018. Creative processes of impact making: Advancing an American pragmatist methodology. *Qualitative Research in Organisation and Management.* doi:10.1108/QROM-03-2017-1506. ISSN: 1746-5648 (In Press).

Kelemen, M., Phillips, M., Moffat, S., and James, D. 2017. Performing the legacy of animative and iterative approaches to co-producing knowledge. In: K. Facer and K. Pahl, eds. *Valuing Interdisciplinary Collaborative Research: Beyond Impact*, Bristol: Policy Press, 107–130.

Kelemen, M., Surman, E., and Dikomitis, L. 2018. Cultural animation in health research: An innovative methodology for patient and public involvement and engagement. *Health Expectations*, 1–9.

Kennedy, J., Ashmore, J., Babister, E., and Kelman, I. 2008. The meaning of 'build back better': evidence from post-tsunami Aceh and Sri Lanka. *Journal of Contingencies and Crisis Management*, 16(1), 24–36.

138   *Yiwen Lin et al.*

Lam, B., Phillips, M., Kelemen, M.L., Zamenopoulos, T., Moffat, S., and de Sousa, S. 2018. Design and creative methods as a practice of liminality in community-academic research projects. *The Design Journal*. ISSN 1460–6925 (In Press).

Lloyd-Jones, T. (2007). Building back better: How action research and professional networking can make a difference to disaster reconstruction and risk reduction. In: *Research Symposium 2007, Reflections on Practice: Capturing Innovation and Creativity*. London: Royal Institute of British Architects.

Lorino, P., Tricard, B., and Clot, Y. 2011. Research methods for non-representational approaches to organizational complexity: The dialogical mediated inquiry. *Organization Studies*, 32(6), 769–801.

Mannakkara, S. and Wilkinson, S. 2012. Building back better in Japan-lessons from the Indian Ocean Tsunami experience in Sri Lanka. In: *Conference: International Conference on Disaster Management*. Kumamoto, Japan: International Institute for Infrastructure Resilience and Reconstruction.

Matanle, P. 2011. The Great East Japan Earthquake, Tsunami, and nuclear meltdown: Towards the reconstruction of a safe, sustainable, and compassionate society in Japan's shrinking regions. *Local Environment: The International Journal of Justice and Sustainability*, 16(9), 823–847.

Minami-sanriku Town website. 2012, on-line available at: www.town.minamisanriku.miyagi.jp/index.cfm/6.html (Accessed 09 March, 2018).

National Police Agency of Japan (NPA). 2018. On-line available at: www.npa.go.jp/news/other/earthquake2011/pdf/higaijokyo_e.pdf. (Accessed 09 April, 2018).

Pink, S. and Morgan, J. 2013. Short-term ethnography: Intense routes to knowing. *Symbolic Interaction*, 36(3), 351–361.

Sorensen, A. and Funck, C. eds. (2009). *Living cities in Japan: Citizens' movements, machizukuri and local environments*. London: Taylor & Francis.

United Nations Office for Disaster Risk Reduction website. 2015. Sendai Framework for disaster risk reduction 2015–2030. On-line available at: www.unisdr.org/we/inform/publications/43291 (Accessed 01 February, 2016).

Veszteg, R.F., Funaki, Y., and Tanaka, A. 2015. The impact of the Tohoku earthquake and tsunami on social capital in Japan: Trust before and after the disaster. *International Political Science Review*, 36(2), 119–138.

Weathering the Storm: How communities respond to adversity. 2013. Video available at: https://youtu.be/VkFtTi6M4t8

Wells, P. and Nieuwenhuis, P. 2017. Operationalizing deep structural sustainability in business: Longitudinal immersion as extensive engaged scholarship. *British Journal of Management*, 28(1), 45–63.

Part 3

9 The Professionalisation of the Police in England and Wales

A Critical Appraisal

Simon Holdaway

Introduction

During the last decade, the 43 police forces of England and Wales have managed a significant decrease to their budgets, chief police officers responding to a reduction of 14% in real terms (Institute of Fiscal Studies, 2017). Most savings have affected staffing; overall, police forces now employ about 20,000 fewer police officers.[1] Reduced funding has therefore been an important driver of police organisational change. The initial emphasis of change was on stripping out costs rather than reforming how services are organised and delivered. Only recently, within the last couple of years, police minds have turned to new organisational structures and the delivery of services. Some organisational change is evident, for example, where constabularies have established regional collaborations to share services like firearms, legal services and public order operations. Attention has also been given to documenting public demand for policing, providing rudimentary evidence of the effect of cuts to other public services on policing, those to mental health services, for example (College of Policing 2015a).[2] It was discovered that the majority of calls from the public requesting police assistance are unrelated to crime. Apparently unknown to generations of chief police officers, research revealed a similar pattern of demand many years ago (Punch, 1979). This particular lack of knowledge is indicative of a wider aspect of police responses to budget reductions.

One important reason for the recent documentation of overall public demand on police services has been that it is no longer convincing for police chiefs to argue that significant cuts to their budgets had led to an increase in crime. During the last decade, official statistics and victim surveys throughout Europe and North America documented what criminologists have called 'the crime drop' (Farrell, Tilley et al., 2014). The latest crime figures indicate that the number of some crime types has risen, but an overall picture of reduction remains (Office of National Statistics, 2018). The historical argument that 'more police means less crime' cannot be argued with ease to influence government decisions about budget cuts (Holdaway, 1977).

Government power to reduce police budgets could provide the home secretary with levers to direct the use of resources in particular ways, which would not be inconsistent with previous Home Office policies. It had for years been commonplace for the Home Office to put in place priorities, targets, plans and many other objectives for constabularies. Before the election of the 2010 Conservative government, Labour's 13 years in office had included a police policy based on Home Office direction of constabularies, chief constables responsible for responding to numerous centrally defined targets and similar instruments (McLaughlin, 2005). The Home Office steered how police services should be organised and, therefore, budgets allocated. Chief constables implemented related policies within constabularies. This was another influence on chief officers' lack of innovative thinking as they responded to the cuts.

Teresa May, the 2010 newly appointed conservative home secretary, steered police policy in a new direction. Centrally defined targets and similar instruments were withdrawn. The Conservative government would no longer intervene so strongly in the police use of resources. The management of budgets was a matter for chief constables overseen by police and crime commissioners. During her address to the 2010 Police Federation conference, May offered a 'new deal' to the police service (Home Office, 2010). The Home Office would stand back from routine intervention in constabularies through objective setting and the like. Labour's days of intervention were over. May certainly steered police strategy when she told chief officers to prioritise crime reduction, but that was all. Contrasting her government's policy with that of previous Labour administrations, she offered the police a deal in which the Home Office would distance itself from routine intervention in police policy. That meant, she stated,

> getting rid of the centralised bureaucracy that wastes money, saps morale and crushes innovation. . . . and free the men and women of our police forces to do what they are trained to do, want to do and the public expect them to do—make our society safer.
>
> (Home Office, 2010)

There would be, she said, "freedom to the police professionals; more power to the people".

The phrase, "freedom to police professionals; more power to the people" was telling, marking the beginning of a new period of police reorganisation associated but not integral to the policy of reduced police budgets. At face value, May's rhetoric echoed the distancing of the government from interference in citizens' lives. Certainly, she and subsequent conservative Home Secretaries did not reintroduce Labour's policies by another name. Inherent to any provision of freedom to act, May's policy was framed implicitly by a notion of police responsibility fitting for a profession. Freedom has limits, and the Home Office would intervene if what she called 'police professionals' did not deliver an adequate service—"by giving local people a real say over how their streets are policed"—by which she meant primarily did not respond to priorities determined locally by police and crime commissioners following public consultation. Central to this paper is an analysis of what, at the time May gave her Police Federation speech, was a novel idea. The police are to be regarded as a profession and, therefore, police officers of all ranks as professionals.

In this chapter, the notion of the police as a profession will be examined and the wider policy context within which the idea was introduced by Teresa May will be considered. The definition of the police as a profession is not new, and the ways in which its meanings have varied will be documented. Particular claims to professional status evident in the contemporary context will therefore be analysed. The sociological literature about professions will be analysed to clarify, criticise and refine police common-sense ideas of their occupational status. Particular attention will then be given to the idea of a profession as a form of regulation. Undoubtedly, the recent definition of the police as a profession raises important questions about the regulation and related accountability of constabularies (Holdaway, 2017). Police professionalisation is central to a new framework of police governance in England and Wales, raising significant policy and related theoretical questions.

The Claim to Be a Profession

Mundane claims to be the member of a profession, to be a professional, often refer to completing a task satisfactorily. Anybody employed in an occupation can consider they are a professional by invoking this idea, but that description of the police as a profession, however, was not in Teresa May's mind in 2010. She invoked the notion of the police as akin to the classic professions, medicine, the law, "I'm not going to presume to tell you how to do your job . . . any more than I would tell a surgeon how to operate—or an engineer how to build a bridge" (Home Office, 2010). May was arguing that the police are a profession in a more precise sense, an opinion buttressed by a similar view found in an influential report she commissioned about police leadership and training, where the argument that the police *needed to become* a profession was central (Neyroud, 2011).

No matter the historical view of police professionalisation taken, May and Peter Neyroud, the author of the report she commissioned, were not the first to claim professional status for the police. In his history of the police in England, published in 1967, Critchley argued that changes to policing during the 1960s demonstrated that the police were a profession. This meant a return to Peelian principles (Critchley, 1967). Critchley's argument was not supported by detailed evidence, but it seems that he had in mind a notion of the police as a profession related to Peel's adage,

> The police are the public and the public are the police; the police being only members of the public who are paid to give full-time attention to duties which are incumbent on every citizen in the interests of community welfare and existence.
>
> (Critchley, 1967)

Here, a profession is committed to public service and therefore free from self-interest, implying public trust in officers.

Later, in the 1970s, Robert Mark, Commissioner of the Metropolitan Police, articulated a different perspective on professions. In a nationally broadcast lecture, he put it that officers had been artisans, but their status had now changed within his contemporary context. Mark put it that

> I suppose you could sum it all up by saying that in Britain certainly, and I have no doubt elsewhere, the time has come when the police are abandoning their artisan status and are achieving by our ever-increasing variety of services, our integrity, our accountability and our dedication to the public good, a status no less admirable than that of the most learned and distinguished professions.
>
> (Mark, 1977)

Whilst commissioner of the Metropolitan Police, Mark tackled serious police corruption. The integrity he regarded as a hallmark of a profession, however, has been re-established, as has accountability through the work of police authorities. Further, like medicine and the law, the police apparently share a body of learned knowledge on which their practices are based. Later during the same decade, we find another, different claim to professional status, focusing more upon the educational qualifications and managerial prowess of senior officers and fast track, direct entrants to officer rank (Holdaway, 1977).

More recent, influential arguments have resonated with Mark's or Critchley's confidence in the professional standing of the police. Importantly, in his 2011 report about police leadership and training, commissioned by Teresa May, former chief constable Peter Neyroud reiterated police assertions of professionalism. He put it that "wide-ranging developments over the last two decades secure the police as a profession" (Neyroud, 2011). Developments to strengthen professionalisation are needed—a professional body registering its members, more evidence-based research and practice and continuing professional development programmes, for example. Neyroud's argument was that the police display fundamental attributes of a profession, which should be extended and strengthened as the foundation of contemporary policing, not least to demonstrate that the public trust officers' integrity. He defined the police as a profession akin to medicine, the law and other bodies because they share their classical traits, a code of ethics, accredited qualifications, a foundation of systematic 'scientific' research and more.

The argument so far is that authoritative definitions of the police as a profession have differed over time. We find claims made for professional status repeated at particular times. Mark was concerned about public perceptions of police integrity, Holdaway documented police officers' claims to managerial competencies and high educational qualifications as indicators of a profession and, more recently, Neyroud pointed to existing professional traits like evidence-based practices that need to secure finally the police as a profession. When offering her deal to the police, Teresa May was making a claim as one voice in a process of re-professionalisation, by which I mean periodic, authoritative, public declarations that the police are a profession (Holdaway, 2017).

Understanding the Police as a Profession

Criminological research about the police does not assist our understanding of the process of re-professionalisation or its social context. Publications by academics have not engaged with the sociological literature about professions or attempted to map the contemporary context within which professional claims have been made. Rather, there has been an implicit acceptance that the police might be or is a profession and, therefore, it is not necessary to probe further (Fleming, 2014; Sklansky, 2014; Tilley and Laycock, 2014). The notion of the police as a profession has found broad, uncritical acceptance within academe, government and the police. Re-professionalisation, however, captures a different, public declaration in which particular attributes of a profession are emphasised and related, implicitly or explicitly, to the social context within which they are articulated. It is argued that, amongst other matters, a lack of trust in police integrity and new government policies intended to distance the home secretary from the regulation of constabularies are key aspects of a renewed emphasis on the idea that the police are a profession.

This chapter, therefore, offers a distinct analytical standpoint, questioning the taken for granted status of the police as a profession. Contemporary claims to professional status are probed to identify the contexts within which they are made; meanings ascribed to actions establishing the police as a profession are analysed; the intended and unintended consequences of such meanings and related actions are scrutinised. First, the policy context within which a renewed interest in the police as a profession has developed is described. Insights from the sociology of the professions to the re-professionalisation of the police are then discussed. The chapter ends with a critique of contemporary views of the police as a profession.

The Contemporary Context of Police Professionalisation

Robert Mark's claim to police professional status was made when questions about police corruption were in the public domain. At the same time, and as Holdaway noted, further problems of adequate police leadership and management were also apparent (Holdaway, 1977). Both of these circumstances were evident when the new Conservative government was elected in 2010 and renewed claims for the police as a profession were made.

The Neyroud Review

Neyroud's 2011 review of police leadership and training was commissioned in 2010, very soon after the election of a Conservative government, and is key to understanding the contemporary re-professionalisation of the police in England and Wales. His terms of reference indicate that during their years in opposition, the Conservative party had been considering radical reforms to policing, including the creation of a professional body and associated policies (Neyroud, 2011, p. 9).

Neyroud was clear that the police exhibit the characteristics of a profession. Radical change to become a profession was not needed, but the consolidation and development of a number of areas of work were required to provide the organisational structure and related ethical standards demonstrated by professions. Before that work could begin, clarity about which police body has responsibility for establishing professional standards of work and the ethics on which they are based was needed. When he wrote his report the Home Office, the Association of Chief Police Officers (ACPO), the Police Federation, Her Majesty's Inspectors of Constabulary (HMIC) and, at times, other bodies published national guidance for the police (Neyroud, 2011, pp. 66–7). Before his retirement from the police, Neyroud had been chief executive of the National Police Improvement Agency, which was also charged with issuing guidance and direction about best practices to constabularies. His experience of the tensions of working in such a disparate context was evident in his report. The home secretary wanted clear advice rather than a welter of sometimes discordant information about diverse subjects provided by ACPO and other bodies (Neyroud 2011, p. 64).

A new, professional body for policing, Neyroud argued, would provide a single source for the definition and dissemination of national police standards, foster greater external scrutiny of proposals for standards, and a great deal more. Its governing body, including 'lay members' and a chair from outside policing, would provide oversight to enhance public accountability of the professional body's work. Importantly, the ability of other groups that previously developed advice about police standards, the Police Superintendent's Association and the Police Federation, for example, would be removed. When established in 2012, the College of Policing was to be the body that 'defined and disseminated core knowledge about 'what works in policing', national policing standards, professional practice and local best practice (Neyroud 2011, pp. 93–4).

Police Ethics and Integrity

Controversy about ethical standards in policing had troubled the home secretary for a considerable time, well before her ideas of professional policing were articulated in 2010. The Hillsborough case, for example, which takes us back to 1989, saw the integrity of Sir Norman Bettinson, Chief Constable of West Yorkshire Police, called into question. It was alleged that, when working in South Yorkshire Police, Bettinson had overseen the drafting of sanitised statements about the death of 96 and injury to 766 fans at a football match and required officers to sign them. Bettinson retired from his force after considerable public and media pressure (Wright, 2015). The manner in which South Yorkshire Police, not least its chief officers, dealt with and investigated the deaths became the subject of a highly critical, independent inquiry and, separately, a formal investigation by the Independent Police Complaints Commission (Hillsborough, 2012). An inquest following the independent inquiry returned a verdict that the 96 fans had been killed unlawfully.

The 1993 Stephen Lawrence murder investigation, etched deeply into the contemporary history of troubled police race relations in England and Wales, drew similar, lasting media and public attention (Sir William Macpherson of Cluny, 1999). Other, significant but less high-profile cases involving, for example, the chief and deputy chief constables of Cleveland Police, who in 2012 were dismissed from office for gross misconduct, added to government concern, keeping the ethics of policing in Home Office sight (Independent, 2012a; Independent, 2013). In North Yorkshire, during the same year, the chief constable faced disciplinary charges related to nepotism when recruiting staff. His deputy was implicated in the offences and retired (Independent, 2012b). The integrity and managerial competence of chief officers, including the ability of ACPO to foster acceptable ethical standards amongst its membership, was brought to the attention of the government by these and other cases. With this point in mind, Neyroud was able to argue that the police required a code of professional ethics, the development of which would be central to the work of the proposed professional body.

Ethical problems were also raised by cases involving lower police ranks. The 2012 'Plebgate' case involved a fracas between constables on duty outside the prime minister's residence and a cabinet minister whom, it was alleged, swore at them (Independent, 2014). Accusations of police illegal and unethical behaviour were made by the cabinet minister and other members of parliament. The House of Commons, Home Affairs Select Committee called Police Federation officials to a special hearing about the incident and were highly critical of their evidence. Questions about public trust in the police tracked Plebgate for several months, drawing attention to the lower police ranks and their representative body, strengthening evidence of the need for a code of police ethics and a professional body for policing to oversee it. Professional bodies typically publish codes of ethics for their membership, and it was no doubt important symbolically for the police professional body to act similarly. The College of Policing's early work, therefore, included the publication of a code of ethics for policing.

Expectations of police ethical standards were strengthened by additional changes. The erstwhile Independent Police Complaints Commission (IPCC), with its mandate to investigate serious public complaints against police officers, had an impact on unethical police conduct but, inevitably, after the event.[3] Investigation and, possibly, disciplinary action follow a complaint, implying an officer's behaviour should change. A more basic and pervasive measure to prevent misconduct before it occurred was also required, and a code of ethics was seen as central to this. Substantial extra funds to restructure and strengthen the IPCC's work were provided by the government in 2014 (House of Commons, 18th Dec. 2013). A new Independent Office of Police Conduct was launched in 2018, replacing the commission. A code of ethics and the reform of the IPCC were aspects of the wider project to regulate police behaviour more effectively and, implicitly, to professionalise the service.

Neyroud's strong recommendation that the police should strengthen their institution as a profession resonated with the home secretary's concerns about police standards. Professions publish codes of ethics, partly to increase public confidence in their members. A lack of clarity about who sets policing standards, the demonstrable lack of high ethical standards amongst the senior and junior ranks and a political view that the state should distance itself from policing policy, allowing officers to take greater responsibility for their work, strengthened the argument for professionalisation. The crucial, initial step required to begin this ambition was the establishment of a professional body for the police of England and Wales.

The College of Policing

Established in 2013, the College of Policing is the professional body for policing and a major feature of the new landscape of police professionalism. As seen, previous attempts to construct professional standing depended on a range of police and related criteria, articulated by chief officers as if they were solid and irrefutable. In contrast, the College was the first organisation within policing to be given the responsibility to create professional status for the police. It has a five-year strategy with objectives that include "Identifying, developing and promoting ethics, values, and standards of integrity", "identifying, promoting and supporting practice based on evidence" and "setting standards of professional practice" (College of Policing, 2014). More than this, the College has the ambition for the public to be confident that, "police officers adhere to a national code of professional policing practice and receive professional development throughout their careers" (College of Policing, 2015c).

A Board of Governors, with a majority of lay members, oversees these far-reaching objectives covering major areas of police work and, on behalf of the board, a Professional Committee oversees national standard setting and supports the College's wider strategic objectives. It is, of course, possible and may be usual for policy to be changed as it is implemented in constabularies, because each chief constable is legally independent.

One particular responsibility for these groups is, as a College objective states, "identifying, promoting and supporting practice based on evidence". Professions, medicine is an example, develop by placing research findings into policies and practices. Similarly, the police should practice what is now recognised as evidence-based policing (EBP).

Evidence-Based Policing

Policy based on 'what works' has been an aspect of government thinking for some time, beginning with New Labour's ideas about 'evidence-based policy'. Subsequently, a Behavioural Insights Team, initially based in Downing Street, was formed in 2010 by the Tory government, drawing on behavioural science to redesign public services. At this time, the Economic and Social Research Council emphasised research with an impact on national policy, This national setting provided the College of Policing with an opportunity to devote resources fostering 'evidence-based policing' and, therefore, a body of knowledge characteristic of a profession.

EBP has its origins in the USA, reaching back over 20 years. One of its major features has been the Campbell Collaboration that publishes systematic reviews of criminal justice interventions, many of them in policing (see www.campbellcollaboration.org/). The collaboration has defined standards of research design and analysis which, it is argued, secure evidence of 'what works' (http://camp.ostfold.net/artman2/uploads/1/Research_Design_Policy_Brief.pdf). From this perspective, criminology is akin to the natural sciences, and its methods of research should be as similar as possible. Accordingly, the Maryland Methods Scale places in a hierarchy of scientific rigour a number of different social science methods of quantitative inquiry. Systematic reviews based on scores associated with the Maryland Scale are attributed with the highest validity, and the strongest empirical method is the randomised control trial. Following that, studies measuring outcomes before and after an intervention, with a number of control sites, one or, perhaps, no control lead down the hierarchy of validity to a before and after evaluation without the inclusion of any control. These are criteria reflecting the work of the Cochrane Collaboration, which preceded Campbell and is a major source of research findings that 'work' in medicine, a profession with a distinct body of research knowledge and related practice at its heart.

This understanding of research chimed clearly with the College of Policing, which from the outset had to demonstrate to the Home Office that it was adopting policies associated with a profession. What might be called a hard version of evidence-based policing, accepting wholeheartedly the Campbell Collaboration approach, was advocated by the College and for some time remained in the ascendency. One major advocate of evidence-based policing, Professor Larry Sherman, was appointed to the College Board, providing a senior, academic voice about the nature and purpose of criminological research (Sherman, 1998; Sherman, 2009). In papers and other communications, Sherman likened the place of evidence-based research in policing to its position in medicine. There should, he argued, be university Faculties of Policing, with posts for officers and academics. A Society for Evidence-Based Policing was launched. Academics and chief officers were nominated for an American Hall of Fame for their contributions to evidence-based policing. Clinical professorships of criminology should be created in criminal justice agencies. Police officers interested in and practising EBP were named pracademics, providing a status associated with key professional work. In his inaugural lecture as Professor of Criminology at the University of Cambridge, Sherman made the claim with certainty that the rigours of the Campbell Collaboration research rules would preserve our liberty, freeing us from the dangerous constraints of 'unscientific' policies and practices (Sherman, 2009).

The Sociology of Professionalisation the Police as an Example

At its 2015 annual conference, the College of Policing's chief executive, Alex Marshall, stated that work completed to establish a body of knowledge about 'what works' in policing, the publication of a code of ethics for the police, a programme of continuous professional development and the licencing and accreditation of officers have secured the police as a classic profession (College of Policing, 2015b). His view chimes clearly with a long-standing

sociological approach to the professions based on the definition of characteristics that separate them from occupations (Carr-Saunders and Wilson, 1933;
Greenwood, 1957). Professions have a professional body, a code of ethics,
evidence-based practice and accredited employment, for example. This was
also the approach accepted by Neyroud, who identified these traits as synonymous with those of the classic professions, law and medicine being two.

Criticisms of the trait approach to professions are well established, not the
least of which has been the creation and revision of increasingly long lists of
traits, their importance sometimes weighted, to include and exclude occupations (Millerson, 1964). The title of Wilensky's influential paper, 'The Professionalisation of Everyone', captured the essence of this criticism (Wilensky,
1964). My main reservation about this analytical approach, however, is that
it is static. When compared to a list of professional traits, an occupation
either is or is not defined as a profession. The wider social context—like
that described earlier in this chapter—within which entitlements to professional status are developed is not considered; processes of claims-making are
neither described nor analysed; and the meanings of claims of professional
standing, some with implicit or explicit regulatory effects, are not taken into
account.

The meanings and effects of claims to professional status, however, are central to Johnson's analysis of professionalisation as a process of constructing
an ideology to enhance the authority and power of an occupation (Johnson,
1972). Johnson argued that the self-serving interests of authority and power
are central to professional status. His analysis challenged Freidson, who
argued that professionals' commitment to an ethic of service was consistent
with disinterested self-regulation (Freidson, 2001). Johnson's understanding
of professions directs our attention to forms of authority sought when claims
to professionalisation are made in particular contexts and is helpful to an
analysis of police professionalisation in the contemporary context described.

There is, however, an important feature of the present context of police
professionalisation that is in tension with Johnson's analysis. Authority to
regulate membership of the police profession has certainly been given to the
College of Policing. Related powers to check and, if needs be, override decisions based exclusively on the authority of police officers as professionals
have nevertheless also been given to the College's lay-dominated governing
council, HMIC, with its majority of 'lay inspectors', and the Independent
Police Complaints Commission. This suggests countervailing opportunities
for the police to make claims to self-regulation through professionalisation
and a moderation of Johnson's argument.

Basing her argument on Foucault's notion of the power of rhetoric, Valerie
Fournier has argued that "the disciplinary logic of professionalism" creates
the identity of the professional and prompts actions related directly to it
(Fournier, 1999). Defined police competencies required for membership of
the College of Policing, for example, create officers who regard themselves
as professionals. This perspective has the advantage of directing attention
to the ways in which professional status is claimed and practices related
to it cloaked with authority. Fournier argues that such claims are fragile

and need to be asserted frequently. In this sense, she embraces the notion of re-professionalisation, but her fundamental argument proposes the over-determination of identity and related actions that create a professional. We know from research that police identity is not uniform. We also know that a distinction should be made between senior and junior police ranks' ideas about policy and practice; written policy does not translate into practice straightforwardly (Holdaway, 1983; Loftus, 2009; Gundhus, 2012).

Julia Evetts has analysed the changing processes of professionalisation or, as she calls it, 'professionalism', offering a perspective that embraces the notion of re-professionalisation (Evetts, 2003). In harmony with Becker's and Hughes' perspective of symbolic interactionism (Hughes, 1958; Becker, 1970; Hughes, 1994), she argues that professionalism is most adequately understood as symbolic processes in which claims for status and authority about occupational values are made by advocates. 'Professionalism', however, is not a wholly symbolic construction. Instrumental changes to action and to the structure of organisations are also fundamental. Evetts provides an argument avoiding the crudity of the trait perspective, Johnson's over-reach when conceptualising the authority and power allowing professionals to regulate themselves, and problems of over-determination presented by Fournier.

Interestingly, Evetts makes a distinction between assertions for 'professionalism from below' and 'professionalism from above' (Evetts 2011). The former refers to practitioners' claims about their status and authority, more usually concerned with autonomy and aspects of self-regulation. The gains from 'professionalism from above', initiated by senior managerial staff and government, are different, more concerned with standardisation, bureaucracy, assessment, the codification of ethics, continuing education related to a body of professional knowledge, collegial authority, a strong sense of purpose and, crucially, regulation (Muzio and Kirkpatrick, 2011). These are features of police professionalism from above but, as will be argued, they are fragile within the organisational context of policing in England and Wales.

Conceptualising the Police as a Profession

A lack of attention to the sociology of the professions when considering contemporary policing has an implicit consequence similar to that created by the trait approach. A profession is conceptualised as object-like, a phenomenon that might gather to itself new characteristics but is basically objective. From this standpoint, the police either are or are not a profession. The sociology of the professions offers alternative views, helping us to understand police professionalisation by drawing attention to a number of underlying features and consequences of professional status that are not evident if we afford social phenomena object-like significance.

When the contemporary social context within which claims to be a profession are articulated is taken into account, ethical and regulatory matters become prominent. It is significant that during the 1970s Robert Mark and, later, Teresa May and others found the erosion of claims to high ethical standards of professional police work to be of importance. Further, a deficiency of clarity about who set standards of policing, coupled with a wish to distance the Home Office from regulatory control of constabularies, also gave impetus to the claims to professionalisation noted.

Although not unleashed entirely from government constraint, the current standing of the police as a profession is, as Johnson and, differently, Fournier argue, a conferring of authority and, in some contexts, power. The College of Policing has authority to set ethical and related standards of practice for all officers; it requires them to engage with continuing training and relates police practice to research findings secured by 'scientific methods'. These are clear, instrumental functions of professional status. Johnson's argument would be that professional status is an overt strengthening of the authority of the police to regulate themselves, a lessening rather than strengthening of public accountability and not, as Teresa May argued, the state distancing itself from the police. The Home Office retains the authority to legislate and in other ways influence police decision-making. For Johnson, the professionalisation of the police is a transfer of Home Office authority to an already powerful institution.

A further, concealed aspect of the authority and power of police professionalisation, however, is its creation of imagery of an institution working to high moral standards, thus shoring-up damage to public confidence in the police. Fournier would argue that this is a disciplinary process, adding new techniques of public control to policing. The so-called traits of a profession, a setting of standards of work and a code of ethics, for example, are understood as disciplinary resources for the police to foster public trust and confidence. The public appearance of a profession betrays its private reality.

Fournier also argues that professionalisation is a process with implications for the occupational identity of its members. The College of Policing, like other professional bodies, creates a structure of internal governance to discipline its members. Police officers of all ranks come to regard themselves as professionals subject to the disciplines of their governing body. Their occupational identity becomes that of a professional. Drawing on Foucault's ideas, the rhetoric and associated actions of chief officers and others who sustain the notion of the police as a profession disciplines the identity and action of all officers. Professional status is of relevance to the external, public appearance of the police and the officers' occupational identity.

Johnson and Fournier draw our attention to important features of professionalisation, authority and power, the rhetoric of status and occupational identity. Their analyses, however, are also limited, too deterministic and lacking empirical support. Take Johnson's claim that professions are afforded authority and power, reducing public accountability. This has not been the case within contemporary policing. Teresa May's proposal to withdraw Home Office interference from constabularies and to establish the College of Policing as the single agency establishing policing standards appeared to provide greater autonomy to a professional police. This has not been the outcome of her policies. A new, hybrid structure of police accountability and governance has replaced the dominant position of the Home Office

(Holdaway 2017). An increased number of organisations have begun to regulate the police, providing, in theory, checks and balances to the potential of a profession to regulate itself.

Police and crime commissioners, elected to represent the publics of 42 constabulary areas, set a police and crime plan for each chief constable and, in theory, holds him or her accountable for its delivery. Her Majesty's Inspectors of Police undertake thematic and more generic inspections regularly, calling chief officers and, by implication, police and crime commissioners to account (HMICFRS 2018). They do not necessarily evaluate police performance against College standards when they rate each constabulary, grade it and require changes before their next inspection. The Independent Office of Police Conduct has been established recently to investigate serious public complaints against the police. Their work calls the chief and other officers to account, drawing attention to poor practices and requiring a change to them. Further, The Police Chiefs Council, which represents all chief officers has numerous committees and sub-committees with a membership of senior officers, considers all police policy from The College of Policing, the Home Office and itself issues advice about policing matters to its members. Many different agencies are now located within this new police landscape, each with regulatory functions, calling chief officers to account. They do not form a hierarchical system of regulation, neither are they coordinated. PCCs, for example, can disagree with the advice of Her Majesty's Inspectorate; Her Majesty's Inspectorate might but does not necessarily refer to the College of Policing Standards when assessing and regulating constabularies. One could chart the overlapping responsibilities of these actors, all having a significant degree of autonomy within what is suitably described as a loosely coupled system of police regulation (Weick 1976). The professionalisation of the police is certainly crucial to but not dominant within these arrangements. It has added to but not structured significantly the contemporary system of police regulation in England and Wales, requiring an adaptation of Johnson's thesis.

Fournier's argument is similarly problematic because she does not account for long-standing research evidence about the occupational culture of the lower ranks (Manning 1977; Holdaway 1983; Loftus 2009). We know from research evidence that lower-ranked officers sustain a strong occupational identity that is not oriented towards evidence-based practice, ethical codes or the professional management ideas of senior and chief officers. Cynicism about rather than confidence in senior officers is apparent (Manning 1977; Holdaway 1983; Loftus 2009; Loftus 2010; Bacon 2014). Policing in England and Wales is based on a hierarchical structure of rank. Chief officers issue policies that, it is assumed, flow down a constabulary to be implemented by the lower ranks. Substantial research about the occupational culture of the lower ranks, however, reveals a world in which 'police commonsense' is dominant. Speed, excitement, action, crime work, control of disorder and cynicism take precedence over a more considered managerial approach that frames the world of senior and chief officers. The worlds of senior and lower-ranked officers are distinct. Managerial instructions, policies, rules and law are refracted through the occupational culture and implemented by the lower ranks who deliver police services to communities (Holdaway 1979; Loftus 2009).

From its inception, the College of Policing has been dominated by and associated with the work of chief officers. The police code of ethics, statements of professional standards and best research-based practices have been issued to the lower ranks without substantive consultation with the lower ranks, apart from a formal period when written comments on proposed policies have been invited. The assumption has been that professional standards flow from the College into constabularies, down the ranks to implementation on the streets. No account has been taken of the lower ranks' occupational culture.

Extensive research into how professional standards and associated phenomena are understood and used by the lower ranks has not been undertaken, but there are studies and other evidence suggesting a considerable cultural fissure between the understandings of professionalism amongst the lower ranks, chief officers and the College of Policing. Officers' attitudes to ethics have been found in two consecutive studies to be rather different from those implied by the College Code of Ethics (Westmarland, 2005; Westmarland and Rowe, 2016). Evidence-based policing, another core idea of the police as a profession, has also faced significant difficulties, not least because the definition adopted initially by the College mirrored that of medicine. Randomised control trials, used widely in medicine, are not readily suitable for policing, and there are many strong arguments to challenge both the assumptions of realist criminology and its methods that define EBP (Sampson, 2010). More importantly for understanding the professionalisation of the police, rank and file officers do not understand social science methods and the problems of applying research findings to practice which contrasts sharply with police common sense. In a small study of officers' views of a training programme to introduce EBP, Jenny Fleming found practitioners observed that the organisational structures and resources required to implement EBP were not currently in place. She recommended that they are enabled and empowered to influence policy from the bottom up and request the organisational structures and resources required to engage in EBP activity (Fleming and Wingrove 2017). Fleming has also argued that much of policing requires craft-like knowledge and skills, which are presently not incorporated into the formally rational, scientific notion of EBP (Fleming and Rhodes 2018).

Finally, lower-ranked officers who use social media have expressed their disappointment with and scepticism about the College. An influential blog written by a serving police inspector, for example, argued that the College was distant from the world of the lower ranks and needed to listen to their perspective, engage them and work in collaboration if the College was to be successful (Constable 2017a, 2017b). Rachel Tuffin, Interim Chief Executive of the College, replied at length, pointing out how greater communication between the rank and file and the College was desirable and that a number of channels had been opened (Tuffin 2017). Lumsden's recent research about the meaning of professionalisation to serving officers uses qualitative interview data to suggest that Tuffin's view is not entirely adequate. The problem of engaging officers with the College of Policing is more than one of inadequate communications. The occupational culture continues to create a tension between the attitudes, values and related actions implicit in professional notions of policing. Lumsden's central point is that "the resilience of characteristics of the police role and culture mean that the transformation in policing such as professionalisation will remain incomplete" (Lumsden, 2017, p. 16). The current re-professionalisation of the police has so far not addressed significant organisational, resource and, crucially, cultural problems that, ironically, have been made known by research for decades. They are substantial and will test the extent to which the College can respond to all ranks within the police workforce, influencing officers' beliefs, attitudes and related actions.

A Professional Police in England and Wales

This chapter has addressed a recent, important claim that the police are a profession. Long-standing traits from sociology that designate occupations as professions have provided common-sense criteria to justify the claims of the home secretary and chief police officers. Neglecting the claims, social context and related processes to create and sustain an occupation as a profession, the trait approach has been found wanting. Problematic police ethics, contested authority to define best police practice through written guidance and other circumstances contextualise the current discussions about police professionalisation.

Once these circumstances are taken into account, the certainty of the trait approach and the question, 'Is the police a profession?' falls away. A more appropriate question is what are the conditions and claims made to construct an imagery of the police that can be described as a profession. A new ethical code, an established College of Policing, continuing professional development and other features of the contemporary police landscape have been analysed as constituents of professional status. These circumstances, however, do not secure professional status. The question, 'Is the police a profession?' cannot be answered 'Yes' or 'No' because claims to such a designation are created and sustained by the attribution of particular meanings to fragile phenomena. The authority of the College of Policing to issue best practice guiding police policy and action is precarious for a number of reasons. A new, hybrid structure of police governance has created a plural rather than a single, authoritative institution to issue guidance (Holdaway 2017). The written Code of Ethics is not yet consistent with research evidence documenting officers' views of it (Westmarland and Rowe 2016). Long-standing evidence about the occupational culture of the lower ranks secures constabularies as fundamentally complex, divided organisations (Loftus 2009). Policy issued by senior and chief police officers is distinct from policy as it is put into practice by the lower ranks. Research evidence, Karen Lumsden's work on police professionalisation being the most recent (Lumsden 2017), is clear that police professional status is indeed contested by the lower ranks and fragile.

The certainty of current police claims to re-professionalise their institution cannot be taken for granted. They are, as Lumsden argues, 'incomplete', and the evidence from social science research indicates that they will remain so.

Notes

1 The reduction of non-police officer staff has been greater than that for officers. Summarising the more recent situation, the Institute of Fiscal Studies put it that "Current estimates of police force revenues in 2016–17 show that the government has done as it promised so far: police budgets remained broadly flat in cash terms between 2015–16 and 2016–17. However, this does mean that real-terms revenues have continued to fall" (Ibid., p. 1).
2 Some changes have been made to accommodate public demand for policing. In the area of mental health problems, for example, in many constabularies social and mental health workers work in a team with police officers. The point made here, however, is that these are initiatives scattered throughout the country rather than part of a basic, strategic consideration of appropriate responses to demand for police services.
3 The Policing and Crime Bill 2015–16 includes wide-ranging provisions for the revision of the IPCC. They will not, however, have an impact on the points made above. The commission was replaced by the Independent Office of Police Conduct in 2018.

References

Bacon, M. (2014). Police culture and the new policing context. In *The Future of Policing*. J. M. Brown. Abingdon and New York, Routledge.
Becker, H. S. (1970). *Sociological Work*. Chicago, Aldine.
Carr-Saunders, A. M. and P. A. Wilson (1933). *The Professions*. Oxford, Clarendon Press.
College of Policing. (2014). *Five Year Strategy*. Coventry, College of Policing.
College of Policing. (2015a). *College of Policing Analysis: Estimating Demand on the Police Service1*. London, College of Policing.
College of Policing. (2015b). "College of Policing Annual Conference." from www.college.police.uk/News/College-events/Pages/College-of-Policing-Annual-Conference-2015.aspx
College of Policing. (2015c). "Integrity in Policing." from www.college.police.uk/What-we-do/Ethics/integrity-in-policing/Pages/Integrity-in-policing.aspx
Constable, N. (2017a). "Canary in the Mine." from https://nathanconstable.word press.com/2017/11/03/canary-in-the-mine/
Constable, N. (2017b). "Listening to the Canaries." from https://nathanconstable.wordpress.com/2017/12/15/listening-to-the-canaries/
Critchley, T. (1967). *A History of the Police in England and Wales*. London, Constable.
Evetts, J. (2003). "The Sociological Analysis of Professionalism: Occupational Change in the Modern World." *International Sociology* 18(2): 395–415.
Evetts, J. (2011). "The New Professionalism? Challenges and Opportunities." *Current Sociology* 59(4): 406–422.
Farrell, G., N. Tilley, et al. (2014). "Why the Crime Drop?" *Crime and Justice* 43(1): 421–490.
Fleming, J. (2014). The pursuit of professionalism: Lessons from Australia. *The Future of Policing*. J. M. Brown. Oxford, Routledge: 355–368.
Fleming, J. and R. Rhodes (2018). "Can Experience Be Evidence? Craft Knowledge and Evidence-Based Policing." *Policy & Politics* 46(1): 3–26.

Fleming, J. and J. Wingrove (2017). "We Would If We Could but Not Sure If We Can: Implementing Evidence-Based Practice The Evidence-Based Practice Agenda in the UK." *Policing: A Journal of Policy and Practice* **11**(2): 202–213.

Fournier, V. (1999). "The Appeal to 'Professionalism' as a Disciplinary Mechanism." *The Sociological Review* **47**(2): 280–307.

Freidson, E. (2001). *Professionalism, the Third Logic: On the Practice of Knowledge.* Chicago, University of Chicago Press.

Greenwood, E. (1957). "Attributes of a profession." *Social Work* **2**: 44–55.

Gundhus, H. I. (2012). "Experience or Knowledge? Perspectives on New Knowledge Regimes and Control of Police Professionalism." *Policing* **7**(2): 178–194.

Hillsborough, I. P. (2012). "Hillsborough: The Report of the Independent Panel." from http://hillsborough.independent.gov.uk/repository/report/HIP_report.pdf

HMICFRS. (2018). "Annual, All Force Inspections (PEEL Assessments)." Retrieved 13.7.2018, 2018, from www.justiceinspectorates.gov.uk/hmicfrs/our-work/article/peel-assessments/

Holdaway, S. (1977). "Changes in Urban Policing." *British Journal of Sociology* **28**(2): 119–137.

Holdaway, S. (1979). Police-Black Relations: The Professional Solution. In *The British Police*. S. Holdaway. London, Edward Arnold: 66–82.

Holdaway, S. (1983). *Inside the British Police: A Force at Work*. Oxford, Blackwell.

Holdaway, S. (2017). "The Re-professionalization of the Police in England and Wales." *Criminology & Criminal Justice* **17**(5): 588–604.

Home Office. (2010). "Police reform: Theresa May's Speech to the Police Federation." from www.gov.uk/government/speeches/police-reform-theresa-mays-speech-to-the-police-federation

House of Commons. (18th December 2013). *Column 112WS*, House of Commons.

Hughes, E. C. (1958). *Men and Their Work*. London, The Free Press.

Hughes, E. C. (1994). *On Work, Race and the Sociological Imagination*. London, University of Chicago Press.

Independent, P. C. C. (2012a). "Cleveland Police Deputy Chief Constable dismissed following IPCC managed investigation." from www.ipcc.gov.uk/news/cleveland-police-deputy-chief-constable-dismissed-following-ipcc-managed-investigation

Independent, P. C. C. (2012b). "Recruitment Campaign—North Yorkshire Police." from www.ipcc.gov.uk/investigations/recruitment-campaign-north-yorkshire-police-0

Independent, P. C. C. (2013). "Cleveland Police Chief Constable Sean Price Dismissed Following IPCC Investigation." from www.ipcc.gov.uk/news/cleveland-police-chief-constable-sean-price-dismissed-following-ipcc-investigation.

Independent, P. C. C. (2014). "Andrew Mitchell—Metropolitan Police Service, West Midlands Police, West Mercia Police and Warwickshire Police." from www.ipcc.gov.uk/investigations/andrew-mitchell-metropolitan-police-service-west-midlands-police-west-mercia-police

Institute of Fiscal Studies (2017). *Police Workforce and Funding in England and Wales: IFS Briefing Note BN208*. London, The Institute of Fiscal Studies.

Johnson, T. J. (1972). *Professions and Power*. London, Macmillan.

Loftus, B. (2009). *Police Culture in a Changing World*. Oxford, OUP.

Loftus, B. (2010). "Police occupational culture: Classic themes, altered times." *Policing and Society* **20**(1): 1–20.

Lumsden, K. (2017). " 'It's a Profession, it Isn't a Job': Police Officers' Views on the Professionalisation of Policing in England." *Sociological Research Online* **22**(3): 4–20.

Manning, P. (1977). *Police Work*. Cambridge, Mass, M.I.T. Press.

Mark, R. (1977). *Policing a Perplexed Society*. London and George, Allen and Unwin.

McLaughlin, E. (2005). "Forcing the Issue: New Labour, New Localism and the Democratic Renewal of Police Accountability." *The Howard Journal of Criminal Justice* 44(5): 473–489.

Millerson, G. (1964). *The Qualifying Associations*. London, Routledge and Kegan Paul.

Muzio, D. and I. Kirkpatrick (2011). "Introduction: Professions and Organizations—A Conceptual Framework." *Current Sociology* 59(4): 389–405.

Neyroud, P. (2011). *Review of Police Leadership and Training*. London, Home Office.

Office of National Statistics. (2018). *Crime in England and Wales: Year ending September 2017*. London, Office of National Statistics.

Punch, M. (1979). The secret social service. In *The British Police*. S. Holdaway. London, Edward Arnold.

Sampson, R. J. (2010). "Gold Standard Myths: Observations on the Experimental Turn in Quantitative Criminology." *Journal of Quantitative Criminology* 25: 489–500.

Sherman, L. W. (1998). *Evidence-based policing. Ideas in American policing*. Washington, The Police Foundation.

Sherman, L. W. (2009). "Evidence and liberty: The promise of experimental criminology." *Criminology and Criminal Justice* 9(1): 5–28.

Sir William Macpherson of Cluny. (1999). *The Stephen Lawrence Inquiry: Report of an Inquiry by Sir William Macpherson of Cluny*, London, HMSO.

Sklansky, D. A. (2014). The Promise and Perils of Police Professionalism. In *The Future of Policing*. J. Brown. London, Routledge.

Tilley, N. and G. Laycock (2014). The police as professional problem solvers. *The Future of Policing*. J. M. Brown. Oxford, Routledge.

Tuffin, R. (2017). "Listening to the Canaries." from www.college.police.uk/News/College-news/Pages/Rachel_Tuffin_blog_response_December_2017.aspx

Weick, K. (1976). "Educational Organisations as Loosely Coupled Systems." *Administrative Science Quarterly* 21(1): 1–12.

Westmarland, L. (2005). "Police Ethics and Integrity: Breaking the Blue Code of Silence." *Policing and Society* 15(2): 145–165.

Westmarland, L. and M. Rowe (2016). "Police Ethics and Integrity: Can a New Code Overturn the Blue Code?" *Policing and Society*, 1–17.

Wilensky, H. (1964). "The Professionalization of Everyone?" *American Journal of Sociology* 70: 137–58.

Wright, S. (2015). "Hillsborough Police Chief Keeps £1m Pension and Escapes Misconduct Charges Because He Retired Last Year." from www.dailymail.co.uk/news/article-2300437/Hillsborough-police-chief-Sir-Norman-Bettison-keeps-1m-pension-escapes-misconduct-charges.html

10 Changing Landscapes, Challenging Identities—Policing in England and Wales

Sarah Charman

Introduction

These are unique times for British policing. The widespread use of body-worn video cameras by police officers combined with the almost universal ownership of personal camera phones mean that police and public encounters are under more public and organisational scrutiny than ever before. Alongside this enhanced scrutiny into current routine police work, we have also witnessed in recent years the report of the Leveson inquiry into press standards, which called into question the relationship between the press and the public, the jailing of police officers over selling information to newspapers, a major inquiry launched into the controversial activities of undercover police officers and the verdict of unlawful killing of 96 Liverpool football fans at Hillsborough in 1989 (Leveson, 2012; Haria and Turvill, 2015; House of Commons, 2015; Conn, 2016). These and other policing controversies have been highlighted by sociologists of policing through the lens of policing cultures for many years. The academic literature on the prevailing cultures within the police remains overwhelmingly negative. Police culture(s) are routinely described as being sites of hegemonic masculinity, racism, prejudice, discrimination and exclusion (Reiner, 2010; Loftus, 2009). Combining all of this with a reduction in police officer numbers, a more complex pattern of emerging crime and the knock-on effect of budgetary cuts to public service elsewhere, it would appear to suggest that these are indeed extremely challenging times for the police service.

However, there are also some other interesting countervailing developments within the social and cultural landscape of policing in England and Wales. Statistics from a recent Crime Survey for England and Wales indicated that the percentage of those who think that their local police were doing a good or excellent job had risen from 47% in the year ending March 2004 to 62% in the year ending March 2017 (Office for National Statistics [ONS], 2017). During 2017, we also witnessed the very positive public and media reactions to the police in the aftermath of a number of terrorist incidents in London and in Manchester (Fox and Taylor, 2017; Griffiths, 2017). This chapter will therefore consider the changing policing landscape over recent years which has faced the challenges of, like many other public services, a reduced workforce, an increased workload and increasing efforts to pursue an agenda of 'professionalisation'. The changing external policing environment will be considered alongside the changing internal policing cultures which together perhaps form a 'new policing identity'.

Hales and Higgins (2016) have identified four major national changes that have impacted upon policing in recent years—remit, governance, values and austerity—which will provide a useful framework for identifying the changing political and economic policing landscape. This chapter will address each of these. However, it will also argue that a changing social and internal policing landscape has also played a significant role in shifting the real and assumed boundaries of police work and has impacted upon a further, relatively neglected area of police reform, that of policing cultures. It will do this by also drawing on some of my own recent research, namely a four-year longitudinal research project of new recruits to the police service which examined the changing identities and changing cultures of police officers and the policing organisation (Charman, 2017).

The Changing Political and Economic Landscape of Policing

The Police Reform and Social Responsibility Act (2011) fundamentally altered the governance arrangements between police forces, local police authorities and central government. This legislation purported to end an era of unaccountable local police authorities and centrally determined targets in favour of a more localised, accountable form of governance through publicly elected police and crime commissioners (PCC) for each force area. The public, however, greeted this dawn of enhanced local accountability with very little enthusiasm (although they were provided with very little information), as shown by a 15% turnout at the first elections in 2012 and a 27% turnout at the second elections in 2016 (Electoral Commission, 2013; Electoral Commission, 2016). The advent of PCCs fundamentally shifted the balance of power in the tripartite relationship of chief constable, central government and local police authorities (replaced by PCCs) much more away from chief police officers and towards PCCs. The Home Office (representing central government) significantly withdrew from the relationship, ending both their setting of national targets and their involvement in disputes between the other two parties. The outcome of this withdrawal is that the powers of PCCs to develop local crime and policing plans, as well as their role in appointing and terminating the contracts of chief officers, meant that the power dynamics lay very much in the direction of these newly elected public figures. To further enhance their sovereignty, the introduction at the same time of police and crime panels (not dissimilar to the original local police authorities themselves), which were designed to scrutinise the decisions of the PCC, have been frustrated by poor levels of funding, high member turnover and limited powers (Lister, 2014).

These fundamental changes to police governance arrangements and target setting came at exactly the same time as substantial and ongoing budgetary cuts to the police service. Hales and Higgins refer to the police service losing "the twin comfort blankets of being told what was most important, and being given more resources to deliver on it" (2016, p. 7). Most of the funding for each police force in England and Wales is obtained from a central government grant with the additional monies raised from council tax. Nationally, this council tax revenue makes up almost a quarter of police expenditure, although this varies from force to force (Johnston and Politowski, 2016). After a sustained period of investment, the police service in England, Wales and Northern Ireland saw budgetary cuts of 22% in real terms between 2010 and 2016. This amounted to a £2.2 billion budget reduction (National Audit Office, 2015). In terms of workforce reductions, this amounted to a loss of 37,400 staff from March 2010 to March 2015. This was accounted for by a 12% reduction in police officers and a 20% reduction in police staff (Johnston and Politowski, 2016). Forces dealt with the cuts in different ways, but one force, Norfolk Constabulary, took the decision to remove the role of police and community support officer in its entirety (Norfolk Constabulary, 2018).

There were widely predicted estimates of 20%–25% further cuts expected at the 2015 Autumn Statement and Spending Review from the then Chancellor of the Exchequer, George Osborne. However, following the coordinated terrorist attacks in Paris in November 2015 resulting in 137 deaths, the chancellor announced that there would be real-term protection for police funding and no further cuts (Osborne, 2015). Since that and subsequent announcements on police funding, there has been criticism of the claims made by the Conservative government that police funding was actually increasing. In 2016 and again in 2018, the Statistics Authority have twice conversely identified a *decrease* in central government grants where it had been suggested by the government that there was an increase (Dilnot, 2016; Norgrove, 2018). Additionally, Her Majesty's Inspectorate of Constabulary (HMIC) published one of their annual police effectiveness, efficiency and legitimacy reports, which highlighted a 'deep-red warning flag' over various aspects of policing, including investigation and neighbourhood policing (HMIC, 2017a, p. 4). There was concern from HMIC over decisions being taken, such as not arresting people, that were "the unintended consequence of changes that forces have made, often in response to the challenge of austerity" (HMIC, 2017a, p. 5). Controversially, Policing Minister Brandon Lewis denied that the funding cuts were a contributing factor and instead argued that "forces still clearly have more work to do . . . I expect to see rapid improvements" (Lewis, 2017).

Individual police forces have in the past not always favoured public criticism of government strategies (Savage, Charman, and Cope, 2000), but funding cuts have changed this with some chief constables making statements about insufficient budgets (Rayner and Hope, 2017), others, including the commissioner of the Metropolitan Police, turning to social media (Perraudin and Travis, 2017), and Avon and Somerset Constabulary entitling their report on organisational threats 'The Tipping Point', arguing that these are "perilous times" (2017, p. 3). One reason for these dramatic claims from within policing, as we shall now see, relate not only to a decrease in funding but also to an increase in both the demands and the complexity of policing modern Britain.

The Changing Social Landscape of Policing

Tabloid newspaper reporting and opinion polls measuring fear of crime suggest that the public believe rates of UK crime continue to rise inexorably. However, official crime data from either the Crime Survey for England and Wales (CSEW) or from the discredited, but nonetheless useful, police recorded statistics appears to show that crime as a whole has been falling since the mid-1990s and now remains relatively stable (ONS, 2018). What the overall crime data hide, however, is the enormous change that has taken place within crime categories and the emergence of new forms of crime that have previously not been counted.

Although more traditional acquisitive crimes such as burglary and theft have seen a steady decline since the mid-1990s, in more recent years crimes involving violence and sexual offences have been rising (ONS, 2018). Although impacted by changes to recording rules plus a surge in reporting following a number of high-profile non-recent sexual abuse allegations, police recorded statistics in the area of sexual offences show an increase of 157% from 2003 until 2017 (ONS, 2018). In the same period, violent crime as a whole had seen a rise of 90% (ONS, 2018). In addition to rises in certain categories of crime, there are also newer categories of crime to be considered.

The CSEW has been asking questions to the public about their experiences of fraud and cyber-enabled crime only since 2015–16, and this remains experimental data. What these tentative figures already reveal, however, is the seemingly huge migration from 'traditional' acquisitive crime to cyber-enabled and cyber-dependant crime. Figures from the 2018 victim-based CSEW show that of the 10.6 million offences taking place in the year ending December 2017, 4.6 million of them were fraud or cyber-enabled crime (ONS, 2018). In terms of other types of offences, the police are dealing with a significant rise in the online sharing of indecent images (Child Exploitation and Online Protection [CEOP], 2013), nearly 6000 active organised crime groups in the UK (National Crime Agency [NCA], 2017) and an estimated 10,000–13,000 victims of human trafficking in the UK (HM Government, 2017), to name but a few areas.

All of these fluctuations in crime frequency and crime types will inevitably have an impact on the demand for policing services and the focus for the police service. This also has to be considered alongside the changes to police officer numbers as outlined above. However, the College of Policing has suggested that 999 emergency calls to the police fell by 23% from 2006/7 until 2013/14 at the same time as police-recorded crime was also falling (College of Policing, 2015). Even taking into account the continuing drop in police officer numbers, the more considerable fall in police-recorded crime meant that if recorded crime was to be taken as the tool for measuring police activity, we have seen a decrease in the number of recorded crimes per officer since 2003 (College of Policing, 2015). However, what this particular measure does not take into account is the changing complexity of the crimes and 'harms' that are now coming to the attention of the police. The National Police Chiefs' Council (NPCC) has argued that we must look beyond 'calls for service' as an indicator of the demands placed upon the police and instead consider demand to be categorised into three distinct areas—public demand, protective demand (both of which could be aligned with reactive and proactive policing styles) and internal demand (NPCC, 2017).

What we have also witnessed, therefore, has been a change in response and focus from the police towards these new types of crime in terms of both approach and language towards what the priorities of the police are. Although, as discussed earlier in this chapter, PCCs are now responsible for the setting of local crime plans for each force area, there is still remarkable consistency between these plans (Hales and Higgins, 2016). The focus for the police is moving away from high-volume crime and its reduction towards low-volume but high-harm offences which have remained relatively hidden from the public gaze (Higgins and Hales, 2016). This would include child sexual exploitation, domestic and sexual abuse, human trafficking, organised crime and terrorism. The activities associated with policing now focus much more upon managing risk, harm, threat and vulnerability. Fraud, however, is still not a focus of local police force activity. Although there are other national bodies such as the National Crime Agency and the Department for Work and Pensions who are involved in the investigation of fraud, less than 1% of police officers are dedicated to this area of criminal activity (Button et al., 2014).

Much of the discussion above has been in relation to the types and forms of criminal activity that the police are involved with and called to respond to. However, a concentration on crime neglects a considerable and growing area of policing demand for local police forces. Research from the College of Policing (2015) indicates that *non-crime related incidents* account for 83% of all 'command and control' calls that come into call centre staff. Additionally, based upon data received from a small number of forces, it is suggested that 'public safety and welfare' incidents now make up the largest category of reported incidents to the police, more than both crime and anti-social behaviour. What this demonstrates is that the demands upon policing organisation are seemingly going in two directions—on the one hand towards a more complex and largely hidden area of low-volume, high-harm offences and on the other hand towards a high volume of non-crime related incidents. This could be considered a *bifurcation of policing activities*.

As part of my research into changing police landscape and officer culture, I interviewed two cohorts of new police officers four times over a period of four years to understand more about the process of identity formation and occupational socialisation (Charman, 2017). One area of questioning surrounded their views of the challenges to policing. A particular concern of the majority of the new recruits was the amount of already limited resources that were being taken up by incidents that were not felt to be policing matters. This particularly revolved around issues that the police felt should be dealt with by other agencies, most notably social services. There were two particular areas of concern from the respondents: missing people and mental illness. Officers were aware of the concerns of sexual exploitation that are attached to missing persons and understood the necessity of their actions.

However, they also expressed frustration at a system which required the statutory reporting of missing older teenagers, particularly from residential care and often only when late returning back, where there was no evidence of any concerns (Charman, 2017).

Research published by the National Crime Agency would support the view from the new police officers that this type of police work involves considerable time. Data received from 42 English and Welsh police forces indicated that there were 375,694 people reported as missing or absent in 2015–16, a 23% increase since 2012–13 (NCA, 2017). Although there are variations across the country, this equates to 917 missing or absent people per day per force. There are disproportionately high numbers of 12–17 year olds who are reported as missing or absent, and this age group is not permitted to be graded as low risk and not requiring immediate action. Of the incidents of missing or absent children, 59% are repeat cases (NCA, 2017).

Estimates from the Independent Commission on Mental Health and Policing suggested that 20% of police time is accounted for by mental illness issues, rising to 40% if the definition is widened to vulnerable people more generally (2013). In his annual review of policing, HMIC Chief Inspector Tom Winsor referred to the police service being used as the 'first resort' for people with mental health problems (HMIC, 2017b, p. 8).

'Failures to act' have been added to wrongful convictions as a significant contributory factor in miscarriage of justice cases (Savage, 2007). Whilst 'failure to act' for social services or for NHS hospital accident and emergency departments would mean not informing the police of an absconded patient or a missing teenager, this then translates to an 'obligation to act' for the police on all incidents that are passed down the line to them. This 'obligation to act' is governed by the fear of what might happen should inaction follow. There are very limited further options for the police in passing these incidents on to any other agency. In many situations, the 'line' goes no further than the police.

Although relationships between the emergency services are generally viewed by the practitioners themselves as positive (Charman, 2013, 2014), there are considerable statutory and non-statutory requirements on these and other services to reduce crime and protect the public which add to the demand placed upon the police. According to the College of Policing, these protective statutory requirements, such as Multi-Agency Public Protection Arrangements (MAPPA) and Multi-Agency Risk Assessment Conferences (MARAC) have increased significantly, and growth is expected to continue (College of Policing, 2015). Additionally, the Policing and Crime Act 2017 places a 'high level duty to collaborate' on all three emergency services in the pursuit of efficiency and effectiveness and additionally allows PCCs to take on the responsibilities of the fire and rescue authority. Partnership work and collaboration is increasingly being called for within the broad remit of policing services (Karn, 2013). These arrangements add to the demands and complexity of policing organisations.

Alongside the changes to crime, the focus upon managing risk, harm, threat and vulnerability plus the changing demands placed upon the police service, the organisation is also undergoing changes to its own internal landscape. Part of this is a requirement to react to the issues discussed within this and the previous section. But, as the following section will demonstrate, very significant elements of these changes are derived from a rather different source—the drive to 'professionalise' the occupation and thereby move it from being considered a 'trade' or 'craft', with its associated 'artisan status', to being considered a 'profession'.

The Changing Internal Policing Landscape

It is not the intention of this chapter to discuss at length the propensity of the police service to regularly seek to re-invent itself through an official or unofficial 'professionalisation' agenda. The issue of the 'professionalisation' or 're-professionalisation' of the police has been extensively discussed by Simon Holdaway (Holdaway, 2017, and in the present volume). However, it is important to acknowledge that many of the police reforms are centred on this debate. The College of Policing (CoP), the professional body for policing, was established in 2012. The CoP is responsible for standards within policing including the Code of Ethics, the broad education and training of police officers and the 'What Works Centre for Crime Reduction'. It remains, however, a challenge to encourage forces to comply with both statutory codes and best practice guidance in addition to a more general lack of acceptance of the work of the College (House of Commons, 2016). One area of significance which the CoP has responsibility for is the Police Education Qualifications Framework (PEQF) which is currently being implemented. What is required by the PEQF is that at entry level, all new recruits are expected to either complete a police constable degree apprenticeship, a specific pre-join professional policing degree or, for existing graduates, a graduate conversion programme.

The PQEF has been a long time in the making. There has long been a desire on the part of various governments to secure a role for higher education institutions to support the development of new police recruits. This was seen very clearly in the Flanagan Review of Policing commissioned by the Labour government and published in 2008 and the Neyroud Review of Police Leadership and Training commissioned by the coalition government and published in 2011. Both called for closer relationships between the police and higher education institutions (Flanagan, 2008; Neyroud, 2011). The basis for this argument appears to come from two strands.

First, it is argued that the type of learning which police officers require to operate in the modern world is that most closely associated with the learning that takes place within a university setting. Second, it is argued that 'similar' professions, such as nursing and education, not only require its new recruits to have a university degree but to have financed this degree themselves before application and selection (Flanagan, 2008). Neyroud specifically recommended a pre-entry national qualification with delivery being split between HEIs which would focus upon the wider context of policing in society and police training centres which would focus on more practical policing skills (2011).

The potential ramifications of these proposals are significant and cannot be speculated upon here. There were, however, concerns around reducing the diversity and accessibility of the police service, including from minority ethnic communities, older applicants and those with caring responsibilities (Tong and Halenberg, 2017). At the time of writing, there are still considerable ongoing negotiations between the CoP and the higher education sector, but there is no doubt that change will occur.

The importance of a police workforce capable of addressing the complex needs of its population, as outlined above, cannot be underestimated. As Loveday has noted, this should not always be conceptualised in terms of police numbers alone; police leadership "must adequately differentiate between police *capacity* and police *capability*" (2017, emphasis as in original). In a digital era characterised by greater mobility and migration, a focus on the requisite skills to police a complex and fast-changing world are essential. But, as this chapter has already discussed, while there has been a movement of attention from high-volume routine crime towards low-volume and high-harm (and less visible) offences, there has also been a change of focus to low-level social problem policing which is characterised by its non-criminal nature. This *bifurcation of policing activities* calls for a close consideration of what the role of the police actually is and what the public (and various other stakeholders) expect from the service.

According to Higgins and Hales (2016), the effectiveness of the police relates very much to what the public wants the police to achieve. They point to two schools of thought in this regard. First, there is the crime reduction goal which focuses upon the measuring of outputs and 'what works'. Second, there is the increasingly popular reference to how legitimate the police are in the eyes of those who are policed. The goal here is the social legitimacy of the police, measured through a public confidence agenda and focused upon the principles of community policing. Their own conclusions, based upon a four-year action research project, were firmly in favour of the latter approach with limited police resources being targeted at specific locations, engaging with partner agencies and seeking to engage the community through legitimate policing practices.

From a relatively straightforward legal and organisational perspective, the police are tasked with the maintenance of law and order, the protection of the public and their property, and the detection, investigation and prevention of crime. But we also know that the realities of policing involve a much less clearly defined role, indeed a much less crime-focused role which concentrates upon dispute management, order maintenance and welfare concerns. Bittner's often quoted account of what the police do is as relevant today as when it was first written. Police officers find themselves responding to and intervening regularly in situations. This is a reactive response to events and represents "something-that-ought-not-be-to-happening-and-about-which-somone-had-better-do-something-now" (Bittner, 1990, p. 249).

The public sector cuts that were felt from 2010 onwards in the fields of health and social care and mental health services brought into sharp focus the enormous range of non-crime-related activity which the police are associated with. Brodeur (1983) has distinguished between two policing tasks—'high policing' and 'low policing'. 'High policing' is perhaps more readily associated with the role of the police that is often portrayed in fictional crime dramas and indeed by the police themselves when engaged in the cultural storytelling that is often a feature of their profession. This involves intelligence-related policing activities which utilise both human and technological intelligence apparatus. 'Low policing' refers to the more mundane day-to-day reality of much of the policing role, which focuses upon responding to criminal or potentially criminal incidents, order maintenance, reassurance and community engagement.

Millie (2013) has conceptualised this further by dividing 'low policing' into 'wide policing' and 'narrow policing'. He argues that historically, but most notably since the early 1990s, the role of the police has become ever wider and encompasses the diverse and multifaceted demands of anti-terrorism, reassurance, fear of crime, catching criminals, crime prevention and crime reduction. Neighbourhood policing, reassurance policing, problem-oriented policing, zero tolerance policing and intelligence-led policing are just a few examples of the many styles of policing which the police are required to adopt depending on the political context of the time. Millie (2013) calls for a more 'narrow' definition of policing. He notes Reiner's (2000) distinction between *preserving* social order and *producing* social order and maintains that the latter could well be passed to other agencies. Millie stops well short of Theresa May's version of 'narrow policing' (when in the role of home secretary) with her demands for the police to be "tough, no-nonsense crime-fighters" (May, 2011) but argues that by considering the police as *one of a group* of agencies associated with social control rather than *the only group* responsible for social control, there is the potential for less conflict over policing priorities and for less role confusion due to a reduced range of activities (Millie, 2013).

If there is confusion about the extent and limits of the policing role, there is also confusion over who the officers are to perform those roles. A House of Commons Home Affairs Committee report indicated that government pledges to protect 'front-line policing' were hampered by poor and unsatisfactory definitions from HMIC of what the 'front-line' actually constituted (Home Affairs Select Committee [HASC], 2011). A subsequent report from HMIC (2011) outlined its interpretation of 'front-line' policing (which included visible and non-visible, available and non-available staff), but the term appears to be loosely interpreted and poorly understood.

My recent research (Charman, 2017) of new recruits to the police service found an interesting change in the perception of these new officers towards their role. Officers were interviewed four times over the course of the first four years serving as police constables. One group of questions sought to understand their views on what they felt was the role of the police. Their answers fell broadly into three categories. First, there were roles associated with crime such as apprehending offenders, making arrests, gathering evidence and crime reduction. Second, there were wider public service sentiments about public protection, visibility and reassurance. Third, there was the more specific role of 'helping' and safeguarding vulnerable people, whether this was due to their status as a victim of crime or in their inherent vulnerability due to their age or their mental ill health. At the initial stages of this research, there was more adherence from the new recruits to the notions of crime fighting, crime prevention and catching criminals. But those narratives about the role of policing changed throughout the course of the research so that, after four years in the job, for example when asked about the role of the police, 85% of the statements made concerned vulnerability and safeguarding, up from 16% in the first few weeks of their job. Likewise, statements about the role of the police being crime-related fell from 35% at the time of the first interview to 9% at the time of the fourth and final interview.

This dramatic change from a focus on the role of the police as concerned with crime and the broad principles associated with public protection to a role focused specifically on vulnerability appears to be a reflection of three mutually dependent factors. First, there is the changing role of the police which has not only become wider and more diverse (Millie, 2013), incorporating both the preservation and the production of social order (Reiner, 2000), but has also been affected by budgetary cuts elsewhere within the public and care sectors. Second, there is the changing realisation from the new recruits of what the role of the police *actually* entails. Many of them initially felt that their role was to 'improve society', but the more time they serve, the greater the 'reality shock' as to the limits of their influence, the nature of the more regular activities that they are involved with and the limits of their time. The level of disappointment at the perceived gap between the expectations of the job and the realities of the job has the potential to produce a more cynical, suspicious, alienated officer who displays lower levels of empathy and higher levels of authoritarianism (Charman, 2017). There is therefore a third explanation as to why the recruits express such a dramatic change in their views on the role of the police and that is influenced by the appearance of cynicism. There is a strong and growing sense of cynicism from officers which is displayed regularly and knowingly as their length of service increases. This has the capacity to influence their attitudes towards both their work and the public that they respond to. This issue of cynicism appears to one of the most long-standing and geographically widespread features of policing cultures. It has been found in research which has spanned decades (Reiner, 1978, 2010; Crank, 1998; de Lint, 1998; Scripture, 1997; Loftus, 2008, 2009), is identified in most corners of the globe (Crank, 1998; Chan, 2003; Steyn and Mkhize, 2016; Sollund, 2008) and is exhibited in both verbal behaviour and in written blogs (Atherton, 2012).

The changing external political and social landscape of policing combined with the internal response to those changes has the potential to impact considerably upon the identities and cultures of those working within the organisation. Loftus (2009) suggested that subtle changes in policing cultures were disguising much more persistent and steadfast elements of the occupational culture. There is indeed research evidence which points to those enduring themes (Kiely and Peek, 2002; Christensen and Crank, 2001). However, to suggest that there is continuity within policing culture not only suggests that there has been no change but precludes the *opportunity* for cultural change. Chan (1997) argues that any successful theory of police culture must take into account the possibility for change and not just opposition to change. The following section analyses that potential for change within policing identities.

Changing Policing Identities

The identity of policing as an organisation and of officers working within that organisation is inevitably affected by the political, economic and social landscape of policing which has been discussed in this chapter. It is also affected by the changing internal landscape of policing. But policing has a significance beyond the actual realities of the organisation and its work. The British police (whether fairly or unfairly, whether negatively or positively) are without doubt a dominant symbolic and cultural icon in the UK, and that status has not diminished despite vast social, cultural and political change. In a similar vein to the royal family, both newspaper editors and TV programme commissioners know that policing in its factual and fictitious forms fascinates and excites the public. The public hold a firm belief in *their* ownership of the British police and in their desire to maintain its supposed historic status as the guardians of public order—the 'thin blue line'.

Loader (1997) is one of a handful of policing scholars who has attempted to reinvigorate the *sociology* of policing and has in particular focused upon the strong position held by the police with regard to their symbolic power. Drawing upon the work of French sociologist Pierre Bourdieu's work on symbolic power, Loader has sought to evaluate the significance of policing as a cultural category. Bourdieu's analysis of symbolic power is that whilst it is invisible, it is nonetheless an active agent in the relationships between those who exercise power and those who submit to that power (Bourdieu, 1991). This is not necessarily a harmonious relationship but a continual struggle whereby different groups are attempting to impose their definitions of the social world upon the social order. This struggle is based not only on words but also upon the power of symbolism.

Symbolism and symbolic power are an active and not a static process and play a role in the maintenance of social order. According to Durkheim, what is essential to the building of solidarity amongst groups is the sharing of this symbolic system (1893/1984). Symbolism therefore has a social function in addition to a dividing function. Where there is an 'out-group' (in the case of the symbolic power of the police, this would be those who seek to undermine the consensus and order established by the police), there is also an 'in-group' (in this case the police acting to protect the public from harm). When that dominant culture in the form of the police has the symbolic power associated with order, stability and morality, then all other subcultures will struggle for acceptance. The police do not have to coerce and manipulate the public into an acceptance of their position as the moral guardians of social order. Whilst attempts are made by policing bodies to portray and promote policing in a positive light, they are assisted by strong historical, cultural and fictional icons and artefacts which all contribute to the strength of the symbolic power of British policing.

It should not be forgotten, however, that within this seemingly benign symbolic status of the police lie other voices that therefore are not heard or are ignored. Where the police voice is deemed legitimate, other voices will be deemed illegitimate. Where the police claim to offer an inclusionary vision for all citizens, there will also be those who are excluded. It is for this reason therefore that a consideration of the cultures of the police, of their either static or changing identities, those working on a day-to-day basis with members of the public, is so vitally important. Manning has argued vociferously that policing studies has become too preoccupied with 'fixing' policing, too close to the police themselves and too willing to research whatever is recently fashionable in policing circles (2010). The result of this has been "too much on the police and too little on the context or culture of policing" (Manning, 2010, p. 100). So the question therefore must be asked, Has the changing external and internal political, economic and social landscape of policing changed the dominant cultures within policing or do they remain immutable and steadfast, characterised in much of the literature in the area as being dominated by exclusion, discrimination and prejudice?

Findings from the research focused upon new recruits to the police service indicate that cultural change did appear to be apparent (Charman, 2017). The research revealed officers who were keen to learn, not necessarily through more formal learning channels but more notably from their peers and their tutors. It revealed officers who were motivated to make a difference but frustrated by their inability to do so. It revealed officers who have close bonds with one another but who, unlike their predecessors, tend to equate policing with a 'job for now' rather than a 'job for life'. It also revealed officers who place 'public protection' and 'safeguarding' at the forefront of their role and, with that, seek to utilise the tools of communication and empathy rather than physical strength and authority. These selected results are, I would suggest, the new and enduring cultural characteristics of policing at the lower ranks— *cynicism, communication, comradeship, code of self-protection, categorisation* and *compassion.*

More recent police recruits bring with them not just demographic diversity but also a diversity of experiences and cultures. They also adhere much less to the narrative of their identity as a police officer defining who they are. They are therefore as likely to be influenced by their previous pre-police experiences and their future non-police experiences. Change might therefore be slow, incremental and potentially largely unnoticeable, but change will nonetheless be occurring.

Table 10.1 The enduring and emerging characteristics of policing—adapted from Charman (2017)

Cynicism	The new recruits highlighted cynicism as something that they observed in other colleagues and also were aware of as a growing feature of their own identities. After four years, 100% agreed or strongly agreed that police officers were cynical. Cynicism functions to provide a recognisable language to other group members, to provide an exclusive and shared humour which cements the group's boundaries and strengthens the group's bonds, and can be used as a technique to cope with the nature of the job itself and the nature of the disappointment about the job.
Communication	The research demonstrated that either when officers were provided with a list of attributes to choose from or when asked to discuss the key skills associated with being a 'good' police officer, communication came out on top. It was not simply acknowledged the most important skill associated with policing or the most important characteristic of a police officer, it was also regularly highlighted by the new recruits as a feature of their policing style which was most effective.
Comradeship	The most positively referred to characteristic of policing cultures was comradeship. It was cited as a reason for joining the police in the first place, and when the new recruits were questioned about the aspects of the job that they were most enjoying, 'team-work' came out as one of three answers, including job variety and working with victims. It must be noted, however, that the benefits of comradeship that a new recruit might take advantage of are not entirely freely given. The established workforce offer solidarity and with it, the ability to 'watch your back'. In exchange for that, the new recruits must 'fit in' with the working culture of the organisation.
Code of self-protection	The new recruits disagreed with this traditional notion of protecting fellow officers—often referred to as the 'blue code of silence'. There are two opposing explanations for why this might be the case. First, it could be argued that police officers become more sophisticated in their 'storytelling' to 'outsiders'; that they become more politically aware of the dangers of betraying the more negative aspects of a policing culture. Second, it could also be argued that the changing nature of policing has had an effect. The changing structures of policing in relation to accountability means that there is now a heavy focus upon professional standards, the routine escalation of complaints, a fear of 'doing the wrong thing' and a fear of little to no management support when things do go wrong. This can be coupled with a changing social environment of policing. This is characterised by a lack of tolerance for unacceptable policing behaviours and a belief in integrity, which was mentioned frequently by the new recruits as a feature of a 'good' police officer. This would appear to indicate that the traditional 'blue code of silence' seems to have been replaced by 'the blue code of self-protection'.

(Continued)

Table 10.1 (Continued)

Categorisation	As is a regular occurrence within organisations with high levels of solidarity, where there is an 'in' group, there will also be an 'out' group. Police officers engage in categorisation in a variety of ways. There was the potential for anyone (external or internal to the policing organisation) to be part of the 'them'. Externally, the new recruits referred to the public, the media, social services and other parts of the criminal justice system as being an occupational challenge. Internally, the new recruits identified a sharp divide portrayed between police officers on the 'front line' and more senior police managers whom they perceived to be 'different' because of their role, their lack of understanding of the issues faced by more junior police officers and the perceived lack of support in difficult circumstances. This tendency towards categorisation is also seen when officers are discussing the public that they are policing. Officers sharply delineate between what they see to be 'deserving' and 'undeserving' victims—using the label of 'genuine victims' to describe those who fulfil the normative criteria of what it is to be an ideal-type victim of crime (e.g. being vulnerable, often older, female and 'hard-working').
Compassion	In an article entitled 'Passionate Professionals', Maurice Punch has argued that there is a further story to be told about officers who are "driven by concern and compassion for the victims and their relatives" (2016, p. 27). There is evidence here to begin that story. The new recruits cited community service principles or as they termed it, 'making a difference', as the key motivator for joining the police service and indicated that this an aspect of the job that they were most enjoying. The skills that they felt were the most important for a police officer to possess and indeed the skills that made a 'good' police officer were all related to the themes of empathy, understanding, integrity and compassion.

Future Challenges

This chapter has indicated that change is apparent across all aspects of the police service. Fundamental political and economic change within the service and within the frameworks of policing governance have created a more localised, less target-driven approach to policing but one that is inevitably struggling with both a reduced budget and a reduced workforce. In isolation, these changes would already be considered significant. However, these changes are occurring within the wider context of further considerable change. A long and continuing period of austerity, driven by the Coalition and Conservative governments of 2010, 2015 and 2017, has disproportionally affected the levels of spending of local government and public services more generally, which in turn has impacted significantly upon the police. As mentioned earlier in this chapter, whilst the police have generally been recognised as the 'service of last resort', they are also now increasingly being used as the 'first resort' (HMIC, 2017b, p. 8). This difficult period in terms of increasing non-crime-related workload has been combined with fundamental changes to not only types and patterns of offending behaviour but also to the more hidden locations of offending and public sensibilities of harm and vulnerability. This *bifurcation of policing activities*, as discussed earlier in this chapter, has resulted in a police service under considerable strain. Sajid Javid's address to the Police Federation conference as home secretary in May 2018 marked the first acknowledgement of this strain from a Conservative minister in many years and may herald the beginning of a new and less fraught relationship between the Conservatives and the police service (Javid, 2018). If we acknowledge the complexities that this bifurcation of policing activities may bring, then inevitably there needs to be a close consideration of what the role of the police actually is and what the public want from the service.

The misinformed belief in the fundamental role of the police to engage in the 'fight against crime' impacts negatively in two different ways. First, it impacts upon the public when that fight is never won, in terms of both their levels of satisfaction in the police and their rational and irrational levels of fear of crime. Second, it impacts upon the police themselves, who struggle to embrace the more routine aspects of the police role, who attempt to downplay the important social function of policing and who act to reframe their identity with more crime-fighting narratives.

The overall pattern is confusing and multifaceted. On the one hand lies the cultural symbolism of the police, which is influenced by a number of sources. It is held in the abstract beliefs of the public. It is found in the media representations of policing, both fictional and non-fictional. It has been encouraged by various governments (Loader refers to the UK coalition government of 2010–2015 seeing itself as "releasing the police's inner crime-fighter" (2014, p. 43)). It is also found in the physical icons of policing. On the other hand, there are the changing realities of the policing role. How the identities of an organisation are constructed and developed is in an interpretation of these meanings, which we can see are attributed to policing from a large variety of sources. The interpretation of these meanings is part of the sensemaking of the police occupational culture (Rantatalo, 2016). Making sense of this confusion, during this period of considerable change, is an ongoing negotiation for police officers. However, although this period of upheaval can be an organisational and individual challenge, it does appear to indicate something more fundamental. What we must consider perhaps is that the changing political, economic and social landscape of policing, coupled with internal organisational change and a new perspective on policing cultures, may together form the beginnings of a 'new policing identity'.

All of this takes us back to the work of Higgins and Hales (2016) in their consideration of the effectiveness of the police, which relates so closely to what the public want the police to achieve. As discussed earlier in this chapter, they point to two schools of thought in this regard. First, the goal of crime reduction and second, the goal of social legitimacy. The legitimacy of the police is not only influenced by the *outcomes* of police actions but crucially in the *processes* that lead to those outcomes. This then shifts the focus strongly from a more quantifiable measure of policing effectiveness to an emphasis much more on the social and cultural aspects of legitimacy in policing—an emphasis on *procedural justice*. Enhancing police legitimacy is no easy task. The police are being asked to wage an unwinnable war ('fighting crime') with largely unworkable tools (e.g. 'the power to arrest'). A change in focus to an emphasis on the social and cultural aspects of legitimacy in policing and around what it means to be a police officer and what it means to be effective as an organisation is not necessarily something that is supported or encouraged either externally from those controlling the police or internally from those managing the police. That, perhaps, remains the challenge for both.

References

Atherton, S. (2012). Cops and Bloggers: Exploring the Presence of Police Culture on the Web. *Internet Journal of Criminology*. Retrieved from https://media.wix.com/ugd/b93dd4_e3fafc746b864462936d254a7c7251c9.pdf

Avon and Somerset Constabulary. (2017). *The Tipping Point*. Retrieved from the Avon and Somerset Constabulary website: www.avonandsomerset.police.uk/media/29964806/safe-sustainable-policing-report.pdf

Bittner, E. (1990). *Aspects of Police Work*. Boston: Northeastern University Press.

Bourdieu, P. (1991). *Language and Symbolic Power*. Cambridge: Polity Press.

Brodeur, J.P (1983). High Policing and Low Policing: Remarks About the Policing of Political Activities. *Social Problems*, 30(5), 507–520.

Button, M., Blackbourn, D. and Tunley, M. (2014). 'The Not So Thin Blue Line After All?' Investigative Resources Dedicated to Fighting Fraud/Economic Crime in the United Kingdom. *Policing*, 9(2), 129–142.

Chan, J. (1997). *Changing Police Culture*. Cambridge: Cambridge University Press.

Chan, J. (2003). *Fair Cop: Learning the Art of Policing*. Toronto: University of Toronto Press.

Charman, S. (2013). Sharing a Laugh: The Role of Humour in Relationships Between Police Officers and Ambulance Staff. *International Journal of Sociology and Social Policy*, 33(3–4), 152–166.

Charman, S. (2014). Blue Light Communities: Cultural Interoperability and Shared Learning Between Ambulance Staff and Police Officers in Emergency Response. *Policing and Society*, 24(1), 102–119.

Charman, S. (2017) *Police Socialisation, Identity and Culture: Becoming Blue*. London: Palgrave.

Child Exploitation and Online Protection. (2013). *Threat Assessment of Child Sexual Exploitation and Abuse*. Retrieved from www.norfolklscb.org/wp-content/uploads/2015/03/CEOP_Threat-Assessment_CSE_JUN2013.pdf

Christensen, W. and Crank, J. (2001). Police Work and Culture in a Nonurban Setting: An Ethnographic Analysis. *Police Quarterly*, 4(1), 69–98.

College of Policing. (2015). *College of Policing Analysis: Estimating Demand on the Police Service*. Retrieved from www.college.police.uk/News/College-news/Documents/Demand%20Report%2023_1_15_noBleed.pdf

Conn, D. (2016, April 26). Hillsborough Inquests Jury Rules 96 Victims were Unlawfully Killed. *The Guardian*. Retrieved from www.theguardian.com/uk-news/2016/apr/26/hillsborough-inquests-jury-says-96-victims-were-unlawfully-killed

Crank, J. (1998). *Understanding Police Culture*. Cincinnati, OH: Anderson Publishing Co.

De Lint, W. (1998). New Managerialism and Canadian Police Training Reform. *Social and Legal Studies*, 7(2), 261–285.

Dilnot, A. (2016). Police Grant 2016–17 [Letter written March 9, 2016 to Rt Hon Andy Burnham MP]. Retrieved from www.statisticsauthority.gov.uk/wp-content/uploads/2016/03/Letter-from-Sir-Andrew-Dilnot-to-Andy-Burnham-MP-090316.pdf

Durkheim, E. (1984). *The Division of Labour in Society*. Basingstoke: Macmillan. (Original work published 1893).

Electoral Commission. (2013). *Police and Crime Commissioner Elections in England and Wales*. Retrieved from www.electoralcommission.org.uk/_data/assets/pdf_file/0003/154353/PCC-Elections-Report.pdf

Electoral Commission. (2016). *The May 2016 Police and Crime Commissioner Elections*. Retrieved from www.electoralcommission.org.uk/_data/assets/pdf_file/0019/215074/2016-PCC-elections-report.pdf

Flanagan, R. (2008). *Review of Policing: Final Report*. London: HMSO.

Fox, A. and Taylor, J. (2017, June 29). Hero Policeman Reveals for First Time How He Fought Three London Bridge Terrorists Armed Just with his Baton. *The Mirror*. Retrieved from www.mirror.co.uk/news/uk-news/hero-policeman-reveals-first-time-10703665

Griffiths, E. (2017, June 5). A Dancing Policeman Stole the Hearts of One Love Manchester Viewers. *Radio Times*. Retrieved from www.radiotimes.com/news/2017-06-05/a-dancing-policeman-stole-the-hearts-of-one-love-manchester-viewers/

Hales, G. and Higgins, A. (2016). *Prioritisation in a Changing World: Seven Challenges for Policing*. London: The Police Foundation. Retrieved from The Police Foundation website: www.police-foundation.org.uk/publication/prioritisation-in-a-changing-world/

Haria, R. and Turvill, W. (2015, July 28). Jailed for More than 20 Years: The Sources Convicted of Selling Stories to Journalists. *Press Gazette*. Retrieved from www.pressgazette.co.uk/jailed-more-20-years-sources-convicted-selling-stories-journalists/

Her Majesty's Inspectorate of Constabulary. (2011). *Demanding Times*. London: The Stationery Office.

Her Majesty's Inspectorate of Constabulary. (2017a). *PEEL: Police Effectiveness 2016, a National Overview*. Retrieved from www.justiceinspectorates.gov.uk/hmic/wp-content/uploads/peel-police-effectiveness-2016.pdf

Her Majesty's Inspectorate of Constabulary. (2017b). *State of Policing: The Annual Assessment of Policing in England and Wales*. Retrieved from www.justiceinspectorates.gov.uk/hmic/wp-content/uploads/state-of-policing-2016.pdf

Higgins, A. and Hales, G. (2016). Cutting Crime in the 21st Century: Informed Proactivity in the Midst of Social and Organisational Change. London: The Police Foundation. Retrieved from The Police Foundation website: www.police-foundation.org.uk/uploads/holding/projects/changing_world_paper_1.pdf

HM Government. (2017). *2017 UK Annual Report on Modern Slavery*. Retrieved from https://assets.publishing.service.gov.uk/government/uploads/system/uploads/attachment_data/file/652366/2017_uk_annual_report_on_modern_slavery.pdf

Holdaway, S. (2017). The re-professionalization of the police in England and Wales. *Criminology & Criminal Justice*, 17(5), 588–604

176   Sarah Charman

Home Affairs Select Committee. (2011). *The New Landscape of Policing*. London: The Stationery Office.
House of Commons. (2015, March 12). *Written Statement (HCWS381) made by The Secretary of State for the Home Department*. Retrieved from www.parliament. uk/documents/commons-vote-office/March%202015/12%20March%202015/31. HOME-Undercover-policing.pdf
House of Commons. (2016). *College of Policing: Three Years On*. Retrieved from https://publications.parliament.uk/pa/cm201617/cmselect/cmhaff/23/23.pdf
Independent Commission on Mental Health and Policing. (2013). *Independent Commission on Mental Health and Policing Report*. Retrieved from www.turning-point. co.uk/media/621030/independent_commission_on_mental_health_and_policing_main_report.pdf
Javid, S. (2018). *Home Secretary Police Federation Speech 2018*. Retrieved from www.gov.uk/government/speeches/home-secretary-police-federation-speech-2018
Johnston, N. and Politowski, B. (2016). *Police Funding*. House of Commons Library Briefing Paper 7279. Retrieved from http://researchbriefings.parliament. uk/ResearchBriefing/Summary/CBP-7279
Karn, J. (2013). *Policing and Crime Reduction: The Evidence and its Implications for Practice*. London: The Police Foundation. Retrieved from The Police Foundation website: www.police-foundation.org.uk/uploads/holding/projects/policing_and_crime_reduction.pdf
Kiely, J. and Peek, G. (2002). The Culture of the British Police: Views of Police Officers. *The Services Industries Journal*, 22(1), 167–183.
Leveson, B. (2012). *Leveson Inquiry—Report into the Culture, Practices and Ethics of the Press*. Retrieved from www.gov.uk/government/publications/leveson-inquiry-report-into-the-culture-practices-and-ethics-of-the-press
Lewis, B. (2017). *Response to HMIC Report*. Retrieved from https://homeofficemedia. blog.gov.uk/2017/03/02/response-to-hmic-report/
Lister, S. (2014). Scrutinising the Role of the Police and Crime Panel in the New Era of Police Governance in England and Wales. *Safer Communities*, 13(1), 22–31.
Loader, I. (1997). Policing and the Social: Questions of Symbolic Power. *British Journal of Sociology*, 48(1), 1–18.
Loader, I. (2014). Why do the Police Matter? Beyond the Myth of Crime-Fighting. In J. Brown (Ed.), *The Future of Policing* (pp. 40–51). London: Routledge.
Loftus, B. (2008). Dominant Culture Interrupted: Recognition, Resentment and the Politics of Change in an English Police Force. *British Journal of Criminology*, 48(6), 756–777.
Loftus, B. (2009). *Police Culture in a Changing World*. Oxford: Oxford University Press.
Loveday, B. (2017). *The Worrying State of Policing in England and Wales after Seven Years of Austerity*. Retrieved from http://blogs.lse.ac.uk/politicsandpolicy/policing-in-england-and-wales-2017/
Manning, P. (2010). *Democratic Policing in a Changing World*. Boulder: Paradigm Publishers.
May, T. (2011). Speech to the Conservative Party Conference. Retrieved from www. politics.co.uk/comment-analysis/2011/10/04/theresa-may-speech-in-full
Millie, A. (2013). The Policing Task and the Expansion (and Contraction) of British Policing. *Criminology and Criminal Justice*, 13(2), 143–160.
National Audit Office. (2015). *Financial Stability of Police Forces in England and Wales*. HC 78, London: NAO. Retrieved from www.nao.org.uk/wp-content/uploads/2015/06/Financial-sustainability-of-police-forces.pdf

National Crime Agency. (2017). *National Strategic Assessment of Serious and Organised Crime*. Retrieved from www.nationalcrimeagency.gov.uk/publications/807-national-strategic-assessment-of-serious-and-organised-crime-2017/file

National Police Chiefs' Council. (2017). *Better Understanding Demand—Policing the Future*. Retrieved from www.npcc.police.uk/2017%20FOI/CO/078%2017%20 CCC%20April%202017%2024%20Better%20Understanding%20Demand%20 Policing%20the%20Future.pdf

Neyroud, P. (2011). *Review of Police Leadership and Training*. London: Home Office. Retrieved from www.gov.uk/government/publications/police-leadership-and-training-report-review

Norfolk Constabulary. (2018, March 29). *Police Chief Pays Tribute to PCSOs as 2020 Plans Take Effect*. Retrieved from www.norfolk.police.uk/news/latest-news/ 29-03-2018/police-chief-pays-tribute-pcsos-2020-plans-take-effect

Norgrove, D. (2018). [Letter written March 20, 2018 to Rt Hon Louise Haigh MP]. Retrieved from www.statisticsauthority.gov.uk/wp-content/uploads/2018/03/ Police-Funding-DN-to-Louise-Haigh.pdf

Office for National Statistics. (2017). *Crime in England and Wales: Annual Supplementary Tables*. Retrieved from www.ons.gov.uk/peoplepopulationandcomm unity/crimeandjustice/datasets/crimeinenglandandwalesannualsupplementary tables

Office for National Statistics. (2018). *Crime in England and Wales: Year Ending December 2017*. Retrieved from www.ons.gov.uk/peoplepopulationandcommunity/ crimeandjustice/bulletins/crimeinenglandandwales/yearendingdecember2017 #main-points

Osborne, G. (2015). *Chancellor George Osborne's Spending Review and Autumn Statement 2015*. Retrieved from www.gov.uk/government/speeches/chancellor-george-osbornes-spending-review-and-autumn-statement-2015-speech

Perraudin, F. and Travis, A. (2017, June 20). Cressida Dick Calls for More Money for the Met after Terrorist Attacks. *The Guardian*. Retrieved from www.theguardian. com/uk-news/2017/jun/20/cressida-dick-calls-for-more-money-for-the-met-after-terrorist-attacks

Punch, M. (2016). *Passionate Professionals: The Dutch Police Response to the Shooting Down of Malaysian Airlines' MH17 in the Ukraine. (2014)*. Paper presented at the Third International Conference on Law Enforcement and Public Health. Amsterdam: The Netherlands. Retrieved from https://cleph.com.au/application/ files/1115/2641/9027/Passionate_Professionals_MH17_rev_30_09_mp.pdf

Rantatalo, O. (2016). Media Representations and Police Officers' Identity Work in a Specialised Police Tactical Unit. *Policing and Society*, 26(1), 97–113.

Rayner, G. and Hope, C. (2017, September 12). Police Chiefs Claim they will have to Cut Bobbies on Beat to Pay for 2% Pay Award. *The Telegraph*. Retrieved from www.telegraph.co.uk/news/2017/09/12/breaking-government-announces-end-1-per-cent-cap-public-sector/

Reiner, R. (1978). *The Blue-Coated Worker*. Cambridge: Cambridge University Press.

Reiner, R. (2000). *The Politics of the Police* (3rd ed.). Oxford: Oxford University Press.

Reiner, R. (2010). *The Politics of the Police* (4th ed.). Oxford: Oxford University Press.

Savage, S. (2007). Putting Wrongs to Right: Campaigns Against Miscarriages of Justice. *Criminology and Criminal Justice*, 7(1), 83–105.

Savage, S., Charman, S., and Cope, S. (2000). *Policing and the Power of Persuasion*. London: Blackstone Press.

Scripture, A. (1997). The Sources of Police Culture: Demographic or Environmental Variables? *Policing and* Society, 7 (3), 163–176.

Sollund, R. (2008). Tough Cop-Soft Cop? The Impact of Motivations and Experiences on Police Officers' Approaches to the Public. *Journal of Scandinavian Studies in Criminology and Crime Prevention*, 9(2), 119–140.

Steyn, J. and Mkhize, S. (2016). 'Darker Shades of Blue': A Comparison of Three Decades of South African Police Service Culture. *SA Crime Quarterly*, 57, 15–26.

Tong, S. and Halenberg, K. (2017). Education and the Police Professionalisation Agenda: A Perspective from England and Wales. In C. Rogers and B. Frevel (eds.) *Higher Police Education: An International Perspective*. London: Springer International.

11 From Extreme to Mundane? The Changing Face of Paramedicine in the UK Ambulance Service

Jo Brewis* and Richard Godfrey

Introduction

Although management and organisation studies (MOS) has paid little attention to the occupation, there is an enormous literature on paramedics and paramedicine in other disciplines. Unsurprisingly, most of this focuses on timely, successful and cost-effective pre-hospital care, "the technical and physical aspects of varying trauma management" (Williams, 2013a, p. 512). Still, a considerable number of studies do consider paramedics' experience of their occupation. On the whole these represent it as a form of 'extreme work' (Granter et al., 2005)—physically and psychologically risky, perhaps traumatic; intensely effortful; fast-paced and target driven; ethically demanding; based on problematic shift patterns; carrying an unpredictable workload; and having a persistently low status amongst healthcare occupations.

In this chapter we begin by outlining this representation. We then discuss the significant changes in UK paramedicine in more recent times. In particular, the last 15 years have seen a marked movement away from a 'scoop and run' model, where critically ill or injured patients are stabilised before a dramatic lights and sirens race to an emergency department, to a 'treat and refer' or 'treat and discharge' approach. In part, this reflects the increasing trend for 999 calls to the English ambulance service being made for or by people with mental health problems, social care needs, minor injuries and/or symptoms of chronic conditions, rather than emergency cases. At the same time, demand for ambulances increases year on year—so much so that volunteer first responders are now routinely used across the country.

To address these challenges, new paramedicine specialisms are emerging, including those where incumbents deliver primary healthcare. The scope of the profession is also expanding more generally to encompass community-based assessment, management and treatment of patients. The most recent example at the time of writing is new legislation enabling paramedics to independently prescribe medication for their patients (College of Paramedics, n.d.). Moreover, the route into UK paramedicine has changed. Currently,

* Correspondence E-mail ID: joanna.brewis@open.ac.uk

the minimum entry qualification is a higher education diploma, and the first diploma graduates are now entering the profession. However, in March 2018, the Health and Care Professionals Council ratified a recommendation from their Education and Training Committee to raise the threshold level of qualification for entry as a paramedic to degree level. This will come into effect from 2021 (Health and Care Professionals Council, 2018).

After mapping these changes, we review preliminary findings as to the new demands they pose for paramedics, and conclude by tracing some of the ways in which MOS researchers could address significant gaps in the literature on this rapidly changing occupation. These build on already-established MOS concepts such as workplace emotions, occupational stress and dirty work. Research of this kind is important because of its implications for understanding how changes to paramedic work may affect job satisfaction, retention and—of course—patient care.

Paramedicine as an 'Extreme' Occupation

As we have suggested, the overwhelming representation of paramedicine in the extant literature is of an extreme form of work, with very high injury and fatality rates, as well as excessive rates of medical retirement compared to other healthcare jobs. For example, Bentley and Levine (2016) suggest levels of ill health and poor fitness rose significantly amongst US paramedics between 1999 and 2008. One reason for this high occupational risk is that paramedics may be working on patients with infectious diseases, with needles and bodily fluids and in scenarios like natural disasters and terrorist attacks (e.g. Corman, 2017; Garus-Pakowska et al., 2017a, 2017b). Equally, paramedicine is physically demanding and ergonomically problematic, involving a lot of lifting, stretching, twisting and bending, often in cramped conditions like the back of a moving ambulance or in patients' homes. Loading and unloading patients into and from ambulances is often carried out solo in urgent situations due to time pressures; and obese, non-cooperative or unconscious patients pose especial challenges during stretcher transfer. As such, musculoskeletal disorders are very common amongst paramedics (e.g. Fischer et al., 2017; Garus-Pakowska et al., 2017b; Prairie et al., 2017). Equally, patient transport is often undertaken at high speed, involving drivers who may be tired from shift work. Paramedics also frequently need to eschew seatbelts whilst attending to patients in transit. And wearing seatbelts carries ergonomic risks because of the need to physically compensate by tensing within the restraint when the ambulance decelerates or accelerates (e.g. Maguire and Smith, 2013; Arial et al., 2014).

Another risk factor in paramedicine is vicarious trauma—the work necessitates proximity to life-threatening injuries, illnesses and death, sometimes on a mass scale and often with a patient's family or other bystanders watching triage and treatment efforts (e.g. Brady, 2015; Clompus and Albarran, 2016). Paramedics are also commonly the targets of violence from patients and their families and bystanders—including intimidation, sexual harassment, and verbal, physical and sexual assault (e.g. Corman, 2017; Maguire et al., 2018; van Erp et al., 2018). Taylor et al. (2016, p. 156) suggest male paramedics especially may under-report such violence for fear of appearing weak. This connects to claims around the masculinist occupational culture of paramedicine, discussed later. They add that female paramedics can be seen as soft targets, and that many of their US respondents see violence as part of the job, perhaps not warranting an official report. And yet these respondents felt largely untrained for such risks. Research by Boyle and McKenna (2016, 2017) amongst Australian paramedic students also indexes violence experienced during placements, adding that these respondents often failed to disclose this because they worried about the career repercussions.

Furthermore, paramedicine involves working on patient, bystander and one's own emotions, to ensure patients remain as calm as possible, receive excellent medical care and feel listened to. As Ahl and Nyström (2012, p. 34) suggest, paramedics therefore need to be able to "deal with patients' vulnerability, anxiety and suffering". Similarly, Ayub et al.'s (2017) study of US paramedics identified challenges associated with "family-member presence and providing information to the family during interventions" (p. 233) when treating children. As for the paramedics themselves, emotional processing can continue afterwards, especially following distressing cases (e.g. Wireklint Sundström and Dahlberg, 2012; Avraham et al., 2014). Unlike staff in emergency departments, paramedics also typically work in small teams and lack the information, equipment or medication available in hospitals (e.g. O'Hara et al., 2015; Harenčárová, 2017). Relatedly, research identifies the ethical challenges involved in decisions around resuscitating or treating end-of-life patients (e.g. Tataris et al., 2017; Leibold, 2018; Waldrop et al., 2018) or working in rural areas, where the paramedic may know the patient or their relatives, so managing professional boundaries becomes difficult (e.g. Jervis-Tracey et al., 2016; Pyper and Paterson, 2016). Likewise, self-harming patients present specific dilemmas of balancing their right to refuse treatment with "the state's interest in the preservation of life" (Rees et al., 2017, p. 65).

Further, paramedics are shift-workers who have to be constantly alert, responsive and flexible because their workload is largely unpredictable. They have to be "prepared for the unprepared" (Wireklint Sundström and Dahlberg, 2012, p. 573), and of course the decisions they make—often in conditions of significant uncertainty—can be a literal matter of life and death (Corman, 2017; Harenčárová, 2017). Relatedly, fatigue is predictive of levels of depression, anxiety, stress, burnout and post-traumatic stress disorder (PTSD) amongst paramedics. Early morning starts, split shifts, night shifts and quick turnovers between shift patterns are especially problematic in this respect.

Ambulance service performance targets and their potentially inimical effects are also noted as potential stressors. One example from the UK is 'Call Connect', introduced in August 2008 to NHS ambulance trusts in England and Wales. This required ambulance services to respond to 75% of life-threatening 'category A' calls in 8 minutes, and 95% of urgent 'category B' calls in 19 minutes. The clock started when the call was routed to the ambulance dispatch team. Perverse outcomes have been reported as a result, like a paramedic suggesting *"As an ambulance service if you get to a patient in 8 minutes and if they die, you succeed; but if you get there in 9 minutes and the patient survives, you fail"* (quoted by Wankhade, 2012, p. 385, original emphasis). Equally, sometimes rapid-response vehicles, driven by a single paramedic, were dispatched and recorded as hitting the response target quickly, but the nature of the patient episode may involve a further wait for a dual-staffed ambulance to enable transportation. Paramedics often describe being alone with a patient for long periods, such as Anne's experience of 90 minutes waiting for an ambulance, when the patient was "completely grey, had no radial pulse, [and I] couldn't get a line in cos he was completely shut down" (quoted in Clompus and Albarran, 2016, p. 4). More recently, the Ambulance Response Programme sets out revised response 'standards', but these are actually tighter than those in Call Connect. Category 1, to patients with life-threatening illnesses or injuries, require a response within 7 minutes on average; and category 2 calls to emergency cases within 18 minutes (Webber, 2017).

Time is a factor in another sense. Corman quotes 'Jake' on the subject of medical assessment on arrival at a scene: "We're trying to play a chess match, [to think] 3, 5 moves ahead. . . [it's] contingency planning all the time. The what-ifs" (2017, p. 608, original brackets and ellipsis). And, if paramedics don't have detailed or reliable information from dispatchers, they need to assess emergency patients especially extremely quickly to decide on a care pathway (e.g. Fjeldheim et al., 2014; O'Hara et al., 2015). The pressure of targets can mean less time to spend with patients, whether at the scene or handing over at the emergency department, which UK targets suggest should be done within 15 minutes (Clompus and Albarran, 2016). Simpson et al. (2017) report accounts from paramedics whereby delays in 'off-loading' at hospital affect transportation decisions, the severity of a patient's condition notwithstanding. Their respondents also talked about receiving 'welfare checks' from dispatch when they were nearing the performance indicator of 20 minutes at a scene, regardless of the patient's medical needs. They perceived these as 'hurry ups'. Similarly, McCann et al. (2013) suggest their paramedics were hurried back out to answer calls immediately after handing patients over to emergency department colleagues.

Additionally, the literature on paramedicine as an occupation discusses its persistently low status, identifying a lack of respect from other healthcare professionals and patients alike, a view that paramedics provide little more than a patient transportation service and their perceived lack of influence at work (e.g. Hansen et al., 2012; O'Hara et al., 2015). In the UK, McCann et al. (2013) suggest that, despite ever-increasing clinical expectations, paramedicine's recognition as a profession in 2000, a legally protected title and the 2009 establishment of a professional association, "paramedics are still struggling to secure those meaningful forms of status, occupational closure, and work autonomy associated with other emerging professions" (p. 751). As regards autonomy especially, the paramedics' fear of litigation or making errors, and/or feeling unsupported by their managers, meant they often self-limited their behaviour at work. For instance, one respondent discussed the records he keeps of explanations for departing from standard protocol, such as a recent memo on oxygen administration. These participants were also constantly under technological surveillance whilst on the road, via radio connections to base and remote monitoring of the position of ambulances.

It is therefore unsurprising that several studies investigate the incidence of drug and alcohol abuse, depression, anxiety, burnout, post-traumatic stress symptoms and full-blown PTSD among paramedics (e.g. Pilgrim et al., 2016; Luftman et al., 2017; Regehr and LeBlanc, 2017). An online survey, conducted by MIND as part of their Blue Light programme, saw 69% of UK ambulance service personnel reporting work-related mental ill health. Thirty-nine per cent suggested they would be treated negatively at work should they disclose this (College of Paramedics, 2016). Stanley et al. (2016, p. 26) observe that, vicarious trauma aside, the occupational experiences of paramedics "may also lower [their] fear of death", so they are more likely to consider, attempt or succeed in suicide. Of course they also have access to "highly lethal suicide means" (ibid.). The MIND survey found that 35% of respondents had considered suicide because of occupational stress (College of Paramedics, 2016). In contrast, Brady (2015, p. 32) suggests being "constantly reminded of death, dying, human fragility and their own mortality" makes paramedics more prone to death anxiety than those in other caring jobs. He claims students in particular may feel unable to reveal death anxiety to colleagues for fear of appearing weak.

Other work examines factors said to affect paramedics' vulnerability to mental ill health, such as gender, educational level, length of service, level of resilience, confidence in coping with stressful situations, social and organisational support, sense of occupational purpose, being involved in mass casualty events and surviving childhood abuse (e.g. Michael et al., 2016; Rybojad et al., 2016; Stanley et al., 2016). Coping strategies of varying effectiveness are also discussed, including debriefings; venting negative emotions; peer or management support; counselling; disassociation, detachment, denial and compartmentalisation; telling war stories; black humour and banter; and unburdening to family and friends (e.g. Boyle, 2005; Charman, 2013, 2014; Ogińska-Bulik and Kobylarczyk, 2015; Tangherlini, 2000).

Equally, there are claims around the 'tough guy' or 'John Wayne' culture in paramedicine, despite it being a caring profession. This is said to create challenges for paramedics because of the emphasis on emotional control during calls and 'back-stage' (e.g. Williams, 2012, 2013a, 2013b; Avraham et al., 2014; Stanley et al., 2016). Boyle's (2005) study of Australian paramedics suggests this culture may mean those who express distress or 'inappropriate' emotions to colleagues are ostracised or harassed. She underlines the tensions here: "As part of their duties as 'caring' paramedics, the . . . on-road staff are expected to perform as emotionally complex individuals while simultaneously adhering to a strict hegemonically masculinist code of conduct" (p. 49). There is other evidence of a poor employment culture in paramedicine, including bullying, intimidation and sexual harassment of female paramedics by their colleagues (Bigham et al., 2014).

Altogether, paramedics emerge from this occupational research as quantitatively and qualitatively overloaded. As well as the personal costs of physical and psychological ill health, the literature emphasises employer costs around sick days, early retirement and labour turnover plus the negative effects on performance and patient outcomes. A reader of the preceding pages might therefore think incumbents in this profession are in terrible distress. However, as this chapter will go on to show, UK paramedicine is changing fairly radically and in many ways is becoming increasingly advanced as its professionalisation project expands. The portrayal of ambulance services as sites of extreme work is—in many important ways—becoming less and less accurate.

Paramedicine as a Changing Occupation

From Secondary to Primary Care

One very commonly cited statistic from the Department of Health's (2005, p. 8) *Taking Healthcare to the Patient* review of the ambulance service is that only 10% of 999 calls involve life-threatening cases. The review asserts that

> Many patients have an urgent primary (or social) care need. This includes large numbers of older people who have fallen in their homes (around 10% of incidents attended), some with no injury; patients with social care needs and mental health problems; and patients with a sub-acute onset of symptoms associated with a long-term condition such as diabetes, heart failure and chronic obstructive pulmonary disease (around a further 10% of incidents attended).

Indeed in England during 2013–2014, something like a third of 999 calls to the ambulance service saw the patient being assessed and treated where necessary at the scene, with no transfer elsewhere in the NHS resulting (Quigg et al., 2017, p. 365). The Department of Health review also suggests demand on the British ambulance service is rising by 6%–7% annually due to an ageing population; public confusion over alternatives to calling 999, like NHS 111 and urgent care centres; reduced out-of-hours provision by GPs; and under-recruitment of GPs and fewer healthcare workers per se (e.g. Andrews and Wankhade, 2014; Evans et al., 2014; O'Hara et al., 2015).

Indeed, as Armstrong et al. (2012, p. 64) suggest, "Some patients who are marginalised by ill health and/or financial burdens use the ambulance service instead of their general practitioner". These groups are often referred to in the literature as 'superusers'. Scott et al. (2014) undertook a systematic review of literature focusing on superusers. Common themes were that they have not suffered any trauma but instead call an ambulance because of an existing medical problem. Scott et al. remark that it is nonetheless important not to demonise superusers because they actually have complex health and social care needs. Ford-Jones and Chaufan (2017) agree, emphasising the need to scrutinise claims that the increasing number of 'mental health calls' represent an abuse or misuse of emergency healthcare provision. Otherwise, we fail to acknowledge that what look like mental health problems might actually be *"reasonable* responses to increasing social exclusion, as the neoliberal state retreats from providing more basic social services toward promoting expanding opportunities for capital accumulation" (p. 3, original emphasis).

Specialisation in Paramedicine

In order to address these demands on the ambulance service and improve patient care, new specialisms in paramedicine are developing, such as critical care paramedics, advanced care paramedics, intensive care paramedics, emergency care practitioners, community paramedics and extended care paramedics. These specialists are trained to a higher level or in a wider skill set. In the UK, they work in GPs' surgeries, nursing homes, emergency departments, minor injury units, urgent care centres and walk-in clinics as well as pre-hospital emergency care (e.g. Evans et al., 2014; O'Hara et al., 2015; Simpson et al., 2017; Bennett et al., 2018). Critical, advanced or intensive care paramedics are trained in procedures like fracture or joint reduction, surgical airways, ultrasounds, central venous access, thoracotomies and thoracostomies. The intention is to reduce preventable pre-hospital mortalities and ease the burden on other healthcare services. The community-based roles—emergency care practitioners, community paramedics and extended care paramedics—fill gaps in primary care provision, identify and treat low acuity patients, provide preventative care like cervical smear tests and health promotion, look after patients with mental health problems or drug impairment and provide on-site medical care for those in residential homes. They are said to be especially useful in rural areas with little access to out-of-hours primary or emergency care, where no other primary medical care exists locally and where higher levels of smoking, obesity, substance abuse and serious injury are likely (e.g. Mulholland et al., 2014; Choi et al., 2016; O'Meara et al., 2016).

Overall, these specialisms move paramedicine from the 'scoop and run' approach of stabilising critically ill or injured patients and transporting them to definitive care towards providing more 'wrap around' healthcare in situ. Indeed, the occupation's scope of practice is widening across the board, so generalist paramedicine increasingly involves community-based assessment, treatment and management per se, without further referral where possible (e.g. Heath and Wankhade, 2014; Wankhade and Brinkman, 2014; O'Hara et al., 2015). However, as observed by management and organisational scholars in research on many workplace settings undergoing change, these changes are also creating unexpected outcomes and knock-on effects. As paramedics are increasingly drawn into unplanned primary care in particular, many report concerns that their critical care skills are deteriorating. This last observation leads us to the new landscape of paramedic experience.

Changing Demands in Paramedicine

With the shift to more primary care provision especially, there are some intriguing if under-developed findings about paramedicine which describe the challenges this creates. In a development not dissimilar from those explored in policing by Bacon and by Charman in the present volume, Campbell and Rasmussen (2012) suggest their Canadian paramedics did not want to deal with patients' psychosocial issues and expressed concern that their duties had expanded to include 'a lot of social work, counselling', as one put it (pp. 93–94). Examples included patients with addictions or mental health problems and vulnerable elderly people. These respondents felt the skill sets required for paramedicine and for social work were too divergent 'to be done well simultaneously' (p. 94). Equally, Prener and Lincoln (2015, p. 613, original ellipsis) cite Mannon's observation that

> bringing into the healthcare system those who otherwise would not get there, giving care and attention to the neglected and forgotten . . . the counterpart of the social worker in the field of health care seems to be the urban EMT[1] and paramedic.

Similarly, McCann et al.'s (2013) UK ethnography found that paramedics are now being called more frequently to patients who are drunk or high on drugs, and that the level and intensity of the abuse to which they are subject have risen as a result. These paramedics said they are often 'left to sweep up' in particular cases because they might be the only emergency service available (p. 767). Also in the UK, Clompus and Albarran (2016, p. 4) discuss their paramedics' reactions to non-emergency calls to patients with mental health issues, social needs or substance use problems. Carol remarked,

> I still have to go on blue lights to a fall . . . someone on the floor who is not usually hurt . . . there's a great gap in the system where nobody picks up [*these*] people . . . So they send an ambulance . . . I get really angry thinking "why are you wasting all our time?"
>
> (original ellipses, emphasis and brackets)

Ann, relatedly, talks about losing her compassion when she is called out to patients who are drunk and won't cooperate. Taylor et al.'s (2016, p. 157) US paramedic and EMT respondents made similar comments, referring to being treated as a taxi to hospital for non-emergent cases, and even being called out to help somebody to reach a remote control. They say there are no repercussions for callers who abuse the system, and that these people don't seem to realise that emergency medical staff have to respond to all 911 calls in the same way—i.e. driving at full speed, with lights and sirens. As we have discussed, transport of this kind is risky in and of itself. Similarly, Boyle (2005) says most of the calls her paramedics dealt with were non-urgent, especially during the day and the early part of night shifts. These required high levels of emotional labour, especially surface acting—like maintaining a neutral expression to entice intoxicated patients into the ambulance. Like the respondents in Clompus and Albarran's study, Boyle's paramedics expressed discomfort about dealing with non-urgent cases, describing elderly patients as 'humpers' or 'geries' (2005, p. 53) or likening the work involved to taxi driving, as did Taylor et al.'s participants.

On the other hand, Corman (2017) discusses how some calls may necessitate persuading a patient that they *do* need to be transported to the emergency department. Julie talked about

> a fellow who's having a heart attack and he refused to go, and my way to convince him was I said, "Well I'll just stand here and wait for you to die then. And then when you die (pause) I'll have all the consent I need. And I will zap you back to life and then I'll take you to hospital." . . . I had to be the biggest bitch to get him to go to the hospital with me.
>
> (p. 618, original brackets and ellipsis)

Strategies for this vary, Corman adds, so at other times being very charming is more appropriate. The situation is complicated by the fact that these Canadian paramedics have limited discretion to leave patients at home/on scene, seemingly regardless of the severity of their condition. Nonetheless, again they differentiate between 'good' or 'holy hairy' and 'shit' or 'bogus' calls which might involve a spot that has burst or trapped wind (Corman, 2017, 2018). Jake also remarked that he much preferred night shifts because "you don't get the BS that you get during the day" (2017, p. 619), like answering calls for nursing home patients.

In a much earlier study, this time from the US, Palmer (1983) calls his paramedic respondents 'trauma junkies' because "calls involving multiple casualties, physical trauma and fast-paced action were deemed to be the 'real work' of emergency medical services personnel. Calls evoking less sophistication of response behaviour are devalued" (p. 162). Palmer talks of the 'high' that 'real work' produced because it allowed the paramedics to use their most advanced skills and preserve the most 'extreme' part of the occupational self-image. Donnelly et al. (2015) agree that emergency medical services personnel tend to be thrill seekers. They quote one EMT as saying, "There's nothing cooler in this world than a Ford F350 Ambulance driving code three[2] . . . the wrong way down a two way street as people look at you in awe is really cool" (Brian, p. 216, original ellipsis). Klee and Renner (2013) also suggest paramedics may have a 'rescue personality', including a predilection for risk taking. On the other hand, Palmer cites respondents discussing 'pukes', where calls involve a patient who may literally be vomiting but equally could be exaggerating the severity of their symptoms. He quotes Metz to the effect that these calls are seen as "nonessential calls, abuse calls, nothing calls, non-emergency calls, and nuisance calls" (p. 167). Like Boyle and Clompus and Albarran, Palmer suggests paramedics resent such calls and may even become hostile, handling patients roughly or assessing them carelessly. In such conditions, paramedics' storytelling and griping about an undeserving public, pointless call-outs and illogical, risk-averse call prioritising sounds very similar to what is shown in dozens of studies of 'police culture' (see Charman, this volume).

However, the only studies we located which foreground these issues are the aforementioned work by Prener and Lincoln (2015) and research on Australian paramedics by Simpson et al. (2017). Prener and Lincoln's US paramedics and EMTs saw many patients with mental health problems. These participants report that patients often smelled bad due to alcohol consumption or incontinence, say, as well as having to keep their guard up lest patients became combative. They also questioned whether cases involving patients with psychiatric issues represented actual emergencies. One respondent suggested, "If a homeless alcoholic is found—there's nothing really wrong with him. I do not know who's supposed to take care of that guy, but definitely not us" (p. 616). As Prener and Lincoln point out—echoing others—where patients are labelled as misusing or outright abusing the system this may affect the treatment they receive. Some respondents said they were less compassionate with these patients. They were also aware, however, that onlookers could react badly to this, with one commenting,

> When I walk up to that guy and go "hey, get in" . . . [bystanders] don't know that that's probably the second time I've taken him today and the last time I took him he shit all over himself and the stretcher, so it's not good for anybody. It doesn't put a good image forward for EMS, and we're not actually helping [the patient].
>
> (p. 617, original ellipsis and brackets)

Respondents also said attending to these patients meant ambulances were sometimes not available for real emergencies, and—like Taylor et al.'s participants—felt responding to 'psych' calls reinforced that it is acceptable to call 911 in these instances.

Turning to Simpson et al. (2017), despite acknowledging that Australian paramedicine increasingly involves attending non-emergent patients, their respondents still regarded 'high acuity', 'good' or 'sexy' calls as 'legitimate' work. One commented,

> generally as ambulance practitioners, we like the blood and guts and gore and the glory jobs and the front page of the paper jobs and . . . the routine stuff where picking people off the floor can be a little bit—it's not glamorous, it's not fun, there's no adrenalin rush involved in it.
>
> (p. 5)

These calls are described as 'frustrating', 'annoying' and 'routine', and—once more—as possibly taking staff away from 'real work' (p. 8). The wider point Simpson et al. make, echoing Prener and Lincoln, is that these perceptions of what real paramedicine is explain whether a specific call is deemed legitimate. This then informs how staff approach each case. On the other hand, some participants reported a felt need to 'cover their arses' by taking all patients to hospital so they would not be "hung out to dry"—the "you call, we haul" approach (p. 9). Granter et al. (2018) discuss the complexities of the ambulance responder role in terms of the 'edgework' involved in navigating between the desire for interesting, worthwhile, high acuity patient episodes on one side and the need for an easier, less demanding shift on the other.

Like the overwhelming majority of 'police culture' studies, much of the above literature portrays ambulance work as retaining a lot of its traditional blue-collar work culture. But that culture is changing fast. The recent introduction of a higher education degree route into paramedicine is now producing its first graduates. Kennedy et al. (2015), noting the paucity of research on students transitioning into the profession, emphasise the lack of attention during degree programmes to the emotional impact of this occupation (also see Williams, 2012, 2013a, 2013b). They observe a generalised anxiety about the job's demands in interviews with new Australian graduates, also noting their desire to 'fit in'. Many feel a sense of separation from their older, more experienced colleagues, who—they think—expect graduates to enter fully equipped for everything paramedicine can throw at them. Simpson et al.'s (2017, p. 6) participants also talked of lacking education in managing older fallers, and educators in the sample confirmed this. As such, a belief that these cases were not 'real work' was reinforced by this gap in their training, which carried over into inattention to a recent protocol introduced to support decision-making during such calls.

Ross et al. (2016, p. 2) suggest media representations of paramedicine are influential in perpetuating the stereotype of "lights, sirens, and dramatic resuscitations". Their study of Australian paramedic students concludes that these participants chose their degree based on wanting to help people, but also having an exciting career and saving lives. Again, this points to a potential gap between what entrants expect and the realities of the occupation. And O'Meara et al. (2016, p. 7, original ellipsis) quote a Canadian paramedic educator in Ontario as follows:

> A lot of people who come into my program are looking for the lights and sirens and trauma and excitement, and when we start talking about something with a slower pace in community paramedicine, then we take them back . . . a lot of students sort of walk in the door going, I want to drive fast, lights and sirens and car crashes and all that good stuff, and when you say, well in actual fact that's about five percent of your career, 95 percent of your career looks much more like community paramedicine.

Having now established what seems to be the new face of contemporary paramedicine, in the UK and elsewhere, we now discuss how MOS scholars can contribute to what is as yet an understudied set of occupational demands.

Discussion

Johnston and Acker (2016, p. 3) suggest stereotypes of the paramedic include trauma junkies, rescue personalities, silent heroes and lifesavers, yet also index "the shift towards low acuity patient pathways and primary care interventions". They remark that, as the profession changes, there is a real need to question these images in terms of the professional identities of contemporary paramedics. It is precisely this kind of research which MOS scholars are well-equipped to undertake. We now identify some key directions in this regard.

Emotions

Academic literature on emotions and organisations is potentially highly relevant to the pre-hospital field. While emotional distress and emotional regulation are widely associated with emergency work, there are also some other avenues of research that are also germane but less typically associated with ambulance work. For example, the literature on emotions and organisations is now paying more concerted attention to boredom as an emotion with workplace implications. Skowronski (2012), for example, identifies consequences of workplace boredom, including alcohol abuse, lower job satisfaction, absenteeism, reduced performance and counterproductive behaviours. He develops a theoretical framework to research coping strategies, focused on how workers look to raise their levels of stimulation. It rests on classifying boredom as a stressor. These coping strategies, Skowronski suggests, may have positive and negative effects on organisations, and he singles out worker autonomy as a potentially important mediator.

Van Hooff and van Hooft (2014) also develop a theoretical framework of the consequences of workplace boredom, differentiating between bored behaviour as a response and the consequences of boredom (including depression and counterproductive behaviours). For them, bored behaviour is unlikely to ameliorate boredom. Something which they think will have this effect, however, is 'job crafting'—the ability to change the boring characteristics of one's work, which has clear parallels with autonomy. Similarly, Mael and Jex (2015) develop a model for assessing both antecedents and consequences of boredom at work. Their starting point is that boredom "has been called a socially devalued emotion, one considered trivial by others. . . [which] is also likely to elicit little managerial sympathy and may be blamed on the employee himself or herself" (p. 132). But they suggest it nonetheless generates 'maladaptive' responses including job dissatisfaction, accidents and counterproductive work behaviours. Mael and Jex provide a multifaceted definition of boredom, distinguishing between 'episodic' and 'chronic' boredom, for example, as well as 'situational' (specific to certain job stimuli, say) and 'global' (much more pervasive in an individual's life) boredom.

Our first observation is that these psychologistic models of workplace boredom are ripe for application to paramedicine, for example to assess whether they can be used to analyse aspects of its shift towards more primary and social care. Skowronski's (2012) claim that some jobs allow much less leeway for interest enhancement seems germane here, as this seems to be increasingly true of paramedicine. Van Hooff and van Hooft's (2014) suggestion that job crafting comprises a positive way to ameliorate workplace boredom is unlikely, on the other hand, to be relevant because paramedics typically have almost no discretion in deciding which calls they answer. Mael and Jex (2015) imply that episodic boredom—which might well be experienced in response to non-emergent calls in paramedicine, and which they say characterises police work—is probably less harmful. However, expectations play a significant role here, so workers may "experience considerable boredom when jobs do not always live up to expectations" (p. 145). The nascent literature on how paramedics experience non-emergent calls and some of the material on paramedic education suggest these were not the sorts of cases they hoped for or expected. Equally, Simpson et al. (2017, p. 7) identify the possibility of "getting 'burnt out' on low acuity work". They also point out that assuming such calls are routine is risky for the patient because it could well produce "a cursory examination, poor information gathering, and sub-optimal clinical decisions".

The second observation is that more sociologically informed studies of emotions and organisations have had little or nothing to say about workplace boredom (for a notable exception, see Phillips (2016) on boredom in the police service). Some work has been done on emotional labour and associated concepts in paramedicine (e.g. Boyle, 2005; Williams, 2012, 2013a, 2013b), but this largely understands the occupation as extreme. We see an interesting opportunity here to explore emotional labour and emotion work in more depth as they relate to non-emergent cases.

Occupational Stress

In their systematic review of research testing the job demand-control model, Häusser et al. (2010) establish that the additive effects of job demands and job control predict both job satisfaction and emotional exhaustion. Job demands include time pressure, quantitative or qualitative overload, role conflicts and physical and emotional demands. Job control (which roughly overlaps with autonomy) encompasses someone's ability to use particular skills at work, but also decision authority—"the extent to which a person is autonomous in task-related decisions, such as timing and method control" (p. 3). The model proposes that high-demand, low-control occupations will produce higher levels of stress and lower well-being, and vice versa. Paramedicine is particularly interesting in this regard because it can combine qualitatively high workload—tasks which are difficult in themselves—with episodes of quantitatively high workload on busy shifts. But it also requires its incumbents to manage the transition from dealing with a trauma case, say, to one where an elderly person has fallen, as well as coping with stop-start work flow. As such, paramedicine appears to generate highly variable emotional, not to say physical, demands, often within one shift, as our discussion of boredom also indicates.

More than this, however, paramedics continue to have some opportunity to use the skills they were trained in—i.e. treating emergent patients—but this is not the case across the board. They also report dealing with cases for which they feel significantly under-prepared, like Prener and Lincoln's (2015) 'psych' calls. Equally, they have almost no decision authority when it comes to timing—in particular how quickly they have to answer a call, although they often retain discretion (sometimes considerable levels of discretion) over how long they spend on scene or the duration of patient handover. The complexities of the job demand-control model as it applies to paramedicine therefore warrant further investigation.

Another interesting concept in the occupational stress literature is what Semmer et al. (2015) describe as illegitimate tasks, which "do not conform to what can appropriately be expected from someone in terms of his or her role" (p. 33). They suggest illegitimate tasks have received little attention in this discipline and report the results from their empirical investigations of this phenomenon. Semmer et al. are careful to point out that tasks become illegitimate when employees feel they should not be doing them. They also differentiate between tasks which are categorised as unreasonable—seen to lie outside the worker's occupational ambit, expertise, authority or experience—and tasks which are categorised as unnecessary, perhaps because of organisational inefficiencies. One central point is that "illegitimate tasks affect one's professional identity, and thus, the self, because role expectancies are violated" (p. 49). These findings suggest illegitimate tasks are predictive of levels of employee well-being and strain at work. Again, this concept offers an interesting avenue for occupational stress researchers to study paramedicine. Some studies suggest paramedics regard certain cases as illegitimate tasks, 'pukes', 'humpers', 'geries', 'bogus' and 'psych' calls amongst them. In other words, these are unreasonable. This perspective also connects to the literature modelling workplace boredom but takes a slightly different (although still psychologistic) approach.

Dirty Work

In Ashforth and Kreiner's (1999) influential development of Hughes' (1958, 1962) original formulation of dirty work, dirt derives from three socially constructed forms of 'taint': physical, where work is deemed dirty in itself or carried out in dangerous or unsanitary conditions; social, where workers interact with stigmatised groups or undertake menial or servile tasks; and moral, rendering the work morally repugnant or focusing on the dubious means needed to carry it out. The dirty work literature has been instructive across a broad range of occupations, including studies on professions in the same ballpark as paramedicine, such as policing, nursing and social care.

However, what is intriguing about paramedicine for dirty work researchers is the changing nature of the profession allied with what might be seen as its dirty qualities. Emergent cases could be deemed physically dirty of course, because they involve dealing with bodily fluids and excretions, blood especially. Paramedics can also work in very risky situations and are vulnerable to violence. But there is also the dirt which may attach to the bulk of their workload, the cases which involve, to reprise Prener and Lincoln's (2015, p. 613) argument, "the neglected and forgotten". Hughes' (1958, p. 51, 1962, p. 7) argument that dirty work consists of socially necessary activities which most of us nonetheless disdain is relevant here, as well as McMurray's (2012, p. 127) suggestion that dirty work becomes dirty *precisely because* it involves tasks that the majority of us neither want to acknowledge nor undertake. There may well be a social taint operating in these non-emergent cases because the patients involved are indeed 'the neglected and forgotten'. As such, the work of a paramedic could be likened to that done by the Samaritans. In McMurray and Ward's (2014) study, these volunteers spoke of taking calls from people who had been banned from accessing public services like community mental health provision and had no other avenue for expressing their distress.

Equally, paramedics may resent the physical dirt entailed in treating non-emergent cases. Recall, for example, the remark made by one of Prener and Lincoln's (2015) respondents about a patient defecating on a stretcher. We suggest they may react differently to the same bodily fluid or excretion depending on the case, with emergent patients perhaps being seen as less dirty because they have a legitimate reason for their excretions as well as for the emergency call being made at all.

Conclusion

This chapter has established that research on paramedics is overwhelmingly focused on the various elements which affect the quality of pre-hospital emergency care. However, the literature that considers the experience of paramedicine as work usually presents it as an extreme occupation—fast-paced and highly time-pressured; risky; involving significant levels of vicarious trauma and the need to manage one's own and others' emotions; characterised by problematic shift patterns; involving considerable ethical decision-making; and undeservedly lacking in status. Incumbents suffer disproportionately from work-related physical and psychological complaints, and paramedicine has concomitantly high levels of occupational fatality, injury and medical retirement. Notably, very little of this occupational research has been carried out by MOS scholars.

But the profession is also moving away from the traditional 'scoop and run' model. Demands for ambulances continues to rise and, to tackle this, new critical care and community specialisms are being introduced in paramedicine. The generalist paramedic's scope of practice is also widening. There are some indications in the extant research that this poses quite different demands from those associated with emergency cases. But this theme is under-developed. There is a genuine need to understand more about how paramedics in the UK—and elsewhere—experience non-emergent calls as they make up more of their workload. This changing caseload could also have significant implications for job satisfaction (consistently reported as low), labour turnover (consistently reported as high) and patient care. MOS researchers sensitive to the qualitative complexities of the social context in which work happens (including the real and perceived roles of, for example, professional, occupational and managerial identities, and the behaviours and symbols of 'the public' or 'the street') are—we contend—ideally positioned to address these gaps in the literature as the research base on this fascinating occupation continues to grow.

Notes

1 Emergency medical technician.
2 The US term for driving with lights and sirens.

References

Ahl, C. and Nyström, M. (2012) 'To handle the unexpected—the meaning of care in pre-hospital emergency care', *International Emergency Nursing*, 20: 33–41.

Andrews, R. and Wankhade, P. (2014) 'Regional variations in emergency service performance: does social capital matter?', *Regional Studies*, 49 (12): 2037–2052.

Arial, M., Benoît, D., and Wild, P. (2014) 'Exploring implicit preventive strategies in prehospital emergency workers: a novel approach for preventing back problems', *Applied Ergonomics*, 45 (4): 1003–1009.

Armstrong, K., Akroyd, K.V., and Burke, L. (2012) 'Short reports. The role of the emergency care practitioner in the provision of health advice and promotion to patients within the UK National Health Service', *Journal of Interprofessional Care*, 26 (1): 64–65.

Ashforth, B.E. and Kreiner, G.E. (1999) ' "How can you do it?": Dirty work and the challenge of constructing a positive identity', *Academy of Management Review*, 24 (3): 413–434.

Avraham, N., Goldblatt, H., and Yafe, E. (2014) 'Paramedics' experiences and coping strategies when encountering critical incidents', *Qualitative Health Research*, 24 (2): 194–208.

Ayub, E.M., Sampayo, E.M., Shah, M.I., and Doughty, C.B. (2017) 'Prehospital providers' perceptions on providing patient and family centered care', *Prehospital Emergency Care*, 21 (2): 233–241.

Bennett, K.J., Yuen, M.W., Merrell, M.A. (2018) 'Community paramedicine applied in a rural community', *Journal of Rural Health*, 34: s39–s47.

Bentley, M.A. and Levine, R. (2016) 'A national assessment of the health and safety of emergency medical services professionals', *Prehospital and Disaster Medicine*, 31 (s1): s96–s103.

Bigham, B.L. Jensen, J.L., Tavares, W., Drennan, I.R., Saleem, H., Dainty, K.N., and Munro, G. (2014) 'Paramedic self-reported exposure to violence in the emergency medical services (EMS) workplace: A mixed-methods cross-sectional survey', *Prehospital Emergency Care*, 18 (4): 489–484.

Boyle, M. and McKenna, L. (2016) 'Paramedic and midwifery student exposure to workplace violence during clinical placements in Australia—a pilot study', *International Journal of Medical Education*, 7: 393–399.

Boyle, M. and McKenna, L. (2017) 'Paramedic student exposure to workplace violence during clinical placements—a cross-sectional study', *Nurse Education in Practice*, 22: 93–97.

Boyle, M.V. (2005) ' "You wait until you get home": Emotional regions, emotional process work, and the role of onstage and offstage support', in C.E.J. Hartel, W.J. Zerbe and N.M. Ashkenazy (eds) *Emotions in Organizational Behavior*, Mahwah, N.J: Lawrence Erlbaum.

Brady, M. (2015) 'Death anxiety among emergency care workers', *Emergency Nurse*, 23 (4): 32–36.

Campbell, H. and Rasmussen, B. (2012) 'Riding third: Social work in ambulance work', *Health and Social Work*, 37 (2): 90–97.

Charman, S. (2013) 'Sharing a laugh. The role of humour in relationships between police officers and ambulance staff', *International Journal of Sociology and Social Policy*, 33 (3/4): 152–166.

Charman, S. (2014) 'Blue light communities: Cultural interoperability and shared learning between ambulance staff and police officers in emergency response', *Policing & Society*, 24 (1): 102–119.

Choi, B.Y., Blumberg, C., and Williams, K. (2016) 'Mobile integrated health care and community paramedicine: An emerging emergency medical services concept', *Annals of Emergency Medicine*, 67 (3): 361–366.

Clompus, S.R. and Albarran, J.W. (2016) 'Exploring the nature of resilience in paramedic practice: A psycho-social study', *International Emergency Nursing*, 28 (September): 1–7.

College of Paramedics. (2016) 'MIND press release—one in four emergency services workers has thought about ending their lives', 20th April. Online. Available at: www.collegeofparamedics.co.uk/news/mind-press-release-one-in-four-emergency-services-workers-has-thought-about-ending-their-lives

College of Paramedics. (n.d.) 'Independent prescribing'. Online. Available at: www.collegeofparamedics.co.uk/publications/independent-prescribing

Corman, M.K. (2017) '*Street medicine*—assessment work strategies of paramedics on the front lines of emergency health services', *Journal of Contemporary Ethnography*, 46 (5): 600–623.

Corman, M.K. (2018) 'Titrating the rig: how paramedics work in and on their ambulance', *Qualitative Health Care*, 28 (1): 47–59.

Department of Health. (2005) *Taking Healthcare to the Patient: Transforming NHS Ambulance Services*, London: Department of Health. Online. Available at: www.nwas.nhs.uk/media/79142/taking_healthcare_to_the_patient_1.pdf.

Donnelly, E.A., Siebert, D. and Siebert, C. (2015) 'Development of the Emergency Medical Services Role Identity Scale (EMS-RIS)', *Social Work in Health Care*, 54 (3): 212–233.

Evans, R., McGovern, R., Birch, J., and Newbury-Birch, D. (2014) 'Which extended paramedic skills are making an impact in emergency care and can be related to the UK paramedic system? A systematic review of the literature', *Emergency Medicine Journal*, 31 (7): 594–603.

Fjeldheim, C.B., Nöthling, J., Pretorius, K. Basson, M., Ganasen, K., Heneke, R., Colete, K.J., and Seedat, S. (2014) 'Trauma exposure, posttraumatic stress disorder and the effect of explanatory variables in paramedic trainees', *BMC Emergency Medicine*, 14 (23rd April), doi:10.1186/1471-227X-14-11.

Ford-Jones, P.C. and Chaufan, C. (2017) 'A critical analysis of debates around mental health calls in the prehospital setting', *Inquiry*, 54: 1–5.

Fischer, S.L., Sinden, K.E., MacPhee, R.S., and The Ottawa Paramedic Service Research Team (2017) 'Identifying the critical physical demanding tasks of paramedic work: Towards the development of a physical employment standard', *Applied Ergonomics*, 65: 233–239.

Garus-Pakowska, A., Górajski, M., and Szatko, F. (2017a) 'Awareness of the risk of exposure to infectious materials and the behaviors of Polish paramedics with respect to the hazards from blood-borne pathogens—a nationwide study', *International Journal of Environmental Research and Public Health*, 14 (8), doi:10.3390/ijerph14080843.

Garus-Pakowska, A., Szatko, F., and Ulrichs, M. (2017b) 'Work-related accidents and sharp injuries in paramedics—illustrated with an example of a multi-specialist

196   *Jo Brewis and Richard Godfrey*

hospital located in central Poland', *International Journal of Environmental Research and Public Health*, 14 (8), doi: 10.3390/ijerph14080901.

Granter, E., McCann, L., and Boyle, M. (2005) 'Extreme work/normal work: Intensification, storytelling and hypermediation in the (re)construction of 'the New Normal', *Organization*, 22 (4): 443–456.

Granter, E., Wankhade, P., McCann, L., Hyde, P., and Hassard, J. (2018) 'Multiple dimensions of work intensity: Ambulance work as edgework', *Work, Employment and Society*, OnlineFirst, doi: 10.1177/0950017018759207.

Hansen, C.D., Rasmussen, K., Kyed, M., Nielsen, K.J., and Andersen, J.H. (2012) 'Physical and psychosocial work environment factors and their association with health outcomes in Danish ambulance personnel—a cross-sectional study', *BMC Public Health*, 12 (July), doi:10.1186/1471-2458-12-534.

Harenčárová, H. (2017) 'Managing uncertainty in paramedics' decision making', *Journal of Cognitive Engineering and Decision Making*, 11 (1): 42–62.

Häusser, J.A., Mojzisch, A., Niesel, M., and Schulz-Hardt, S. (2010) 'Ten years on: A review of recent research on the Job Demand-Control (-Support) model and psychological well-being', *Work & Stress*, 24 (1): 1–35.

Health and Care Professions Council (2018) 'Changes to SET 1 for education providers'. Online. Available at: www.hpc-uk.org/education/standards/set1changeseducationproviders/

Heath, G. and Wankhade, P. (2014) 'A balanced judgement? Performance indicators, quality and the English ambulance service; some issues, developments and a research agenda', *Journal of Finance and Management in Public Services*, 13 (1). Available at: www.cipfa.org/policy-and-guidance/the-journal-of-finance-and-management-in-public-services

Hughes, E.C. (1958) *Men and Their Work*, Westport, CT: Greenwood Press.

Hughes, E.C. (1962) '*Good people and dirty work*', Social Problems, 10 (1): 3–11.

Jervis-Tracey, P., McAuliffe, D., Klieve, H., Chenoweth, L., O'Connor, B., and Stehlik, D. (2016) 'Negotiated policy spaces: Identifying tensions for rural professionals in delivering their statutory responsibilities', *Journal of Rural Studies*, 45: 123–133.

Johnston, T.M. and Acker, J.J. (2016) 'Using a sociological approach to answering questions about paramedic professionalism and identity', *Australasian Journal of Paramedicine*, 13 (1): 1–7.

Kennedy, S., Kenny, A., and O'Meara, P. (2015) 'Student paramedic experience of transition into the workforce: a scoping review', *Nurse Education Today*, 35 (10): 1037–1043.

Klee, S. and Renner, K-G. (2013) 'Short communication. In search of the "Rescue Personality": A questionnaire study with emergency medical services personnel', *Personality and Individual Differences*, 54 (5): 669–672.

Leibold, A., Lassen, C.L., Lindenberg, N., Graf, B.M., and Wiese, C.H.R. (2018) 'Is every life worth saving: Does religion and religious beliefs influence paramedic's end-of-life decision-making? A prospective questionnaire-based investigation', *Indian Journal of Palliative Care*, 24 (1): 9–15.

Luftman, K., Aydelotte, J., Rix, K., Ali, S., Houck, K., Coopwood, T.B., Teixeira, P., Eastman, A., Eastridge, B., Brown, C.V.R., and Davis, M. (2017) 'PTSD in those who care for the injured', *Injury*, 48 (2): 293–296.

Mael, F. and Jex, S. (2015) 'Workplace boredom: an integrative model of traditional and contemporary approaches', *Group & Organization Management*, 40 (2): 131–159.

Maguire, B.J., O'Meara, P., O'Neill, B.J., and Brightwell, R. (2018) 'Violence against emergency medical services personnel: a systematic review of the literature', *American Journal of Industrial Medicine*, 61 (2): 167–180.

Maguire, B.J. and Smith, S. (2013) 'Injuries and fatalities among Emergency Medical Technicians and paramedics in the United States', *Prehospital Disaster Medicine*, 28 (4): 376–382.

McCann, L., Granter, E., Hyde, P., and Hassard, J. (2013) 'Still blue-collar after all these years? An ethnography of the professionalization of emergency ambulance work', *Journal of Management Studies*, 50 (5): 750–776.

McMurray, R. (2012) 'Embracing dirt in nursing matters', in R. Simpson, N. Slutskaya, P. Lewis and H. Höpfl (eds) *Dirty Work: Concepts and Identities*, Houndmills, Basingstoke: Palgrave Macmillan, pp. 126–142.

McMurray, R. and Ward, J. (2014) "Why would you want to do that?': Defining emotional dirty work', *Human Relations*, 67 (9): 1123–1143.

Michael, T., Streb, D., and Häller, P. (2016) 'PTSD in paramedics: Direct versus indirect threats, posttraumatic cognitions, and dealing with intrusions', *International Journal of Cognitive Therapy*, 9 (1): 57–72.

Mulholland, P. Barnett, T., and Spencer, J. (2014) 'Review article. Interprofessional learning and rural paramedic care', *Rural and Remote Health*, 14 (3): 1–13.

Ogińska-Bulik, N. and Kobylarczyk, M. (2015) 'Relation between resiliency and posttraumatic growth in a group of paramedics: The mediating role of coping strategies', *International Journal of Occupational Medicine and Environmental Health*, 28 (4): 707–719.

O'Hara, R., Johnson, M., Sirwardena, A.N., Weyman, A., Turner, J., Shaw, D., Mortimer, P., Newman, C., Hirst, E., Storey, M., Mason, S., Quinn, T., and Shewan, J. (2015) 'A qualitative study of systemic influences on paramedic decision making: care transitions and patient safety', *Journal of Health Services Research & Policy*, 20 (Supplement 1): 45–53.

O'Meara, P., Stirling, C., Ruest, M., and Martin, A. (2016) 'Community paramedicine model of care: an observational, ethnographic case study', *BMC Health Services Research*, 16: 39. doi:10.1186/s12913-016-1282-0.

Palmer, C.E. (1983) ' "Trauma junkies" and street work: Occupational behavior of paramedics and emergency medical technicians', *Urban Life*, 12 (2): 162–183.

Phillips, S. (2016) "Police discretion and boredom': What officers do when there is nothing to do', *Journal of Contemporary Ethnography*, 45 (5): 580–601.

Pilgrim, J.L., Dorward, R. and Drummer, O.H. (2016) 'Drug-caused deaths in Australian medical practitioners and health-care professionals', *Addiction*, 112 (3): 486–493.

Prairie, J., Plamondon, A., Larouche, D., Hegg-Deloye, S., and Corbeil, P. (2017) 'Paramedics' working strategies while loading a stretcher into an ambulance', *Applied Ergonomics*, 65 (November): 112–122.

Prener, C. and Lincoln, A.K. (2015) 'Emergency medical services and "psych calls": Examining the work of urban EMS providers', *American Journal of Orthopsychiatry*, 85 (6): 612–619.

Pyper, Z. and Paterson, J.L. (2016) 'Fatigue and mental health in Australian rural and regional ambulance personnel', *Emergency Medicine Australia*, 28 (1): 62–66.

Quigg, Z., McGee, C., Hughes, K., Russell, S. and Bellis, M.A. (2017) 'Violence-related ambulance call-outs in the North West of England: A cross-sectional analysis of nature, extent and relationships to temporal, celebratory and sporting events', *Emergency Medicine Journal*, 34 (6): 364–369.

Rees, N., Rapport, F., Snooks, H., John, A., and Patel, C. (2017) 'How do emergency ambulance paramedics view the care they provide to people who self-harm? Ways and means', *International Journal of Law and Psychiatry*, 50: 61–67.

Regehr. C. and LeBlanc, V.R. (2017) 'PTSD, acute stress, performance and decision-making in emergency service workers', *Journal of the American Academy of Psychiatry and the Law*, 45 (2): 184–192.

Ross, L., Hannah, J., and Van Huizen, P. (2016) 'What motivates students to pursue a career in paramedicine?' *Australasian Journal of Paramedicine*, 13 (1): 1–7.

Rybojad, B., Aftyka, A., Baran, M., and Rzońca, P. (2016) 'Risk factors for posttraumatic stress disorder in Polish paramedics: a pilot study', *Journal of Emergency Medicine*, 50 (2): 270–276.

Scott, J., Strickland, A.P., Warner, K., and Dawson, P. (2014) 'Frequent callers to and users of emergency medical systems', *Emergency Medical Journal*, 31 (8): 684–691.

Semmer, N.K., Jacobshagen, N., Meier, L.L., Elfering, A., Beehr, T.A., Kälin, W., and Tschan, F. (2015) 'Illegitimate tasks as a source of work stress', *Work & Stress*, 29 (1): 32–56.

Simpson, P., Thomas, R., Bendall, J., Lord, B., Lord, S., and Close, J. (2017) '"Popping nana back into bed'—a qualitative exploration of paramedic decision making for older people who have fallen', *BMC Health Services Research*, 17 (21st April), doi:10.1186/s12913–017–2243-y.

Skowronski, M. (2012) 'When the bored behave badly (or exceptionally)', *Personnel Review*, 41 (2): 143–159.

Stanley, I.H., Hom, M.A., and Joiner, T.E. (2016) 'A systematic review of suicidal thoughts and behaviors among police officers, firefighters, EMTs, and paramedics', *Clinical Psychology Review*, 44 (March): 25–44.

Tangherlini, T.R. (2000) 'Heroes and lies: storytelling among paramedics', *Folklore*, 111 (1): 43–66.

Tataris, K.L., Richards, C.T., Stein-Spencer, L., Ryan, S., Lazzara, P., and Weber, J.M. (2017) 'EMS provider perceptions on termination of resuscitation in a large, urban EMS system', *Prehospital Emergency Care*, 21 (5): 610–615.

Taylor, J.A., Barnes, B., Davis, A.L., Wright, J., Widman, S., and LeVasseur, M. (2016) 'Expecting the unexpected: a mixed methods study of violence to EMS responders in an urban fire department', *American Journal of Industrial Medicine*, 59 (2): 150–163.

Van Erp, K.J.P.M., Gevers, J.M.P, Rispens, S., and Demerouti, E. (2018) 'Empowering public services workers to face bystander conflict: Enhancing resources through a training intervention', *Journal of Occupational and Organizational Psychology*, 91 (1): 84–109.

Van Hooff, M.L.M. and van Hooft, E.A.J. (2014) 'Boredom at work: Proximal and distal consequences of affective work-related boredom', *Journal of Occupational Health Psychology*, 19 (3): 348–359.

Waldrop, D.P., McGinley, J.M., and Clemency, B. (2018) 'The nexus between the documentation of end-of-life wishes and awareness of dying: A model for research, education and care', *Journal of Pain and Symptom Management*, 55 (2): 522–529.

Wankhade, P. (2012) 'Different cultures of management and their relationships with organizational performance: evidence from the UK ambulance service', *Public Money & Management*, 32 (5): 381–388.

Wankhade, P. and Brinkman, J. (2014) 'The negative consequences of culture change management: Evidence from a UK NHS ambulance service', *International Journal of Public Sector Management*, 27 (1): 2–25.

Webber, R. (2017) 'The best response, first time', *National Health Executive*, 13th December. Online. Available at: www.nationalhealthexecutive.com/Comment/the-best-response-first-time

Williams. A. (2012) 'Emotion work in paramedic practice: the implications for nurse educators', *Nurse Education Today*, 32 (4): 368–372.

Williams, A. (2013a) 'A study of emotion work in student paramedic practice', *Nurse Education Today*, 33 (5): 512–517.

Williams, A. (2013b) 'The strategies used to deal with emotion work in student paramedic practice', *Nurse Education in Practice*, 13 (33): 207–212.

Wireklint Sundström, B. and Dahlberg, K. (2012) 'Being prepared for the unprepared: A phenomenology field study of Swedish prehospital care', *Journal of Emergency Nursing*, 38 (6): 571–577.

12 Decision-Making at the Front Line

The Role of Choice Architecture in NHS Paramedic Judgements Over Patient Conveyance

Andrew Weyman* and Rachel O'Hara

Scope

This chapter articulates contemporary insights into non-clinical considerations that impact on paramedic decision-making over patient treatment and (non-)conveyance to hospital emergency departments. It is informed by the authors' recent empirical work with the NHS emergency ambulance service[1] but, necessarily, draws upon the invaluable complementary insights of broader published findings on extrinsic influences on paramedic decision-making. After introducing the concept and role of choice architecture, it moves on to provide a flavour of tensions surrounding extrinsic influences on decision-making over care destinations for patients, in the context of rising demand for services, scarcity of resources and worries over blame and accountability.

What Do We Mean by Choice Architecture?

Paramedics working in the UK's National Health Service (NHS) are expected to make clinical judgements and perform treatments that were formerly the preserve of hospital-based clinicians, while at the same time playing a gatekeeper role in rationing rates of conveyance to hospital. While the clinical judgement is key in decision-making over whether a patient should be treated at the scene and conveyed to an emergency department or some other type of care provider, there are grounds for believing that it is not the only criterion applied. The choice architecture of availability of alternative care destinations; perceptions of professional vulnerability; institutional and employee beliefs over accountability and blame; features of the service delivery performance regime, potentially play a role in framing and directing paramedic decision-making over patient conveyance.

Borrowing, and broadening, the concept of choice architecture from Thaler and Sunstein (2008), the nudges that will be articulated in this chapter relate to elements of workplace climate/context that induce paramedics to make

* Correspondence E-mail ID: A.Weyman@bath.ac.uk

predictable choices. Of key interest are effects that can be characterised as engendering perverse motivations, i.e. effects that are in tension with patient interests and service delivery objectives.

Against a background and in part as a consequence of unprecedented rises in demand, the 21st-century UK ambulance service is now expected to play a key role in triaging patients, dispensing care in the community and managing scarce resources while maintaining public confidence (NHS England, 2013). This represents a major and fundamental broadening of the role that society expects the ambulance service and its employees to perform. The chapter aims to provide an appreciation of an array of associated headline issues and tensions, notably in the areas of responsibility, accountability and managing public expectations, with particular emphasis on institutional and professional *coping strategies*. Arising implications for patient care and ambulance personnel well-being and service resources are discussed.

Paramedics are routinely placed in situations where they have to make time-pressured decisions, based on presenting information that is often incomplete, against a backdrop of finite resources, the complexities of alternative care pathways and professional and service provider boundaries that characterise the modern NHS (O'Hara et al., 2014). Appropriate, high-quality, evidence-based clinical decision-making embodies notable challenges, yet this is not our primary focus within this chapter. Rather, it is on the organisational climate and socio-technical context in which these decisions take place (Trist and Bamforth, 1951; Reason, 1995; Carayon, 2015), specifically how these elements conspire to configure the choice architecture (Thaler and Sunstein, 2008) within which ambulance paramedics operate and which impact upon the choices they make over patient care, with arising implications for patient, employee and paramedic well-being.

The Modernisation Agenda: A Rise in Intrinsic and Extrinsic Job Demands

Reflecting experiences within most advanced economies, recent decades have witnessed calls for 'new models of care'; a 'transformation of emergency care' giving rise to an unprecedented broadening of the scope and breadth of care delivered by UK emergency ambulance services (Radcliffe and Heath, 2010; NHS England, 2013, 2015). Beginning in the 1970s but becoming the subject of overt government policy since the 1990s DoH, 2005), the role and remit of the service and its staff have expanded from a primary orientation around conveyance and non-invasive stabilisation of patients to engagement in diagnosis and treatment at a level previously reserved for clinicians.

Equipping ambulance personnel "with a greater range of competencies that enable them to assess, treat, refer, or discharge an increasing number of patients and meet quality requirements for urgent care" (DoH, 2005, p. 44) has, inevitably, brought with it a major rise in intrinsic job demands. This includes broadening/enhancement of core skills, the need to demonstrate continuous professional development and delivery of new treatments/techniques, for both long-serving employees to be able to make the transition to paramedic status and newer entrants to this *new* profession. The evolution of the ambulance service in terms of role remit, combined with the strong policy emphasis on reducing the demand for care in emergency hospitals, adds a further layer of complexity to the decision-making context. The study by O'Hara et al. (2014) highlights the complexity of decisions to transport or leave at scene.

The decade of professionalisation took place against, and partly because of, an unprecedented peace-time rise in demand for emergency care. Emergency calls increased by 3.36 million (42%) between 2002 and 2011 (Ambulance Services England, 2013). The basis for the rise has been, variously, attributed to the UK's ageing demographic; the shift from institutional care to community living for vulnerable adults (closure of traditional care institutions); closure of community clinics and functionally equivalent non-emergency care facilities; changes to general practice working hours and rising waiting times (Marsh, 2017; NHS England, 2017; Booker et al., 2017; Coster et al., 2017); as well as claims of rising inappropriate call-outs by the public, sponsoring the, unsubstantiated, conclusion that *the public are the problem* (see, for example, McCann, 2011).

Whether attributable to structural changes within the NHS, prevailing funding levels, staff shortages, demographic shifts or changes in public orientation, the net result is that demand for ambulance services is outstripping supply and to an unprecedented (peace-time) degree. A primary impact on paramedics is that the rise in demand means that road crews have effectively become peripatetic clinicians, transitioning from one call-out to the next, routinely only returning to base at the end of their shift.

Thus, while ostensibly reflecting the public policy intent of improving patient outcomes, by reducing the time frame for care delivery in life-threatening situations necessitating conveyance to hospital, treatment at scene and non-transport addresses the arguably more pressing public policy objective of reducing rates of conveyance and, thereby, the demand for hospital care. The two decades of professionalisation have, therefore, witnessed not only a rise in intrinsic job demands (technical skills) of ambulance personnel, but also the extrinsic components: rises in work-rate, changes to working hours[2] and active participation in the rationing of scarce resources, against a background of profound funding austerity (post-2010), staff shortages and an intensified regulatory focus on performance management and accountability of professionals and service providers.

We consider the distinction between intrinsic[3] and extrinsic[4] components of job demands important (Siegrist, 1996). At a fundamental level, the intrinsic components of the ambulance paramedic role—interaction with the patients and carers, decisions over treatment, risk of musculoskeletal injury, shift work, exposure to, at times, stressful and fatiguing situations, etc.—represent core features of the job, for which staff need to be suitably trained and supported to manage. Extrinsic components relate to the configuration of work and related systems; headline examples include length and configuration of shift patterns, availability of resources, time pressure arising from operational performance objectives and measures; quality and usability of systems, e.g.

record keeping and software; and social support/isolation. A key distinction is that intrinsic components are essentially immutable, although supportable, whereas extrinsic components are mutable, i.e. there is significantly greater scope for intervention to address the load imposed by extrinsic components.

For ambulance service employers, external contingencies, notably funding levels, structural labour shortages (exacerbated by contemporary UK government immigration policy) and the need to meet challenging service delivery performance targets limit the scope for addressing undesirable impacts on staff of extrinsic job demands. The performance regime, in particular, gives rise to an array of institutional *coping strategies* that contribute to the extrinsic load on front-line personnel, e.g. greater (ir)regularity of shifts; longer shifts; higher rates of lone working[5] leading to greater social isolation; as well as perceived and overt pressure to meet response time targets.[6]

The arising conclusion is that the last decade has witnessed an unprecedented rise in both intrinsic and extrinsic job demands for ambulance service personnel. While meeting the former can be challenging, much resting upon the adequacy of training, it does not present as unduly problematic; rather it is elements relating to extrinsic components that feature prominently within paramedics' accounts of their capacity to meet their job demands, worries and concerns over their personal vulnerability and ultimately why they leave the service 'early', routinely in their early to mid-50s (Weyman and Roy, 2017). Critically, the rise in job demands is not limited to elements arising from the design and configuration of work; it extends to the need to become actively involved in the process of rationing scarce resources (see, for example, Imison et al., 2017).

Paramedics as Managers of Scarcity?

Irrespective of the underpinning rationale, the objective of reducing non-emergency call-out rates has intensified the focus on triaging potential ambulance consumers. While front-line paramedics are now expected to play a key role in the field with respect to decisions over conveyance, the process of triage begins earlier in the system, with emergency call handlers within the traditional 999 service and the recently introduced non-emergency care 111 public helpline. Both make use of digital decision support software (the NHS Pathways clinical assessment software, NAO, 2011; or the older Medical Priority Dispatch System, Clawson, 1983), operated principally by lay call handlers. The respective call handlers prioritise the calls based on the output from the decision software, backed up by recourse to a clinical hub of health professionals. These clinicians (generally paramedics and nurses) resolve calls over the phone where it is transparent that an emergency ambulance response is not needed. They also act as a sounding-board resource to support paramedics' at-the-scene decision-making. Direct calls to the ambulance service from the public and health professions (principally general practitioners) involves triaging by an ambulance trust clinician who, adhering to the guidelines provided in the *Ambulance Care Pathway* procedure, will resolve the call over the phone or dispatch an ambulance. Triaging at the scene by ambulance paramedics may result in treatment and/or convey-ance to an accident and emergency hospital or a suitable alternative destina-tion, e.g. non-emergency care facility. Within the boundaries of ambulance service policies, protocols and guidance, paramedics are required to exercise considerable discretion, with limited formal (control centre clinician) deci-sion support.

Reflecting the state's ambition to reduce ambulance transports to hos-pital emergency departments, NHS England's Urgent and Emergency Care Review (2013) called for the ambulance service to adopt 'new models of care'. At the core of this hierarchical model was an intensified emphasis on resolving patient health issues over the phone ('hear and treat'); treating and discharging patients at the scene ('see and treat'); and transporting patients to non-hospital destinations (e.g. community services and non-emergency care facilities). A notable feature of UK provision, however, is that the array of options for non-emergency care destinations exhibits notable variation by locale (O'Hara et al., 2014). For example in England, local clinical com-missioning groups (CCGs)[7] play the role of choice architect, in so far as they play a key role in configuring the range of health and social services in a given locale that constitute viable alternatives to hospital emergency departments.

Transparently, realisation of this vision embodies the potential to increase the burden on ambulance services and their personnel in the area of profes-sional responsibility and accountability in respect of patient care-outcomes. Moreover, evidence regarding the effectiveness of 'hear and treat' and to some degree 'see and treat' indicates that this tends to be bounded by restricted access to non-emergency care resources/destinations, as well as the time/resource penalty for negotiating access, the latter being principally born by the ambulance service (Eastwood et al., 2015).

The intersect between the NHS 111 non-emergency helpline and the emer-gency ambulance service has proved to be controversial. Set up and rolled out in England and Scotland between 2012 and 2015, the 111 service reflects the general perspective that the key, if not the only, purpose of the system is to reduce public demand for NHS emergency services, particularly accident and emergency admissions. However, evidence of its effectiveness is mixed, some sources claiming no reduction in ambulance call-out rates (Turner et al., 2013) and others, more disturbingly, claiming that it has actually sponsored an increase (Nuffield Trust, 2017). The latter has been widely attributed to the deployment of non-clinical call handlers and their consequent heavy reliance on the Pathways decision support software, giving rise to claims of excessively risk-averse triaging. Implicit implications are that this is either a product of the limited medical knowledge and expertise of call handlers or attributable to some systematic bias within the software algorithm(s) (Pope et al., 2017; Nuffield Trust, 2017). A counter-intuitive and unexplained find-ing, in relation to NHS 111 service triaging, given that the profile of patient demand for care essentially reflects a hierarchy[8] of need, is that a "consist-ently higher number [sic] of people [are] sent to ambulance services com-pared to A&E" (National Health Executive, 2017).

Arising intuitive conclusions, transparent in the accounts provided by commentators, are that arising issues are resolvable through up-skilling call handlers, increasing rates of health professional involvement and/or enhancement of the Pathways decision support software (Turnbull et al., 2014; National Health Executive, 2017). There is quite likely scope for both, and potentially to good effect. Equally, discounting the public policy objective of reducing call-out rates, a decision support tool that that exhibits a bias favouring caution would seem to be preferable to its alternative.

Whether arising from working practices and culture within the 111 service, software limitations/systematic bias or the significant political and resource-related pressure on ambulance service employers to reduce rates of conveyance, the net result is an increased reliance upon paramedics in the field to determine whether presenting health needs are most appropriately addressed through treatment and discharge at the scene, treatment and conveyance to a hospital/alternative care institution or referral to other care services.

For the majority of cases, presenting health status will likely render the appropriate course of action transparent (Colver, 2012). Our central interest, however, is in the smaller proportion of cases where there is sufficient doubt and ambiguity over the status of the patient and their needs that the most appropriate course of action necessitates deliberation, most acutely over whether to convey (see Porter et al., 2007, 2008; O'Hara et al., 2015). Clinically, this can involve complex decisions over patient status, particularly in the context of rising rates of co-morbidity, e.g. amongst the growing proportion of elderly patients, but can also require careful consideration of social and psychological components. Often tending to be overlooked within biomedically focused accounts, relevant skills extend beyond issues of practitioner technical competence and confidence to issues of knowledge and availability of potential care/destination options, managing social interactions with the public and their expectations against a background of scarce resources (both within their own ambulance service and other care services) and high-profile performance objectives.

Evidence relating to the role played by consideration of non-medical criteria and non-technical skills (Shields and Flin, 2013) in at-the-scene paramedic decision-making over conveyance is sparse, although a number of authors make reference to it (Snooks et al., 2005; Colver, 2012). Moreover, we have not found any evidence from our empirical work indicating that patient well-being has been sacrificed due to overt pressure on road crews to reduce rates of conveyance, or the need to meet measured service performance objectives despite their high profile within the service and the broader public arena. With reference to the latter, reflecting alignment with findings reported by others (notably Colver, 2012), a pervasive impression is that the strength of paramedics' commitment to meeting presenting patient needs typically sponsors robust responses to prioritising patient care over performance considerations, e.g. pressure from ambulance control centres to dispatch an ambulance crew to a new call (Weyman and Nolan, 2018). However, it remains the case that all personnel with an involvement in triage will have an awareness of, and are unlikely to be wholly immune from effects arising from the background institutional rhetoric of, the *need* to reduce rates of conveyance and are operating in a decision environment framed by a choice architecture of relative scarcity/availability of road-based resources and destination care-facility capacity (Colver, 2012; O'Hara, 2014).

The burden and consequences of a non-conveyance decision resulting in harm to a patient transparently rest disproportionately upon ambulance personnel at the scene. While these professionals may be best placed to make an informed judgement, they are also the group who will experience the greatest sense of loss and arising consequences (to patients and personally) in the event that they make what turns out to be a poor decision. Intrinsically, such demands are not new; rather the central issue rests with the fact that there has been a rise in, and need to take account of, extrinsic elements. However, evidence relating to claims of unreasonably risk-averse decision-making amongst front-line paramedics seems to be mixed and, plausibly, may owe something to cultural differences within the different service provider organisations (Colver 2012; O'Hara et al., 2014; Simpson et al., 2017; Weyman and Nolan, 2018).

Risk, Blame and Accountability

The potential for unreasonably risk-averse clinical judgements amongst ambulance crews does not present, primarily, as the product of shortfalls in technical expertise, although this can obviously be an issue particularly amongst inexperienced personnel. Rather, there are claims that unreasonable risk aversion owes more to worries over the personal consequences of 'getting it wrong' (Colver, 2012; O'Hara et al., 2014; Weyman and Nolan, 2018).

Indeed, it would be surprising not to encounter worries over accountability and blame, given reports of the prevalence of such amongst professionals and organisations within sectors tasked with the management of, for the most part, rather less fundamental challenges to public well-being. Claims of over-cautious decision-making abound within social care, state education, passenger transport and recreational facilities (Ruch, 2005; Spielman, 2017; Weyman et al., 2006; Broadhurst et al., 2010). Causal influences have variously been ascribed to over-interpretation of health and safety regulations, high-profile judicial judgements, a cultural shift in public perspectives on tolerability, insurance company policy and compensation claim marketing within the legal profession and self-protective practices on the part of employers. Irrespective of the cause, a central claim is that increasingly professionals and their employers operate in a climate of possibly unreasonable and disproportionate focus on accountability and apportionment of blame in the event of failure (Beck, 1992; Giddens, 1999; Power, 2004; Young, 2010).

While evidence of an increase in rates of litigation and prosecutions has, for the most part, been found wanting, an arising conclusion is that their social profile owes more to media focus and hyperbole surrounding a relatively small number of high-profile cases rather than any widespread change; its legacy has a reality in the institutional and individual reactions to produce an amplified belief in their vulnerability (Power 2004; Young, 2010; Williams, 2014). As Williams notes,

> The fact that there may be no objective proof that we live in an increasingly 'blame and sue' society is beside the point when an 'urban myth' to the contrary is said to have taken hold. Thus, whatever the actual likelihood of being the target of litigation, many increasingly believe themselves to be at heightened risk of being unfairly sued.
>
> (Williams, 2014, p. 2)

Evidence of the prevalence of such amongst ambulance service personnel and their managers was apparent within the authors' empirical work (O'Hara, 2014; Weyman and Nolan, 2018), as well as Snooks et al. (2005) and Colver's (2012) accounts of impacts on personnel behaviour.

Before moving to consider contemporary insights into circumstances identified as giving rise to a culture of excessive risk aversion, it is perhaps worth reflecting that while ambulance services are potentially subject to the same believed or actual amplified focus on blame and accountability as other sectors, the issue for them and their employees is not limited to beliefs. Changes to ambulance service response options to produce alignment with the public policy objective of minimising conveyance and managing demand has a material impact on corporate vulnerability and potentially the vulnerability of service employees, i.e. any reduction in the proportion of conveyances will potentially have the effect of increasing the probability of undesirable outcomes for patients. It is perhaps noteworthy that this fact is under-articulated, and conspicuous by its absence, within the contemporary public policy rhetoric, which tends to frame the issue as one of *delivery of better care; providing the most appropriate ambulance response* (see, for example, NHS England 2013).

In some degree, the policy drive for greater autonomy over clinical and related conveyance decisions by paramedics contrasts with the shift towards greater prescription encountered in other sectors with responsibility for public well-being, e.g. social care, education, transport. In these and many other organisations, recent decades have witnessed a drive to reduce employee decision latitude over risks to the public (Beck, 1992; Giddens, 1999; Power, 2004). Indeed, the requirement for greater autonomy in paramedic decision-making presents as being in some tension with the strong prescriptive tradition of close compliance with standard operating procedures (SOPs) within the service (see Colver, 2012). Not surprisingly, paramedic accounts highlight amplified perceptions of personal vulnerability (Colver, 2012; O'Hara et al., 2014; Weyman and Nolan, 2018).

Reports of employee responses to the introduction of the 'Treat and Refer' (T&R) model of care (Department for Health, 2005), aimed at reducing non-emergency conveyances, highlight an array of coping strategies that present as alleviating the dissonance experienced, i.e. the presence of decision criteria go some way to alleviating paramedic worry and concern over the defensibility of their decisions, in the event that this should be challenged.

Identified coping strategies include reversion to established SOPs, extracting signed consent from patients for non-conveyance, verification of treat and leave decisions with more senior practitioners, a tendency to over-triage or wholesale retreat from engagement with the initiative (Snooks et al., 2005; Gray and Wardrope, 2007; Deakin et al., 2006; Burrell, Noble, and Ridsdale, 2012; Colver, 2012; O'Hara et al., 2014). If generalisable, such coping strategies foreseeably represent a challenge to the realisation of the public policy objective of ambulance services playing a key role in managing public demand for unscheduled health care. Ultimately, conveyance to an accident and emergency hospital represents "the safest (lowest personal risk) option for a paramedic, as all alternatives require a justification for the decision made in the event of a negative outcome for the patient" (O'Hara et al., 2014, p. 57).

A notable feature of ambulance employee orientations to, essentially, safety rules and procedures, that contrasts with the air of resentment that tends to characterise reactions in many other sectors (Jeffcott et al., 2006; Ruch, 2005; Spielman, 2017), is the seemingly widespread perspective that the capacity to demonstrate an audit trail (written or electric) of compliance affords significant protection against the spectre of claims of poor clinical judgement and/or negligence. Indeed, the accounts reported by Colver (2012), Snooks et al. (2005), Gray and Wardrope (2007) and O'Hara et al. (2014) indicate what presents as a widespread (although not universal) desire, amongst front-line ambulance personnel, for more prescription (guidance and formalised decision criteria) rather than less. As Gray and Wardrope (2007) note, the presence of non-transport (T&R) guidance also affords a degree of medico-legal protection for ambulance service employers, in defending *themselves* with respect to the practice of their staff.

A related contrast with accounts from other sectors seems apparent with respect to employee perceptions of the volition and appropriateness of guidance and SOPs. Elsewhere it is common to encounter the belief that a primary volition relates to protection of the employer from liability, most acutely with respect to the audit trail that accompanies demonstrable compliance (Weyman et al., 2006). This is not to say that the ambulance service has not experienced the rising tide of audit culture (Beck, 1992) found in other sectors. Employee accounts testify that the time and effort burden of associated record keeping can be resented, that not all SOPs are necessarily practicable and workable, or that ambulance personnel do feel vulnerable in keeping up with changes to procedures (O'Hara et al., 2014); however, suspicions surrounding the motivations of their architects (policymakers and employers) do not seem to feature prominently in the accounts of operational staff (Weyman and Nolan, 2018).

Arguably a fundamental feature, if not prerequisite, for broadening the role remit of emergency ambulance personnel relates to the role of trust, in an array of inter-related domains: employer and public trust in the ability and judgement of paramedics, and the paramedic trust in their employers.

Evidence relating to employee trust in service employers is modest and presents as mixed, possibly reflecting differences between the organisations studied. Colver (2012) and O'Hara et al. (2014) both articulate evidence of paramedics feeling alone and unsupported by their managers in the event of an adverse patient incident arising from a non-conveyance decision. Colver, however, nuances this in commenting, "Interestingly the participants did not report personal experience of being subject to investigation or discipline but talked of other peoples' experiences"; nevertheless, "this is likely to have an impact on how they practice and the level of decision-making they are prepared to take" (Colver, 2012, p. 32) This is not uncommon and potentially generalises to reports of related worries over Health and Care Professions Council (HCPC)[9] action (Colver, 2012; O'Hara et al., 2014).

Insights from the broader workplace safety and risk literature highlight how employees' perceptions of the personal consequences of failure are routinely vague and impressionistic. Moreover, the salience of a small number of cases tends to be amplified, particularly where they align with, and therefore have the effect of reinforcing, extant suspicions. By contrast, Nolan et al. (2018) report probing the issue of management style with respect to accountability and blame in the event of negative impacts on patients arising from triaging and treatment decisions, excepting evidence of professional negligence, conveyed the impression of notable confidence that, if challenged, their decisions and actions would receive support and be defended by more senior staff. However, reflecting findings reported by Colver and O'Hara, paramedics did feel vulnerable in the area of compliance with rules and procedures, e.g. a number expressed worry over *missing something important*, due to the intensity of their workload and, partly as a consequence, of their relative social isolation.

Weyman and Nolan (2018) also concluded that their case study ambulance service line managers and senior managers conveyed an impression of notable trust and confidence in the judgement and decision-making of their front-line personnel. Underpinning this was what presented as significant insight and empathy with respect to the pressures that are experienced by front-line staff. In some degree, it seems plausible that the traditional career structure and promotion structure within the service may contribute to this, i.e. a notable feature of the ambulance service, that contrasts with the trend of increasing professionalisation of the management function in other sectors, is that most senior personnel routinely have a career history in the service, having progressed through the ranks.

Reinforcing the point highlighted earlier, employee beliefs, accurate or otherwise, are important as they tend to impact on orientation and behaviour in relation to risk (Morgan, Fischoff, and Bostrom, 2008; Weyman et al., 2006, 2012). As, O'Hara et al. (2014) report,

> A particular consideration is the action [and beliefs about actions] taken by the [employing] Trust in the event of an incident. . . . Specifically staff disclosed circumstances in which they felt that what was best for the patient conflicted with service policy and they feared the ramifications of not adhering to guidelines or policy.
>
> (O'Hara et al., 2014, p. 57)

In a similar vein, Porter et al. report,

> Even where the crew did not think that the patient should go to hospital and the patient did not want to go, crew members were still bothered by the fear of a possible comeback if it turned out to be the wrong decision.
>
> (Porter et al., 2007, p. 35)

The salience of trust, however, is not limited to the repercussions following incidents; where a climate of mistrust prevails, there is a very real risk that employees will be inhibited from reporting near misses, unsafe practices, routine deviations from procedures and similar where "they feel the organisation is more likely to blame them than support them" (O'Hara et al., 2014, p. 64). The capacity to recognise such vulnerabilities, and the necessary organisational climate to achieve such, is widely acknowledged as a core feature of organisational learning to enhance resilience in high reliability organisations (Perrow, 1984; HSE, 2011).

Consideration of ambulance sector findings on issues of blame and accountability in the event of failure with reference to experiences in other high-profile sectors charged with managing public well-being is that, to date, while failures in triage/treatment and service standards regularly receive notable media and judicial attention, against a rumbling discourse of a system in crisis, this does not seem to generate the same intensity of outrage amongst the public that it has in other sectors (Jeffcott et al., 2006; Ruch, 2005; Samuel, 2014; Spielman, 2017). Similarly, the widespread publicity, which extends to active media advertising campaigns, over the need to reduce rates of conveyance, carries with it an implicit message that decisions are being made by health professionals over the distribution of scarce resources. There appears to have been some success over propagating and gaining public buy-in to the claim that there is a need to stem the rate of inappropriate ambulance call-outs/conveyances and that service users appear to trust that non-conveyance decisions are based on medical considerations, rather than subsidiary criteria (O'Hara, 2014).

In this respect, broader findings on public orientations to UK state sector health care would seem to be of relevance. In short, the amassed evidence is that the high regard and high social capital, seemingly almost universally, vested in the NHS and those who work for it owes much to what is perceived to be the altruistic nature of its intent, combined with the notion that its product is provided free at the point of need (see Pidgeon et al., 2003). Intentionally sidestepping debates that question the veracity of this, the issue of public beliefs represents our central interest here. The net result appears to be that while litigation against individuals and employers within the sector do occur, the predominant profile is one of the public tending to be more forgiving of errors (excepting clear cases of negligence) on the part of the service and its employees than in other sectors, tending to be more disposed to make external attributions, blaming failures on shortage of staff, resources, underfunding and, ultimately, the UK government as the architect of this.

Conclusions

Recent decades, gathering pace since the turn of the century, have witnessed fundamental changes to what the UK state and society expect of NHS ambulance services and their staff. The shift of emphasis to dispensing treatment at the scene and referral to non-emergency care providers, underpinned by structural pressure to reduce rates of conveyance to accident and emergency hospitals, reflects a major shift in responsibility and arising vulnerabilities for ambulance service employers and their staff.

The challenge is multifaceted, extending significantly beyond the intuitive need to enhance the technical skills of front-line personnel with the introduction of the paramedic qualification and professional registration. It includes mastery of non-technical skills, notably the capacity to interact effectively with patients, as well as non-emergency health and social care organisations, combined with sufficient confidence and preparedness to make decisions with potentially high personal consequences in the event of poor patient outcomes.

The UK state's strong desire to reduce rates of conveyance to emergency hospitals, combined with the implicit expectation that the role of emergency ambulance services has broadened to encompass a much wider range of care within the community, necessarily requires a high degree of autonomous decision-making on the part of paramedics. This is a big ask for these professionals, with respect to their professional vulnerability. Indeed, realisation of the policy objective may come to owe much to the degree to which the workplace climate and choice architecture within which conveyance/non-conveyance decisions are made supports autonomous decision-making or sponsors a defensive, self-protective risk-averse response. The consequences of an inappropriate conveyance of a patient to an accident and emergency department are significantly less than an inappropriate non-conveyance decision.

Reference to the wider context of professional and institutional accountability sponsors the conclusion that the drive towards greater employee autonomy presents as swimming against the tide, i.e. in other sectors, whether born of a desire to reduce primary risks to the public or secondary risk to the employer, a strong drive towards greater standardisation and proceduralisation has become a dominant feature of organisational culture. The latter has been cast as a defensive strategy on the part of employers, and one that can have the effect of increasing the vulnerability of front-line personnel, in extremis, where operating rules and procedures are more strongly orientated around avoidance of corporate culpability than protection of employees and the public.

Evidence relating to public perceptions of the need to reduce rates of conveyance is scant, but indicates some success in propagating the rhetoric that resolution lies in reducing the number of trivial/inappropriate (non-emergency) 999 calls. To date, it seems that a non-conveyance recommendation is not regarded with suspicion of reflecting a financial imperative, in the same way as denial of access to certain drugs and treatments tends to be. However, this does not mean that the current public orientation is necessarily stable and not subject to change, particularly should the issue become the subject of media attention and social amplification.

Beyond the moderating influence of accountability and blame, the drive to minimise rates of conveyance hinges upon the availability of alternative care provision. The post-2010 world of health care has been one of significant restructuring and austerity, including unprecedented cuts to local authority budgets for social care, in the context of rising demand. Paramedics' accounts suggest that the practicalities of finding and making contact with alternative (non-emergency) care providers willing to accept patient referrals can be problematic. The time implications of negotiation alone is foreseeable as a disincentive for front-line paramedics, as well as reducing emergency response capacity.

A corollary of the post-2010 restructuring, austerity and rising demand for care is that the ambulance service has, in some degree, found itself filling the arising voids in care provision, notably with respect to timely access to patient assessment and treatment. Indeed, all else being equal, there may be merit in deploying mobile healthcare services in this way within the community, provided there are sufficient resources to support it, i.e. such that paramedics play a key role in triage and patient transitions to appropriate care. Realisation of this potential would require something of a paradigm shift with respect to the role and remit of the emergency ambulance service and paramedics, but one that reflects the growing reality of current practice. However, its realisation transparently requires large-scale investment, not just in the ambulance service, but in the health and social care services it interacts with. Neither appears to be likely to be forthcoming in the near future.

Notes

1 Decision making and safety in emergency care transitions (2012–2013), O'Hara et al., funder: NIHR Health Services and Delivery Research Programme (project number 13/54/75). *Extending Working Lives in the NHS*: Opportunities, Challenges and Prospects (2014–2018) Nolan et al., funder: Medical Research Council.
2 Compressed hours leading to longer shifts, typically 10–12 hours.
3 Intrinsic job demands defn, Elements that relate to professional role, e.g. skill, expertise and stresses associated with their deployment and arising consequences.
4 Extrinsic job demands defn, Elements relating to organisation of work, e.g. pace of work, resources, configuration of working hours, performance criteria.
5 Although only in part attributable to the need to meet response time targets, ambulance employers have increased the use of non-ambulance transport, including cars, motorcycles and bicycles.
6 *Measuring Patient Outcomes: Clinical Quality Indicators*, https://aace.org.uk/uk-ambulance-service/national-performance/
7 CCGs were set up under the Health and Social Care Act 2012 to organise the delivery of NHS services in England. This function is performed by Health Boards in Scotland, Wales and Northern Ireland.
8 The number of cases requiring conveyance by ambulance is subset of A&E all cases; similarly, the number of A&E admission is a subset of all injuries / individuals requiring care, in a given time frame.

9 The Health and Care Professions Council (HCPC) is an independent UK regulatory body responsible for setting and maintaining standards of professional practice for health sector employees.

References

Ambulance Services England (2013) NHS Digital. https://digital.nhs.uk/data-and information/publications/statistical/ambulance-services/ambulance-services-england-2012-13.

Beck, U. (1992) From Industrial Society to the Risk Society: Questions of Survival, Social Structure and Ecological Enlightenment. *Theory Culture and Society* 9(1); pp. 97–123.

Booker, M.J., Purdy, S., and Shaw, A. (2017) Seeking ambulance treatment for 'primary care' problems: a qualitative systematic review of patient, carer and professional perspectives. *BMJ Open*. https://bmjopen.bmj.com/content/7/8/e016832. Accessed 28/8/18.

Broadhurst, K., Hall, K., Wastell, D., White, S., and Pithouse, A. (2010) Risk, instrumentalism and the humane project in social work: Identifying the informal logics of risk management in children's statutory services. *British Journal of Social Work* 40(4); pp. 1046–1064.

Burrell, L., Noble, A., and Ridsdale, L. (2012) Decision making by ambulance clinicians in London when managing patients with epilepsy: A qualitative study. *EMJ*. online March 20th; doi:10.1136/emermed-20110200388.

Carayon, P., Hancock, P., Leveson, N., Noy, I., Sznelwar, L., and van Hootegem, G. (2015) Advancing a sociotechnical systems approach to workplace safety—developing the conceptual framework. *Ergonomics* 58(4); pp. 548–564.

Clawson, J. (1983) Medical priority dispatch: It works!! *Journal of Emergency Medical Services (JEMS)* 8(2); 29. www.emergencydispatch.org/articles/medicalprioritydispatch1.htm. Accessed 20/7/18.

Colver, K. (2012) Ambulance Service Treat and Refer Guidelines: A Qualitative Investigation into the Use of Treat and Refer Guidelines by Ambulance Clinicians. Thesis Submitted to the University of Stirling for the Degree of Master of Philosophy School of Nursing, Midwifery and Health.

Coster, J. E., Turner, J. K., Bradbury, D., and Cantrell, A. (2017). Why do people choose Emergency and Urgent care services? A rapid review utilizing a systematic literature search and narrative synthesis. *Academic Emergency Medicine*, 24; pp. 1137–1149.

Deakin, C. D., Sherwood, D. M., Smith, A., and Cassidy, M. (2006) Does telephone triage of emergency (999) calls using advanced medical priority dispatch (AMPDS) with Department of Health (DH) call prioritisation effectively identify patients with an acute coronary syndrome? An audit of 42 657 emergency calls to Hampshire Ambulance Service NHS Trust. *Emergency Medicine Journal* 23(3). https://emj.bmj.com/content/23/3/232.full. Accessed 20/7/18.

Department of Health. (2005) Taking healthcare to the patient: Transforming NHS ambulance services, June.

Eastwood, K., Morgans, A., Smith, K., and Stoelwinder, J. (2015). Secondary triage in prehospital emergency ambulance services: A systematic review. *Emergency Medicine Journal* 32; pp. 486–492.

Giddens, A. (1999) Risk and responsibility. *The Modern Law Review* 62(1); pp. 1–10.

Gray, J.T. and Wardrope, J. (2007) Introduction of non-transport guidelines into an ambulance service: A retrospective review. *Emergency Medicine Journal* 24(10); pp. 727–729.

Health and Safety executive (HSE). (2011) High reliability organisations. A review of literature. Research report RR899. www.hse.gov.uk/research/rrpdf/rr899.pdf. Accessed 21/6/18.

Imison, C., Curry, N., Holder, H., Castel-Clarke, S., Nimmons, D., Appleby, J., Thorlby, R., and Lombardo, S. (2017). Shifting the balance of care. *Research report*. Nuffield Trust.

Jeffcott, M., Pidgeon, N., Weyman, A., and Walls, J. (2006) Risk, Trust, and Safety Culture in U.K. Train Operating Companies. *Risk Analysis* 26(5); pp. 1105–1121.

Marsh, S. (2017) More patients waiting longer than a week for GP appointments. *The Guardian*. www.theguardian.com/society/2017/jul/06/more-patients-waiting-longer-than-a-week-for-gp-appointments. Accessed 18/9/18.

McCann, N. (2011) The ten worse reasons to call an ambulance. BBC News 15th September. www.bbc.co.uk/news/uk-northern-ireland-14930507. Accessed 18/9/18.

Morgan, G., Fischoff, B., and Bostrom, A. (2008) Risk Communication a mental models approach. Cambridge, UK.

National Audit Office (NAO). (2011) Transforming NHS ambulance services. London: National Audit Office. www.nao.org.uk/wp-content/uploads/2011/06/n10121086.pdf. Accessed 18/9/18.

National Health Executive. (2017) Risk averse 111 service sending more callers to struggling A&E and ambulances, 22nd February. http://www.nationalhealthexecutive.com/Care-Pathways/risk-averse-111-service-sending-more-callers-to-struggling-ae-and-ambulances

NHS England. (2013) High Quality Care for All, Now and for Future Generations: Transforming Urgent and Emergency Care Services in England—Urgent and Emergency Care Review End of Phase 1 Report. www.nhs.uk/NHSEngland/keogh-review/Documents/UECR.Ph1Report.FV.pdf. Accessed 20/8/18.

NHS England. (2015) Transforming Urgent and Emergency Care Services in England. Clinical Models for Ambulance Services. www.england.nhs.uk/wp-content/uploads/2015/06/trans-uec.pdf. Accessed 20/8/18.

NHS England. (2017) Referral to treatment (RTT) waiting times statistics for consultant-led elective care. 2016/17 Annual Report. www.england.nhs.uk/statistics/wp-content/uploads/sites/2/2017/06/RTT-Annual-Report-2016-17-v0.9-final.pdf. Accessed 18/9/18.

Nuffield Trust. (2017) NHS 111 sending increasing number of callers to A&E and ambulances. Press release 22nd February. https://www.nuffieldtrust.org.uk/news-item/nhs-111-sending-increasing-number-of-callers-to-a-e-and-ambulances.

O'Hara, R., Johnson, M., Hirst, E., Weyman, A., Shaw, D., Mortimer, P., Newman, C., Storey, M., Turner, J., and Mason, S. (2014). A qualitative study of decision-making and safety in ambulance service transitions. *Health Services and Delivery Research* 2(56).

O'Hara et al. (2015) A qualitative study of systematic influences on paramedic decision making: Care transitions and patient safety. *Journal of Health Services Research and Policy* 20(1); pp. 45–53.

Opportunities, Challenges and Prospects. Report to the UK Medical Research Council.

Perrow, C. (1984) *Normal accidents: Living with high-risk technologies*. New York: Basic Books.

Pidgeon, N., Walls, J., Weyman. A., and Horlick-Jones, T. (2003) Perceptions of and Trust in the Health and Safety Executive as a Risk Regulator. Health and Safety Executive Research Report 093. HSE Books.

Pope, C., Turnbull, J., Jones, J., Pritchard, J., Rowsell, A., and Halford, S. (2017) Has the NHS 111 urgent care telephone service been a success? Case study and secondary data analysis in England. *BMJ Open*. https://bmjopen.bmj.com/content/7/5/e014815. Accessed 18/9/18.

Porter, A., Snooks, H., Youren, A., Gaze, S., Whitfield, R., Rapport, F., and Woolard, M. (2007) 'Should I stay or should I go?' Deciding whether to go to hospital after a 999 call. *Journal of Health Services Research & Policy* 12; pp. 32–38.

Porter, A., Snooks, H., Youren, A., Gaze, S., Whitfield, R., Rapport, F., and Woollard, M. (2008) "Covering our backs": ambulance crews' attitudes towards clinical documentation when emergency (999) patients are not conveyed to hospital. *Emergency Medicine Journal* 25(5); pp. 292–295.

Power, M. (2004) The risk management of everything. *The Journal of Risk Finance* 5(3); pp. 58–65.

Radcliffe, J. and Health, G. (2010) Implication of the changing role of the ambulance paramedic for the interpretation of inappropriate calls: A review of the literature. *PAC Conference Proceedings*, Nottingham Trent University, Nottingham.

Reason, J. (1990) *Human Error*. Cambridge: Cambridge University Press.

Ruch, G. (2005) Relationship-based practice and reflective practice: holistic approaches to contemporary child care social work. *Child and Family Social Work* 10; pp. 111–123.

Shields, A. and Flin, R. (2013) Paramedics' non-technical skills: A literature review. *Emergency Medicine Journal* 30(5); pp. 350–354.

Siegrist, J. (1996) Adverse health effects of high-effort/low-reward conditions. *Journal of Occupational Health Psychology*, 1, 27.

Simpson, P., Thomas, R., Bendall, J., Lord, B., Lord, S., and Close, J. (2017) 'Popping nana back into bed'—a qualitative exploration of paramedic decision making when caring for older people who have fallen. MC Health Services Research. https://bmchealthservres.biomedcentral.com/articles/10.1186/s12913-017-2243-y. Accessed 18/9/18.

Snooks, H.A., Kearsley. N., Dale, J., Halter, M., Redhead, J., and Foster, J. (2005) Gaps between policy, protocols and practice: a qualitative study of the views and practice of emergency ambulance staff concerning the care of patients with non-urgent needs. *BMJ Quality and Safety* 14; pp. 251–257. https://qualitysafety.bmj.com/content/qhc/14/4/251.full.pdf

Spielman, A. (2017) Ofsted's Chief Inspector writes about safety culture in schools. www.gov.uk/government/speeches/ofsteds-chief-inspector-writes-about-safety-culture-in-schools. Accessed 18/9/18.

Thaler, R. and Sunstein, C. (2008) *Nudge improving decisions about health, wealth and happiness*. New Haven, Connecticut, Yale.

Trist, E.L. and Bamforth, K.W. (1951) Some social and psychological consequences of the longwall method of coal getting. http://journals.sagepub.com/doi/pdf/10.1177/001872675100400101.

Turnbull, J., Halford, S., Jones, J., May, C., Pope, C., Prichard, J.S., and Rowsell, A.C. (2014). The work, workforce, technology and organisational implications of the '111'single point of access telephone number for urgent (non-emergency) care: a mixed-methods case study. *Health Services and Delivery Research* 2(3).

Turner, J., O'Cathain, A., Knowles, E., and Nickoll, J. (2013) Impact of the urgent care telephone service NHS 111 pilot sites: A controlled before and after study. BMJ Open. https://bmjopen.bmj.com/content/bmjopen/3/11/e003451.full.pdf. Accessed 18/9/18.

Weyman, A., Meadows, P., and Buckingham, A. (2013) Extending working life Audit of research relating to impact on National Health Service employees. NHS Working Longer Review. www.nhsemployers.org/~/media/Employers/Documents/Pay%20and%20reward/WLR%20-%20Extending%20Working%20Life%20-%20An%20audit%20of%20research%20relating%20to%20impacts%20on%20NHS%20Employees%20May%202013.pdf. Accessed 18/9/18.

Weyman, A., Pidgeon, N., Jeffcott, M., and Walls, J. (2006) *Organisational dynamics and safety culture in UK train operating companies*. Health and Safety executive. Bootle: HSE Books.

Weyman, A.K.; Wainwright; D; O'Hara, R. & Buckingham, A. (2012) Extending Working Life Behaviour Change Interventions. Department for Work and Pensions Report 809. https://assets.publishing.service.gov.uk/government/uploads/system/uploads/attachment_data/file/193404/rrep809.pdf

Weyman, A. and Roy, D. (2017). Should I stay or should I go?–Exploring relative drivers of employee early-exit from the NHS. *Annual Conference of British Psychological Society Brighton.*

Weyman, A. and Nolan, P. (2018) Paramedics drivers of early exit from the NHS – Penetration to Ambulance Sector Working Group, UNISON Headquarters, Euston Road London, 31st October.

Williams, K. (2014) State of fear: Britain's compensation culture reviewed. *Legal Studies* 25(3); pp. 499–515.

Young, Lord of Graffham (2010) Common sense common safety. HM Government. https://assets.publishing.service.gov.uk/government/uploads/system/uploads/attachment_data/file/60905/402906_CommonSense_acc.pdf. Accessed 18/9/18.

13 A Comparative Appraisal of Recent and Proposed Changes to the Fire and Rescue Services in England and Scotland

Peter Murphy,* Katarzyna Lakoma,
Kirsten Greenhalgh and Lynda Taylor

Introduction

Scottish firefighters and fire brigades have been an integral part of the fire services in the UK since James Braidwood established the first municipal service in Edinburgh. He was the first to develop systematic methods of controlling and fighting fires rather than simply (and sometimes chaotically) responding to individual incidents (Ewen, 2010). Braidwood went on to establish the London Fire Engine Establishment in 1833, which was the precursor to the Metropolitan Fire Brigade of 1866. As Taylor et al. (2018, p. 191) acknowledge,

> from the early 19th century to the end of the 20th there was little to differentiate the scale scope and nature of the service in Scotland from those south of the border, as the Edinburgh 'model' was adopted by in all the great Victorian cities, such as Glasgow, Manchester, Liverpool, Birmingham, Leeds and many more.

The heart of the early 21st century modernisation of the fire service by the New Labour administrations and the subsequent development of policy and service delivery was the Fire and Rescue Services Act 2004 and the Civil Contingencies Act 2004. These two acts were developed and came into force at the same time. Scotland actually had its own Fire and Rescue Services Act of 2005, but this is almost identical to the English Fire and Rescue Services Act 2004 in terms of principles, objectives and the extensive changes to policy and practice that followed the commencement of the act.

At this time, both systems changed the basis for their assessment of risk from a system based primarily on evaluating risks to premises, buildings and property to a system based upon evaluating risks to people and communities (Bain et al. 2002). Amongst other things, the act introduced an Integrated Risk Management Planning process (IRMP) together with Integrated Risk Management Plans, which by statute have to be produced and regularly updated in both countries. Although a great number of changes have subsequently happened to the fire service in both England and Scotland, the

* Correspondence E-mail ID: peter.murphy@ntu.ac.uk

one thing that has not changed in either service since its introduction is the requirement to assess risk based on an IRM process and the requirement to produce an IRM plan.

Financial Resources

Both regimes and administrations have also been subject to the same severe financial constraints under the coalition government's macro-economic approach to 'austerity' (Blyth, 2015; O'Hara, 2015; Schui, 2014). This was a UK-wide policy that has been operationalised at service and local levels through successive financial settlements and short-term cutback management.

Although the policy of cutback management (Wilks, 2010; Scorsone and Plerhoples, 2010) was intended to be 'short term' and originally intended to address the 'structural deficit' in the UK's finances, it has persisted since the emergency budget and the governments' Spending Review of 2010. Cutback management is usually a short-term policy response to major spending shocks or crises, last seen in the UK in the 1980s. It is questionable whether it is an efficient or effective policy in the short term; there is no doubt that it is an inefficient long-term economic policy. It has been implemented in the UK through a series of short-term sub-optimal adjustments instead of through a coherent and robust long-term strategic approach. The result has been an increase in the national debt, which exceeded £1.5 trillion at the end of the 2015–16 financial year (HMT, 2018a).

The government's long-term single departmental spending plans are laid out at the Spending Review 2015 (HM Treasury, 2015) for the period 2015 to 2020 (Home Office, 2016a). These plans described the new governments' objectives and are intended to ensure that each government's department's plans and spending reflected the priorities of the 'whole of government' priorities. The departmental expenditure limits for the Home Office in England and for Scotland are shown (in cash terms and in billions) in Table 13.1. They effectively show a medium-term reduction in cash terms, and a greater reduction in real terms, for public services in both countries, both recently and in the foreseeable future.

Although these departmental plans were updated in December 2017 (Home Office, 2017a), together with the latest annual 'supply', estimates presented

Table 13.1 Resource (DEL excluding depreciation) 2015 Spending Review Departmental Expenditure Limits (HM Treasury p. 77).

Departmental Expenditure Limit	2015–16	2016–17	2017–18	2018–19	2019–20	2020–21	Cumulative Real Growth
Home Office	10.3	10.7	10.6	10.6	10.6	*	−4.8%
Scotland	25.9	26.1	26.3	26.3	26.5	*	−5.0%
Wales	12.9	13.0	13.1	13.2	13.3	*	−4.5%

to the House of Commons by HMT in April 2018 were still based upon the 2015 Spending Review, and the latest 'Spring Statement' in March 2018 (HM Treasury, 2018b) made no new spending announcements.

Thus the 'resource envelope' upon which the fire and rescue services is dependent in both countries in the period from 2010 to 2018 and in the foreseeable future up until 2020/21 is remarkably similar. It is contracting.

A Watershed

The common approach to policy and the delivery of fire and rescue services changed radically after the election of a Conservative-led coalition government in England in May 2010, and First Minister Alex Salmond launched the Christie Commission on the Future Delivery of Public Services in Scotland (Scottish Parliament, 2011a).

The latter was to examine how Scotland's public services could be delivered in order to secure improved outcomes for communities across the country. The following year, the Scottish National Party won the May 2011 elections to Holyrood with an overwhelming majority. The Christie Commission produced its report with the chairman Dr Campbell Christie urging the government to "act quickly and decisively", claiming that "the way forward is clear, and it is now essential that the Scottish Government exercises its leadership by initiating a fundamental public service reform process" (2011, p. vi).

The period from 2010 to 2015 then saw considerable changes to public policy and management as well as service delivery across the whole public sector throughout the UK. Nowhere was it better exemplified by the respective changes in the two fire and rescue sectors. The next three sections of this chapter will therefore compare changes in the policy development, service delivery and public assurance arrangements in England and Scotland, before drawing some conclusions in the final section.

Policy and Leadership

The fundamental differences in the policy approach to fire and rescue services was almost immediately apparent from the first policy documents published after the respective elections in 2010 and 2011. Both governments proposed new legislation and initiated consultation exercises. These resulted in new legislation and the issuing of new national frameworks for fire and rescue services based upon competing visions of public services. Policy development at both national and local levels changed and has continued to contrast between the two countries.

In Scotland, the Christie Commission had focused on how to secure improved outcomes from public services. The Scottish government was urged to show leadership and "act quickly and decisively" to improve public services.

Before the end of 2011, and admittedly benefiting from all party general support, the Scottish government had published a consultation on the future of the Scottish fire and rescue services (Scottish Government, 2011a), an initial options appraisal report on possible structural reform (2011b) and an outline business case (Scottish Government, 2011c) for the creation of a single national services. The latter, to be through the amalgamation of the eight existing services and the national training centre, had quickly become the preferred option.

These were followed by the 2012 Police and Fire Reform Act (Scotland), which required the establishment of a single national service by April 2013, when a national policy framework (Scottish Government, 2013a) and a new governance and accountability framework for fire and rescue services (Scottish Government, 2013b) were also published. In retrospect, it is clear that the Scottish government took an immediate grasp of fire and rescue service policy and sought to develop it in an open collaborative manner reminiscent of earlier calls in England for the co-production of policy.

This practice of collaboratively producing policy with the services and organisations that have to deliver the policy, and allowing significant time for public consultation and reflection upon representations received, is one that has endured into the latest round of national policy. At the time of writing this chapter, the Scottish parliament are in the course of undertaking 'Post-legislative Scrutiny of the Police and Fire Reform (Scotland) Act 2012' (Scottish Parliament, 2018); Audit Scotland (2018) have published an update of their audit report on the first two years of the fire and rescue reforms (Audit Scotland, 2015), the Scottish FRS are consulting on their future strategy (SFRS, 2018) and HMI Fire Service Inspectorate, partly motivated by the Grenfell tragedy, have completed a national Fire Safety Enforcement Inspection (HMFSI, 2018).

What emerges from all of this activity is not only the continuing difference in their policy content and underlying principles but also the difference in the way the processes are being conducted.

The open, consultative, inclusive and reflective process in Scotland contrasts with the equivalent in England. In England, independent third parties find it difficult to contribute to the process, consultation periods are as limited as statute allows and key national policy documents such as a draft new national framework (Home Office, 2017b) are published to a "silent fanfare of absent publicity" (Murphy and Glennon, 2018, p. 22), to be followed almost immediately by a national framework (Home Office, 2018) that has taken a minimal amount of notice of the limited response.

In their analysis of the period up to 2015, Taylor et al. (2018) noted that the early initiatives reflected a strong orientation towards notions of public value, new public service theory and traditional interpretations of public service (2018, p. 194), where the users of public services are seen as citizens with responsibilities as well as rights, rather than 'customers' of services. They also give the impression that the public's voice is valued, heard and acted upon.

The latest policy documents embrace and further embed these notions as the government attempts to operationalise the next stage of service reform and build on the approach adopted over the reforms to date. Scotland, at least in terms of its fire and rescue service, has witnessed a successful start to its transformation project that has demonstrated individual and collective leadership within a strategic and holistic approach to the service (Taylor et al., 2018; Audit Scotland, 2015, 2018).

> Board and management display mutual respect, a constructive tone and genuine shred ownership of issues.
>
> (Audit Scotland, 2018, p. 5)

Finally, at the local level, policy development, partnership working and community working continues to be effective (Audit Scotland, 2015, 2018; Taylor et al., 2018).

> The SFRS has successfully maintained effective relationships at a local level through local senior officers (LSOs) who liaise with the 32 Scottish councils and community planning partnerships. The council officers and councillors that we interviewed during our audit consistently said that they valued the enthusiasm and contribution of the LSOs very highly, particularly in relation to their community work on prevention and protection.
> LSOs lead the development of local fire and rescue plans for each Community Planning Partnership. These plans are more tailored to local risks than previous plans and are focused on improving outcomes for local people, such as better home safety.
>
> (Audit Scotland, 2018, p. 23)

In England, policy development took a different turn from the moment the new fire minister in the coalition government announced a strategic review of the fire and rescue sector and the government's role within it (DCLG, 2010). A new policy regime for public services that has been described as 'austerity localism' (Lowndes and Pratchett, 2012) was established by the Localism Act 2011 and the Open Public Services White Papers (Cabinet Office, 2011, 2012). This was a return to the notions of new public management, neoliberalism and the advocacy of greater exposure of public services to markets and price competition. The emergency services were no exception.

The national framework for fire and rescue services that followed (DCLG, 2012) included a significantly reduced role for the government in policy development and support for the delivery of fire services (Murphy and Ferry, 2018). This was accompanied by a significant loss of capacity and coherence in the sector, which compromised strategic alignment at the national level (Ferry and Murphy, 2015; NAO, 2015a). The government also abolished the Audit Commission and most of the 'improvement' infrastructure, losing significant amounts of data and intelligence in the process (see also Chapter 9). At the local level, it introduced a 'light touch' self-governing model for local fire and rescue authorities and implemented a commissioner/provider split with the fire and rescue service.

The result was effectively an abdication of individual and collective leadership by the government, with only limited and unplanned restructuring of service delivery, as only two pairs of county service amalgamations took place at the local level despite continuous policy encouragement. By the time of the general election in 2015, the system was in disarray and quickly became unacceptable to both parliament and the government.

In 2016 the Public Accounts Select Committee had reported,

> The Department for Communities and Local Government has not had a strong understanding of the capacity of individual fire authorities to absorb further reductions through efficiency savings, or of the impact of reducing fire prevention work. By not providing more active support and guidance, the Department exacerbated the risk that fire authorities would miss opportunities to improve value for money . . . There are weaknesses in the local scrutiny by fire authorities which raise concerns about their operational performance and safeguarding value for money; this is more serious because of the lack of an external inspectorate.
>
> (2016b, p. 3)

The government announced that responsibility for fire and rescue services would henceforth be transferred to the Home Office, and in one of her last speeches as home secretary, the future prime minister admitted,

> fire and rescue landscape are still beset by poor governance and structures (they are) a service that requires further reform to improve accountability, bring independent scrutiny and drive transparency.
>
> (Home Office 2016b, p. 2)

Mrs May's proposed solution was to adopt the approach that she had previously taken to the reform of the police services with the introduction of police and crime commissioners who would now ('subject to a local case being made') be encouraged to take over governance and policy responsibility for local fire and rescue services. She therefore announced that emergency amendments would be added to the Policing and Crime Bill, then at third reading in the House of Commons, accepting and incorporating all of the recommendations of the PAC report.

Chapter 9 describes in more detail the introduction of police and crime commissioners and the resultant changes in the organisational landscape in England that resulted from what became the Crime and Policing Act 2017.

To examine how policy changed, we need only look at the new national framework for fire and rescue services (Home Office, 2018) that was published after the act. We have of course already commented on the process adopted and the limitations of the consultation arrangements. What the framework includes and what it excludes are both instructive.

There is no mention in the minister's foreword or in the introduction to the National Audit Office or the Public Accounts Committee reports that drew attention to inadequacies in the sponsorship, leadership, financial control and infrastructural support for the service. There is also no explicit mention of the long-term planned future reductions in financial support. The new framework is, however, very clear that the government's overall policy approach has not changed.

> The National Framework will continue to provide an overall strategic direction to fire and rescue authorities, but Whitehall will not run fire, and fire and rescue authorities and their services remain free to operate in a way that enables the most efficient and effective delivery of their services, drawing upon their considerable skills and experience to best reduce the risks from fire.
>
> (Home Office, 2018, p. 4)

The framework re-confirmed that the basis of policy development would remain the IRMP process. Similarly, it confirmed that the role of national government in the national resilience arrangements is to identify any gaps in provision. It remains the responsibility of fire and rescue authorities to assess all foreseeable risks that affect their communities—whether they are local, cross-border, multi-authority and/or national in nature, from fires to terrorist attacks—and to address any gaps.

While the act and the framework clearly acknowledge the services' contributions to wider social policy issues and wish to encourage wider collaborative working, both the act and the framework are primarily concerned with changes in the arrangements for public assurance and service delivery rather than public policy.

Service Delivery

There are a number of characteristics or issues relating to service delivery through which we can compare the two countries: management and performance, ways of working, the priority afforded to protection and prevention as opposed to reactive services, and of course, the governance and delivery structure.

The clear contrast in the service delivery structure is the simplest to describe in the two countries since it has already arisen in both this chapter and in Chapter 9.

The amalgamation of services, primarily to achieve economies of scale and make more sophisticated specialist services and appliances universally available, had been a recurrent feature in both countries, since 'modernisation' at the turn of the century.

John Prescott, the politician most responsible for the Fire and Rescue Act 2004 and the Civil Contingencies Act when he was secretary of state and deputy prime minister, was often accused of trying to apply his regional agenda to all public service reform, and the fire and rescue service was no exception. His project to replace 46 local fire control centres with nine purpose-built regional centres was a particular disaster that became a political albatross (NAO, 2011; PAC, 2011) for regionalisation long before and after the scheme had to be abandoned. The coalition government, however, remained committed to encouraging voluntary amalgamations. So much so that in 2015 Lyn Brown MP, then shadow fire minister, published a consultation about the future of fire services in England that was based explicitly on three options for the horizontal integration and amalgamation of services (Brown, 2015).

As we know from Chapter 9, this did not happen in England. In Scotland, however horizontal integration across the sector had all-party support in principle and ultimately resulted in the creation of the Scottish fire and rescue service, which is the largest service in the UK and the fourth largest in the world.

There are, however, three aspects of service delivery that have remained constant across both countries, although even in these areas minor differences are starting to appear. The first is a firefighting establishment with a mixture of service personnel consisting of whole-time and part-time (or 'retained') personnel and volunteers. The second is the deployment of this personnel via the 'watch' and station structure, and the third is the need for collaborative working both across the emergency services and more widely with key partners such as local authorities.

These three aspects reflect almost universal characteristics of fire services across the globe. Although both countries share these characteristics, the approach to flexible rostering of personnel, the use and retention of stations and other premises and the nature of their collaborations is starting to change because of policy differences.

Scotland is effectively implementing a resource- or asset-based strategy— valuing its assets and attempting to optimise its use of available resources while evaluating inputs, outputs and outcomes against the creation of both public and private value. England, as the new national framework (Home Office, 2018) and the new inspection proposals demonstrate (HMICFRS, 2018), is implementing a financially led strategy, through a shrinking resource envelope, allied to evaluating services and initiatives against the financial return on investment primarily (but not exclusively) in the short term. Scotland is essentially retaining assets and estate and seeking to make better use of them, often in collaboration with the other emergency services. England is actively rationalising and disposing of its assets and estates, where possible, to meet financial targets.

The second emerging difference results from the balance of investment within the respective services and countries, in terms of investment in national and local 'protection and prevention services' on the one hand, and fire response services on the other.

Both countries acknowledge the importance of maintaining fire protection and prevention services, and overall, both services are subject to approximately the same level of reducing resources. However, in terms of proportionate reductions, the overall balance tends to favour investment in emergency response in England, while in Scotland it favours the protection and preventative services because of alternative service and financial policies between the two countries.

In terms of collaborative working, the service in England is clearly moving towards much closer collaboration with the police in particular, although the government was so concerned about the extent of collaboration across the emergency services that it introduced a statutory requirement to collaborate in Chapter 1 of the Policing and Crime Act 2017.

In Scotland, collaboration between the government, the SFRS, the emergency services and other key stakeholders such as the local authorities has been relatively successful and is considered to be improving. The geographical co-terminus boundaries between police, fire and ambulance services in Scotland undoubtedly help collaborative working at the strategic level, while coterminous boundaries with local authority areas clearly assist operational collaboration.

Finally, we are able to compare the management and performance of the two services, as both have been subjected to extensive external independent scrutiny and review over the last eight years, not least by their external auditors (NAO, 2015a, 2015b; Audit Scotland, 2015, 2018) but also by their respective parliamentary scrutiny arrangements (PAC, 2016; Scottish Parliament, 2011b, 2018).

In terms of both financial and service performance, the contrast is surprisingly stark.

While Scotland has been characterised as having strong financial management with a 'good approach to long term financial management' (Audit Scotland, 2018, p. 5), in England the NAO (2015a, 2015b) found significant inadequacies in financial management and value for money, which were reiterated by the PAC (2016) and acknowledged by the government (Home Office, 2016b).

In Scotland, the auditors initially reported that the Scottish government and the Scottish fire and rescue service managed the 2013 merger of the eight fire and rescue services effectively and that there was no impact on the safety of the public during or as a result of the merger. There were no additional funds to help with the merger but, nevertheless, in the first phase from 2013 to 2015 the performance of the Scottish fire and rescue service improved and was continuing to improve (Audit Scotland, 2015). By 2018 the auditors were still positive if more cautious; "the SFRS continues to deliver emergency and prevention service while progressing a complex and ambitious programme of reform" (2018, p. 1). Audit Scotland was, however, by this time *inter alia* calling for an increase in the pace of reform, the introduction of well-developed performance management systems and more robust monitoring evaluation and reporting of the impacts of community safety activity.

Public Assurance

In Scotland, there is a comprehensive system of parliamentary and governmental scrutiny over the fire and rescue services. The government appoints an arms-length independent board, who are responsible for the corporate governance of the SFRS. The senior management of SFRS reports to the board, and they in turn are accountable to the Scottish government through the Department of Community Safety who are, *inter alia*, responsible for 'delivering fit-for-purpose police and fire services'. The external audit is the responsibility of Audit Scotland, who now audit 224 public bodies including the Scottish parliament central government bodies, the 32 councils and the 23 NHS bodies.

Parliamentary scrutiny in Scotland is largely based on the Westminster system, which is a model of scrutiny through a series of all-party backbench select committees that largely mirror government departments. The fire service in Scotland is scrutinised primarily by the Local Government and Communities Committee but, as in England, can be called upon by other select committees. In addition, Scotland also has a Public Audit and Post-legislative Scrutiny Committee. This committee scrutinises the performance of the Scottish government and public bodies, considers issues arising from their accounts and specifically reviews the implementation and effectiveness of recent legislation. As mentioned earlier, the Local Government and Communities Committee is currently scrutinising building regulations and fire safety in Scotland, largely as a result of the Grenfell Tower disaster (Grenfell Tower Inquiry, 2016), while the Public Audit and Post-legislative Scrutiny Committee is investigating issues arising out of the 2018 Audit Scotland update of the Scottish FRS (Audit Scotland, 2018).

In England, since 2016, the Home Office has been responsible for the fire and rescue services. However, the minister of state for policing and the fire service, in his foreword to the new national framework, states that the national framework will continue to provide an overall strategic direction to fire and rescue authorities. 'Whitehall will not run fire', thus signalling a continuation of the policy and practice that was evident from 2010 to 2015 under the previous Department of Communities and Local Government (Home Office, 2018).

The Home Affairs Committee and the Public Accounts Select Committee provide parliamentary scrutiny, although both of their remits are much wider than that of their Scottish counterparts. Fire and rescue services are therefore a much smaller part of their respective portfolios. For example at the time of writing, the Home Affairs committee has 14 ongoing inquiries, none of which involves the fire and rescue service, while the PAC has 29 ongoing inquiries with the only one affecting fire and rescue a review of the process for replacing the 'Airwave' emergency communication system.

Fire and rescue authorities in England can appoint their own auditors, who cover the authority's financial statements and the assessment of value for money under the Local Audit and Accountability Act 2014. The act only applies to England, where the audit of organisational performance has increasingly relied on the development of the concept and practice of 'armchair auditors' or interested members of the public taking direct evaluative interest in services rather than regular public assessment and reporting from professional auditors. There is now considerable independent research to question the effectiveness of this reliance on 'armchair auditors' (Ferry and Murphy, 2017; Ferry et al., 2018).

In a speech shortly before she became prime minister, Mrs May promised to put in place the right framework of institutions and processes to ensure operational integrity, as well as greater accountability and transparency for the fire service (Home Office, 2016b). She referred in particular to the lack of an independent inspectorate, a regular audit of performance and the limited available data on performance over time or between areas.

External independent inspection of the fire and rescue service was terminated on the announcement of the abolition of the Audit Commission. The Audit Commission had taken over independent inspection from Her Majesty's Fire Service in 2007. Between 2007 and 2018, England was the only country in Europe without an inspectorate. Scotland had retained Her Majesty's Fire Service Inspectorate for Scotland throughout.

Shortly after the Policing and Crime Act 2017 received royal assent, the minister (Brandon Lewis) announced further details about the new inspectorate (Home Office, 2017c). He said that a new 'suitable' inspectorate for fire and rescue services would be modelled on Her Majesty's Inspectorate of Constabulary (HMIC), and that, like HMIC, it would have a focus on efficiency and effectiveness.

It would have the power to undertake joint inspections with HMIC and thematic inspections as well as organisation inspections and service inspections. Like HMIC, it would report to government through the Home Office. The home secretary has the power to commission and direct inspections and the chief inspector's annual report will be presented to parliament via the Home Office.

Emerging as Her Majesty's Inspectorate of Constabulary and fire and rescue services, it was established in April 2018 with a chairman and board inherited from its predecessor the HMIC.

Any ambitions for robust independence were further deflated with the publication of the consultation on the new inspectorate's proposed inspection framework and initial programme of inspections (HMICFRS, 2017). Emulating the practice adopted by the Home Office with the national framework, it was published in the week immediately prior to Christmas in 2017 (Murphy and Glennon, 2018). Following a minimal statutory consultation process that took little notice of the limited representations received, it was quickly followed in March 2018 by the formal framework (HMICFRS, 2018).

In Scotland, the chief inspector (HMFSI) is appointed by Order in Council and operates independently of ministers and the SFRS.

The purpose of the Scottish Inspectorate is to "give assurance to the Scottish people and to Scottish ministers that the Scottish FRS is working in an efficient and effective way and to promote improvement in the SFRS" (Audit Scotland, 2016, p. 1). The inspectorate has to have regard to "the principles of public focus, independence, proportionality, transparency and accountability" (Audit Scotland, 2016, p. 2). By statute, the chief inspector has a duty to make 'independent' determinations and is obliged to collaborate and align the work of the inspectorate with key stakeholders such as Audit Scotland, the Ombudsman and the Procurator Fiscal Service.

The Scottish Inspectorate is conceptualised and established as part of the scrutiny arrangements of governance rather than being part of the government. The new HMICFRS in England is clearly conceptualised and strategically positioned closer to the government. Although it is too early to judge in this case, history suggests that the more independent an inspectorate is, the more robust open and effective the scrutiny it provides.

Mrs May's speech in 2016 also drew attention to the limited available data on service performance available to the government, key stakeholders, collaborators and the public. Some would regard this as a tacit acknowledgement of the failure of the armchair auditor initiative. The loss and degradation of performance data and intelligence has been an issue since the announcement of the demise of the Audit Commission. It was further exacerbated by the closure of the Improvement and Development Agency and a range of non-departmental public bodies that were part of the so-called Bonfire of the Quango's (Ferry and Murphy, 2015; NAO, 2015a; Murphy et al., 2018). As a result of these changes, there was a huge loss of publically available data, intelligence and historical knowledge and an irreplaceable back catalogue of individual reports and inspections. In addition, the tools and techniques, capacity and capability to analyse and interrogate this information was also lost.

Conclusions

In retrospect, it appears somewhat ironic that the policy priority in Scotland of improving public services and in particularly improving outputs is consistent with the policy emphasis in England prior to the 2010 general election. Horizontal integration to achieve economies of scale and greater efficiencies were an ambition of the New Labour administrations. Indeed, some of the changes in Scotland might well have emerged as a logical next stage or at least a policy option had the general election not intervened.

Similarly, the ambition to integrate local policy objectives, and align organisational activities, across locally delivered public services, for example via Local and Multi Area Agreements, was a characteristic of previous Labour administrations. These initiatives were soon abandoned in England after 2010 but found further expression in Scotland through Single Outcome Agreements and community planning. At a more general level, this appears to reflect greater active involvement from central government in service delivery. Scotland also appears to have a more reflective and responsive approach to policy development and service delivery, not least in terms of 'ownership' of issues.

Changes in the structural and organisational landscape in both countries is the most visible contrast between the two countries in terms of service delivery. It will be interesting to see whether the emerging contrasts between estates strategies, the balance of investment between preventative and reactive services and the alternative approaches to collaboration continue to widen and if so, what impact this has on service management and performance. What surprised the authors of this study is how little evidence there appears to be of mutual learning between the respective regimes.

The crucial issue is how well the services are performing, how efficiently they are spending the public's money and ultimately how safe their communities are as a result.

The current evidence may be limited, but the findings of our investigations tend to favour the approach in Scotland. And this is the case even if you allow for competing objectives.

It is clear that England has financial management and expenditure targets as its central priority. Yet, in terms of value for money and financial targets (which are equally challenging in both countries), it is Scotland that appears to have been more successful to date. Whether the changes emerging from the Crime and Policing Act 2017 and the new national framework in England have a positive or negative impact on this comparison is a matter for a future study.

Finally, in terms of public assurance, we found clearer lines of accountability between the government and the service; more and more focused parliamentary, national and local scrutiny; and more robust and effective frameworks for inter-agency working in Scotland than exist or are emerging in England.

References

Audit Scotland. 2015. *Scottish Fire and Rescue Service*, Audit Scotland: Edinburgh.

Audit Scotland. 2016. *Memorandum of Understanding for Cooperation Between Audit Scotland, on Behalf of the Auditor General for Scotland, and HM Fire Service Inspectorate in Scotland (HMFSI)*, Audit Scotland: Edinburgh.

Audit Scotland. 2018. *Scottish Fire and Rescue Service an Update*, Audit Scotland: Edinburgh.

Bain, G, Lyons, M, and Young, M. 2002. *The Future of the Fire Service; Reducing Risks Saving Lives: The Independent Review of the Fire Service* Norwich: TSO.

Blyth, M. 2015. *Austerity: The History of a Dangerous Idea*, Oxford: Oxford University Press.

Brown, L. 2015. *The Future of Fire and Rescue Services in England*. London: House of Commons.

Cabinet Office. 2011. *Open Public Services White Paper*. London: Cabinet Office.

Cabinet Office. 2012. *Open Public Services White 2012*. London: Cabinet Office.

Christie Commission. 2011. *Commission on the Future Delivery of Public Services*. Norwich: TSO.

DCLG. 2010. *Leading a Lean and Efficient Fire and Rescue Service, Fire Minister Bob Neill's Speech to Fire and Rescue 2010 Conference*, Harrogate, England.

DCLG. 2012. *Fire and rescue national framework for England*. London: TSO.

Ewen. S. 2010. *Fighting Fires: Creating the British Fire Service 1800–1978*. Basingstoke: Palgrave Macmillan.

Ferry, L., Glennon, R., and Murphy, P. 2018. Chapter 3: *Local Government* in Public Service Accountability: Rekindling a Debate. Cham, Switzerland: Palgrave Macmillan.

Ferry, L., and Murphy, P. 2015. *Financial sustainability, accountability and transparency across local public service bodies in England under austerity. Report to National Audit Office*. Nottingham: Nottingham Trent University.

Ferry, L., and Murphy, P. 2017. What about financial sustainability of local government! A critical review of accountability, transparency, and public assurance arrangements in England during austerity. *International Journal of Public Administration*, 41(8), 619–629.

Grenfell Tower Inquiry. 2016. *Ongoing*. Available at www.grenfelltowerinquiry.org. uk/ [Accessed 18/09/2018]

HM Fire Service Inspectorate. 2018. *Fire Safety Enforcement by the Scottish Fire and Rescue Service*. Edinburgh: HMFSI.

HMICFRS. 2017. *Proposed Fire and Rescue Services Inspection Programme and Framework 2018/19*. London: HMICFRS.

HMICFRS. 2018. *Fire and Rescue Services Inspection Programme and Framework 2018/19*. London: HMICFRS.

HM Treasury. 2015. *The Spending Review 2015*. Norwich: TSO.

HM Treasury. 2018a. *Public Expenditure Statistical Analyses 2018*. Norwich: TSO.

HM Treasury. 2018b. *Spring Statement 2018: Speech* [Online]. Available at: www. gov.uk/government/speeches/spring-statement-2018-philip-hammonds-speech [Accessed 07/09/2018].

Home Office. 2016a. *Single Departmental Plans for 2015 to 2020* [Online]. Home Office. Available: www.gov.uk/government/collections/single-departmental-plans-for-2015-to-2020#single-departmental-plans-2015-to-2020 [Accessed 20/08/2018].

Home Office. 2016b. *Home Secretary Speech on Fire Reform* (at REFORM event 24/ 05/2016. [Online]. Available at: www.gov.uk/government/speeches/home-secretary-speech-on-fire-reform [Accessed 17/09/2018].

Home Office. 2017a. *Home Office Single Departmental Plan.* [Online]. Available at: www.gov.uk/government/publications/home-office-single-departmental-plan/home-office-single-departmental-plan [Accessed 19/09/2018].

Home Office. 2017b. *Fire and Rescue National Framework for England: Government Consultation*. London: TSO.

Home Office. 2017c. *Fire Minister's Speech to Reform*. Available at: www.gov.uk/ government/speeches/fire-ministers-speech-to-reform [Accessed 19/09/2018].

Home Office. 2018. *Fire and Rescue National Framework for England. London: TSO.*

Lowndes V., and Pratchett, L. 2012. Local governance under the coalition government: austerity, localism and the big society. *Local Government Studies* 38(1), 21–40.

Murphy, P., and Ferry, L. 2018. Another turn of the screw: Fire and rescue under the coalition government of 2010–2015. In P. Murphy and K. Greenhalgh (eds.), *Fire and Rescue Services: Leadership and Management Perspectives* (pp. 45–59). London: Springer.

Murphy, P., Ferry, L., Glennon, R., and Greenhalgh, K. 2018. *Public Service Accountability: Rekindling a Debate*. Cham, Switzerland: Palgrave Macmillan.

Murphy, P., and Glennon, R. (2018). Why not take the time to get the fire framework right? *FIRE*, March, 21–23.

National Audit Office. 2011. *The Failure of the Fire Control Project*. HC 1272 2010–2012. London: TSO.

National Audit Office. 2015a. *Financial Sustainability of Fire and Rescue Services*. HC 491, Session 2015–16. London: TSO.

National Audit Office. 2015b. *Variation in Spending by Fire and Rescue Authorities 2011–12 to 2013–14*. London: TSO.

O'Hara, M. 2015. *Austerity Bites: A journey to the sharp end of the cuts in the UK*. Bristol: Policy Press.

Public Accounts Committee. 2011. *The Failure of the Fire Control Project. Fiftieth Report of Session 2010–12*. London: TSO.

Public Accounts Committee. 2016. *Financial Sustainability of Fire and Rescue Services Twenty-third Report of Session 2015–16.* London: TSO.

Schui, F. 2014. *Austerity: The Great Failure,* New Haven: Yale University Press.

Scorsone E. A., and Plerhoples, C. 2010. Fiscal Stress and Cutback Management Amongst State and Local Governments: What Have We Learned and What Remains to Be Learned? *State and Local Government Review,* 42(2), 176–187

Scottish Fire and Rescue Service. 2018. *Your Service Your Voice: A Consultation on the Safe and Planned Future of the SFRS.* Cambuslang: SFRS.

Scottish Government. 2011a. *A Consultation on the Future of the Fire and Rescue Service in Scotland.* Edinburgh: Scottish Government.

Scottish Government. 2011b. *Initial Options Appraisal Report: Prepared for Scottish Fire and Rescue Services Ministerial Advisory Group,* Scottish Government: Edinburgh.

Scottish Government. 2011c. *Reform of the Fire and Rescue Service in Scotland: Outline Business Case,* Scottish Government: Edinburgh.

Scottish Government. 2013a. *Fire and Rescue Framework for Scotland,* Edinburgh: Scottish Government.

Scottish Government. 2013b. *Scottish Fire and Rescue Service (SFRS) Governance and Accountability Framework.* Edinburgh: Scottish Government.

Scottish Parliament. 2011a. *Financial Scrutiny Unit Briefing: The Commission on the Future Delivery of Public Service 11/52.* [Online]. Available at www.parliament. scot/ResearchBriefingsAndFactsheets/S4/SB_11-52.pdf [Accessed 15/09/2018].

Scottish Parliament. 2011b. *Report on the Financial Memorandum of the Police and Fire Reform (Scotland) Bill.* [Online] Available at: www.parliament.scot/ parliamentarybusiness/CurrentCommittees/48609.aspx [Accessed 18/09/2018]

Scottish Parliament. 2018. *Public Audit and Post-Legislative Scrutiny Committee: Scottish Fire and Rescue Service—an Update.* [Online] Available at: www.par liament.scot/parliamentarybusiness/CurrentCommittees/109350.aspx [Accessed 18/09/2018].

Taylor, L., Murphy, P., and Greenhalgh, K. 2018. *Scottish fire and rescue services reform 2010–2015.* In P. Murphy and K. Greenhalgh (Eds.), *Fire and Rescue Services: Leadership and Management Perspectives* (pp. 191–205). London: Springer.

Wilks, S. 2010. Cutback management in the United Kingdom: Challenges of fiscal consolidation for the administrative system. *The Korean Journal of Policy Studies,* 25(1), 85–108.

Part 4

14 Rethinking the New 'Leadership' Mainstream

An Historical Perspective From the National Health Service

Mark Learmonth

Introduction

Today, people working in 'blue light' emergency services—apparently like people in all sectors and organizations—seem obsessed with something called 'leadership'. But what is it? Leadership is often portrayed as different from and in important ways more advanced, more up to date and more virtuous than 'management' or 'administration' (Learmonth & Morrell, 2019). Yet its various traits and meanings should not be uncritically assumed.

Emergency services organisations have faced significant management and operational problems and scandals, such as performance failures in relation to response times, poor care and outdated doctrine; miscarriages of justice; mis-handling of major incidents; entrenched cultures of conflict such as bullying and blame cultures; and hyper-masculinized traditions of authoritarianism and hierarchy. Shortcomings in management seem to be endemic in emergency services, with many surveys, investigations, inspections and so on having reached the media about authoritarianism, target-driven goal displacement and inappropriate behaviours and cultures associated with excessive workloads, harassment, ostracism and bullying. It is hardly surprising, therefore, that the idea of leadership—especially 'compassionate' leadership—has recently come to prominence as a possible antidote to such problems and a reaction to bad publicity, alongside calls to change leadership culture and personnel, including opening up the top ranks of emergency organisations to outsiders with non-uniformed backgrounds. Meanwhile, 'leadership' is also a seductive idea in that it increasingly applies not just to the senior ranks, but to everyone in the organization—to be a leader is to be a competent professional at all levels. Rhetorically, this is another way in which the discourse of 'leadership' feeds further into clinical, policing or firefighting practice.

This chapter, however, demonstrates that this recent turn to leadership has a longer history within the wider National Health Service (NHS). Its history shows that leadership is not necessarily the obvious, natural or desperately needed phenomenon that it might seem. In what follows, the chapter first offers a particular reading of the history of administration, management and leadership in health care since the foundation of the NHS, some 70 years ago. It then speculates on the implications of its historical interpretation for current practices of 'leadership'. As the chapter is based on historical research on the NHS, its arguments are perhaps most germane to ambulance services, but, as I will argue in what follows, the turns towards 'leadership' and 'leaderisim' are relevant to all blue light services and beyond. As such, it is important that 'leadership' in its various forms is not regarded as a simple panacea to entrenched operational problems but is instead subject to in-depth, historical scrutiny in an attempt to understand it critically and holistically.

NHS History

There is a widely received history of management in the English National Health Service that many who have worked in health care (including ambulance services) since the 1970s or 1980s still tell. Similar tales also exist in the academic literature, widely told to students. Other healthcare systems across the world will doubtless have similarly widely received histories. In brief, the English story runs (more or less) as follows:

> From the establishment of the NHS in 1948, hospitals and other health bodies were 'traditionally administered bureaucracies. . . [so they had] an administrative hierarchy that ran parallel to the medical hierarchy': (Sausman, 2001); hospitals were run by a so-called lay administrator, a matron, and the chairman of the medical staff committee. The first major change to this model came in 1974, when 'consensus management' was introduced. Under this system, hospitals (and other NHS services) were managed by teams consisting of a 'full-time Administrator, Nurse, Community Physician and Finance Officer, with the addition of two part-time clinicians (one hospital consultant and one general practitioner)' who had to agree upon a course of action in order for it to get implemented (Harrison, 1982). Thus, between 1948 and the early 1980s, the administrators of the NHS acted primarily as 'diplomats' in that they were 'agents for physicians in a passive alliance, facilitating their practice by solving problems, smoothing conflicts and generally maintaining the organisation'.

Then came the publication of the *NHS Management Inquiry* in 1983, which recommended the introduction of a "clearly defined general management function throughout the NHS" (DHSS, 1983, p. 11). This ensured that managers (not administrators) were put in place at all levels of the NHS. The extent to which these new managers were really 'in charge' (especially of doctors) is a matter of dispute, but the subsequent emergence of competition in the 1990s encouraged these managers (and some doctors, who were persuaded, albeit with mixed success, to get involved with management) to have an increasingly corporate outlook.

Finally, while the market was replaced by supposedly more cooperative forms of working under New Labour from 1997 (though these cooperative arrangements were supplemented by the national performance framework, star-ratings, and other regulatory mechanisms), NHS leaders—whether healthcare professionals or professional 'managers'—became what Davies and Harrison claim they still are today: "agents of government [rather] than . . . facilitators of professionally driven agendas" (Davies & Harrison, 2003, p. 647).

I do not imply that the above account is wrong in a strong sense (though of course, any account is necessarily always a partial telling of the tale). For example, it is a tale told from the administrators' (or managers'/leaders' point of view). It would certainly be possible to write an account from the traditional point of view of healthcare professionals—one which would undoubtedly emphasise more how contested the process was, how contingent on the outcome of various power dynamics. However, the aim of this chapter is both to complement and to problematise any single sort of historical account. It does so by producing a discursive history of NHS 'management' (with 'management', for reasons that will become apparent, quite definitely in scare quotes). Such a discursive history, with the emphasis on *language* rather than *practices*, might run as follows: Since the establishment of the UK National Health Service (NHS) in 1948, there has been a range of shifts in the way that its organising practices have been represented. In the first few decades, administration was the more or less unexamined term for talking and arguing about how certain things got done in the NHS. Until the early 1980s, therefore, people referred to as administrators generally held quite prestigious jobs (and were mostly men). However, by the end of the eighties, NHS workers called administrators had become what they remain today: relatively poorly paid (and mostly women), while 'manager' had turned into a title that conferred substantial status. And especially after New Labour came to power, up until today, similar activities were/are increasingly articulated in the language of leadership. Indeed, by the end of the last century in the NHS, perhaps it was not too much of an exaggeration to claim that 'we are all leaders now' (Ford & Harding, 2007), in the sense that under New Labour, a desire to be (known as) a leader had become an aspiration held widely in the NHS—not merely by (those who were at one time called) lay administrators—but also by many clinical professionals including in ambulance services (Martin & Learmonth, 2012).

For some of those who hold to this history, perhaps these sorts of changes in the dominant terms used are assumed merely to mirror the different practices seen in the NHS over the last 70 years (though commentators such as Davies and Harrison cited above do acknowledge a certain significance to the semantic shifts). However, while terms like leadership, management and administration might well be the names for different things in the world, what this chapter emphasises is that such words also function as discursive resources, discursive resources—particularly as theorised by Jacques Derrida—that in themselves have fuelled change. Grey observes,

> the ascription of the term 'management' to various kinds of activities is not a mere convenience but rather something which has certain effects. The use of words is not innocent, and in the case of management its use carries irrevocable implications and resonances which are associated with industrialism and modern Western forms of rationality and control.
>
> (Grey, 1999, p. 557)

A central claim elaborated throughout this chapter is that the different reso-
nances associated with administration, management and leadership have represented important means by which contrasting normative ideas about the
way healthcare should be organised have come to be naturalised. So rather
than assume that language merely reflects reality, this chapter demonstrates
how such discursive resources "are simultaneously the grounds, the objects,
and the means by which struggles for power are engaged in" (Currie &
Brown, 2003, p. 565). In other words, the focus of this chapter is not so
much upon what administration, leadership and management are (and have
been) as on what these terms do (and have done) with reality and to reality
(cf. Chawla & Learmonth, 2018; Gond et al., 2016; Learmonth, 2004, 2005;
Learmonth & Morrell, 2017).

A range of empirical materials will be examined. These include professional journals read by hospital administrators in the early years of the NHS
up to and including the 1960s; research interviews that, in part, look back
to this period (though they were conducted with NHS trust chief executives
in 1997 and 1998—at the start of New Labour's term of office); and finally
contemporary policy documents. The intent of the analysis is to nurture critical reflection upon how changes in the dominant language for organising the
NHS have rendered it intelligible and contestable in different ways. Furthermore, by exploring historical changes discursively, I particularly seek to problematise the assumptions of continuity and progress that are implicit in many
of the received histories of NHS management. As we shall see, the discursive
approach tends to stress some of the discontinuities—between, for example,
the welfarism of the kindly administrators in the 1940s and the tough management job that chief executives had come to represent themselves as doing by
the 1990s. There is a particular emphasis, too, upon how the terms administration, leadership and management have been deployed by (people known today
as) NHS 'managers' (and also 'leaders') in struggles with medical and other
healthcare professions (although distinctions between 'leaders' and medics is
becoming increasingly unclear) over power and legitimacy.

The chapter proceeds as follows. An introductory discussion of the discursive method used in the analysis is followed by the presentation of empirical
materials relevant to what I represent as three more or less separate eras—the
era of administration, the era of management and, finally, the era of leadership. I conclude the chapter with thoughts about how this approach to the
historical analysis of the 20th-century NHS contributes to how we might
understand the contemporary NHS—especially 'leadership' in ambulance
services.

An Approach to Discursive History

The primary theoretical inspiration for exploring the significance of words
like 'leadership', 'management' and 'administration' comes from a reading
of Jacques Derrida, a thinker whose ideas are of particular value in analyses
concerned with the relationship between language and the world to which
(we might assume) language refers. For Derrida, in a radicalisation of John

Austin's *How to Do Things With Words*, language never only states the way things are, it is also always performative—where performative language is language that 'does something, in actuality, in reality, with reality' (Royle, 2000, p. 9). And it is Derrida's radicalised version of Austin's 'speech acts' theory that I use to understand the words 'leadership', 'management' and 'administration' as performative.

Austin referred to those speech acts he considered merely to set out a state of affairs as constative; but his interest was in speech that, in and of itself, does things—using the term performative for such utterances. Austin's concern, as he put it, was with the: 'performance of an act in saying something as opposed to [the] performance of an act of saying something' (Austin, 1962, p. 99). Instead of considering a statement such as 'there is a bull in the field' (1962, p. 32) primarily as a constative statement—in terms of what it describes about the scenery—Austin privileged what the statement does, asking whether it might be a warning, a request, a complaint and so forth. Derrida's thought has a number of affinities with Austin's in that they both unsettle the traditional image of communication as the straightforward transportation of meaning from one speaker to another. Derrida welcomed Austin's move as an antidote to ideas that underpin, among other things, traditional understandings of empirical inquiry:

> Austin was obliged to free the analysis of the performative from the authority of the truth value, from the true/false opposition. . . . The performative is a 'communication' which is not limited strictly to the transference of a semantic content that is already constituted and dominated by an orientation toward truth.
>
> (Derrida, 1979, p. 190)

However, their ideas diverged when theorising how words do what they do. Austin argued that the 'force' of a performative utterance is provided primarily by the authentic intentions of the speaker, usually allied to the context in which speech is uttered and the lack of ambiguity in the formulation used. So, for Austin, a priest in a wedding ceremony who says, 'I pronounce you husband and wife' would be uttering a speech act which would be successful in doing something (marrying the couple) because of the intentions of the priest and the couple involved—along with the context and the unambiguity of the formulation. In opposition to Austin, however, Derrida made clear that for him the force of a performative speech act is not intention, but citation. The notion of iterability or citation is what for Derrida underlies any 'successful' performative utterance:

> Could a performative utterance succeed if its formulation did not repeat a 'coded' or iterable utterance, or in other words, if the formula I pronounce in order to open a meeting, launch a ship or a marriage were not identifiable as conforming with an iterable model, if it were not then identifiable in some sort of way as a 'citation'?
>
> (Derrida, 1979, pp. 191–192)

To continue the example of a wedding, Derrida is pointing out that a priest can only marry someone because the words spoken are recognisably part of a marriage ceremony: 'I pronounce you husband and wife' must be a citation for it to marry a couple. Citation, Derrida argued, is prior to intention; indeed, it is a condition of possibility for intention to operate. This is not to deny that intention and context have a role in speech acts, but, as Derrida argued, intention and context "will no longer be able to govern the entire scene and system of utterance" (p. 192).

Following Derrida, then, if terms like management, leadership and administration do things in the world, they operate not primarily because the intention of the speaker successfully governs the action of speech, but because these words, in some sort of way, are citations—quotes from previously existing sources. Indeed, it is surely uncontroversial to claim that these terms have become conventional categories to use in representing the organisation of public services like the NHS, such that it is hardly possible to make intelligible statements in the field without recourse to these terms. Derrida's point is that the effects on the world of these terms rely upon the accumulation of academic research, official reports, routine talk and so on in which these terms are deployed. And, as we shall see, these terms did different things in different eras of NHS history because they came to accumulate different conventions surrounding their meanings.

The Era of NHS Administration

The main empirical materials in this section are derived from the May editions of a journal called *The Hospital* (*TH*) which was sampled between 1946 to 1948, 1956 to 1958, and 1966 to 1968 (cf. Learmonth, 1998). During this period, *TH* was the official publication of the Institute of Hospital Administrators (IHA), a body to which the vast majority of hospital administrators belonged. The IHA was primarily a professional membership organisation, setting examinations for apprentice administrators, as well as publishing *TH* in order to meet its members' continuing education needs. Today, incidentally, the successor body to the IHA is known as the Institute of Healthcare Management (IHM)—see www.ihm.org.uk/home—a change of name not without significance, of course, for the arguments in this chapter. In any event, the study of *TH* was conducted not so much to enable an understanding of the formal arrangements and official reports of the time, but was intended to enable inferences to be made about the ways in which the people called administrators thought and acted in this period.

In this regard, during the 1940s and 1950s, the vast majority of the material in the texts was descriptive and prescriptive, articles concerned with what might be described, not entirely unfairly, as recipes for the best way to do things, in the sense that the guidance seemed to have been meant simply to be followed. In other words, complex abstractions were very rarely debated, nor were sophisticated arguments developed; indeed, there was a marked reluctance to engage with anything that sounded "complicated and American in its high falutin' approach", as one commentator put it. It seems then that both what the job of the administrator consisted of and how it should be carried out was assumed to be clear and uncontroversial.

What was also clear in the early part of this period was that "the chief officer of the hospital [is] usually the Medical Superintendent . . . the secretary . . . controls the business side". Indeed, there was never any discussion of the potential for conflict between the business and medical 'sides', and any possible question about whether the administrators' deferential situation was appropriate seems not to have occurred to them. Therefore, the overwhelming majority of articles in the 1940s and 1950s were concerned with minutely detailing recommendations about the best course of action for the conduct of day-to-day arrangements. Matters labelled, for example, "superannuation"; "Lunacy Act 1890 section 287 'Out-county' changes"; "'hospital planning—patients' accommodation'"; "mental health service: changes proposed under the Bill"; "hospital cost accounts: application in practice", all had several pages of dense typeface devoted to them—the articles concentrating on thoroughly elaborating the minutiae of the technicalities involved with each issue.

However, there were a few more conventionally reflective passages. One such, an editorial comment from 1948 that discussed the work of the recently established Institute of Management, is of particular interest for the arguments advanced in this chapter:

> Speaking at the recent Annual Conference of the Institute of Hospital Administrators, Mr. F.A. Lyon mentioned the difficulty of evaluating the content of the respective spheres of administration and management. His conclusion was that a complete separation could not be made, but he made a point of mentioning the danger of laying excessive emphasis on the technical aspects of hospital management, saying that attention must be given in the courses of study of bodies such as the Institute of Hospital Administrators, to the study of 'the pure science and art of administration'.

Here, in contrast to today's assumptions, the comparison between management and administration seems to imply that administration was regarded as a 'higher' discipline than management; management being about mere technical matters. Indeed, from the wider literature on the history of management, it seems possible that in the 1940s and 1950s, 'management' still had (for some) undesirable cultural associations that linked it with being 'in trade' or with household management (Mant, 1982); associations that appear to have been occluded by the language of administration—an art that was practised at that time by top (Oxbridge-educated) civil servants. It is worth noting as an aside that a preference for administration rather than management is still discernible today, surviving as it does in formulations from this period. A notable example is that a higher business degree is still widely known as an MBA: Master of Business Administration.

However, perhaps most striking for me as a contemporary reader was the emphasis throughout the texts that administrators needed to remember the nature of the service they were in and the implication that this had for their personal conduct. For example, in a conference speech, a newly appointed regional hospital board chairman contrasted those services that depended "upon mechanical efficiency" with human social services (including health care) which

> come under a different heading . . . for in that field what is required is not mathematical efficiency but a sympathetic understanding. It is not only what you do that is important; it is the way in which you do it; it is the approach; it is the recognition that you are dealing with human beings and qualities which are required in the administration of that service are something beyond mere intellect; it is the right sort of human emotion.

He went on to describe the personal qualities of a regional chairman, who will require

> the patience of Job; the kindly spirit of a saint, the deafness that will prevent him hearing all the things which might disturb him and a sight which will enable him not to see the things which are better not seen.

This early emphasis on kindliness had disappeared, however, by the 1960s' editions of *TH*. For a start, overt conflicts between the business side and the medical practices of the hospital had emerged. For example, discussing how complaints against medical staff should be handled, one article asks, "should the administrator be involved?" The answer is resonant with Harrison's claim that administrators were diplomats who smoothed out problems for doctors but were essentially subservient to them:

> Yes. If he is a wise administrator his involvement will appear indirect . . . If the medical staff close their ranks against him then there is something wrong. The secret is to build one's personal relationships before the incidents occur. . . . One should deal with consultants personally. An occasional visit to the operating theatre and a cup of coffee in the surgeon's room is a worthwhile practice.

It was also clear from the pages of the 1960s journals that many administrators were now studying for college- or university-based management qualifications (importantly, such qualifications were in management as opposed to administration). These qualifications would have been in addition to their basic IHA examinations, but a number of projects originally conducted for such qualifications were published in *TH*. Perhaps, in part because of the influence of management education (Hunter, 1988), though the term administration was still dominant, routine claims about their work were also starting to be made in the language of management. One article, for example, claims that "all senior staff of whatever category are now thought of as managers", and even the nursing profession were said to be putting "faith in intensive training in management" for their senior staff.

In other words, a tension—between traditional ideas about administration and what, even ten years previously might have been called 'high falutin' management'—was beginning to emerge. This can be seen especially clearly in a debate about the possibility of chief executives for hospitals that found its way into *TH*. Two reports, *Administrative Practice of Hospital Boards in Scotland* (Scottish Health Council, 1966) and *The Shape of Hospital Management in 1980?* (King Edward's Hospital Fund for England, 1967) had both recommended the appointment of a general manager to head district hospitals. Such proposals were opposed by doctors at the time in the most vehement terms. As one letter in the *British Medical Journal* put it,

> The lay take-over of hospital administration by all-powerful general managers, most of whom would be 'lay,' would eventually reduce the status of medical staff to the level of all other groups of hospital workers. . . . The interference with professional freedom and the doctor-patient relationship . . . would unquestionably ruin our health service for all time.
>
> (Blundell & Lowry, 1967, p. 617)

Perhaps predictably, given its cautious attitude to working on complaints against doctors, the commentary to be found in *TH* on the chief executives debate was short and deferential:

> The working party [that had prepared the 1967 King's Fund Report] felt that doctors were non-managers and did not like being managed, but might be prepared to hand over middle management chores.

Still, there was a (gentle) insistence on using the language of management, which contrasts rather starkly with terms like 'lay . . . hospital administration' preferred by the *BMJ*'s correspondents. But in any case, both reports were quietly ignored by the Labour government of the day, and hospital administrators were officially to remain administrators for almost another 20 years. Indeed, although a number of significant changes to NHS organisational arrangements were made in the 1970s—in particular Area and District Health Authorities were established, and with them, as we have seen, so-called consensus management. However, administrators remained administrators and what representing these workers in the language of administration successfully did was to keep them in subordination to doctors throughout this time. Things were set to change in the 1980s, however, when proposals were made again to create a new cadre of people called managers in the NHS. It is to these 1980s proposals, and their effects, to which we now turn.

The Era of NHS Management

In 1983, at the request of the Secretary of State for Health and Social Security, a team of businessmen headed by Roy Griffiths produced the *NHS Management Inquiry*—a document that was widely read as recommending the adoption of "a clearly defined general management function throughout the NHS" (DHSS, 1983, p. 11). As we have seen, similar proposals had been made in the 1960s with no effect. This time, however, within two years, the Thatcher government (the prestige that Thatcher accorded to business people is significant here) announced that general managers had been appointed at all levels of the NHS; albeit in the teeth of bitter opposition from many healthcare professions (Timmins, 1998; Harding & Learmonth, 2000).

Though some commentators were less than enthusiastic at the time, many of the individuals who came to be called managers were themselves deeply committed to what they believed were the new ideals of general management (Strong & Robinson, 1990). This was true even though about 70% of the (supposedly new) managers had previously been known as administrators (Petchey, 1986). The officially sanctioned rhetoric by the late 1980s had come to be that the NHS had been "transformed from a classic example of an administered public sector bureaucracy into one that is increasingly exhibiting qualities that reflect positive, purposeful management" (Best; in Flynn, 1992, p. 47).

The shock waves caused by the *NHS Management Inquiry* were profound. Even though the interviews reported in this chapter were conducted in 1998 to 1999, it was very evident that the informants were still conscious of the significance of this change—the change from being known as administrators to being called managers. The interviews were conducted with 16 NHS trust chief executives in hospitals in the north of England and were intended to investigate how such individuals made sense of their professional world. They were unstructured, qualitative interviews, framed simply by an opening question—'What do you see as the heart of your job?'—continuing by ranging across a wide set of topics in a fluid and informal manner as the participants themselves chose.

As a preliminary to the interviews, each respondent was asked to describe their professional background. Of the 16 interviewees, one was a clinician, two were accountants and one had come into the NHS from another sector in the last ten years. In the case of the other 12, exchanges such as the following two excerpts were typical of the start of the interviews:

Q: If I could just ask you what your professional background is
A: Well administration, health service administration

Q: Right, good. OK first question then, I'd like to ask you to describe the heart of your job
A: Leadership

Q: Right, fine ha. Tell me about leadership
A: Well we, I, am personally accountable for the managerial performance of the organisation, the organisation consists of three thousand people and to achieve my objectives I physically can't do it myself; when I was an administrator I had tasks to do which I did myself but as a leader you inspire, lead, manage others to do the work

Or:

> My professional background? I mean I came into the health service as, at that stage, a career administrator, straight from university; on to the administrators' training scheme and if you like moved into management, as management developed in the NHS, from an administrative background.

The opposition between administration and management was not something that occurred merely at the start of the interviews, though its striking regularity at the start of the interviews was what prompted a search of the transcripts for other examples. In the course of the interviews, the radical differences claimed to exist between administrators from the past and current chief executives were sometimes elaborated at length:

> just as a caricature I would make the observation that many administrators in the '70s and '80s, the top ones, were employed mainly, well mainly, for their brain power per se. As I say, a lot of them were intellectuals, Oxbridge graduates and so on; and the current generation of chief executives are also very clever people but they have their skills are now rooted in common sense and people skills. So it's not just about administering legal or financial affairs which require a certain set of administrative skills and brain power, it's more to do with empowering people and leading people and having those skills. And I've many a time come across in my career people whose intellect has got in the way of their common sense, people skills. So it is they're now different animals.

Thus, a belief in the essential inferiority of administration and the concomitant prestige of management had clearly become established by this time. This relationship between the two terms can also be seen in the fact that when the term administrator occurred (outside ruminations about the past), it was typically deployed as an insult. The next excerpt illustrates this. In this example, a chief executive was talking of the top management team immediately before her appointment (including the former chief executive). According to her, these people had been unable to cope with the new demands of partnership working, such that

> there [had been] no radical or strategic thinking enough to do that sort of work; [name of hospital] used to be peopled by a bunch of administrators basically.

And, according to another respondent, 'administrator' was a term that could also be used to similar disparaging effect by medical staff:

> . . . when consultants actually want to diminish what I do they call me an administrator.

Q: Yes, I remember that from the early eighties.

A: Still do, still do, because that's about your job is to support what we do; accepting that I'm actually a chief executive gives me a leadership position.

By the 1990s then, in contrast to the 1960s, it seems that words associated with management had come to do things, in the sense that these words constructed and legitimated an organisational world in which chief executives felt they had supremacy. Administrator, on the other hand, had come to do things that undermined the prestige and authority such people would like. These sorts of insights are reinforced and further explained by the next excerpt in which some of the history of the power relations between doctors and managers (or should we say administrators?) are represented in more detail:

. . . earlier on in my career where the successful administrators in the sixties and seventies were those which were actually able to facilitate what the doctors wanted to do, that's how you were judged.

Q: Right, not influence it at all?

A: Well you might influence it provided you didn't tell people you were influencing it; it was actually quite a clever game—you let the doctors think that it was their idea but actually your skills were in terms of making it happen and using the process or whatever. Of course the real skill was that you didn't make happen those things that you didn't want to make happen, but if you made nothing happen then you were not a good administrator and you would alienate the doctors and then you would be unsuccessful.

As we have already noted, prior to the *NHS Management Inquiry*, administrators were widely seen (by themselves and by the medical staff) as doctors' support workers. Any prestige they might have had arose from their success in fulfilling doctors' wishes rather than from the activities they chose independently. But one way of reading this excerpt is to see it as an implicit statement that the re-labelling from administrator to manager that was licenced by the *NHS Management Inquiry* was not one that necessarily altered the substance of administrators'/managers' activities. Senior administrators of the past and chief executives in the 1990s could be represented as carrying out much the same activities—according to this excerpt, making things happen, more or less as they felt appropriate. However, individuals called administrators had to make sure that what they did appeared to be done in the service of others. Their self-identity was therefore continuously defined as subservient and secondary—the need to be able to subvert the apparent relationship by playing 'quite a clever game' no doubt merely reinforced this identity (Learmonth & Humphreys, 2011). Of course, the implicit corollary to the status of the administrator is that what being called a manager does is legitimate the (so-called) manager acting in a way that is independent of "what the doctors want"; thereby radically changing the nature of their respective senses of self.

Thus, the discursive change from administration to management can be understood as a resource to be called upon in struggles for power and legitimacy. In the mid-1990s, this resource often seems to have been used by deploying the term 'management' as an apparently uncontroversial and routine way of talking about all sorts of activities. For example,

> One of the things that I learnt was that we often expect too much of doctors in terms of their ability to manage and also their capacity to manage and their commitment to do the things that managers have to do because their livelihoods depend on it—doctors don't [have to do these things]. And I felt that, [and] the medical director he felt, that the emergence of clinical governance was an opportunity to refocus the doctors' role on clinical management, leadership and the management increasingly of clinical practice informed by evidence, rather than on the management of service delivery and staffing budgets and so on.

In this excerpt, the speaker deploys the term 'management' in at least two senses. There is the more or less conventional contemporary sense of management as the distinctive occupational functions of certain people identified as professional managers by their job titles. Management in this sense is represented as "the management of service delivery and staffing budgets and so on", which the speaker believed doctors need not do. However, in juxtaposition to this, he also uses the same term 'management' to represent rather different functions, functions he considers to be legitimate medical duties: "clinical management, leadership and the management increasingly of clinical practice informed by evidence". But it is not implausible to believe that what he is talking about here could equally have been represented in more traditional language, as part of the ordinary, routine duties that senior medical staff have always carried out in modern times; that is, such duties could have equally been described without recourse to the term 'management'.

The next interview quotation gives a parallel example of this sort of deployment. It occurred after I had asked the respondent to explain (what for me was) her intriguing use of the term 'consultant-managers':

Q: Do you mean all consultants are managers or do you mean that there are certain consultants who are managers like clinical directors or whatever?

A: Okay, I mean both. All consultants are managers; not all consultants would recognise that or recognise the implications of that as readily as others do but they all manage resources, they all manage their time, manage junior medical staff and have therefore particular accountability for them.

One way of interpreting what was being attempted in both these excerpts is that it was a representation of medical work as managerial work. The significance of the change from the point of view of the chief executive being that if managerial language successfully colonises doctors' routine talk and thinking, they are likely to come to understand their own identities as managerial, at least in part. Furthermore, the logic of such an understanding tends to imply that doctors should then be accountable to the professional expert in management (i.e. the chief executive). And not only accountability was at stake, important as it might be. Another implication of the discursive change from administration to management is that more traditional considerations for the NHS, especially ones based on welfarism, caring and compassion (values consistently stressed in the 1940s and 1950s) can plausibly be played down and rendered subservient to the tough job of ensuring good management.

The Era of NHS Leadership

But did the discursive change from administration to management have the effects on medical staff's allegiances that was seemingly desired? It seems that its effects were limited. Perhaps, in part, this was because for individual chief executives, even those who have never been administrators themselves, the discursive history of the term 'manager' in the NHS always has the denigrated shadow of the administrator behind it: people called managers in the NHS are intrinsically vulnerable to being cast as 'mere' administrators. One might speculate then that it was the negative associations accumulated by management and administration by the end of the 1990s that underlay the popular and officially sanctioned turn to leadership that occurred at that time, not just in health but in many other parts of the public sector (Ford, 2004). It may well also account for other discursive shifts in the NHS that reduced the need to deploy the terms 'manager' and 'management', especially in clinical matters. Prominent examples from the early New Labour era included senior nurses being described as modern matrons or nurse consultants (rather than as nurse managers) and the control of clinical activities being officially designated clinical governance (rather than clinical management).

At the beginning of New Labour's first term of office (when the interviews were conducted), the discourse of leadership was clearly available to chief executives in the NHS in the sense that the word was regularly mentioned—in fact, it occurs in most of the excerpts used in this chapter. However, whereas management was made intelligible by opposing it to administration, at this stage, leadership was not generally constructed through sharp distinctions with management—the two terms seemed to have been used more or less as synonyms. But this situation seems to have changed by the close of the century: as Parker has pointed out, under "New Labour . . . management itself . . . [was] beginning to go out of fashion (now being discursively articulated as something rather like administration) and leadership . . . [was] the new panacea" (Parker, 2004). Thus by 2002, on the National Nursing Leadership's Project website, a government minister could say,

> Good clinical leadership is central to the delivery of the NHS Plan. We
> need leaders who are willing to embrace and drive through the radical

transformation in services that the NHS requires. Leaders are people who make things happen in ways that command the confidence of local staff. They are people who lead clinical teams, people who lead service networks, people who lead partnerships, and people who lead organisations.

(National Nursing Leadership Project, 2002)

Such statements about 'clinical leadership' bear comparison with the respondents' talk of 'clinical management' cited earlier. Both sorts of statements were no doubt intended to represent the world as it is: nurse "leaders are people who make things happen"; consultants "manage resources, they all manage their time, manage junior medical staff". But again, understanding either statement only as empirical claims overlooks (and thereby reinforces) what such words do. Deploying leadership in this way seems more or less calculated to have the effect of "regulating employees' 'insides'—their self-image, their feelings and identifications" (Alvesson & Willmott, 2002, p. 622). Indeed, throughout the public sector, the official endorsement of leadership to represent organisational practices can be interpreted in part, as a growing recognition that calling activities 'leadership' does more than calling them 'management' (and, it goes without saying, more than 'administration') in terms of encouraging individuals to identify with policy aims. This is because leadership's relative lack of negative associations (at least its lack of negative associations so far—who knows how things will change) made leadership a term likely to be inoffensive, perhaps attractive to many healthcare professionals as the new central resource in the construction of their self-image.

By the end of the Blairite period then, leadership for many in the NHS had become "a way of being" (Ford, Harding, & Learmonth, 2008, p. 4), rather than merely a job. But it was a way of being that was disciplinary, in the sense that in order to maintain this sense of self, individuals had to conform to the demands of those who define what good leadership is (Learmonth, 2011). For according to the above excerpt, being a good leader is not just about romantic notions such as an ability "to drive through . . . radical transformation in services". Axiomatic to being a 'good' leader is also compliance with official definitions of what "the NHS requires".

In the last few years then, rather than managerialism being the dominant way people with power think about their influence, what O'Reilly and Reed (2010, p. 962) call 'leaderism' has taken its place. As they argue,

> whereas management necessarily involves the conundrum of aligning principal and agent, the change in discourse to leadership resolves this conundrum through re-definition by making the issue the establishment of a passion for a common goal between leaders and led.
>
> (2010, p. 962)

Indeed, the word leadership is now used for pretty much any kind of activity that is thought of by officials as 'positive' so that it is becoming an almost meaningless term (see McCann, 2017). Indeed, the rhetoric is so widespread that as Morrell and Hewison (2013, p. 70) in the context of the Darzi report show, "it becomes impossible to see an alternative to "leadership" . . . leadership is, seemingly, anything and everything".

Discussion and Conclusion

It follows then that many activities carried out by NHS staff today—including in ambulance services—'are' leadership (or administration, or management) in the sense that they are currently given these names. However, the contribution of this historical analysis is to show that these same activities are always potentially not management or not leadership in the sense that they can always be called by other names—and, as we have seen, they have been given different names in times past. What a particular activity 'is' does not rely on some essence within it—things like leadership, management or administration (indeed all categories through which we experience the world) are human creations, a reflection of conventional ways of apprehending the world and not a reflection of what the world is 'really like'. What leadership, management and administration have come to represent therefore has been made to appear self-evident through an inescapably arbitrary process of inclusion and exclusion of significance, a process held together only by convention and power. So the problems with seeing leadership, administration and management as more or less unproblematic terms representing different things in the world is that typically, in both practitioner and academic accounts, leadership is preferred—there is a hierarchy amongst the terms. Calling certain practices administration, others management and yet others leadership is not simply to name them. The practice does things to them, most obviously perhaps, in the sense that it values them in different ways.

One of the big problems, particularly with 'leadership', is that the cultural associations of the term make it seem 'better' than management in the sense that leadership can plausibly be associated with terms like 'servanthood' or 'compassion' in ways that management does not lend itself to; and the trouble with terms like 'compassion' or 'servanthood' is that they are extremely seductive and easy to signal, but in reality very hard to do.

What I want to argue then is that one way of doing historical analyses of organisational phenomena is to focus on the *effects* of dominant discourses rather than whether these discourses were 'true'. In this case, constructing a certain sense of self is something that any appeal to be an administrator, a manager or a leader does; something likely to be missed if such words were to be read merely as potentially true or false claims about the changing nature of workplace duties. Understanding oneself as a leader (not a manager) provides positive cultural valences that enable one to construct an affirmative reflexive understanding of self. It is good to be able to think of oneself as a radical and strategic manager or an empowering leader—not as (merely) administering something like paperwork. Furthermore, and relatedly, being known as a leader (and not a manager) is more likely to construct the sort of public image that others may see as legitimate—and to which they will therefore acquiesce. As Clarke and Newman (1997) have pointed out, the "discourse of managerialism . . . is part of the process through which 'administrators', 'public servants' and 'practitioners' come to see themselves as 'business managers' . . . 'strategists', 'leaders' and so on" (p. 92).

All this is important because it may well not be in the interests of health-care professionals to define themselves as leaders or to use the language of leadership—as attractive as it may be on certain levels so to do. After all, identifying as a leader involves conformity to the wider logics of leadership: an acceptance of the legitimacy of the top leader's (the chief executive's) right to lead, as well as an acquiescence to the elites who get to define "what the NHS requires". Doctors who insult chief executives by calling them 'administrators' (are there still people who do this?) seem to be aware of this particular danger. Indeed, I would go so far as to argue that the currently taken-for-granted status of the language of leadership might well constitute a form of what Pierre Bourdieu has called "structural symbolic violence"; the resultant domination is "something you absorb like air, something you don't feel pressured by; it is everywhere and nowhere and to escape from that is very difficult" (in Catley & Jones, 2002, p. 28).

So what should we do in the light of this debate, faced today with the hegemony of the language of leadership for the representation of organising in emergency services? On the one hand, we cannot use terms like 'leadership' and 'management' without their automatic appropriation, by one side or another, for doing things in the conflicts over language to which I have drawn attention. On the other hand, we must use these sorts of terms to make ourselves intelligible (Learmonth, 2009). One possibility for a research agenda that takes these problems seriously would proceed not by relativising terms such as 'leadership' and 'management' so that any distinction is denied, but rather by the detailed scrutiny of the precise points at which distinctions are invoked so that easy and comfortable assumptions about their implications cannot be made. We might examine what invoking distinctions do rather than what the distinctions are. And in particular, perhaps, examine whose interests are favoured and whose denied when strong distinctions are made to appear to be plausible.

References

Alvesson, M., & Willmott, H. (2002). Identity regulation as organizational control: Producing the appropriate individual. *Journal of Management Studies* 39(5), 619–644.

Austin, J.L. (1962). *How to Do Things with Words*. Oxford: Oxford University Press.

Blundell, J., & Lowry, J. (1967). Managing the Hospitals. *British Medical Journal* (9 December), 617.

Catley, B., & Jones, C. (2002). Deciding on violence. *Reason in Practice: The Journal of Philosophy of Management* 2(1), 23–32.

Chawla, G., & Learmonth, M. (2018). The wicked problem of leadership in the NHS. In Thomas, W., Hujala, A., Laulainen, S., & McMurray, R. (Eds.), *The Management of Wicked Problems in Health and Social Care*. New York: Routledge. 51–61.

Clarke, J., & Newman, J. (1997). *The Managerial State: Power, politics and ideology in the remaking of social welfare*. London: Sage.

252   *Mark Learmonth*

Currie, G., & Brown, A.D. (2003). A narratological approach to understanding processes of organizing in a UK hospital. *Human Relations* 56, 563–586.

Davies, H.T.O., & Harrison, S. (2003). Trends in doctor-manager relationships. *British Medical Journal* 326: 646–649.

Derrida, J. (1979). Signature event context. *Glyph* 1, 172–197.

DHSS. (1983). *NHS management inquiry* DA(83)38. Stanmore Middlesex: DHSS (Leaflets).

Flynn, R. (1992). *Structures of Control in Health Management*. London: Routledge.

Ford, J. (2004). A feminist critique of leadership and its application to the UK NHS. In Learmonth, M. (Ed.), *Unmasking Health Management: A Critical Text* (pp. 41–55). New York: Nova Science.

Ford, J., & Harding, N. (2007). Move over management: We are all leaders now. *Management Learning* 38, 475–493.

Ford, J., Harding, N., & Learmonth, M. (2008). *Leadership as Identity: Constructions and deconstructions*. Houndmills: Palgrave Macmillan.

Gond, J.P., Cabantous, L., Harding, N., and Learmonth, M. (2016). What do we mean by performativity in organizational and management theory? The uses and abuses of performativity. *International Journal of Management Reviews* 18(4), 440–463.

Grey, C. (1999). 'We are all managers now' 'We always were': On the development and demise of management. *Journal of Management Studies* 36(5), 561–585.

Harding, N., and Learmonth, M. (2000) Thinking critically: The case of health policy research. *Technology Analysis & Strategic Management* 12(3), 335–341.

Harrison, S. (1982) Consensus decision-making in the national health service: A review. *Journal of Management Studies* 19(4), 377–394.

Harrison, S. (1988) *Managing the NHS: Shifting the Frontier*. London: Chapman & Hall.

Hunter, D.J. (1988) The impact of research on restructuring the British national health service. *The Journal of Health Administration Education* 6(3), 537–553.

Learmonth, M. (1998) Kindly technicians: Hospital administrators immediately before the NHS. *Journal of Management in Medicine* 12(6), 323–330.

Learmonth, M. (2004) "The violence in trusting trust chief executives: glimpsing trust in the UK National Health Service." *Qualitative Inquiry* 10(4), 581–600.

Learmonth, M. (2005) Doing things with words: the case of 'management' and 'administration.' *Public Administration* 83(3), 617–637.

Learmonth, M. (2009) 'Girls' working together without 'teams': How to avoid the colonization of management language. *Human Relations* 62, 1887–1906.

Learmonth, M. (2011) "When science and philosophy meet: One explication of the relationship between evidence and theory in management research". In Cassell, C. and Lee, B. (Eds.), *Challenges and controversies in management research*. New York: Routledge. 212–224.

Learmonth, M. and Humphreys, M. (2011) Blind spots in Dutton, Roberts and Bednar's "Pathways for positive identity construction at work": "you've got to accentuate the positive, eliminate the negative." *Academy of Management Review* 36, 424–427.

Learmonth, M., and Morrell, K. (2017) Is critical leadership studies 'critical'? *Leadership* 13(3), 257–271.

Learmonth, M., and Morrell, K. (2019) *Critical Perspectives on Leadership: The Language of Corporate Power*. New York: Routledge.

Mant, A. (1982) *The Rise and Fall of the British Manager*. Harmondsworth: Penguin.

Martin, G., and Learmonth, M. (2012) A critical account of the rise and spread of 'leadership': the case of UK health care. *Social Science & Medicine*, 74(3), 281–288.

McCann, L. (2017) 'From management to leadership'. In Edgell, S., Gottfried, H., and Granter, E. (Eds.), *The Sage Handbook of Sociology of Work*. London: Sage.

Morrell, K., and Hewison, A. (2013) Rhetoric in policy texts: The role of enthymeme in Darzi's review of the NHS. *Policy and Politics* 41, 59–79.

National Nursing Leadership Project. (2002) http:www.nursingleadership.co.uk [accessed 15.05.02].

O'Reilly, D., and Reed, M. (2010) 'Leaderism': An evolution of managerialism in UK public service reform. *Public administration* 88, 960–978.

Parker, M. (2004) Structure, Culture and Anarchy: Ordering the NHS. In Learmonth, M. (Ed.), *Unmasking Health Management: A Critical Text* (pp. 171–185). Hauppage, New York: Nova Science Publishers.

Petchey, R. (1986) The Griffiths reorganisation of the national health service: Fowlerism by stealth? *Critical Social Policy* 17(3), 87–101.

Royle, N. (2000) What is Deconstruction? In Royle, N. (Ed.), *Deconstructions: A User's Guide* (pp. 1–13). Houndmills: Palgrave Macmillan.

Sausman, C. (2001) New roles and responsibilities of NHS chief executives in relation to quality and clinical governance. *Quality in Health Care* 10 (Suppl II), ii13–ii20.

Scottish Health Council. (1966) *Administrative Practice of Hospital Boards in Scotland*. Edinburgh: The Scottish Office.

Strong, P., and Robinson, J. (1990) *The NHS under new management*. Milton Keynes: Open University.

Timmins, N. (1998). A tale out of school, or reflections on the management of the national health service. In Best, R. (Ed.), *The Quest for Excellence—What is Good Health Care: Essays in Honour of Robert J. Maxwell* (pp. 67–76). London: Kings Fund.

15 Public Confidence in the Police

A Critical Review and Interrogation of Construct Clarity

Basit Javid* and Kevin Morrell

Introduction

The month after her appointment as home secretary in May 2010, Theresa May publicly announced to the Association of Chief Police Officers (ACPO) the immediate abolition of what was at the time the last remaining policing target: to increase public confidence in the police (*The Independent*, 29 June 2010). She told chief officers, after warning them about coming cuts, that their role was simply to cut crime. Despite the home secretary's scrapping of the last remaining target from New Labour, confidence remains an important measure in policing. In the Crime Survey for England and Wales, measures include an assessment of confidence in the police.[1] This, despite government policy changes, is one reason for the continued importance placed by police organisations on the issue of public confidence in policing. 'Confidence' is such a basic imperative that every police force across England and Wales remains concerned, to some extent at least, with measuring and improving public confidence.

The press and wider media have increasingly played a pivotal role in the concerns and debate around public confidence in policing. In December 2012, Keith Vaz MP, then chair of the Commons Home Affairs Select Committee, was reported as saying public confidence in the police has been hurt by a 'dangerous cocktail' of controversies, such as the critical Hillsborough report and the Andrew Mitchell 'Plebgate' row (BBC News, 30 December 2012).[2] Speaking at the same time, Sir Bernard Hogan-Howe, then commissioner of the Metropolitan Police, said, "I want Londoners to love, respect and be proud of their Met" (*The Telegraph*, 26 September 2013).[3] This was after a series of alleged scandals were said to have damaged confidence in the police.

The history of policing as an institution is sometimes seen through either the lens of scandal or the lens of tragedy. In contrast, though, the media often shape our perceptions of police work by representing it in terms of heroism and sacrifice. These contrasting perspectives are core to the phenomenon of public confidence, and they illustrate that relations between the police and the public are extremely complex. Sir Bernard's vision of love, respect and be

* Correspondence E-mail ID: b.javid@west-midlands.pnn.police.uk

proud was bold and expansive—and also one that strikes us admirably clear. Yet understanding what public confidence 'really' means is not quite so clear, and this has important consequences for how we understand this crucial service and its relation to the public.

Understanding Public Confidence in Policing

Since the early 1980s, when the British Crime Survey (now the Crime Survey for England and Wales) began, there has been a growing number of studies on public confidence in policing. Most tend to focus on a particular theme and its relationship with confidence, such as police visibility, fairness, treatment or community engagement. No studies can claim a perfect, complete understanding of public confidence; their findings overlap with important similarities as well as differences. Some of these differences are functions of a lack of clarity in relation to the core meaning of confidence. We can call this a lack of 'construct clarity'.

For example, analysis of the way *confidence* is used in government texts suggests a multiplicity of meanings. Fleming and McLaughlin (2012) highlight continual slippage between the terms *confidence, satisfaction* and *trust*. Others also point out the crossover between terms such as *confidence* and *satisfaction* (Myhill and Quinton, 2010), including confusion over the sense of popular survey phrases such as 'doing a good job' (Stanko et al., 2012). This in itself can lead to ambiguities and confusion amongst researchers and practitioners when discussing confidence within the context of policing. Fitzgerald (2010) suggests confidence can also mean different things to different sections of the public in different places at different times.

These differences in terms of the sense and reference of confidence suggest that future work could benefit from greater construct clarity. A more precise operational definition of confidence could help to direct research in ways that would help contribute to the study and practice of policing. Without such clarity, these sources of crossover and confusion could serve to undermine our collective efforts to understand confidence in policing.

The importance of defining confidence more clearly can be illustrated with reference to a phenomenon known as the *perception gap*. This is an expression of the difference between (i) expectations of the quality of service one believes will be delivered by public services and (ii) actual experience—which leads to someone's satisfaction or dissatisfaction. Often, the public tends to be satisfied with their *local* services and with encounters with—say—their last hospital visit but hold a more negative view of the same public services if asked about them in general terms (what might someone think about 'the NHS' or a particular school versus 'education' or 'schools' and so on). A similar gap has been identified in surveys across a number of public services, and it is a particularly interesting topic in policing (Fleming and McLaughlin, 2012; Millie and Herrington, 2005). This is because the gap can actually open up after an encounter—perhaps because victims of crime or those needing police services have unrealistically high expectations of what can be delivered.

The confidence gap seems to reflect a lack of public recognition that their public services in general provide quality outcomes. This has frustrated both the government and the police service for decades (Barnes and Eagle, 2007). It is this which in part prompted the 2008 home secretary, Jacqui Smith, to publish the Policing Pledge. The now defunct pledge focused on restoring public faith, through the confidence drivers of fairness, dignity and respect; engagement and consultation; responsiveness and reliability; transparency; and accountability. With a remit across all territorial police forces of the UK, it offered promises from local police to their communities. In effect, it was a type of contract.

These efforts to be clear about policing and what the communities of the UK could expect were later discredited (Fleming and McLaughlin, 2012). Nonetheless, the Policing Pledge at least made an effort to define more clearly what the public could expect from their local police. This clarity around expectations appears to be missing somewhat when it comes to deciphering and defining confidence. For example, when surveys ask the question, 'Do you have confidence in your local police?', no actual explanation of the term confidence is given and it is often left for the respondent to apply their own meaning to the word.

Since we know there is a lack of construct clarity in relation to confidence, a starting problem for such surveys is their consistency and interpretation. One potential solution could be to ask members of the public what 'confidence in the police' means to them by adding a series of specific sub-questions in the survey. These could then be used to ask the respondent to describe what would improve their confidence in the police (visibility, responsiveness and so on).

The question of clarity about the construct confidence is not just a question for researchers, it is important to practitioners too. Lowe and Innes (2012) make the important point that English and Welsh police forces spend much of their time worrying about what the public make of their local police. In their article 'Can we speak in confidence?', they discuss a case study of an innovative community engagement methodology, which was intended to allow and encourage citizens to voice their concerns. They suggest that sharpening the focus of localised police interventions can improve public understanding and perceptions of crime, disorder and policing with a positive effect on public confidence and overall community well-being. However, they also suggest that such improvements do not necessarily result in generalised public confidence. Initiatives of the nature described are considered both resource intensive and hard work, which can be considered a dilemma for the police service at a time of austerity.

The most common and interchangeable word with the term confidence is *trust*, with the two often being used hand in glove and generating much debate in the social sciences (Stanko et al., 2012). Stanko and colleagues suggest there is overlap between the two concepts but refer to the notion of confidence as one that suggests, "an overall attitude or orientation that people *have* towards the police, one that summarises their assessment of its ability to perform the range of different functions that constitute its role and position in society" (Stanko et al., 2012, p. 321). This is contrasted with trust being described by them as something "that people do—or do not". They suggest to trust in the police is to hold specific beliefs about the ability of the police overall, and also to have expectations about how officers will act in certain situations; confidence, on the other hand, is an overall summary judgment of the job that the police are doing is one that citizens can rely on.

Jackson and Bradford (2010) describe trust and confidence as having three separate dimensions: trust in police effectiveness, trust in police fairness and trust in police engagement and shared values. Their work suggests that believing (or trusting) the police to be effective is less important in predicting overall confidence than more socio-relational aspects of shared values and the fairness of interpersonal treatment. They advocate that overall confidence be based on trust that is rooted in a particular social alignment and shared values between the police and the community. They conclude that overall confidence is entrenched in perceived fairness and that its effect could be channelled through motive-based trust (see also Bradford and Jackson 2010). Whilst this description could be considered to blur the lines between trust and confidence, it does recognise the important link between the two terms and acknowledges how, in the eyes of many, the two are synonymous.

Does Confidence Matter?

Setting aside for a moment the potential confusion as to what the construct 'confidence' actually means in a theoretical sense, it is clear that police forces have been trying to measure (and increase it) for more than a decade. Some of the more practical benefits for police forces achieving public confidence are discussed by Sindall et al., (2012). Using repeated cross-sectional survey data from the British Crime Survey (BCS) in order to apply a time-series regression analysis, they show how confidence in policing can change for the aggregate population over a period of time. Their findings suggest time-series analyses reveal that confidence in the police is not related to aggregate worry about crime and perceptions of social cohesion or informal social control, but only to perceptions of crime and the property crime rate.

Sindall et al. state that if citizens do not have confidence in the police, they are less likely to comply with police authority, report crimes, act as witnesses or obey the law themselves (see also Hough and Roberts, 2004; Tyler, 2004). There is a potential paradox or unintended consequence here if improved confidence leads to more crime reporting. This would mean that the crime rate increases, which is reported to the public who then have less confidence in the police due to the increase in crime. This would suggest a kind of homeostatic effect, which means the relationship between police and public is always taken back to where it started.

There is the potential for a broader set of benefits as highlighted by Stanko et al. (2012, p. 320), who advocate "there is considerable evidence that trust in the police is linked to concrete behaviours—cooperation with officers, compliance with law and engagement in informal social control". As well as these police-related benefits, Jackson et al. (2009, p. 101) also point towards the wider implications of greater legitimacy. This can encourage people to "do all the other things that the criminal justice system relies on in order to function effectively". These observations highlight that the value of confidence is not just about crime.

Even so, the relationship between public confidence in policing and public perceptions of crime remains relevant. In asking the question, 'Does the fear of crime erode public confidence in policing?', Jackson et al. (2009, p. 109) conclude by saying, "the answer we have come to—on the basis of the data we have at our disposal—is therefore largely no". They propose a different explanation for levels of confidence, suggesting that both fear of crime and confidence are rooted in members of the public's assessment of non-criminal aspects of their neighbourhood. They suggest that people look to the police to defend community norms and values, especially when those norms and values are seen to be declining.

The positive policy implication of defending norms and values is that dealing with low-level issues that people find important could result in an uplift in confidence. However, there is also a clear expectation from policymakers and the public alike that the police effectively deal with the more direct forms of crime (burglary, robbery, violent crime etc.). The consideration here becomes what is the appropriate, first-order strategic priority for UK policing—crime or confidence? The current period of austerity does not allow for everything to be a priority, and there is certainly a danger of spreading resources too thin. Whilst there is a consensus that confidence does matter, there is no clear route to high levels of confidence.

Another way to consider these interrelationships is to see public confidence in the police as something that is important to the public generally as citizens. A positive image of the police is important for the police to function effectively within the community they serve, but attributions of policing matter more widely in the context of what we understand a democratic society to be (Ren et al., 2005; Cao and Stack, 2004). Fleming and McLaughlin (2012, p. 261) expand on this democratic importance by highlighting the fact that "the police are the most visible and symbolic domestic agents of coercive governmental authority in advanced liberal democratic states", suggesting what the public thinks and feels about the police as well as police attitudes to the public can stand as a key indicator of confidence in the state's ability to fulfil its side of the social contract.

Without public support, the police are seriously limited in their ability to effectively bring offenders to justice, deal with local neighbourhood problems, maintain law and order and build effective partnerships (Rosenbaum et al., 2005). The public's trust and confidence in the police matters to the extent that without their support, the police will find their task near on impossible. Rigid performance regimes have also held police leaders to account, ensuring that they understand confidence matters. Those same police leaders whose job is to deliver increased confidence seek a simple solution. As described by Stanko et al. (2012, p. 326), they seek a "bottled formula, but such a magic solution rarely exists".

What the public thinks of their police has been on the top of the policy agenda for successive governments in the UK for decades, clearly stating they want to see improvements confidence, as measured by the BCS, since it started in 1982. Myhill and Bradford (2012) suggest that significant doubts remain as to how this enormous task might be achieved, even questioning whether it is indeed possible for police to improve public confidence in any straightforward way. Whilst their questioning of this demand placed upon the police is valid, the challenge is nevertheless unlikely be abandoned by current or future policymakers. The benefits of improved confidence are clear, and as such one must conclude that confidence does matter. The question however remains, how do police organisations go about achieving confidence in the most effective way?

Engagement and Contact

Various confidence-related studies have focused on the issue of public engagement and contact, an element of confidence that is more in line with the theme of this study. In their article on the role of public attitude surveys in understanding public confidence, Bradford, Stanko and Jackson suggest they "have strong evidence that contact matters" (2009, p. 147). They suggest communication with the public is another form of contact, which can contribute to the way people feel about their local police service. They argue that "the provision of such information may reassure that the police are taking the matter seriously, or justify what might otherwise be seen as arbitrary or unjust behaviour" (Bradford, Stanko and Jackson, 2009, p. 146). The conclusion here is that contact is important, but of greater importance is getting contact right if the ambition is to influence positive feelings towards the police.

Whilst Bradford, Stanko and Jackson (2009) also report that communication between officers and the public—of information, of fairness and respect, and of police presence—appears to be of central importance, there can also sometimes be negative implications arising from direct contact. Their findings highlight evidence that well-handled contacts can have a small but positive impact; however, they also suggest that personal contact with the police can be associated with lower levels of public confidence. In a separate study, Bradford, Jackson and Stanko (2009) summarise evidence on contact and confidence from the BCS and surveys by the Metropolitan Police Service (MPS), suggesting that reductions in confidence may not be due to the increased levels of police-public encounters, but because increasingly more of those encounters are felt to be unsatisfactory in some way.

Myhill and Bradford (2012) suggest fears that contact inevitably has an adverse impact on confidence are overstated; suggesting that improving the way officers handle encounters might lead to enhanced trust and confidence. The ability of the police to improve trust and confidence in a straightforward way is questioned. They present evidence that strongly concurs with prior work in finding that unsatisfactory contact with the police is strongly associated with lower confidence. Based on their findings using panel data, they find that "when officers get things wrong—or are perceived to get things wrong—significant damage to public trust can result" (2012, p. 419).

Other studies have also found that contact, even where it is well received by the public, does not always have a consistent, positive effect, with some even suggesting that the police are limited in what they can do to improve public opinions by improving the quality of their interactions with them (Skogan, 2006). In moving the focus from more general contact to victims of crime, according to Skogan, one consistent finding is that victims are less *outcome*-orientated than they are *process*-orientated. That is, they are less concerned about someone being caught or (in many instances) getting stolen property back than they are about how promptly and responsibly they are treated by the authorities. According to Skogan, police are judged by what physicians might call their *bedside manner*. Factors like how willing the police are to listen to people's stories and show concern for their plight are very important, as are their politeness, helpfulness and fairness (see also Tyler and Huo, 2002). These opportunities are clearly within the gift and control of the police. To not deal with people with a higher degree of professionalism can be seen as a missed opportunity to improve confidence.

In their study on the impact of public encounters with the police, Bradford, Stanko and Jackson (2009) are motivated by the question, Can well-handled encounters have a positive effect on public confidence in policing?' Their findings suggest that not only is it important that the police do things properly, but that it is also important that they are seen to do them properly. Bradford et al. argue that it may be easier for police to improve visibility and communication than contact experience, implying that no form of contact is straightforward.

According to Skogan (2006), who used data from the 1992 BCS (as well as studies from various US cities), the likely outcomes of direct contact are questionable in the sense that positively assessed encounters (on whatever basis the assessment is made) fail to result in improvements in confidence; while negatively assessed encounters continue to have the predicted effect. The suggestion here is that the impact of contact is damaging at worst and negligible at best. Ren et al. (2005), in their US study on police confidence, found their data showed that more contacts between citizens and the police led to higher levels of confidence in the police in general, although their findings were also found to be consistent with prior evidence that negative contacts served to lower public confidence in the police.

Whilst the experience of direct contact with the police is an important one, also of importance is a recognition that the vast majority of the public either do not have and/or do not want interaction with the police (Barnes and Eagle, 2007; Stanko et al., 2012; Skogan, 1990). Of the BCS sample 2009–2010, 71% had not come into contact with the police in the last 12 months (Stanko et al., 2012). With the measure of confidence routinely being taken from randomly selected public surveys, the only way to influence the wider population through consultation and engagement is through a wider reach.

Myhill's (2012) review of the literature advocates a strong theoretical case for community engagement in policing. He suggests that informal mechanisms of social control play a greater role in building confidence than more formal and traditional mechanisms, such as reactive and enforcement-based policing. He cites many potential benefits of engagement, which include increasing trust and confidence. This is further supported by Jackson et al. (2009), who discuss the various components and drivers for public confidence, listing *engagement with the community* as being the most central. In a more practical sense, this means that in order to drive public confidence, the police need to engage as a part of the community, represent community values, norms and morals. Dealing with the issues that matter the most to the community, whilst being visible and accessible, may also serve well to address both fear of crime and public confidence in policing.

Socio-Demographic Considerations

Research shows that people more generally support the police and on the whole tend to be satisfied with the way the police perform their duties (Miller et al., 2004; Cao et al., 1996). Research also shows that not all segments of society hold equally positive opinions, and various demographic considerations need to be made in light of the different views people may have depending not only on their experience of the police, but also their social or demographic footing. BCS results have regularly shown that people's experiences of the police and their associated assessment of services provided were consistently related to factors such as age, race and gender (Skogan, 1990). Early research on the relationship between the public and the police focused on demographic determinants of confidence in the police (Ren et al., 2005). Race, age, gender, socio-economic status and education were seen as the principal predictors, with race receiving the greatest attention. Most studies showed that minorities were more critical and less likely to have confidence in their police (see also Dowler, 2003).

White people tend to view the police more positively than do their black and minority ethnic (BME) counterparts. Previous research on this subject matter has typically concluded that direct contact with the police is the major reason why residents, especially minorities, hold negative views of the police (Rosenbaum et al., 2005). Rosenbaum and colleagues also highlight the problem with this conclusion, in that the majority of these studies are cross-sectional and therefore unable to substantiate a causal relationship between contact and attitudes or determine the order of causality.

Their study sought to overcome these limitations by collecting attitudinal data before and after contact with the police. The results did not support previous research. Over the period of a year, they found an absence of effect for changes in attitudes based on direct contact, which was consistent across racial and ethnic groups. They did, however, find some evidence that different racial and ethnic groups may receive and process information about the police differently in light of some combination of prior experience, stereotypes and access to different sources of information. These findings prove useful in better understanding confidence in the context of a multi-cultural society, such as the UK.

Using survey data from 1000 randomly selected residents in the city of Cincinnati, Cao and colleagues (1996) found consistencies with other research, in that while minorities express less favourable attitudes towards to police than do white people, they still possess favourable attitudes. In addition, they found that respondents' gender, age and income were statistically significant determinants of confidence in the police. Especially, females and older individuals were more likely to express higher levels of confidence than males and younger respondents. Income levels were also positively related to confidence, whilst level of education was not. They do suggest, however, that community context is the most important determinant of confidence.

When their findings were taken together, Cao et al. concluded that attitudes towards the police might not be regulated by a person's race per se, but by the social context in which the person is situated. This throws open the question of whether minority groups or people view the police less favourably, given that, in their study, race was not significant when contextual variables were controlled. This may well suggest that it is indeed possible that much of the previous research, which did not include contextual variables, had based findings on unreliable models.

Using telephone interview data from 2058 community residents in a medium-sized midwestern US community, Huebner et al. (2004) contrasted samples of white and African American citizens in order to better understand how demographic, experiential and neighbourhood contextual factors shape perceptions of police services. They found that African American citizens were strongly influenced by their demographic attributes and the *stake* they held in their neighbourhoods, while the perceptions of white citizens were more a product of their neighbourhood, suggesting a "uniform approach may not work for members of all racial groups" (Huebner et al., 2004, p. 133). The implications of such a suggestion can be far reaching within the UK, if such a consideration is applied through different levels of service. Whilst valuing the difference of our communities sits at the forefront of UK policing policy, the moral dilemma associated with even considering different levels of service provision needs to be thought through and considered with a great deal of care, or disregarded altogether.

A Home Office commissioned report (Bradley 1998) analysed focus groups with a broad cross section of the general population. This suggested the needs and priorities of the public should be assessed in a clear and distinct social context, identifying key social groups for policing. These were, in the main, groups defined in terms of age/life stage, socio-economic class and ethnicity. Analysis of these focus group suggested that whilst the police already had a good working relationship with some social groups, others, particularly young people and ethnic minorities, believed that the police failed to address their concerns. In order to address these failings, the report proposed that the police service should regard the public not as a single entity, but as a number of distinct publics. This suggestion—proposing that the police treat different sections of the community in a different manner and different styles—is more palatable than any implication that they might apply different standards of service. The report clearly suggests a form of *segmented* policing: appropriate to the specific group, aimed at targeting negative perceptions. This model of policing has no doubt developed and been encouraged in the form of local or neighbourhood policing over the last ten or so years.

Local Policing

Myhill and Beak (2008) of the National Policing Improvement Agency list neighbourhood policing as one of the most important factors associated with the public being confident in the police. They suggest the most important factor (by far) identified from those who took part in their study is "agreeing that the local police are dealing with the things that matter to local people" (2008, p. 6). Contemporary UK policing has been moulded by programmes such as *citizen focused policing, reassurance policing* and *neighbourhood policing*, all interchangeable terms, which are generally referred to collectively as *local policing*. Government bodies and the police initiated a more localised style of policing as a direct reaction to findings from the BCS over the past decades, with aim to improve public confidence in policing (Wünsch and Hohl, 2009).

In examining police reform, Innes (2005) considered why it is that *soft* policing functions appear so troublesome for the police to perform. He defines *soft* policing as "the non-coercive aspects of police-led social control encompassing the provision of a visible presence of authority, persuasion, negotiation and community interaction" (2005, p. 157). Innes suggests 'soft policing' is where the police power is based. This power is based less on the direct enactment of coercion and rests instead upon a persuasive mode of social control. Innes also identifies with the more traditional approach of *hard policing*, suggesting the occupational culture of street cops tends to value the conduct of hard policing functions, such as pursuing *real* criminals, public order policing and so forth, whilst treating the less coercive aspects of the police role with disdain.

Whilst in the past police reform has been seen to oscillate between these two distinct approaches to policing (hard and soft as described by Innes), the coalition government and its successor have been more clear in their support for a more localised approach to policing, along with the associated benefit of securing public support and confidence. This could be seen by some as a handover of power to communities, as the police become more responsive to public demands. The question of priorities, focus and approach are still being considered at a time when policing is being cut back at a considerable level.

The current neighbourhood policing model was a product of the National Reassurance Policing Programme (NRPP), which was first implemented in 16 neighbourhoods in England and Wales between 2003 and 2005. The programme involved intensive local activity, which was focused on visibility of the police, community engagement and problem solving. The outcomes were intended to be reduced fear of crime, increased sense of safety, reduced anti-social behaviour, improved quality of life, improved social capacity and improved public satisfaction with confidence in the police (Tuffin et al., 2006). The model is now fully operational in all forces in England and Wales (Lowe and Innes, 2012), with a design to render local policing more directly responsive to public concerns and needs. As the landscape of UK policing has once again changed through the implementation of police and crime commissioners (PCCs), government influence and budget cuts, maybe it is an opportune time to consider whether the expensive focus on local policing is in need of review.

Media and Communication

Opinions about the police are derived from people's own experiences, what they hear from others, and what they see and read about the police. In their review, which drew upon representative public opinion surveys to examine the state of public confidence in justice around the world, Hough and Roberts (2004) state that a great deal of research has been gathered on media coverage of crime and justice, with the subject providing a rich harvest of newsworthy stories, even if there is a good deal of selectivity in the process. Hough and Roberts suggest that this literature reveals several features of media coverage that are likely to have a negative impact on public confidence, such as an emphasis on violent and sexual crimes, an emphasis on street crime, limited coverage of statistical trends to place individual incidents in context and a focus on the steepest increases in crime rates, where trends are reported.

In using BCS data to look at the public's attitude towards the police, Skogan (1990) concluded that the media had the most influence on those who had no direct contacts with the police and some effect upon those who did. Western society is fascinated with crime and justice. From films, books, newspapers, magazines and television to everyday conversations, we are constantly interested in crime (Dowler, 2003). The public's perception of crime and law enforcement is largely determined by the mass media, and more recently social media. The influence of these mean it is essential that the effects the media has on attitudes towards crime are considered in our efforts to understand and manage their impact on confidence. Dowler's suggestion that the police and the media engage in mutually beneficial relations is becoming even more of a reality in a modern age, with forums like Facebook, Twitter and YouTube allowing an opportunity for immediate access by the police to the wider public. Every police force in the UK has a form of communication/media department, which employs experts in the field to maximise opportunities to benefit from this potentially mutually beneficial relationship.

According to Fleming and McLaughlin (2012), the last Labour government was very much aware of the role that the news media could play on issues that posed questions about government power and legitimacy. This awareness played a crucial role in their positive approach to boost public confidence in policing through effective use of the media. The media, however, can also have a damaging effect on the police's public image. According to Fleming and McLaughlin, in March 2010 the Labour government's *Public Confidence Agenda* suffered when the Advertising Standards Agency concluded that Policing Pledge advertisements that had cost the public purse £1.9 million had also been misleading in their promise of what the public could expect from their police force. They suggest that Labour stood accused of not just spin, but also of deliberately deceiving the public. This cautionary tale is still relevant, in the sense that the current media climate offers opportunities but also has the potential to inflict reputational damage for the police and for the government.

In their study of public opinions of the police, Miller et al. (2004) asked the question, 'Is the media's portrayal of the police an important determinant of public opinion of the police'? Whilst they conclude that citizen's opinions of the police are positive over time, at least in the absence of significant shifts in police policy or media scandals, they also found that police managers' routine management of media coverage may not have a profound impact on public opinion (see also Innes, 2004). They suggest focusing on improving the quality of police-public interactions may be more effective, certainly in periods where there are no major police scandals. Efforts to improve the quality of police-public interactions in general are likely to be more important to public confidence. To some extent, the view taken by Miller et al. (2004) is thrown into question by Rosenbaum et al. (2005), whose study of 2500 randomly selected Chicago residents found that positive information about the police produced larger attitudinal effects than did negative information. They advocate that the public learning something positive about the police may be newsworthy and unexpected.

These findings have an important implication in modern-day policing within the UK. While there is little doubt about the importance of direct communication with the public, there is also uncertainty about how and what kind of communication and information provision is effective in enhancing confidence (Millie and Herrington, 2005; Wünsch and Hohl, 2009). According to Wünsch and Hohl (2009), a number of studies attribute low confidence in the police to a deficit in the public's knowledge about actual crime figures and a lack of understanding of police work in general. They suggest that information provision aimed at educating the public might both narrow knowledge and improve confidence. The challenge is to know with more certainty what type of information will have the greatest impact on improving confidence and the least on damaging it. This is an area of media and communication yet to be studied in sufficient detail and would clearly benefit from further research, within the context of community policing within the UK.

Drivers for Improved Confidence

Using a range of qualitative and quantitative research methods, the MPS Strategy, Research and Analysis Unit (SRAU) have since 2004 used tracking studies, undertaken field observations on Safer Neighbourhoods (SN) teams and held focus groups with members of the public (Rehman, 2009). This work has been underpinned by the MPS's own London-wide public attitude surveys, which capture key evidence on what factors influence people's perception of crime, disorder and policing. In an effort to positively impact on public confidence, the SRAU have been able to develop practical guides to advise their SN teams. The MPS model shows three key drivers of public confidence in policing: the public's perception on how *effective* the police are at dealing with crime and disorder; how *fair* the police are when dealing with the public; and how they *engage* with the public correlate with confidence in the police, with engagement being the most important aspect (see also Jackson and Bradford, 2008; Stanko and Bradford, 2009).

In 2007, the London Borough of Hammersmith and Fulham and the MPS jointly ran an initiative with the objectives of reducing crime and disorder and improving local residents' perception of crime and disorder (Rehman, 2009). The results of the initiative illustrated the benefits of localised enhanced policing by focusing police efforts on community concerns and effective engagement. The SRAU research has shown that the public are more concerned about local issues than they are about the level of crime at a borough or national level. Rehman suggests that by providing an engaging, fair and effective police service that focuses on local issues and concerns, the police can improve and maintain public confidence.

Increased focus on public perception measures has led senior officers to ask what drives confidence, with researchers seeking to better understand how people form generic assessments of the police and to what effect (Myhill and Quinton, 2010; Bradford, Stanko and Jackson, 2009). Understanding the links between the more practical approach and academic research is an important factor in determining key drivers for improved confidence.

Of the different components to public confidence, Jackson et al. (2009) found engagement with the community to be the most central. They state, "in practice this means that in order to improve public confidence, the police need to re-engage as an active part of the community, representing and defending community values, norms and morals" (2009, p. 108). Whilst much of the research has found engagement, communication and feedback to be the key drivers for building confidence (Lowe and Innes, 2012; Jackson et al., 2009), visibility is also seen by some to be a key driver (Myhill and Bradford, 2012). However, Tuffin et al. (2006) argue that improved confidence requires more than officers simply being visible. Their evaluation of the NRPP showed that improvements in confidence were only realised in those sites where visible patrol was targeted and accompanied by a level of proactive community engagement, with associated problem solving.

A key policy document for reassurance was Her Majesty's Inspectorate of Constabulary's (HMIC) report entitled 'Open All Hours' (Povey, 2001). The report highlighted three key elements for an effective reassurance approach: visibility, familiarity and accessibility. Povey also made the valid point that whilst the police need to be seen, the visibility must exist beyond a simple 'drive by' approach. Officers also need to be familiar faces within local neighbourhoods and accessible (see also Millie and Herrington, 2005; Barnes and Eagle, 2007).

Whilst the drivers listed above do not form a complete list, they do present a good deal of relevance to this focus of this study. The importance of police-initiated engagement has already been highlighted and cannot be understated in being considered to be the most useful and effective tactic in driving public confidence.

Emerging Issues and the Need for Empirical Research

The clear focus of studies relating to public confidence in policing should, in part, be to provide police leaders and policymakers with evidence and incentive to improve public confidence. Empirical evidence arising from previous studies shows fairness is linked to cooperation, compliance and public engagement (Stanko et al., 2012). Public confidence targets are still firmly situated within internal performance management regimes. This may be unlikely to change in the democratic and political climate of governance under the second wave of recently elected PCCs.

Public confidence in policing is a complex and moving landscape. There is as yet, as we have cautioned, no agreed definition of public confidence. Similarly, although there are many recognised strategic and operational drivers (engagement, communication, visibility) and potential organisational and public benefits (compliance with authority, public adherence to the law, improvements in crime management), there are also many potential barriers and conflicts in the existing literature (opportunities and dangers of the media and social media, the influence of communication and direct engagement).

A pressing requirement for the improvement of public confidence in policing is for recommendations on future direction to be based on research, using valid and reliable methods of data collection, with greater clarity as to the core construct 'confidence'.

Notes

1 Office for National Statistics—Accessed 04 May 2013 from www.ons.gov.uk/ons/guide-method/surveys
2 BBC News—Accessed on 04 May 2013 from www.bbc.co.uk/news/uk-20869023
3 *The Telegraph*—Accessed on 01 November 2013 www.telegraph.co.uk/news/uknews/crime/10336479/Respect-the-police-says-Britains-top-officer.html

References

Barnes, I., and Eagle, T. (2007). 'The role of community engagement in neighbourhood policing', *Policing: A Journal of Policy and Practice*, 1 (2): 161–172.
Bradford, B., and Jackson, J. (2010). '*Trust and confidence in the police: A conceptual review*' [online]. Available at: http://papers.ssrn.com/sol3/papers.cfm?abstract_id=1684508. Last accessed: 09 November 2013.
Bradford, B., Jackson, J., and Stanko, E.A. (2009). 'Contact and confidence: Revisiting the impact of public encounters with the police', *Policing and Society: An International Journal of Research and Policy*, 19 (1): 20–46.

Bradford, B., Stanko, E.A., and Jackson, J. (2009). 'Using research to inform policy: The role of public attitude surveys in understanding public confidence and police contact', *Policing: A Journal of Policy and Practice*, 3 (2): 139–148.

Bradley, R. (1998). 'Police expectations and perceptions of policing', *Police Research Series Paper 96*. London: Home Office.

Cao, L., Frank, J., and Cullen, F.T. (1996). 'Race, community context and confidence in the police', *American Journal of Police*, XV (1): 3–22.

Cao, L., and Stack, S. (2004). 'Confidence in the police between America and Japan: Results from two waves of surveys', *Policing: An International Journal of Police Strategies & Management*, 28 (1): 139–151.

Dowler, K. (2003). Media consumption and public attitudes toward crime and justice: The relationship between fear of crime, punitive attitudes, and perceived police effectiveness', *Journal of Criminal Justice and Popular Culture*, 10 (2): 109–126.

FitzGerald, M. (2010). 'A confidence trick?' *Policing: A Journal of Policy and Practice*, 4 (3): 298–301.

Fleming, J., and McLaughlin, E. (2012). 'Through a different lens: Researching the rise and fall of New Labour's 'public confidence agenda'', *Policing and Society: An International Journal of Research and Policy*, 22 (3): 280–294.

Hough, M., and Roberts, J. (2004). *Confidence in Justice: An International Review*. London: Home Office, cited in Sindall, K., Sturgis, P. and Jennings, W. (2012). 'Public confidence in the police: A time-series analysis', *British Journal of Criminology*, 52: 744–764.

Huebner, B.M., Schafer, J.A., and Bynum, T.S. (2004). 'African American and White perceptions of police services: Within- and between-group variation', *Journal of Criminal Justice*, 32: 123–135.

Innes, M. (2004). 'Reinventing tradition?: Reassurance, neighbourhood security and policing', *Criminal Justice*, 4 (2): 151–171.

Innes, M. (2005). 'Why "Soft" policing is hard: On the curious development of reassurance policing, how It became neighbourhood policing and what this signifies about the politics of police reform', *Journal of Community & Applied Social Psychology*, 15: 156–169.

Jackson, J., and Bradford, B. (2008). 'Crime, policing and social order: On the expressive nature of public confidence in policing', *The British Journal of Sociology*, 60 (3): 493–521.

Jackson, J., and Bradford, B. (2010). 'What is Trust and Confidence in the Police?', *Policing: A Journal of Policy and Practice*, 4 (3): 241–248.

Jackson, J., Bradford, B., Hohl, K. and Farrall, S. (2009). 'Does the Fear of Crime Erode Public Confidence in Policing?', *Policing: A Journal of Policy and Practice*, 3 (1): 100–111.

Lowe, T., and Innes, M. (2012). 'Can we speak in confidence? Community intelligence and neighbourhood policing v2.0', *Policing and Society: An International Journal of Research and Policy*, 22 (3): 295–316.

Miller, J., Davis, R.C., Henderson, N.J., Markovic, J., and Ortiz, C.W. (2004). *Public Opinions of the Police: The Influence of Friends, Family, and News Media*. New York: Vera Institute of Justice.

Millie, A., and Herrington, V. (2005). 'Bridging the gap: Understanding reassurance policing' *The Howard Journal*, 44 (1): 41–56.

Myhill, A. (2012). *Community engagement in policing: Lessons from the literature*. National Policing Improvement Agency.

Myhill, A., and Beak, K. (2008). '*Public Confidence in the Police*', National Police Improvement Agency.

Myhill, A., and Bradford, B. (2012). 'Can police enhance public confidence by improving quality of service? Results from two surveys in England and Wales', *Policing and Society: An International Journal of Research and Policy*, 22 (4): 397–425.

Myhill, A., and Quinton, P. (2010). 'Confidence, neighbourhood policing, and contact: Drawing together the evidence', *Policing: A Journal of Policy and Practice*, 4 (3): 273–281.

Povey, K. (2001). *Open All Hours: A Thematic Inspection Report on the Role of Police Visibility and Accessibility in Public Reassurance*, London: Her Majesty's Inspectorate of Constabulary (HMIC).

Rehman, U. (2009). 'The Hammersmith initiative: An example of how to impact and improve public confidence in policing', *Policing: A Journal of Policy and Practice*, 3 (4): 310–317.

Ren, L., Cao, L., Lovrich, N., and Gaffney, M. (2005). 'Linking confidence in the police with the performance of the police: Community policing can make a difference', *Journal of Criminal Justice*, 33: 55–66.

Rosenbaum, D.P., Schuck, A.M., Costello, S.K., Hawkins, D.F., and Ring, M.K. (2005). 'Attitudes towards the police: The effects of direct and vicarious experience', *Police Quarterly*, 8 (3): 343–365.

Sindall, K., Sturgis, P., and Jennings, W. (2012). 'Public confidence in the police: A time-series analysis', *British Journal of Criminology*, 52: 744–764.

Skogan, W.G. (1990). *The Police and Public in England and Wales: A British Crime Survey Report*. Home Office Research Study 117.

Skogan, W.G. (2006). 'Asymmetry in the Impact of Encounters with the Police', *Policing and Society*, 16 (2): 99–126.

Stanko, B., Jackson, J., Bradford, B., and Hohl, K. (2012). 'A golden thread, a presence amongst uniforms, and a good deal of data: Studying public confidence in the London metropolitan police', *Policing and Society: An International Journal of Research and Policy*, 22 (3): 317–331.

Stanko, E.A., and Bradford, B. (2009). 'Beyond measuring "How Good a Job" police are doing: The MPS model of confidence in policing', *Policing: A Journal of Policy and Practice*, 3 (4): 322–330.

Tuffin, R., Morris, J., and Poole, A. (2006). *An Evaluation of the National Reassurance Policing Programme*. London: Home Office.

Tyler, T.R. (2004). 'Enhancing police legitimacy', *Annals of the American Academy of Political and Social Science*, 593: 84–99, cited in Sindall, K., Sturgis, P., and Jennings, W. (2012). 'Public confidence in the police: A time-series analysis', *British Journal of Criminology*, 52: 744–764.

Tyler, T.R., and Huo, Y.J. (2002). *Trust in the law: Encouraging public cooperation with the police and courts*, New York: Russell Sage Foundation.

Wünsch, D., and Hohl, K. (2009). 'Evidencing a "Good Practice Model" of police communication: The impact of local policing newsletters on public confidence', *Policing: A Journal of Policy and Practice*, 3 (4): 331–339.

16 Balancing Formal and Informal Support for Psychological Health in Emergency Services

Creating Multiple Pathways for Ambulance Staff

Ashlea Kellner, Keith Townsend,*
Rebecca Loudoun, Tiet-Hanh Dao-Tran and
Adrian Wilkinson

Introduction and Background

It is well accepted that ambulance work is characterised by employee burnout, high stress, work intensification and exhaustion—physical, mental and emotional (Granter, Wankhade, McCann, Hassard, & Hyde, 2018). A key factor that contributes to these problems is an unavoidable feature of emergency services work, that employees will be regularly exposed to extreme and traumatic events (Bigham et al., 2014; McFarlane & Bryant, 2007; McFarlane, Williamson, & Barton, 2009). Exposure of this kind increases the risk of a number of mental health conditions such as depression and anxiety (Izutsu, Tsutsumi, Asukai, Kurita, & Kawamura, 2004) and post-traumatic stress disorder (Bennett et al., 2005; Grant, Dutton, & Rosso, 2008; Huizink et al., 2006). There is a significant cost—financial, social and emotional—of mental health conditions to emergency services organisations, patients, the community, and to employees, and their friends, families and peers.

For emergency services organisations, mental health problems are associated with increased incidence of employee burnout and long-term sick leave (Brattberg, 2006), deteriorated health and well-being (Berger et al., 2007) and increased employee turnover (Patterson et al., 2010). It is of increasing importance to emergency services organisations to invest resources in preventing and managing mental health problems. There is also a particular historical culture which can both create stress for individuals while contradicting support mechanisms. For example, many professions that are male-dominated and uniformed tend to have a strict hierarchy, a masculinist 'man up' approach with a culture of blame, fear, bullying and poor industrial relations. While these factors appear to be changing with time, they are still a major part of the stressful working lives of paramedics.

* Correspondence E-mail ID: k.townsend@griffith.edu.au

Research suggests a range of factors can influence the prevalence and severity of consequences associated with trauma exposure and promote positive outcomes. Formal systems of employee support, such as access to professional counselling services and resilience training, can positively influence employees' health and well-being (Rajaratnam, Sears, Shi, Coberley, & Pope, 2014; Richmond, Pampel, Wood, & Nunes, 2017). Informal support via relationships with co-workers and family can be instrumental in reducing the severity of symptoms and encouraging positive post-traumatic growth (Oginska-Bulik, 2015; Prati & Pietrantoni, 2010; Somville, De Gucht, & Maes, 2016). Additionally, these formal and informal elements feed into the 'psychosocial safety climate' that can potentially influence employees' physical and psychological state of health (Zadow, Dollard, McLinton, Lawrence, & Tuckey, 2017).

In this chapter, we examine the formal and informal support systems of two Australian state emergency services cases, with a specific focus on the formal employee assistance and peer support officer programmes and the informal colleague, family and front-line manager support. Using interview data, we explore the components of a balanced support model and identify strengths and weaknesses of support within the cases. We find these components work together as a network of complementary support functions that can reduce the severity and assist in the management of mental health problems in the ambulance service. A balance of complementary formal and informal support mechanisms can temper the climate and provide a holistic approach to supporting employees that responds to individual preferences. In short, we argue that it is not enough to provide formal support systems which function well in their own right. The different needs of staff and the tendency to want the capacity for informal peer support means we need to see the system in terms of how the formal and informal fit together. We need to better understand how things operate in practice (the interactions of the system in use) rather than in the system codified on organisational policy documents. Understanding the needs and the actual practice of ambulance service employees when in times of need is critical in improving their work health outcomes.

Risk Factors for Mental Health Problems Among Emergency Responders

Front-line emergency services workers frequently perform their work in uncontrolled environments that include exposure to potentially traumatic events (Beaton, Murphy, Johnson, Pike, & Corneil, 2005; Reichard, Marsh, & Moore, 2011). Apart from vicarious trauma from exposure to or involvement in an extreme event, emergency responders are also at high risk of a range of physical incidents that can trigger or lead to mental health problems.

For example, the risk of serious injury for emergency responders is seven times higher than the Australian national average, and the fatality rate is six times higher (Maguire, O'Meara, Brightwell, O'Neill, & Fitzgerald, 2014).

Up to 90% of emergency responders are exposed to workplace violence in some form (Pourshaikhian, Abolghasem Gorji, Aryankhesal, Khorasani-Zavareh, & Barati, 2016), at least half of emergency responders have experienced physical assault (Gabrovec, 2015; Pourshaikhian et al., 2016) and over two thirds have been subject to verbal abuse (Bigham et al., 2014). Additionally, around one in four emergency responders experience sexual harassment or sexual assault on the job (Bigham et al., 2014; Gabrovec, 2015; Pourshaikhian et al., 2016). On the whole, a combination of job-related risk factors is associated with extreme events that present a challenging and at times dangerous work situation for emergency responders. While there is an attempt to influence these factors by public awareness campaigns, the impact of these has been limited.

There are, however, some individual factors and workplace characteristics associated with increased prevalence of PTSD and other psychological conditions over which the organisation can exert some degree of control and influence. For instance, pre-trauma risk factors for PTSD include low levels of education (Rybojad, Aftyka, Baran, & Rzońca, 2016), psychiatric history (Neria, Nandi, & Galea, 2008) and sleep disturbance (Wright, Britt, Bliese, & Adler, 2011). Research also suggests that individuals who are younger (Brewin, Andrews, & Valentine, 2000), female (Skogstad, Heir, Hauff, & Ekeberg, 2016) and non-married (Berger et al., 2007) are at higher risk of developing PTSD. While some characteristics such as psychiatric history are typically already considered in pre-screening checks, other factors noted here may need further consideration in developing employee support programmes that specifically target at-risk groups.

Evidence indicates individual responses to exposure to trauma are difficult to predict and can vary widely. The way individuals cope with trauma may also affect their risk of developing PTSD (Armstrong, Shakespeare-Finch, & Shochet, 2014; Kirby, Shakespeare-Finch, & Palk, 2011). For example, using maladaptive coping strategies such as avoidant emotional coping (Smith, Drevo, & Newman, 2017), distraction (Clohessy & Ehlers, 1999; Sattler, Boyd, & Kirsch, 2014), rumination, suppression and dissociation (Armstrong et al., 2014; Clohessy & Ehlers, 1999) increase the risk of PTSD; hence, the argument that educating employees to understand the difference between adaptive and non-adaptive coping mechanisms is important in helping reduce the risk of mental health disorders.

In the workplace, many factors can contribute to increased rates of PTSD, such as routine work stress (Maguen et al., 2009), organisational stressors (Smith et al., 2017) and employment status (Rybojad et al., 2016). The nature of emergency services work—the types and timing of exposure to traumatic incidents—are also influential. The prevalence of PTSD is higher among those exposed to *more types* of traumatic events (Skeffington, Rees, & Mazzucchelli, 2017; Smith et al., 2017) and those with *earlier and more prolonged* exposure (Perrin et al., 2007; Sattler et al., 2014).

There are opportunities for employers to address many of these workplace centric factors, for example, by addressing administrative or procedural factors that increase job-related stress and by improving job security.

It is generally unfeasible, however, to limit or change factors such as types of trauma individuals are exposed to or the duration of exposure. Rather, emergency services organisations are better served by addressing workplace factors found to reduce the risk of developing psychological conditions or the duration of those conditions and by improving coping skills and post-traumatic growth. For example, a strong psychosocial safety climate can buffer the impact of job demand on mental health problems (Hall, Dollard, Winefield, Dormann, & Bakker, 2013), and the support of colleagues can reduce the incidence of PTSD (Prati & Pietrantoni, 2010). The focus of this chapter is the provision of support to emergency responders as a means to reduce incidence and better manage psychological conditions associated with trauma exposure. Support, however, is a multifaceted concept; we address it by distinguishing between formal and informal mechanisms. We explore employee perceptions of their formal support system in two Australian case studies of emergency service organisations and how these operate in balance with the informal support system, underpinned by the psychosocial safety climate.

Formal Employee Support

Formal support for employees is often provided under the banner of an Employee Assistance Program (EAP), which is the umbrella term used to capture a range of complementary support services for employees, and sometimes their immediate family members (Scully, 2011). EAPs can be effective through providing preventative health and well-being measures, by reducing the incidence of hospitalisation and long-term absences from the workplace and through improving morale and performance (Richmond et al., 2017). They have been found to have a positive influence on the health and well-being of employees (Rajaratnam et al., 2014; Richmond et al., 2017). Core services in established and well-resourced emergency services organisations include a peer support officer program, 24-hour phone helpline, access to professional counsellors and psychologists, debriefing or defusing sessions post-trauma, and education and training (Scully, 2011; Shakespeare-Finch & Scully, 2008). Access to formal systems of support is critical for emergency response workers to assist them in coping with the trauma that they face.

Informal Social Support

In contrast to formal support practices facilitated by an organisation, informal support refers to ad hoc interactions that can act to 'fill the gaps' of a formal system (Townsend, Wilkinson, & Burgess, 2013). Social support can be defined as "the perceived support that helps to meet social needs due to the presence and accessibility of people [that an individual] can trust" (Semerci, 2016, p. 43). Support can be provided by a number of individuals in the employee's network, including friends, partners, family, colleagues and supervisors. There is substantial theoretical and empirical evidence that points to social support as a significant contributor to individual well-being (see, for instance, Cohen & Wills, 1985; Halbesleben, 2006; Prati & Pietran-toni, 2010).

Social support can improve well-being through two key mechanisms (Cohen & Wills, 1985): it has an immediate *buffering effect* of lessening the impact when a person is subject to a stressful situation, and the accumulation of social resources and integration in a social network acts as a *protective mechanism* that leads to improved well-being over time. These two processes of social support have significant implications for paramedics, reducing immediate and continuing implications of trauma exposure and improving well-being and personal growth.

The Psychosocial Safety Climate

While the regulatory climate and guidance directed at physical health and safety may be well developed, legislation—and as a result organisations—are less well advanced when it comes to job-related psychological or psychosocial hazards (Zadow et al., 2017). The *psychosocial safety climate* is characterised by a number of elements that are both tangible and intangible, formal and informal, and is seen as both a precursor to and outcome of employee support systems. Psychosocial safety climate is measured by employees' perceptions about the degree of management commitment and priority given to matters relating to psychological health, and the way the organisation communicates about and encourages participation in these matters (Dollard & Bakker, 2010; Hall, Dollard, & Coward, 2010). Largely, it is a measure of how a combination of factors combine and create an underlying understanding of how psychological health, safety and well-being is prioritised and promoted in the organisation. These factors could include formal policies and procedures, managerial behaviour and communication, formal organisational communication, and interactions with other peers and within teams.

There is a growing body of evidence indicating a strong psychosocial safety climate can have significant impact on a range of factors in the workplace, by reducing the adverse impact of job demands (Bailey, Dollard, McLinton, & Richards, 2015) and depression (Hall et al., 2013), altering the impact of workplace bullying on PTSD (Bond, Tuckey, & Dollard, 2010) and limiting physical and psychological work injury (Zadow et al., 2017). Given the broad potential effect of the psychosocial safety climate, we consider this in our conceptualisation of employee support as a characteristic that underpins the formal and informal elements of support. In the remainder of this chapter, we explore the notion of a holistic employee support system in emergency services, examining strengths and weaknesses through the lens of two case studies.

A Holistic Perspective of Employee Support

Academic research and findings from our own study suggest both formal and informal support mechanisms are recommended for employees exposed

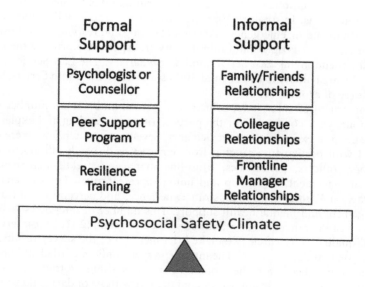

Formal
Support | Informal
Support

| Psychologist or Counsellor | Family/Friends Relationships |

| Peer Support Program | Colleague Relationships |

| Resilience Training | Frontline Manager Relationships |

Psychosocial Safety Climate

Figure 16.1 Employee support system in emergency services

to trauma and stress in the workplace (Beaton, Murphy, Pike, & Corneil, 1997; Prati & Pietrantoni, 2010; Scully, 2011). A balance must exist between robust formal mechanisms and strong effective informal mechanisms to ensure individual preferences and situations can be addressed. This concept has been illustrated in Figure 16.1.

Two Australian Cases

Throughout 2015 to 2018, emergency services organisations in three Australian states participated in a research project on the role of and interactions between people management sub-systems and health and well-being outcomes for ambulance employees and ambulance service operations more broadly. The aim of the project was to better understand how these interactions affect outcomes. Specifically, the project explored how the design and management of organisational systems influence employees' individual outcomes such as job satisfaction, intention to quit and psychological well-being including PTSD. The research design combined data collection via phone surveys, interviews and a range of secondary documents provided by the organisations and unions. While we completed 72 interviews across the three jurisdictions, this chapter reports on findings from the two larger cases only, as data from the third case was too small to sensibly generalise and compare (owing to a small population and only ten interviews).

The services fall under the control of the relevant state government authority. Combined, the services provide assistance to a significant cohort of the

Australian population, across metropolitan, rural and extremely remote and indigenous areas. In total, they attend around one and a half million cases each year, including emergency and crisis planning and response, pre-hospital patient care, and hospital and inter-facility transport. We provide the cases with the pseudonyms *East Service* and *South Service*. The East Service is the largest by area and employs around 3000 staff, while the South Service has a workforce of around 1000.

Semi-structured interviews, primarily in person and a small number over the phone, were conducted for the purpose of understanding and explaining key issues and experiences of participants. Seventy-two interviews were conducted with participants ranging from emergency dispatch officers, patient transport officers, paramedics, front-line managers, middle management, upper management, leadership and union representatives. For this chapter, we draw on 62 interviews to illustrate experiences and perceptions of trauma management and mental health support. This number of interviews is at the high end of the range noted by Saunders and Townsend (2016) for interview-based, qualitative research. We make brief mention of the survey results, but do not use that data in detail. The interviews were audio recorded and professionally transcribed before the content was analysed using a software program, NVivo. This data was examined in conjunction with secondary data to identify key themes in the data relating to barriers to provision of employee support. While each interview was completed by a single researcher, the research team met during the data collection process to discuss findings and refine the interview schedule. Analysis began at the start of the interviewing process and concluded after all data were collected. The researchers engaged in an analytical conversation after the interviews to identify preliminary themes that were emerging, to assess the relevance of existing codes to new data and to examine the relationships between codes (Goetz and LeCompte, 1981). This process fits with the notion of convergent interviewing (Jepson and Rodwell, 2008) which helps improve the internal validity and external and construct validity of qualitative data collection techniques. Interviews were then imported into the data program NVivo (Version 11) for analysis. Thematic content analysis of interview data resulted in the emergence of themes relevant to the effectiveness of formal and informal employee support.

In both our cases, there was a well-resourced and -established formal system of support incorporating all of the elements illustrated in Figure 16.1. Our findings, however, indicate that informal support from colleagues, family and supervisors still played a central and critical role for employees that couldn't be filled by the formal system. The quality of informal support and the nature of interactions are broadly influenced by the psychosocial safety climate that exists in the organisation. This climate facilitates and influences the strength of the front-line manager and relationships between colleagues that support the employee. A strong climate can thereby alleviate pressure on the support relationships with family and friends, as the employee will have much of their support needs addressed within the workplace environment. Where one or more elements is not present, the balance will begin to tip, and the employees' support needs may not be adequately addressed. We explore these aspects of the system through our cases in the following section.

The Formal Support System

In both cases, significant investment is made to developing robust formalised organisational support systems to assist employee resilience and coping. These services include telephone and face-to-face counselling services, education and training, and a peer support programme (which is addressed separately and in more detail in the next section). In general, our response from interviewees indicated a positive overall perception of the formal support programmes in East Service and South Service. There was a sense that the components of the programme were effective individually and fitted together well as a cohesive system. The following interviewee captures the process that followed a critical incident in South Service:

> Once an incident has reached a certain point, there's an automatic [process], you have—managers are coming down to do a debrief, the crew's stood down, they all go back to station. . . . I didn't feel completely ready to download to this manager that I'm going to have to sit in front of in future interviews. . . . So the next thing that happened for us was we got a phone call from one of—we have three psychologists in the city that we can access four times a year. So one of those gave us a call that night and that was quite helpful. . . . But then we got follow up from our team leader. 'How's it going? Everything all right?' Just softly, softly.
>
> (Interview 35, South Service, Paramedic)

This quote mentions an initial debrief procedure (formal debriefs are very rarely reported in either case), follow-up phone call from the external counselling service and informal conversations with the front-line manager. Noted here and in other instances, however, were concerns about future ramifications of having genuine conversations within this support system. This interviewee perceives that having an honest discussion with the manager could compromise their chances of future interviews for promotion, and this was a view echoed in other interviews. For instance,

> I feel like we spend a lot of money on our staff welfare through the peer support program and our EAP, the psychologist who we have available to us. But it seems very closed . . . there's two psychologists that we're allowed to go and see. Now, if you're someone who is thinking I also am applying for this position at the moment and I think this person might be on this panel, I think I just won't go. We're not really given other options.
>
> (Interview 53, South Service, Frontline Manager)

Many paramedics expressed the view that an authentic conversation about an individual's psychological health within the organisations could later result in a bias that affects career progression. These concerns prohibit some individuals from seeking support within the formal system. Some employees indicated they sought psychological support at their own expense, outside of the organisation, to reduce this risk.

Clearly, the debriefing issue is problematic for not only the organisation but also the staff, and ultimately, the patients. While we can interpret this as the illustration of a lack of care/support for staff, we must also recognise that a lack of openness and a fear by paramedics of seeking out a debrief stems from a long-held legacy of the blame culture. Furthermore, in such a culture there is a lack of opportunity for clinical learning as debriefs are not just about helping the employees exposed to trauma or a stressful event, but they are also clinically important as a learning and reflection exercise.

Another core component of the formal support system is education and training to improve resilience and managerial ability to improve coping. We expected to find a fundamental introduction to resilience and coping skills addressed prior to beginning work, during tertiary education. We conducted an examination of the course topics for the ten universities across East and South Service state areas offering the Bachelor of Paramedic Science degree. Our study found only one university that explicitly advertised an offering of a unit with some content relating to understanding the paramedics own mental health in the context of the work environment. Within this course, only one lecture was dedicated to exploring 'our own mental health and care of the self, mental health continuum'. As the director of Employee Support in East Service stated, "what universities offer in that space . . . is concerning given that the majority of new paramedics do not have the level of life experience once common among ambulance officers in decades past".

This deficiency in tertiary preparation places pressure on the ambulance service to build resilience and coping skills into their programmes. Some resilience training is incorporated into the induction programmes in both cases. In South Service and East Service, a half-day programme is provided, but the structure of these is not identical. In South Service, the programme is a half day where managing personal stresses in the workplace, shift work, cumulative stress and acute stress are discussed. Interviewees in South Service desire a more comprehensive approach to resilience training in the induction and over the course of their career. Paramedics suggest "a better system is a bit more than a day's training on psychological stressors" (Interview 29, South Service, Paramedic). While clinical training in South Service is generally well resourced, the provision of resilience training is something desired by many employees.

In East Service, a resilience training programme has been introduced in recent years as part of the induction process, with positive feedback from employees. This is a four-and-a-half-hour programme where participants are provided with resources and activities to complete over the first 12–24 weeks on the road, along with a reflective journal, covering topics such as work-life balance, sleep patterns, coping mechanisms and recognising and managing stress. The programme culminates in a visit with an organisational psychologist to 'close the loop'.

East Service also provide a one-day mandatory training programme for managers, supervisors and acting supervisors, which focuses on trauma and resilience in the workplace. The programme covers legal responsibility for psychological well-being and other topics such as critical incidents, PTSD, anxiety, depression and suicide. Over a period of almost ten years, the programme appears to impact the way managers and supervisors interact with employees around psychological wellness, as demonstrated by the following example of an exercise that has been conducted in the programme since its inception.

> We say to them, what's all the worst things you could say when [paramedics] get back or when they come back to the station? It used to be that there was lots of energy in the room. People would be recounting what had been said to them in the past. There would be a whole heap of things that people would come up with. Interestingly, I really saw a contrast last year. The same scenarios. When you ask them what's all the things that would be helpful, the room would go quiet and you wouldn't hear anything. But last year it was the opposite way around. It struck me because it was the biggest contrast I've seen around a group of managers. All the 'worst things' . . . They were having trouble trying to think of things! And 'what are all the helpful things?' The room got active and they were—they came up with loads of things!
> (Interview 65, East Service, Director Employee Support)

As the previous quote illustrates, there has been a sustained effort to deliver practical skills to help managers conduct positive interactions about mental health and wellness with their employees. Over time, the introduction of this programme has reshaped managerial interactions with employees about mental health and support. It is possible that development of similar skills among employees would enable them to provide enhanced support to colleagues—who our research suggests are the preferred source of informal support for many participants.

The Peer Support Programme

The peer support programme aims to provide employees with early intervention and support following exposure to an incident. Through a number of pathways, employees exposed to critical and traumatic incidents can contact or are contacted by a peer support officer (PSO) soon after exposure to the incident. PSOs are carefully selected and trained in areas such as counselling skills, components of acute stress, psychological trauma, bereavement, suicide and effective communication skills. Typically, the PSO will contact an employee by phone after receiving notification from a centralised service that exposure to particularly traumatic incident such as suicide or paediatric death has occurred.

The PSO programme is well established across East Service and South Service. Our data indicates the programme is generally viewed positively by employees, although some elements of the system are seen as frustrating. For example, the time frame in which a PSO contacts the paramedics, the means of communication and the integrity of the conversations were identified as potential areas of concern.

Firstly, the period between an incident occurring and contact from a PSO was a topic of mixed feelings. While some interviewees prefer time to process the event before speaking about it with a PSO, others believe contact should be made sooner. For instance, a South Service paramedic recounted a call over a day after an incident was like "a slap in the face because it was a significant job the day before in the morning, but over 24 hours later you get a phone call . . . I couldn't hang up quick enough" (Interview 43). The timing of PSO contact is quite nuanced and differs based on the individual preferences. The following interviewee provides a detailed suggestion for an alternative model of contact that allowed the individual to exert more control to shape the contact to their needs:

> I think we need to empower people to use the program and not necessarily enforce the program on people. 'Hi, this is Doug doing a peer support call.' 'I'm fine, thanks. Thanks for the phone call. Appreciate it. See you later.' Is that the right way? I think we need to actually now start talking to our staff and saying, 'what type of peer support do you want?' I think that's where we could use technology to our advantage. So you could generate an automatic message going out. So as soon as peer support is activated, bang, 'hey, Doug, peer support's been activated. Do you need to speak to somebody now? (a) No? (b) Yes.' Bang, it fires back to the person who's doing the peer support activation. Peer support required now.
>
> (Interview 32, South Service, Paramedic)

While the programme is seen as generally effective, more flexibility in how it engages with employees and caters to their support preferences for contact type and timing would be beneficial. This may be through an auto-generated or personalised text message very soon after a critical incident occurs. Such an approach is likely to cater to a subset of employees who indicated that they do not engage with PSOs, but the contact is still important. This is because it is not the two-way communication that is important, but the acknowledgement of the difficult job they have attended. "I feel better that somebody cares, that Comms [The Communications Department] recognised that I had to do something difficult" (Interview 7, East Service, Paramedic). Hence, in some cases, it is not the timing that is particularly important but the contact itself, which may have the same effectiveness in a different format such as an initial text message which gives the employee control of whether and how they choose to respond to support.

Paramedics suggest that the use of a text message—although it can be viewed as impersonal—gives the employee more discretion to make contact at a time that they can ensure they are able to talk privately and when they are ready. The following paramedic discusses this technique as applied by a PSO:

> She'll send you a very gentle text and she'll follow it up in a week's time. . . . So what I like about the texts is . . . if you need me, if you want to—and sometimes—that's the only time I've actually reacted to a PSO and texted back, you know, actually it was an awful job.
> (Interview 45, South Service, Paramedic)

Overall, there was a small but notable degree of concern that employees exposed to major trauma could occasionally 'fall through the cracks' when they are not contacted in a reasonable time period (or at all). This is where the interaction and balance between the formal systems of support and the informal means of support become critical.

Informal Support From Colleagues and Family

Informal support is complementary to the formal system in place in these organisations. In our survey, we found that most employees drew support from colleagues and family and the least from front-line managers. Social support from colleagues and family can be effective at addressing the emotional and informational components of support. Support from colleagues, we found, is valuable for revisiting cases, exploring what happened and the clinical actions taken by the employee. Among each other, colleagues can discuss the technical aspects of often quite traumatic situations to better understand and process the event. This type of support usually cannot be provided by friends and family, who, according to our respondents, are better suited to discussing issues relating to the working conditions or other related stressors.

Our interviews indicated there was high importance placed by staff on the informal interactions by paramedics in the ambulance vehicle or at the hospital following a traumatic event. This casual discussion, often involving 'black humour', replaces the need for formal debrief and allows employees to process information and relieve the state of hyperarousal.

Colleague support is fundamental for assisting coping in employees exposed to critical incident stress. The scope of training seems to centre on self-care, rather than caring for work colleagues, and identifying signs and symptoms of stress-related mental illness and how to respond and provide support to those suffering.

> You might do a case that's very challenging . . . All you really want to do is speak to your peers . . . to go over how you went professionally.
> (Interview 34, South Service, Paramedic)

The role of peers is vital as it fills a space that generally cannot be filled by close friends and family who are less familiar with the trauma associated with emergency service work. As another paramedic summarised, "You can't

go home and tell people, I had a baby die today . . . then they become needy"
(Interview 34, East Service, Paramedic).

As these excepts demonstrate, family are not always a suitable sounding
board for discussing difficult cases—peers are critical for this aspect of support. The difficulty associated with peer support, however, is the high workload experienced by many employees, particularly in the metropolitan areas.
There is very limited down time between cases, so "there's no chance to
defuse after a job because they're bouncing you from job to job, you never
get the chance to process what just happened because you're now onto the
next event" (Interview 11, East Service, Clinical Educator). There can also
be a great deal of inconsistency between the peers rostered on in the same
vehicle, which—particularly in larger stations—can lead to challenges form-
ing lasting relationships.

Informal Support From Front-Line Managers

In our survey, over half of respondents indicated they receive no or little
support from their front-line manager. Low front-line manager support was
also noted in our study to be related to higher incidence of PTSD and intention to quit and lower job satisfaction. As has been shown in a vast array
of previous research, front-line managers play a key role in the experiences
of employees (Hutchinson and Pucell, 2010; Townsend et al., 2012), hence
understanding why front-line managers are not viewed as a primary source
of support is important in further research. Certainly FLMs can and do play
a formal role; however, we focus here on the informal role that they can play
supporting their employees.

Interviewees suggested some key barriers to the provision of informal
social support by front-line managers. These generally related to the front-
line manager's attitude (particularly their expressed empathy), and their
workload as it impacts availability for support. First, issues relating to mindset and attitude are best described by an employee:

> Oh, at [a city station] I had two team leaders, because I split between the
> two [stations], and they were polar opposites. One was very helpful and
> supportive. The other one was an elitist and didn't have any personal
> skills. Didn't know how to communicate with people. Apparently—well,
> not apparently—gave off the feeling he just didn't care. Yeah, it was like
> polar opposites.
>
> (Interview 41, South Service, Paramedic)

While this response was not unanimous, a cohort of employees expressed
perceived deficiencies in front-line managers' core support skills such as
empathy, concern and genuine compassion. This may be a result of a promo-
tional process that does not adequately consider the emotional intelligence
and skill set of front-line managers. Alternately, it may be that front-line
managers are not all receiving the degree of development needed to provide
the type of support that each individual requires.

Another key theme in our data was that the workload or location of the front-line manager was a major hurdle in the provision of adequate support. There is frustration because FLMs "might see [their team] at the start of a shift but they don't get access to the staff because of workload" (Interview 2, East Service, Paramedic). These issues of workload and availability seem to be compounded in some stations where FLMs are also required to spend a period of their day on the road responding to calls. As one regional manager explains,

> Their job was meant to be a team leader, to look after the staff. It wasn't to be a clinician. That was the sort of thing they were going to use if last resort, call these guys for backup if there's no one else. But they have used them and abused them and used them as a resource to treat patients. But in doing that, they now don't do their job properly as a team leader.
>
> (Interview 71, East Service, Regional Manager)

While at times the lack of FLM presence at stations means support cannot be accessed, clearly the seriousness of this issue varies by geographical location. In small regional and rural stations, FLMs' staff interaction can be limited because of time spent driving long distances between remote towns. Other FLMs in regional locations are allocated to work on the road and are rarely in the station themselves. In busy metropolitan stations, the FLM can be subject to such a heavy workload that they are unable to meet with staff particularly where teams are very large. Some FLMs in metropolitan stations in the East Service reported that—as staff here do not return to the station between jobs—it can be impossible to have face-to-face contact unless FLMs visit the nearby hospital and catch employees on the ramp. There is, however, substantial variation and no clear answers that apply consistently across the organisation.

Toward a Balanced Support System

First responders are subject not only to regular trauma exposure but also to a range of work conditions that can create a high level of stress in their everyday lives (Granter et al., 2018; Sterud, Hem, Ekeberg, & Lau, 2008). To achieve the highest level of reliability and safety in the services provided to the community, first responders must operate in an environment where they are adequately supported. For one employee, suitable support may be a chat with a peer support officer following a traumatic incident. For another, it may be a discreet visit to the psychologist or to defuse with friends after work at the pub. The preferred support pathway will change, with time and personal preference, according to the type of trauma exposure or due to other personal events occurring concurrently. Support preferences are changeable, and they are personal. As noted, there is a particular historical culture in the service which can both create stress and mitigate against support. Consequently, changing the system is required. The system (formal and informal interacting) must evolve to be more open and supportive while recognising that systems of support need to align to the workplace as it currently stands and not as it ought to be.

Our research offers messages that will be of value to other emergency service organisations. The formal support systems need to maintain the utmost degree of integrity and separation from management and other processes. If employees are to utilise the system, they must feel confident it is a confidential process and that interaction with it will not be detrimental to their career. Where an aversion to using the formal mechanisms develop among staff, this will place undue pressure on the informal mechanisms, and the support system will become unbalanced.

Some potential improvements to processes and programmes of the formal system are evident from our case studies. Currently, in Australia, resilience training in tertiary studies for emergency responders is limited or non-existent. The responsibility for building employee resilience rests with the organisation. We cannot overstate the significance and value of high-quality initial (during the induction process) and ongoing resilience training for employees, to better enable identification of mental health conditions in themselves and others and to provide tools to assist coping. Additionally, there is added value in developing these programmes to extend, where possible, to the greater network of employees' family and friends, given the importance identified of this support in our research and that of others (Evans, Pistrang, & Billings, 2013).

The support system exists in the context of the psychosocial safety climate of the organisation. To strengthen this component of support, leaders must act to destigmatise conversations around psychological health and to model positive behaviours of self-care, peer support, and facilitating post-traumatic growth. Team leaders and front-line managers are critical here, and support can be improved by developing managerial attitude and mindset and addressing physical availability to employees. While *emotional* support needs appear to be addressed by family, friends, and—to a degree—colleagues, the front-line manager is key in providing the advice, direction and resources that aid recovery and coping. The learning here relates to balance; to minimise employee suffering and promote positive growth, there must be equilibrium between formal and informal support mechanisms available to staff, resting on the psychosocial safety climate. Individual support needs are not identical, and they change over time, hence a robust system with multiple support pathways is the most desirable process.

References

Armstrong, D, Shakespeare-Finch, J, & Shochet, I. (2014). 'Predicting post-traumatic growth and post-traumatic stress in firefighters', *Australian Journal of Psychology*, 66: 1, 38–46.

Bailey, TS, Dollard, MF, McLinton, SS, & Richards, PAM. (2015). 'Psychosocial safety climate, psychosocial and physical factors in the aetiology of musculoskeletal disorder symptoms and workplace injury compensation claims', *Work & Stress*, 29: 2, 190–211.

Beaton, R, Murphy, SA, Johnson, C, Pike, K, & Corneil, W. (2005). 'Exposure to duty-related incident stressors in urban firefighters and paramedics', *Journal Trauma Stress*, 11: 4, 821–828.

Beaton, R, Murphy, SA, Pike, KC, & Corneil, W. (1997). 'Social support and network conflict in firefighters and paramedics', *West Journal of Nursing Research*, 19: 3, 297–313.

Bennett, P, Williams, Y, Page, N, Hood, K, Woollard, M, & Vetter, N. (2005). 'Associations between organizational and incident factors and emotional distress in emergency ambulance personnel', *British Journal of Clinical Psychology*, 44: 2, 215–226.

Berger, W, Figueira, I, Maurat, AM, Bucassio, EP, Vieira, I, & Jardim, SR, et al. (2007). 'Partial and full PTSD in Brazilian ambulance workers: Prevalence and impact on health and on quality of life', *Journal of Trauma Stress*, 20: 4, 637–642.

Bigham, BL, Jensen, JL, Tavares, W, Drennan, IR, Saleem, H, Dainty, KN, et al. (2014). 'Paramedic Self-reported Exposure to Violence in the Emergency Medical Services (EMS) Workplace: A Mixed-methods Cross-sectional Survey', *Prehospital Emergency Care*, 18: 4, 489–494.

Bond, SA, Tuckey, MR, & Dollard, MF. (2010). 'Psychosocial safety climate, workplace bullying, and symptoms of posttraumatic stress', *Organization Development Journal*, 28: 1, 37–56.

Brattberg, G. (2006). 'PTSD and ADHD: Underlying factors in many cases of burnout', *Stress and Health*, 22: 5, 305–313.

Brewin, CR, Andrews, B, & Valentine, JD. (2000). 'Meta-analysis of risk factors for posttraumatic stress disorder in trauma-exposed adults', *Journal of Consulting Clinical Psychology*, 68: 5, 748–766.

Clohessy, S, & Ehlers, A. (1999). 'PTSD symptoms, response to intrusive memories and coping in ambulance service workers', *British Journal of Clinical Psychology*, 38: 3, 251–265.

Cohen, S, & Wills, TA. (1985). 'Stress, social support, and the buffering hypothesis', *Psychological Bulletin*, 98: 2, 310.

Dollard, MF, & Bakker, AB. (2010). 'Psychosocial safety climate as a precursor to conducive work environments, psychological health problems, and employee engagement', *Journal of Occupational and Organizational Psychology*, 83: 3, 579–599.

Evans, R, Pistrang, N, & Billings, J. (2013). 'Police officers' experiences of supportive and unsupportive social interactions following traumatic incidents', *European Journal of Psychotraumatology*, 4: 1, 19696.

Gabrovec, B. (2015). 'The prevalence of violence directed at paramedic services personnel', *Obzornik Zdravstvene Nege*, 49: 4, 284–294.

Goetz, JP, & LeCompte, MD. (1981). 'Ethnographic research and the problem of data reduction', *Anthropology & Education Quarterly*, 12: 1, 51–70.

Grant, AM, Dutton, JE, & Rosso, BD. (2008). 'Giving commitment: Employee support programs and the prosocial sensemaking process', *Academy of Management Journal*, 51: 5, 898–918.

Jepsen, DM, & Rodwell, JJ. (2008). 'Convergent interviewing: A qualitative diagnostic technique for researchers', *Management Research News*, 31: 9, 650–658.

Granter, E, Wankhade, P, McCann, L, Hassard, J, & Hyde, P. (2018). 'Multiple dimensions of work intensity: Ambulance work as edgework', *Work, Employment and Society*, 0950017018759207.

Halbesleben, JR. (2006). 'Sources of social support and burnout: A meta-analytic test of the conservation of resources model', *Journal of Applied Psychology*, 91: 5, 1134.

Hall, GB, Dollard, MF, & Coward, J. (2010). 'Psychosocial safety climate: Development of the PSC-12', *International Journal of Stress Management*, 17: 4, 353–383.

Hall, GB, Dollard, MF, Winefield, A, Dormann, C, & Bakker, A. (2013). 'Psychosocial safety climate buffers effects of job demands on depression and positive organizational behaviors', *Anxiety, Stress, & Coping*, 26: 4, 355–377.

Huizink, AC, Slottje, P, Witteveen, AB, Bijlsma, JA, Twisk, JW, & Smidt, N, et al. (2006). 'Long term health complaints following the Amsterdam air disaster in police officers and fire-fighters', *Occupational and Environmental Medicine*, 63: 10, 657–662.

Hutchinson, S, & Pucell, J. (2010). 'Managing ward managers for roles in HR in the NHS: overworked and under-resourced', Human Resource Management Journal, 20: 4, 357–374.

Izutsu, T, Tsutsumi, A, Asukai, N, Kurita, H, & Kawamura, N. (2004). 'Relationship between a traumatic life event and an alteration in stress response', *Stress and Health*, 20: 2, 65–73.

Kirby, R, Shakespeare-Finch, J, & Palk, G. (2011). 'Adaptive and maladaptive coping strategies predict posttrauma outcomes in ambulance personnel', *Traumatology*, 17: 4, 25–34.

Maguen, S, Metzler, T, McCaslin, S, Inslicht, S, Henn-Haase, C, & Neylan, T, et al. (2009). 'Routine work environment stress and PTSD symptoms in police officers', *The Journal of Nervous and Mental Disease*, 197: 10, 754–760.

Maguire, BJ, O'Meara, PF, Brightwell, RF, O'Neill, BJ, & Fitzgerald, GJ. (2014). 'Occupational injury risk among Australian paramedics: An analysis of national data', *Medical Journal of Australia*, 200: 8, 477–480.

McFarlane, A, & Bryant, R, (2007). 'Post-traumatic stress disorder in occupational settings: anticipating and managing the risk', *Occupational Medicine*, 57: 6, 404–410.

McFarlane, A, Williamson, P, & Barton. CA. (2009). 'The impact of traumatic stressors in civilian occupational settings', *Journal of Public Health Policy*, 30: 3, 311–327.

Neria, Y, Nandi, A, & Galea, S. (2008). 'Post-traumatic stress disorder following disasters: A systematic review', *Psychological Medicine*, 38: 04, 467–480.

Oginska-Bulik, N. (2015). 'Social support and negative and positive outcomes of experienced traumatic events in a group of male emergency service workers', *International Journal of Occupational Safety Ergonomics*, 21: 2, 119–127.

Patterson, PD, Jones, CB, Hubble, MW, Carr, M, Weaver, MD, & Engberg, J, et al. (2010). 'The longitudinal study of turnover and the cost of turnover in EMS', *Prehospital Emergency Care: Official Journal of the National Association of EMS Physicians and the National Association of State EMS Directors*, 14: 2, 209–221.

Perrin, MA, DiGrande, L, Wheeler, K, Thorpe, L, Farfel, M, & Brackbill, R. (2007). 'Differences in PTSD prevalence and associated risk factors among World Trade Center disaster rescue and recovery workers', *American Journal of Psychiatry*, 164: 9, 1385–1394.

Pourshaikhian, M, Abolghasem Gorji, H, Aryankhesal, A, Khorasani-Zavareh, D, & Barati, A. (2016). 'A systematic literature review: Workplace violence against emergency medical services personnel', *Archives of Trauma Research*, 5: 1, e28734.

Prati, G, & Pietrantoni, L. (2010). 'The relation of perceived and received social support to mental health among first responders: A meta-analytic review', *Journal of Community Psychology*, 38: 3, 403–417.

Rajaratnam, AS, Sears, LE, Shi, Y, Coberley, CR, & Pope, JE. (2014). 'Well-being, health, and productivity improvement after an employee well-being intervention in large retail distribution centers', *Journal of occupational and environmental medicine*, 56: 12, 1291–1296.

Reichard, AA, Marsh, SM, & Moore, PH. (2011). 'Fatal and nonfatal injuries among emergency medical technicians and paramedics', *Prehospital Emergency Care*, 15: 4, 511–517.

Richmond, MK, Pampel, FC, Wood, RC, & Nunes, AP. (2017). 'The impact of employee assistance services on workplace outcomes: Results of a prospective, quasi-experimental study', *Journal of occupational health psychology*, 22: 2, 170.

Rybojad, B, Aftyka, A, Baran, M, & Rzońca, P. (2016). 'Risk factors for posttraumatic stress disorder in polish paramedics: A pilot study', *The Journal of Emergency Medicine*, 50: 2, 270–276.

Sattler, DN, Boyd, B, & Kirsch, J. (2014). 'Trauma-exposed firefighters: Relationships among posttraumatic growth, posttraumatic stress, resource availability, coping and critical incident stress debriefing experience', *Stress and Health*, 30: 5, 356–365.

Saunders, M, and Townsend, K. (2016) 'Reporting and justifying the number of interview participants in organisation and workplace research', *British Journal of Management*, 27: 4, 836–852.

Scully, PJ. (2011). 'Taking care of staff: A comprehensive model of support for paramedics and emergency medical dispatchers', *Traumatology*, 17: 4, 35–42.

Semerci, A. (2016). 'The effect of social support on job stress of entrepreneurs', *Academy of Entrepreneurship Journal*, 22: 1, 41.

Shakespeare-Finch, JE, & Scully, PJ. (2008). 'Ways in which paramedics cope with, and respond to, natural large-scale disasters', in *The Phoenix of Natural Disasters: Community Resilience* (pp. 89–100). New York: Nova Science.

Skeffington, PM, Rees, CS, & Mazzucchelli, T. (2017). 'Trauma exposure and posttraumatic stress disorder within fire and emergency services in Western Australia', *Australian Journal of Psychology*, 69: 1, 20–28.

Skogstad, L, Heir, T, Hauff, E, & Ekeberg, Ø. (2016). 'Post-traumatic stress among rescue workers after terror attacks in Norway', *Occupational Medicine*, 66: 7, 528–535.

Smith, RJ, Drevo, S, & Newman, E. (2017). 'Covering traumatic news stories: Factors associated with post-traumatic stress disorder among journalists', *Stress and Health*, 34: 2, 218–226.

Somville, FJ, De Gucht, V, & Maes, S. (2016). 'The impact of occupational hazards and traumatic events among Belgian emergency physicians', *Scandinavian Journal of Trauma, Resuscitation and Emergency Medicine*, 24: 1, 59.

Sterud, T, Hem, E, Ekeberg, Ø, & Lau, B. (2008). 'Occupational stressors and its organizational and individual correlates: A nationwide study of Norwegian ambulance personnel', *BMC emergency medicine*, 8: 1, 16.

Townsend, K, Wilkinson, A, & Allan, C. (2012). 'Mixed signals in HRM: the HRM role of hospital line managers', *Human Resource Management Journal*, 22: 3, 267–282.

Townsend, K, Wilkinson, A, & Burgess, J. (2013). 'Filling the gaps: Patterns of formal and informal participation', *Economic and Industrial Democracy*, 34: 2, 337–354.

Wright, KM, Britt, TW, Bliese, PD, & Adler, AB. (2011). 'Insomnia severity, combat exposure and mental health outcomes', *Stress and Health*, 27: 4, 325–333.

Zadow, AJ, Dollard, MF, McLinton, SS, Lawrence, P, & Tuckey, MR. (2017). 'Psychosocial safety climate, emotional exhaustion, and work injuries in healthcare workplaces', *Stress and Health*, 558–569.

17 Commissioners, Mayors and Blue Lights

Reviewing the Prospects for Integrated Emergency Service Governance

Rachel Ashworth

Introduction

Increasing policy attention has been devoted to the governance of emergency services, with the UK government favouring a shift in accountability in order to drive more effective collaboration between police, fire and ambulance services. Introduced in relation to policing, the elected commissioner model has gained considerable traction in recent years, on the basis that an injection of direct democratic accountability has helped to re-connect public organisations with their communities. Indeed, so much so, that legislation has now been prepared, and enacted, in order to extend the role to police, fire and crime commissioner (PFCC), where appropriate local circumstances prevail. Similarly, the mayoral system has received greater attention, following a high-profile series of elections and the subsequent incorporation of policing and fire services within mayoral responsibilities. However, despite these developments, critics continue to question the value of these new and proposed arrangements, along with the general direction of travel towards an integrated governance system for all three emergency services. Some point to flaws within new accountability systems, such as the PCC model, claiming these elected officials provide for an unhealthy concentration of power, while others suggest that the degree of commonality between the three blue light services is somewhat overplayed, doubting that a single governance framework could adequately guide and oversee two, let alone three, similar, but distinct, emergency services.

This chapter combines an institutional perspective with evidence that includes empirical research on police and crime commissioners and fire and rescue governance, in order to present a critical assessment of governance reform for blue light services. Ultimately, the chapter reviews the prospects for a future integrated emergency service governance system. In doing so, it first emphasises the importance of applying an institutional theory perspective to analyses of governance reform by highlighting the need to consider perceptions of legitimacy from a variety of internal and external audiences. Next, the chapter sets the scene in terms of outlining recent and proposed changes in accountability arrangements for emergency services, before reviewing the somewhat limited evidence that has accumulated to date on the effectiveness of these alterations. Finally, the chapter summarises progress and offers a provisional assessment on the prospects for the legitimisation and long-term institutionalisation of integrated governance arrangements for emergency service organisations in the UK.

Applying an Institutional Perspective to the Reform of Emergency Service Governance

As the integration of the governance of blue light services in the UK indicates a significant institutional change, it seems appropriate to draw upon sociological institutionalism, which promotes the importance of the institutional environment in shaping organisational structures, practices and belief systems. As Scott advocates, "institutional environments are multiple, enormously diverse and variable over time. To neglect their presence and power is to ignore significant causal factors shaping organizational structures and practices" (1987, p. 508). The work of institutional theorists has proved helpful and significant in improving understanding and explanations of patterns of both continuity and change, within and across organisations (Meyer and Rowan, 1977; Greenwood et al., 2014). An additional reason for adopting an institutional approach to assess the likely success of governance reforms to emergency service organisations relates to its emphasis on important societal actors, such as the state and professions, in addition to the influence of cultural interests (Ashworth et al., 2013; Muzio et al., 2013). In this sense, an institutional perspective is more attentive to the layers of organisational complexity that characterise public organisations in their context, layers that are rendered ever more complex by endless waves of public service reform (Ashworth and Entwistle, 2010; Greenwood et al., 2011; Pache and Santos, 2010).

In their attempts to better understand processes of institutionalisation and estimate prospects for success, institutional theorists place significant emphasis on the concept of legitimacy. As Ashforth and Gibbs argue, legitimacy is "a valued but problematic resource" (1990), as in order for any change to become institutionalised, it must be perceived by various audiences to be legitimate (Scott, 1987). Legitimacy is commonly viewed as a precursor for institutionalisation because, once secured, it can provide a basis for re-institutionalization leading to continuity and stability. Without legitimacy, a change process is problematic, as the resulting organisation or institution remains in danger of being viewed as "negligent, irrational or unnecessary" (Sillince and Brown, 2009, p. 1830). For public organisations such as emergency services, authorisation for change from external audiences is critical, but public service reforms also require internal legitimacy if they are to become successfully embedded (Staw and Epstein, 2000). This is especially the case, it is argued, if innovations are governance-based, as these are likely to lead to the development and sustainment of new organisational forms (Suddaby and Greenwood, 2005).

In order to assess whether governance reform in emergency services is likely to be a success and become institutionalised, we first need to consider the concept of legitimacy in more detail. In this chapter, we follow Suchman who in his seminal article defines legitimacy as "a generalized perception or assumption that the actions of the entity are desirable, proper or appropriate within some socially constructed system of norms, values, beliefs and definitions" (1995, p. 574). He goes on to elaborate different types of legitimacy that have become widely established as an underpinning framework for legitimacy analysis (Brown and Toyoki, 2013). These include a short-lived and relatively weak form—*pragmatic legitimacy*—sometimes called 'exchange legitimacy', where organisational actors view change in highly instrumental terms, based on prospects for efficiency and other measures of short-term effectiveness. Suchman contrasts this with *cognitive legitimacy*, where change becomes "taken-for-granted" by various audiences over time as any alternative scenario becomes "unthinkable". He argues that this most powerful, yet subtle, form of legitimacy ensures prospects for successful institutionalisation are high and likely to be sustained.

Of particular relevance to the emergency services context is a third type— *moral legitimacy*—that has a particular resonance within professional settings. Here, the view is that institutional change can only be effective when it aligns with moral and ethical principles underpinning professional and vocational occupations. In this context, change becomes 'the right thing to do', reflecting a 'pro-social logic' that differs fundamentally from self-interest. Research evidence from Sonpar et al. (2010) emphasises the importance of maintaining high levels of moral legitimacy amongst public service professionals at key stages of institutionalisation, whilst Greenwood et al. suggest "it is only when ideas are couched in such a way that they are perceived to be consistent with prevailing values that they appear compelling and legitimate for adoption" (Greenwood et al., 2002, p. 75).

Finally, before we move to consider the context of emergency services, it is important to consider *when* legitimacy becomes important within the context of an institutional change process. Greenwood et al. (2002) suggest this is when a change becomes authorised. They refer to this point as "theorization" when organisational actors become convinced, firstly, that an organisational problem exists and, secondly, that the proposed solution will resolve that problem (Greenwood et al., 2002). Once convinced, audiences can provide their authorisation for change and the system moves to re-institutionalization (Suchman, 1995). However, theorisation is not a straightforward process, as demonstrated by the case analysed by Greenwood et al. (2002) where theorising required "sustained repetition" over almost two decades as ideas are created which are then transported through processes of translation and diffusion (Vaara et al., 2006; Deephouse and Suchman, 2013; Nielsen et al., 2014).

To summarise, for an integrated emergency governance system to be successfully implemented and institutionalised over time, it needs to make sense and be perceived to have value. More specifically, various internal and external audiences need to be convinced of (a) the need for change and (b) the type of change being proposed. Once this has been achieved, and legitimacy has been gained on a pragmatic, moral or cognitive basis, 'authorizing' support could be provided by a range of stakeholders, thereby accelerating the change process and ensuring success. The chapter moves next to a more detailed discussion of the proposed reform of emergency services, before reviewing the prospects for its success.

Reforming the Governance of Emergency Services

Recent developments in emergency service governance have been strongly influenced by the establishment of elected police and crime commissioners (PCCs). The PCC role was created in response to a critique of police accountability that reflected concerns about the effectiveness of police authorities, in addition to assertions of an apparent dislocation between policing organisations and their publics (Lister and Rowe, 2015). The argument for the introduction of PCCs was predicated on the grounds that this new set of citizen representatives offered an improvement on a prior system, where police authorities comprising of local government representatives failed to adequately scrutinise police spending and performance (Gains and Lowndes, 2014). The UK government maintained that the individualised nature of the role would help to re-connect police organisations with their communities, improve police accountability and reduce levels of crime. In order to achieve their objectives, the 41 commissioners were awarded considerable executive powers, which include the capacity to develop a strategic police and crime plan, set the policing budget and hold chief constables to account, with ultimate power to 'hire and fire' (Lister, 2013). Indeed, so significant are the responsibilities of the new PCCs that police and crime panels (PCPs) were established alongside them in order to provide an extra layer of scrutiny, although there is some debate around the level of challenge PCPs provide to PCCs and the degree of robustness within the new policing accountability system (Lister, 2013).

In creating PCCs, the UK government was charged with simultaneously extending and diminishing government "by creating a rival focus of democratic legitimacy" (Jones et al., 2012, p. 236). The reform marked a shock to the wider democratic and political party system, while heightening levels of nervousness and anxiety within policing organisations. Further, the launch of the PCCs took place against a backdrop of political concern, public disinterest, intense media scrutiny and voter apathy—a context which translated into low turnouts for the first PCC elections in November 2012 (not much improved second time around) and a flurry of public (unproven) accusations of cronyism and misconduct (Loveday, 2013). Against this negative backdrop and clearly suffering from a "liability of newness" (Suchman, 1995, p. 586), PCCs certainly faced a difficult scenario in terms of establishing their legitimacy.

In their analysis of PCCs, Jones et al. (2012) predicted a future scenario where their responsibilities could be extended to other policy areas, such as health, the wider criminal justice system and other emergency services, such as fire and ambulance. The Knight Review (2012) also identified the prospect of a better integrated set of emergency service organisations through the establishment of a joint governance mechanism, claiming that a merger between fire and one or more other blue light services could "clarify accountability arrangements"[1]. Meanwhile, a Home Affairs Select Committee report of 2016 concluded that the PCC model was 'here to stay', highlighting a series of benefits associated with clearer lines of accountability and leadership in policing.[2] In addition, despite some examples of good practice from the Emergency Services Collaboration Working Group, concerns were also being voiced regarding evidence of fragmentation, rather than collaboration, between the three services. This was occurring, it was suggested, despite conditions of coterminosity and was often symbolised by examples that indicated slow progress in the shared use of fire, police and ambulance estates.

Together, these developments informed a Conservative Party manifesto commitment designed to assist closer working between fire and police and to expand the role of PCCs. The resulting Policing and Crime Act (2017) placed a statutory duty on police, fire and ambulance services to collaborate, while outlining three key FRS accountability reforms that would enable PCCs to take on fire and rescue governance, create a new national inspection regime and establish a national website containing comparable performance data. The three accountability changes are of significance but, unsurprisingly, the extended PCC role is the element of reform that has attracted most attention (Farrell, 2017). Under the legislation, a PCC can, at a minimum, gain a seat on the local fire and rescue authority under the *Representation Model*. Alternatively, under the *Governance Model*, s/he can adopt the status of the fire and rescue authority and take on its duties and functions, much as they have relative to police authorities. A final model involves PCCs becoming a *Single Employer* for police and fire employees. To extend their role under the Governance or Single Employer models, PCCs have to provide a business case, demonstrating economy, efficiency, effectiveness and public safety gains, which is supported locally. The situation to date is that PCCs in Essex, Mid Staffordshire, West Mercia, Cambridgeshire, Northamptonshire and North Yorkshire have become, or are in the process of becoming, police, fire and crime commissioners, while a further three—Hertfordshire, Norfolk and Lancashire—have proposals in train.

With regard to ambulance services, the emphasis on governance integration has been slightly softer, although it should be noted that there is an appetite amongst certain PCCs to integrate ambulance service governance alongside that for police and fire, while the London Assembly is currently conducting a review of the London Ambulance Service focused in part on its governance arrangements and accountability to the people of London.[3] Nevertheless, despite the slower progress regarding governance, the ambulance service must still uphold the statutory duty to collaborate which has, to date, been pursued through the Association of Ambulance Chief Executives and the Emergency Services Collaboration Working Group.

Finally, it should be emphasised that these governance reforms apply to emergency services in England only. Police, fire and ambulance are devolved in Scotland and Northern Ireland, and while policing is managed across England and Wales, fire and ambulance are devolved to the Welsh government and fire authorities in Wales. The other areas of exception to the arrangement are London and Manchester where, under the mayoral system, the mayor assumes the powers of the PCC and also governs the FRS. The next section of this chapter moves to an evaluation of evidence that draws upon responses to the reform from various audiences, designed in order to facilitate a provisional assessment of the prospects for an integrated model of emergency services governance.

Evaluating the Prospects for Change

Consistent with an institutional perspective and the prior discussion on legitimacy and the process of theorisation, this section focuses on the *policy problem* that has been presented to predicate the proposed change in governance arrangements, before considering the merits of the *proposed solution*. So, first, this section contains a discussion of the argument that suggests blue light services have been slow to integrate and have been in need of improvement, especially in relation to response times. Second, the section goes on to discuss the case for the proposed solution to the problem—an integrated emergency service governance system. In addition to evidence from policy reports and research studies, observations contained in this section of the chapter are also drawn from two specific research projects. The first of these constitutes research conducted with police and crime commissioners during their first elected term and references findings derived from extended semi-structured interviews with 17 PCCs, along with their police and crime plans (Ashworth, 2016). The second research project is work in progress that is focused on fire and rescue service governance reform and comprises a comparative study of a range of alternative FRS governance systems (Ashworth and Farrell, 2018).

The 'Policy Problem'—Fragmentation and Poor Performance

The case for change to emergency service governance rests upon the need to enhance integration and improve performance. In terms of the former, it has long been argued that the three emergency services share similar aims and objectives, operational requirements and occupational conditions and experiences. As such, a strong case has been made for more effective coordination between police, fire and ambulance in order to deliver improved services to the public and identify the operational and efficiency gains that might result from reductions in overlaps and the marshalling of spare capacity. In this sense, reform is designed to build upon previous successes aimed at achieving greater coherence around joint emergency interoperability through JESIP and other mechanisms and reflects an argument that single employer and/or central command and control systems might provide important clarity, particularly in emergency scenarios.

In response to this call for greater integration, many initiatives have been designed and introduced from the 'bottom up' in order to enhance collaborations between services at the local level. In terms of outcomes, we have seen the introduction of tri-service officers in the south-west of England and the

FRS supporting the provision of 'safe and well' checks across the UK, in addition to acting as the key responder to cardiac arrests in areas such as Greater Manchester. While there has been some sustained success in this regard, it is increasingly apparent that these examples of innovation in collaborations tend to be localised and are sometimes ineffective in the longer term, due to their cumulative impact on personnel and lack of fit with the core role of a firefighter/police officer/paramedic. For example, and as briefly referenced by Charman in Chapter 10 in this volume, the challenges of co-responding to cardiac arrest on a continuous basis were not anticipated at the outset of the Greater Manchester initiative. Consequently, the resulting well-being issues amongst firefighters led to the eventual suspension of this particular co-responding trial.

There is a long-running debate that reflects the need to view the three services as separate and distinct from one another, highlighting the need to recognise not only that occupational cultures are complex and distinctive (Andrews and Ashworth, 2017), but also that firefighter, police officer and paramedic roles are continuing to develop at a rapid rate as they become increasingly professionalised (Heath and Radcliffe, 2007; Wankhade, 2011; McCann et al., 2013; Charman, 2013). However, there is also evidence to suggest that accounts of fragmentation and division between the three services might be somewhat overplayed. For example, Charman's continued research on the relationship between police and ambulance professionals highlights the strength of day-to-day working and reports "a strong and positive working relationship, characterised by trust, empathy and respect", along with a series of "cultural characteristics" that are shared in common between the two services (2014, 2015). This type of evidence mitigates against a perception of fragmentation and raises a query over whether further systematic integration is required.

Linked to the discussion of integration is a reference to performance improvement, especially in terms of emergency response and particularly relative to the ambulance service, which has been measured against response times since 1974 (Woollard et al., 2003). The governance of the ambulance service 'by target' is an approach that has been strongly critiqued on the basis that it leads to gaming, poor strategic decision-making, low staff morale and perverse consequences (Bevan and Hood, 2006; Granter et al., 2018; Heath and Radcliffe, 2007; Wankhade, 2012). The need to develop a better set of clinical outcome measures for the ambulance service is clear to all, but some question whether closer collaboration between emergency services (e.g. drafting in related emergency personnel from the FRS) is an appropriate solution in the meantime (Bevan and Hamblin, 2009; Siriwardena et al., 2010). Others point to the influence of a wider context that reflects resource constraint, blockages within the wider health and social care system and widespread problems of mental health (Heath and Radcliffe, 2007). In their article, Bevan and Hood do connect the issue of performance to accountability, highlighting the futility associated with an "arcane and impersonal process of reporting from one bureaucracy to another in a closed professional world", suggesting the need for more "face-to-face" accountability between the public and healthcare providers (2006, p. 534). This indicates that there might be a case for a closer connection between the ambulance service and the public that extends beyond existing fora such as the Patient-Ambulance Liaison Service, although aligning accountability for ambulance with police and fire is unlikely to be a straightforward solution. Similarly, recent evidence from a comparative study of the governance of the FRS indicates that, despite enjoying a strong connection to the public via local authorities, fire authorities can fail to scrutinise sufficiently during their public meetings and sometimes struggle to deliver on the strategic elements of their governance role (Ashworth and Farrell, 2018).

The 'Policy Solution'—an Integrated Emergency Governance System

The alignment of governance and accountability systems across blue light services is the proposed solution to problems of fragmentation and performance. As emphasised above, while researchers, such as Bevan and Hood (2006), have raised concerns regarding the lack of direct connection between citizens and public services, including ambulance, and while PCCs were introduced in response to an accountability problem relative to police authorities, this latest wave of governance reforms has been predicated mainly upon the need for greater collaboration. In other words, for the UK government, governance reform is perceived as a vehicle not necessarily for dealing with a democratic deficit or an accountability crisis but for delivering a faster and more progressive form of service integration. All of which prompts an important question about whether the policy solution in this case will prove to be effective. So, while there is something of a debate over the level and extent of fragmentation, there is an even greater discussion about the merits of an integrated governance model and whether it represents the solution to a problem of fragmented emergency services. Indeed, there is anecdotal evidence to suggest that in some cases, the preparation of a business case and proposed move to governance reform has caused some damage to existing collaborative relationships, e.g. between PCCs and the local county councils (Ashworth and Farrell, 2018).

Unsurprisingly, the proposed move to an integrated form of governance has re-ignited the debate over PCCs and their effectiveness. Some cite the low levels of electoral turnout as an indication of PCCs' lack of connection with the public, while others point to the size of their constituencies and the degree of power concentrated in an individual politician (Lister and Rowe, 2015). Evidence from the PCCs obtained during a research project focused on their first term revealed that they too identified with some of these concerns. For example, one commented,

> I'm kind of very anxious really about the power that invested in PCCs. I've never had so much unbridled power and it worries me quite a lot.

Whereas another acknowledged the power linked to their role but seemed keen to exercise this to shake up the system.

> I'll set kites flying in all sorts of directions with deliberate intent to destabilize so that people end up thinking "what's he going to do or say next?"

In a final example, one PCC reflected that their power could be overplayed, identifying

> The 'big hat, no cattle' thing. Seeming to have real powers but in fact we haven't really got any more powers than the old Police Authority had and in some areas have got less.

Perhaps boosted by their authority, there is evidence to suggest that PCCs have prompted innovation, not only in policing priorities (e.g. with respect to domestic violence and rural crime), but also in terms of governance, on the basis that they have invented novel systems designed to hold police constables to account. They have also worked effectively to shift policing away from a centralised model, characterised by target-based approaches to the delivery and assessment of services. Indeed, for many police officers, the PCC is now perceived to be a proactive champion of the service, when compared with the predecessor Police Authority. This point has not been lost on the Fire Brigades Union (FBU), with examples of local branches writing in support of PCC business cases, based on their perception that, under the current system, the service receives little attention and fire budgets are not always protected.

Finally, it is important to consider whether PCCs perceive themselves as the solution to the problem of improved service integration. When interviewed during their first term, several PCCs seemed to recognise the need for additional joint working but did not necessarily equate this with an extended personal remit. For example, one commented,

> Do I think we could do more to get coordinated? Yes we're working hard on it. Do I want to run the fire service? No thank you. Do I want people on the fire authority to think I would like to? No I blooming don't.

Another suggested that collaboration might move in a different direction, noting the extent to which duties have been already broadened and the way in which boundaries between these services are increasingly blurred:

> There's this view that the Police and Fire Service ought to merge. Whether this is right or wrong, it's on the premise that people wear blue uniforms and have a flashing blue light on their heads, they're the same service. In actual fact policing now has more in common with Children's services and the health service.

For others, it was a matter of responding pragmatically to issues of performance and other practicalities:

> The number of times that police officers take someone to A&E in the back of a police car because they can't get an ambulance. So it's tempting to think 'well, we could sort that out' and I think if the Government was to come and say today, "look can you can take on fire and ambulance yes or no?" I would probably have to say yes because the offer was there.

However, even those that accepted the logic relative to the FRS seemed nervous about integration across all three services:

> I don't think you can take on the ambulance service. I think it's too different and too complicated. I think the tasking is totally different. I think fire and rescue would be easier to do, especially if you are a county force and you've got a county fire brigade.
>
> I have reservations about taking on part of what is the ambulance service or NHS because they are a little bit different but there is more of a synergy between fire and rescue and police.

Concluding Comments

This chapter has combined an institutional perspective with evidence that includes empirical research on police and crime commissioners and fire and rescue governance, in order to present a critical assessment of governance reform for blue light services. This closing section considers the prospects for integrated emergency service governance, relative to the objectives of reform and mindful of the role of legitimacy as a precursor for meaningful institutional change.

With seven police, fire and crime commissioners moving into position and at least a further three on the way, the integrated model of emergency service governance is already beginning to demonstrate signs of success for the UK government, at least in terms of take-up. So, it seems that a number of audiences, including PCCs, chief fire officers, county councils, FRAs, and in some cases the FBU, recognise a problem within the existing system, whether that involves concerns over the future of the FRS and its budget, the need to improve performance or a lack of a direct accountability connection to the public. It is clear though that more collaborative working across emergency services is not the main motivator for change on the ground in this regard. While professionals across the emergency services recognise the importance of working more effectively together, they acknowledge the importance and significance of the structures within which they are currently situated. An example here would be the close connection between the FRS and the wider public service system that is maintained via their accountability link through to local authorities. In this sense, there seems to be something of a disconnect between the stated aims of the reform, the problem it was designed to address and the nature of the governance reform—all of which has implications for the basis and strength of legitimacy associated with the change.

Evidence suggests that various audiences are responding pragmatically to this governance reform due to an identifiable exchange benefit that is apparent to them. For PCCs, the change provides an opportunity to extend their role in a way that seems manageable and appropriate, based upon their interpretation of similarities between police and fire. For parts of the FRS and related audiences, such as local branches of the FBU, the perception is that reform might provide the opportunity for proactive engagement with, and representation of, the FRS. For politicians—both national and PCC—there is a political commitment that also needs to be met. Public service leaders and employees might more broadly recognise the need to work more collaboratively in order to provide better services to the public, but it seems that the clear preference here is for localised, rather than top-down, initiatives. These already prove a challenge to manage, alongside the need to sustain the essence of a service in the face of considerable challenges linked to resource and demand. Further, while there seems to be a moral element to the case for change, it seems that audiences are not quite convinced of integrated governance as the solution to the collaboration problem. Further, there are aspects of this reform that continue to be 'unimaginable', in particular the integration of ambulance governance alongside police and fire, which for many, including some PCCs, is currently seen as a step too far. Ambulance services are delivered by NHS ambulance trusts, organisations who themselves are already linked in complex ways into networks of other organisations via the commissioning system, a system that is about to embark on further major change as 'Integrated Care Systems' start to come into play as part of the new policies of the NHS Five Year Forward View.

The prospects for success are summarised in Table 17.1, relative to legitimacy types and audiences. The table demonstrates that, so far, this reform has gained legitimacy but predominantly of the pragmatic type and, as this is often weak and short-lived, this does not bode well in terms of sustained

Table 17.1 Prospects for institutionalisation

Legitimacy type	Basis	Audience	Prospects*
Pragmatic	Efficacious and accountable blue light services	Government	✔
		Taxpayers	✔
		Citizens	x
		Public service leaders	✔
Moral	Integration to resolve intractable policy problems	Professionals	x
		Citizens	x
		Politicians	✔
	Injection of local democracy	Service users	✔
Cognitive	Reform proposals make sense without question, hard to see an alternative.	Collective audience	x

* This column signifies whether there is evidence to suggest that legitimacy has been achieved and audiences have been convinced. 'x' signifies that audiences have not yet been convinced while '✔' indicates that there is some evidence that they have.

institutional change. There is a clear moral basis to the reform based upon joint working for the public good but, to date, this has not been reflected in the response to change, which is significant given that the reform concerns three prominent and life-changing public services. Unsurprisingly then, and as indicated by the response to the integration of ambulance services, we do not yet have evidence of the reform being legitimised on a cognitive basis, likely due to its embryonic nature and the relatively recent creation of PCCs.

Overall, it seems that the conditions for theorisation are not yet sufficient, as key audiences remain somewhat unconvinced of the appropriateness of the reform. Nevertheless, the move to create PFCCs continues at pace. This serves to remind us of the relative power and influence associated with different audiences, which affects the weight associated with different responses to change. While slowly gaining an enhanced professional status, it is clear that the voice of paramedics, firefighters and police officers remains somewhat muted, depending on the strength of their union/professional association, along with service users who are increasingly frustrated by the problems within our emergency services. As such, this case serves as a reminder of the power of the state, and particularly the UK central government, whose mantra of 'driving integration, further and faster' may yet prove to be sufficient to move emergency services governance to a scenario where no alternative is imaginable.

In closing, it is important to highlight the limitations associated with this discussion. Due to the limited space, the chapter draws only upon selected research when additional perspectives and information could shed further light on the policy problem and proposed solution. Also, the chapter adopts an institutional perspective to analyse the prospects for success, but alternative frameworks might yield different observations and conclusions, especially given that institutional theory has a tendency to overplay stasis and downplay the degree of change. The developments discussed in this chapter emphasise the urgent need for more extensive and detailed analysis of the changes that are unfolding within emergency service governance. In particular, it will be important to gain a sense of the 'legitimacy work' undertaken as the shift from fire authority to PFCC takes place and is experienced on the ground. It is also vital that attention is focused on the governance of the ambulance service, particularly in light of recent developments in London. Finally, and perhaps most significant of all, is the need for emergency service scholars to move beyond their own boundaries in order to work collectively to study the process and practice of integration across police, fire and ambulance services. Greater connectivity is likely to facilitate the compilation of research evidence, in volumes such as this, and will provide us with a greater opportunity to highlight both intended and unintended consequences of reform within our emergency services.

Notes

1 www.gov.uk/government/publications/facing-the-future
2 https://publications.parliament.uk/pa/cm201516/cmselect/cmhaff/844/84402.htm
3 www.london.gov.uk/about-us/london-assembly/london-assemblys-current-investigations/future-londons-ambulance-service

References

Andrews, R., and Ashworth, R. (2017). Feeling the Heat? Management Reform and Workforce Diversity in the English Fire Service. in Greenhalgh, K. and P. Murphy (eds), *The Management of Fire and Rescue Services*, London: Springer Press.

Ashforth, B., and Gibbs, B. (1990). The double-edged sword of organizational legitimation. *Organization Science*, 1, (177), 194.

Ashworth, R. E. (2016). Becoming a Police and Crime Commissioner: Patterns of Identity Work in an Emergent Institutional Context, paper presented at *European Group of Organization Studies*, Naples, July.

Ashworth, R., and Entwistle, T. (2010). The contingent relationship between public management reform and public service work. *Reassessing the Employment Relationship*, 424–444.

Ashworth, R. E., and Farrell, C. M. (2018). No smoke without fire? Evaluating fire and rescue governance in the UK, paper presented at the *International Research Symposium for Public Management*, Edinburgh, April.

Ashworth, R. E., Ferlie, E., Hammerschmid, G., Moon M. J., and Reay, T. (2013). Theorizing contemporary public management: International and comparative perspectives, *British Journal of Management*, 24(S1), S1-S17.

Bevan, G., & Hamblin, R. (2009). Hitting and missing targets by ambulance services for emergency calls: Effects of different systems of performance measurement within the UK. *Journal of the Royal Statistical Society: Series A (Statistics in Society)*, 172(1), 161–190.

Bevan, G., & Hood, C. (2006). What's measured is what matters: Targets and gaming in the English public health care system. *Public administration*, 84(3), 517–538.

Brown, A. D., and Toyoki, S. (2013). Identity work and legitimacy. *Organization Studies*, 34(7), 875–896.

Charman, S. (2013). Sharing a laugh: The role of humour in relationships between police officers and ambulance staff. *International Journal of Sociology and Social Policy*, 33(3/4), 152–166.

Charman, S. (2014). Blue light communities: Cultural interoperability and shared learning between ambulance staff and police officers in emergency response. *Policing and Society*, 24(1), 102–119.

Charman, S. (2015). Crossing cultural boundaries: Reconsidering the cultural characteristics of police officers and ambulance staff. *International Journal of Emergency Services*, 4(2), 158–176.

Deephouse, D. L., and Suchman M. (2013). Legitimacy in organizational institutionalism. in Greenwood, R. C. Oliver, K. Sahlin and R. Suddaby (eds), *The Sage Handbook of Organizational Institutionalism*, Sage: London.

Farrell, C. M. (2017). Governance Matters. *Fire and Rescue Service—Leadership and Management Perspectives*, London: Springer Books.

Gains, F., and Lowndes, V. (2014). How is institutional formation gendered, and does it make a difference? A new conceptual framework and a case study of police and crime commissioners in England and Wales. *Politics & Gender*, 10(4), 524–548.

Granter, E., Wankhade, P., McCann, L., Hassard, J., and Hyde, P. (2018). Multiple dimensions of work intensity: Ambulance work as edgework, *Work, Employment, and Society*, p.0950017018759207.

Greenwood, R., Hinings, C. R., and Whetten, D. (2014). Rethinking institutions and organizations. *Journal of Management Studies*, 51(7), 1206–1220.

Greenwood, R., Raynard, M., Kodeih, F., Micelotta, E., and Lounsbury, M. (2011). Institutional complexity and organizational responses, *Academy of Management Annals*, 5, 317–371.

Greenwood, R., Suddaby, R., and Hinings, C. R. (2002). Theorizing change: The role of professional associations in the transformation of institutionalized fields. *Academy of Management Journal*, 45(1), 58–81.

Heath, G., and Radcliffe, J. (2007). Performance measurement and the English ambulance service. *Public Money and Management*, 27(3), 223–228.

Jones, T., Newburn, T. and Smith, D. J. (2012). Democracy and policing: Key themes in Reiner's work' in T. Newburn and J. Peay (eds), *Policing: Politics, Culture and Control*, Oxford: Hart Publishing.

Lister, S. (2013). The new politics of the police: Police and crime commissioners and the 'operational independence' of the police. *Policing: A Journal of Policy and Practice*, 7(3), 239–247.

Lister, S., and Rowe, M. (2015). Electing police and crime commissioners in England and Wales: Prospecting for the democratisation of policing. *Policing and Society*, 25(4), 358–377.

Loveday, B. (2013). Police and crime commissioners: The changing landscape of police governance in England and Wales: their potential impact on local accountability, police service delivery and community safety. *International Journal of Police Science & Management*, 15(1), 22–29.

McCann, L., Granter, E., Hyde, P., & Hassard, J. (2013). Still blue-collar after all these years? An ethnography of the professionalization of emergency ambulance work. *Journal of Management Studies*, 50(5), 750–776.

Meyer, J. W., and Rowan, B. (1977). Institutionalised organizations: Formal structure as myth and ceremony. *American Journal of Sociology*, 83(2), 340–363.

Muzio, D., Brock, D. M., and Suddaby, R. (2013). Professions and institutional change: towards an institutionalist sociology of the professions. *Journal of Management Studies*, 50(5), 699–721.

Nielsen, J. A., Matthiassen, L., and Newell, S. (2014). Theorization and translation in information technology institutionalization: Evidence from Danish home care. *Management Information Systems Quarterly*, 38(1), 165–186.

Pache, A., and Santos, F. (2010). When worlds collide: The internal dynamic of organizational responses to conflicting institutional demands. *Academy of Management Review*, 35: 455–476.

Scott, W. R. (1987). The adolescence of institutional theory. *Administrative Science Quarterly*, 32(4), 493–511.

Sillince, J. A. A., and Brown, A. (2009). Multiple organizational identities and legitimacy: The rhetoric of police websites. *Human Relations*, 62(12), 1829–1856.

Siriwardena, A. N., Shaw, D., Donohoe, R., Black, S., and Stephenson, J. (2010). Development and pilot of clinical performance indicators for English ambulance services. *Emergency Medicine Journal*, 27(4), 327–331.

Sonpar, K., Pazzaglia, F., and Kornijenko, J. (2010). The paradox and constraints of legitimacy. *Journal of Business Ethics*, 95(1), 1–21.

Staw, B., and Epstein, L. (2000). What bandwagons bring: Effects of popular management techniques on corporate performance, reputation and CEO pay, *Administrative Science Quarterly*, 45, 523–556.

Suchman, M. (1995). Managing legitimacy: Strategic and institutional approaches, *Academy of Management Review*, 20(3), 571–610.

Suddaby, R., and Greenwood, R. (2005). Rhetorical strategies of legitimacy. *Administrative Science Quarterly*, 50(1), 35–67.

Vaara, E., Tienari, J., and Laurila, J. (2006). Pulp and paper fiction: On the discursive legitimation of global industrial restructuring. *Organization Studies*, 27(6), 789–810.

Wankhade, P. (2011). Performance measurement and the UK emergency ambulance service: Unintended consequences of the ambulance response time targets. *International Journal of Public Sector Management*, 24(5), 384–402.

Wankhade, P. (2012). Different cultures of management and their relationships with organizational performance: Evidence from the UK ambulance service. *Public Money & Management*, 32(5), 381–388.

Woollard, M., Lewis, D., and Brooks, S. (2003). Strategic change in the ambulance service: Barriers and success strategies for the implementation of high-performance management systems. *Strategic Change*, 12(3), 165–175.

18 Conclusion

Understanding Emergency Services in Austerity Conditions

Leo McCann,* Paresh Wankhade and Peter Murphy

The chapters in this book cover a wide array of substantive and conceptual issues, showing considerable differences in how management, work and organisation are structured across blue light services. They also document significant changes affecting the nature of work, organisation, managerial scrutiny and professional identity. Some of these changes can be regarded as largely progressive, as emergency work becomes professionalised and develops a more scientific evidence base, as technological capacity grows, as more inter-agency working takes place and as the scope of professional practice broadens. We have also seen some significant developments whereby policy change has led to changed priorities for uniformed work, such as a much greater focus on 'new' forms of crime or harm that have a history of being neglected, such as domestic violence. Emergency organisations are learning and developing, adapting to the changing society around them.

But the chapters equally show just how much these organisations are struggling. Budgetary pressures have been extremely challenging given ten years of austerity measures since the global financial crash of 2007–8. Many emergency service organisations face not only very heavy demand, but also complicated changes in the nature of this demand. They face constant external scrutiny, regular changes in government policy, and a barrage of official reports informing them of the various ways in which they are inadequate and the requirements for change. Austerity conditions have in particular created a climate in which public service providers' demands for increased funding will be received with government scepticism; instead, these bodies can more realistically expect to receive instruction to eliminate 'waste', seek 'efficiency savings', and be 'more effective' with what scarce resources they already have (see for example NHS Improvement, 2018). Reflective of the dominance of neoliberal approaches to governance, the 'gold standards' and 'best practices' for efficiency and effectiveness are to be found primarily in cutting-edge private sector companies (Brown, 2015; Steger and Roy, 2010). It follows from this logic that public sector organisations should emulate multinational corporations and take managerial, accounting and marketing lessons from

* Correspondence E-mail ID: leo.mccann@york.ac.uk

global consulting firms, as if doing so would provide straightforward, uncontroversial, technical fixes.

Emergency service organisations will never enjoy the profile, status, influence and power of global consulting or finance corporations. But one could argue that, nevertheless, they are becoming increasingly high profile. There has always been an enduring public interest in uniformed emergency work as heroic and indispensable, and their public role may become yet more prominent due to what many see as a broader social climate of anxiety and heightened sensitivities to risk, harm and victimhood (Bude, 2018; Linke and Smith, 2009). While financial and operational pressures are unlikely to ease, it could be that the symbolic capital of the 'romantic' or 'heroic' discourses associated with emergency work could be on the rise. Emergency services themselves are becoming increasingly commercialised in their form and structure, relying ever more on subcontractors and volunteer roles, appointing 'business managers' and marketing consultants, and trying to shape their public agenda in an increasingly hypermediated society (Granter et al., 2015).

The pressures they face are immense and multifaceted. The nature of work in today's blue light organisations is akin to life in a "greedy institution" (Coser, 1974)—organizations that "make total claims on their members and which attempt to encompass within their circle the whole personality" (1974, p. 4). While there are potentially large existential rewards associated with being part of an organisation or culture with a lofty mission of serving the public and protecting the vulnerable, the pressures and strains faced by emergency organisations and the professionals who staff them are becoming increasingly troublesome. Senior professionals have bluntly complained that "money is being withdrawn from basic life-giving services".[1] While in some ways their recent experiences of change reflect an increasing sophistication and growing responsiveness to social need, ceaseless operational pressure and strain can create a paradox that those who embody emergency services roles might be becoming ever more alienated in their roles and resentful of governments that provide them with insufficient support and trust.

The chapters of this book, we hope, have gone some way to providing a holistic and critical understanding of the roles of emergency organisations in contemporary society. As editors, it has been a particular pleasure to be able to incorporate the writings and thoughts of experienced emergency service practitioners alongside those of our academic colleagues. We hope that this volume will be of use to both. But, as with any research endeavour, there is always the sense that the book only scratches the surface and there remains much more to learn. If we are to understand the role of these 'basic life-giving services' in the detail they deserve, then we need further collaborative research that is sensitive to the often intense and sometimes unique paradoxes and complexities of emergency service working life.

Note

1 'Huge rise in ambulance callouts as "spice" drug takes toll on homeless', *The Guardian*, 21 September 2018.

References

Brown, W. (2015) *Undoing the Demos: Neoliberalism's Stealth Revolution.* Cambridge: MIT Press.

Bude, H. (2018) *Society of Fear.* Cambridge: Polity.

Coser, L. A. (1974) *Greedy Institutions: Patterns of Undivided Commitment.* New York: The Free Press.

Granter, E., McCann, L., and Boyle, M. (2015) Extreme work/normal work: Intensification, storytelling, and hypermediation in the (re)construction of 'the New Normal, *Organization*, 22, 4: 443–456.

Linke, U., and Smith, D. T. (2009) Fear: A Conceptual Framework, in Linke, U., and Smith, D. T. (eds.), *Cultures of Fear: A Critical Reader.* London: Pluto.

NHS Improvement (2018) *Operational Productivity and Performance in English NHS Ambulance Trusts: Unwarranted Variations.* London: NHS Improvement.

Steger, M., and Roy, R. K. (2010) *Neoliberalism: A Very Short Introduction.* Oxford: Oxford University Press.

Contributors

Rachel Ashworth is Professor of Public Services Management and Dean and Head of Cardiff Business School, Cardiff University. Email: *ashworthre@cardiff.ac.uk*

Cliff Bacon is a doctoral student at Alliance Manchester Business School and a Lecturer in Policing and Forensics, Staffordshire University. Prior to commencing this study, he was a police officer with Greater Manchester Police for 30 years. Email: *clifford.bacon@staff.ac.uk*

Jo Brewis is a Professor in the Department of People and Organizations at the Open University Business School, UK. Email: *joanna.brewis@open.ac.uk*

Sarah Charman is a Reader in Criminology at the University of Portsmouth. Email: *sarah.charman@port.ac.uk*

Carl Daniels, MSc, SR Para is the Deputy Senior Responsible Officer for the Joint Emergency Services Interoperability Programme (JESIP). He joined the programme at its inception in September 2012. Email: *carl.daniels@wmas.nhs.uk*

Tiet-Hanh Dao-Tran is currently a Lecturer in School of Nursing and Midwifery and a post-doctoral research fellow in an ARC-funded research project in the Centre for Work, Organisation, and Wellbeing at Griffith University. Email: *aohanh2001@gmail.com*

Bob Fellows, BSc, PGCE, MA(Ed), FCPara is the Head of Education at the College of Paramedics. Email: *bob.fellows@collegeofparamedics.co.uk*

Richard Godfrey is a Senior Lecturer in Strategy at the Open University Business School, UK. Email: *richard.godfrey@open.ac.uk*

Kirsten Greenhalgh is Associate Professor of Accounting and Chair of the School Teaching and Learning Committee at Nottingham University Business School. Email: *kirtsen.greenhalgh@nottingham.ac.uk*

Lindsay Hamilton is Senior Lecturer in Management and Undergraduate Director at Keele Management School. Email: *l.hamilton@keele.ac.uk*

Graham Harris, BSc, PGCE, MSc, Chartered MCIPD, FCPara, is the National Education Lead at the College of Paramedics. Email: *graham-harris@live. co.uk*

Simon Holdaway is the Professor Emeritus of Criminology and Sociology at the University of Sheffield and part-time Professor of Criminology at Nottingham Trent University. Email: *s.holdaway@sheffield.ac.uk*

Basit Javid is a Chief Superintendent for West Midlands Police. Email: *b.javid@west-midlands.pnn.police.uk*

Mihaela Kelemen is Professor of Management Studies and Public Engagement at Keele University and Director of the Community Animation and Social Innovation Centre (CASIC). Email: *m.l.kelemen@keele.ac.uk*

Ashlea Kellner is a Research Fellow at Griffith University's Centre for Work, Organisation and Wellbeing. Email: *a.kellner@griffith.edu.au*

Katarzyna Lakoma is a research assistant and PhD student in the Emergency Services Unit of the Public Policy and Management Research Group at Nottingham Trent University. Email: *Katarzyna@ntu.ac.uk*

Mark Learmonth is Professor of Organization Studies at Durham University. Email: *mark.learmonth@durham.ac.uk*

Yiwen Lin is a PhD candidate in her final year and a graduate teaching assistant at Keele Management School. Email: *y.lin@keele.ac.uk*

Rebecca Loudoun is Associate Professor at Griffith University and is a leading scholar in health, safety and well-being (including psychosocial safety), shift work and stress. Email: *r.loudoun@griffith.edu.au*

Leo McCann is Professor of Management at the University of York. Email: *leo.mccann@york.ac.uk*

Kevin Morrell is Professor of Strategy and an Associate Dean at the University of Durham. Email: *kevin.morrell@durham.ac.uk*

Peter Murphy is Professor of Public Policy and Management at Nottingham Trent University. Email: *peter.murphy@ntu.ac.uk*

Andy Newton, QAM, FCPara, BSc (Hons), PGCG, Dip IMC, MSc, PhD, is the immediate past Chair of the College of Paramedics and Former Paramedic Director, South East Coast Ambulance Service NHS Trust. Email: *anewton@collegeofparamedics.co.uk*

Rachel O'Hara is a Senior Lecturer at the School for Health and Related Research, University of Sheffield. Email: *r.ohara@sheffield.ac.uk*

Linda Reid, PhD, MSc, BA (Hons), Cert. Ed., M.CIPD, is an associate tutor for the Elizabeth Garret Anderson (EGA) MSc programme at Alliance Manchester Business School, University of Manchester. Email: *linda. reid@manchesters.ac.uk*

Lynda Taylor is Assistant Professor of Accounting at Nottingham University Business School. Email: *lynda.taylor@nottingham.ac.uk*

Keith Townsend is Professor of Human Resource Management at Griffith University, Australia. Email: *k.townsend@griffith.edu.au*

Paresh Wankhade is a Professor of Leadership and Management at Edge Hill University Business School, UK. Email: *Paresh.Wankhade@edgehill.ac.uk*

Andrew Weyman, MIEHF, is a Reader at the Department of Psychology, University of Bath. Email: *A.Weyman@bath.ac.uk*

Adrian Wilkinson is Professor and Director of the Centre for Work, Organisation and Wellbeing at Griffith University, Australia. Email: *adrian. wilkinson@griffith.edu.au*

Roy Wilsher, OBE, QFSM, C.Eng, is the Chair of National Fire Chiefs Council, UK. Email: *roy.wilsher@nationalfirechiefs.org.uk*

Index